D1633137

MANAGEMENT DEVELOPMENT
THROUGH CULTURAL DIVERSITY

This text is a comprehensive introduction to the principles of management and organizational behaviour, as well as a corrective to the Eurocentric bias of most management texts. It develops a transcultural perspective which draws on insights from across the world to examine different management styles, cultures and stages of business development. Distinctive features include:

- management perspectives from the western, eastern, northern and southern parts of the world
- analysis of primal, rational, developmental and metaphysical management
- discussion of management practitioners from America, Scandinavia, Japan, the Far East, southern Africa and elsewhere
- examination of economic, technological, social and cultural factors
- numerous case studies with appropriate examples from a wide range of international organizations

The uniquely wide-ranging perspective makes this a valuable text for all those interested in general management, international business, organizational behaviour and corporate strategy.

Ronnie Lessem is Reader in International Management and Academic Director of the MBA at City University Business School, London. The inventor of the concept of the global businessphere, he is the author of over twenty books including *Managing in Four Worlds* (with S. Palsule, 1997) and consults across the world.

MANAGEMENT DEVELOPMENT THROUGH CULTURAL DIVERSITY

Ronnie Lessem

London and New York

First published 1998
by Routledge
11 New Fetter Lane, London EC4P 4EE

Simultaneously published in the USA and Canada
by Routledge
29 West 35th Street, New York, NY 10001

© 1998 Ronnie Lessem

Typeset in Baskerville by
J&L Composition Ltd, Filey, North Yorkshire
Printed and bound in Great Britain by
TJ International Ltd, Padstow, Cornwall

British Library Cataloguing in Publication Data
A catalogue record for this book is available
from the British Library

Library of Congress Cataloguing in Publication Data
Lessem, Ronnie.
Management development through
cultural diversity/Ronnie Lessem.
p.   cm.
Rev. and updated ed. of: Global management principles. 1989.
Includes bibliographical references and index.
1. Comparative management. 2. Management–Cross-cultural studies.
3. Career development. 4. Organizational change. I. Lessem, Ronnie.
Global management principles. II. Title.
HD30.55.L473   1998
658–dc21   97-45920
CIP

ISBN 0–415–17875–4 (hbk)
ISBN 0–415–17876–2 (pbk)

CONTENTS

ILLUSTRATIONS

Figures

Tables

INTRODUCTION

Management metamorphosis: a global transformation

Why? – in pursuit of metamorphosis

A reader's perspective

Setting out on a journey

Every book, whether on martial arts or on management, is written with a particular reader in mind, and this one is no exception. Having spent 25 years teaching MBAs at business schools in the UK, in continental Europe, in the Middle and Far East, as well as in southern Africa, I have continually asked myself the same questions. Firstly, why do we separate off the so-called 'specialist' business subjects, such as finance and marketing, from so-called general management, that is strategy and organization. It has never made sense to me, cutting such parts away from the whole. Secondly, as I have travelled around the globe, I have also wondered how we can claim that the same MBA syllabus, that we might teach in Boston or Birmingham, is equally relevant in Madrid or Madras. Finally, and perhaps most poignantly for me at this stage of my 'midlife', I ask myself why such a standard curriculum has been worked out for the 28-year-old MBA, whereas nothing equivalent has been formulated for the 38- or even 48-year-old executive.

In contrast to this restrictive conventional focus, this book is aimed at a person who wants to become a truly rounded manager rather than a narrowly bound specialist, who wishes to have a global reach rather than a parochial one, and who wants to be able to manage in their thirties and forties, fifties and sixties, and not only in their twenties. Ultimately, moreover, you will want to be very much your own person, though set within the context of your society, your profession and perhaps your organization.

More specifically, then, you will have begun travelling around the world, at least in your mind's eye, if not yet in actuality. As such a journeyman or woman, you have on the one hand a cosmopolitan outlook, while on the other hand taking pride in your own local heritage. As a result, while setting out on your journey from where you are locally, within your own managerial self, you are at the same time reaching out globally to others – economically and socially, technologically and culturally. In the process, and in the final analysis, you are pursuing managerial mastery, and I want to help you get there if I can.

Pursuing metamorphosis

The pursuit of such a mastery, in effect, involves nothing short of a metamorphosis in your thoughts, feelings and actions. As such, the acquisition of your management knowledge needs to be accompanied by the development of your self as a manager, as well as by the enhancement of your managerial skills. Moreover, you will be well aware of the fact that while such a managerial metamorphosis is a lifelong pursuit, that journey of many thousands of miles has already begun. As part of that continuing journey you may be embarking on a formalized MBA, or on a less formalized path of long-term management development. You will also be aware of the fact that the worldly path you are pursuing will require you to become engaged with pioneering and mature enterprises, as well as with those in between. Similarly, you will need to touch base with both the more youthful and also the more mature sides of your own self. Finally, on the road to actualizing yourself as a manager, in theory if not also in practice, you will need to immerse yourself in both developing and developed societies in all quarters of the globe.

Becoming a master manager

In progressively transforming yourself, then, you will be actively learning to become a master manager, as opposed to passively acquiring a masters in management. You will therefore not only be assimilating concepts, and indeed reflecting on their nature and scope, but also renewing them in particular contexts, and reviewing their appropriateness to yourself, your organization and your society. You will be intent, moreover, on contributing to the development of a continually knowledge-creating organization, and indeed of a learning society. You will therefore want to ensure that such collective learning processes as abstraction, reflection, collaboration and experimentation are built into everyday institutional life. As such a learner, you and your actual or prospective employer – as such a learning enterprise – will purposefully be developing new products and services, processes and systems, as well as effectively mantaining and improving the old ones.

Both you as manager and your organization, and here is the rub, will need to be building upon widely spread, and deeply set, knowledge grounds, with a view to developing new concepts and competencies. With such ends in mind, whereas an ordinary masters student will pursue such conventional MBA subjects as finance and marketing – and the more extraordinary learner focuses on cross-functional aspects of, for example, information or total quality management – your aim is to master the even more wide-ranging, and deeply set, economic and technological, social and cultural, domains of management.

My aim throughout this text is to help you get there, either within or without the context of a formalized masters programme. To the extent that you become a master, then, you will have reached down to the roots of these scientific disciplines, before drawing upon the mainstem management ideas that arise, as well as the branch theories derived from them, thereafter enriching your managerial fruits as well as those of others. In the process, and as will be discussed in much more depth in chapter 21, you and I will be metamorphosing 'the stories we are'. In other words, you will be transforming yourself from a mere 'protagonist', or instinctively oriented primal manager, into a more purposeful 'narrator', or rationally based one; and thereafter into a 'reader', that is an insightfully developmental manager, before becoming an imaginative 're-authorizer' of your managerial self. In order to discover your own 'novelty', you will need to be drawing upon economic and anthropological, social and technical, biological and ecological, aesthetic and epistemological knowledge grounds.

Becoming a citizen of the globe

Ultimately, moreover, your worldliness will be underpinned by the cosmopolitan nature and scope of your thoughts, feelings and activities. You will therefore have uncovered, and subsequently put to work, principles and practices of management drawn from all over the globe. While acknowledging that America continues to be the managerial workshop of the world, you will have become aware that Japan and Western Europe have important managerial tales to tell. Moreover, such emerging markets as Singapore and Malaysia actually, as well as emerging societies such as Brazil and South Africa potentially, have some distinctively different managerial models to facilitate your managerial metamorphosis. Finally, within the European community as a whole, the differentiation between the Anglo-Saxon and the Teutonic, the Latin and the Nordic approaches is becoming ever more evident, notwithstanding their parallel integration.

As a would-be global manager, able to adapt to, and even fuse together, different cultural and economic orientations, you will be seeking after the ultimate in worldlywiseness, that is to participate in the development of 'worlds class' knowledge-creating organizations. In the process, and in the course of scaling what we have termed a 'developmental trajectory', you will have ascended through the primal and rational, developmental and metaphysical, domains of management, of managing, and ultimately of your managerial self. So much for my outer-directed purpose, oriented towards yourselves as students and practitioners of management. What about my own inner-directed purpose, as a management educator, and as a knowledge creator?

A writer's perspective

I felt myself to be a fraud

I was born in southern Africa of northern-European heritage. While having also been subsequently exposed to a Middle Eastern culture, I ultimately pursued a western-oriented business education. As an economics undergraduate in Zimbabwe, therefore, I rapidly discovered that the economic theory I was taught came direct from developed England. As such it had precious little to do with developing Africa. The University of Rhodesia and Nyasaland, as it was then called, was patently not a knowledge-creating organization.

So I set out to study development economics at the avant garde University of Berkeley in San Francisco, but got side-tracked by well-meaning business-minded parents, who proposed that I become an accountant instead. As a dutiful son I reluctantly complied, but after six months of what involved, for me, intellectual and emotional starvation, I gave up accountancy and took up a place at the London School of Economics.

As a postgraduate student there, however, I realized that the 'economics of industry' that I was exposed to had little to do with the business of business. So, after completing my second degree in London, I decided to acquire another so-called 'Masters', this time in 'Business Administration', from Harvard. For I thought that would bring me closer to the business world. It was there that I came to realize that the inert case-study material on offer was a million miles removed from the live substance of management. Patently such Harvard cases failed to arouse the kind of inspiration and panic that has entered into my business and managerial life ever since.

As a result, I graduated from the famed business school two years later, enriched by the cultural experience of having lived in America, but impoverished by my educational experience. For my empirically based education had been divorced from rationally based concepts, from a due variety of social contexts, and from the humanities of life and living. So I returned to Africa for 'southern' nourishment, only to enter a 'northern' world.

After subsequently working for two years in analytically based corporate planning – the topic in which I had majored at Harvard Business School – I was appointed managing director of an offshoot of the family business, a chain of soft-goods stores in South Africa called 'Clothestown'. While the business experience I gained there proved invaluable, and while I kept myself intellectually occupied by pursuing a PhD at the University of South Africa, I felt emotionally extremely ill at ease. In effect I felt an absolute fraud.

For how could I, at the youthful age of 26, call myself a *master* of business? What right did I have, after developing neither my knowledge nor myself as a manager of people – as opposed to as a business administrator – to be called a *managing* director? What knowledge did I have of *business* worldwide, after spending two years in a classroom in one small western corner – that is at Harvard in

Cambridge, Massachusetts – of what I would come to call the global businessphere? Finally, and to the extent that I had been exposed to a maximum number of often superficial cases (and a minimum number of significant concepts), how could I claim to have comprehensively mastered the subject matter of business *administration*? In short, and as not only a managing director of a business, but also as the proud possessor of a Harvard MBA, an MSc in Industrial Economics, and a BSc in Economic Principles, I felt a fraud four times over.

There is a twist, though, to this tale. Some thirty years after this powerful set of experiences I hold the position of Academic Director of City University Business School's Management MBA. In fact I have devoted much of the last ten years of my life to this programme. Moreover, I have now become wholly committed to our men's clothing factory, the thriving family business in Zimbabwe. How then can this be, and what have both outcomes got to do with 'managerial metamorphosis?' Have I in fact donned the very MBA shoes that I spurned as a young man, or is there some other journey to mastery upon which we might embark together, as aspiring managerial travellers?

Knowledge bears fruit in works

Let's then pursue 'the story I am'. For I decided to leave the family business in South Africa two years after I joined. In fact our merchandising manager came up to me one day, a year after I had taken up my post as MD, and said, 'Mr Lessem, feel the cloth'. In fact it was a blue babygrow that I was being invited to savour. I actually 'felt' nothing! The rag trade was not where I belonged physically, mentally or emotionally. In my late twenties, at the tail end of my age of youthful exploration, I felt totally disconnected from the trade I had entered. While the business required me to concentrate on marketing clothing and setting up relevant IT systems, my head and my heart were somewhere else. In fact I had gradually become aware, through teaching organizational psychology part-time at a further education college in Johannesburg, that my passion lay not in soft-goods retailing, set within the technological and commercial context of business, but in management education, set within a social and cultural context. At that point I packed my bags and left for England, where management education was exploding, also somewhat disenchanted with apartheid South Africa, and ended up at City University Business School.

While I was officially taken on as a lecturer in general management, my first unofficial initiative was to launch a short course, for our then MBAs, on 'Management and Mankind'. In fact, this served as a precursor to the managerial metamorphosis in which I am now engaged, at City University in the UK.

For it was Sir Francis Bacon, inventor of scientific method in 1622, who proclaimed that 'knowledge must bear fruit in works', and that 'our empire of hope must be built from out of the common clay'. For me, Bacon – who not only invented scientific method and wrote one of the first texts on *The Advancement of Learning*, but also served as Chancellor of the Exchequer in Elizabethan England

– offered Great Britain a way forward that neither major political party was providing. I therefore saw it as our historic task, at City University, to renew Bacon's original dream, and to serve mankind in that particular way.

London's City University Business School, in fact, is an offshoot of Gresham College, named after one Sir Thomas Gresham, who was a contemporary of Bacon's. As a prominent merchant adventurer of the Elizabethan day, and having amongst other things established the City of London's Royal Exchange, Gresham dedicated his fortune, and thereby his legacy, to the education of the common man. As I saw it, our globally oriented masters degree, following on some four hundred year later, would serve to renew his original vision, as well as Francis Bacon's, as well as indeed my own.

The societal perspective – in search of integrity

The split in the national psyche

Having been born and bred in a developing country, that is Rhodesia, which became Zimbabwe, the notion was instilled in me as a young child that, in the overall scheme of things, the needs of society came first.

These needs are followed by those of the organization, with those of the individual following close behind the other two. Nevertheless, probably because of my combined European and colonial heritages, the place of the individual remained very important, even if relegated to third place in the pecking order of managerial things.

From a social perspective, moreover, it had become clearly apparent to me, growing up in Africa, that the health of economy and society were mutually interdependent. Subsequently I was also to realize, after journeying around the world, that no one nation had mastered this process of mutual development. America, while remaining something of a model in economic terms, is socially a deeply divided nation. Japan, having in recent years risen to remarkable economic pre-eminence, is still somewhat politically immature. Germany, a major source of the European post-war 'economic miracle', was also the perpetrator of the holocaust. My own southern Africa has been responsible for a political miracle and a social maelstrom. Indeed, the country has produced both the most revered statesman in the world today, Nelson Mandela, and also a crime rate that is amongst the worst in the world.

Management and mankind

It seemed to me, therefore, that the only viable business way forward was one which served to combine all these partially flawed national forces into a new transnationally based whole. That was to be my managerial metamorphosis. To be fair, there have been changes in individual nations. Germany, for example, has recognized that the European imperative is a necessary safeguard against the potentially nationalistic excesses of its own *Zeitgeist*. The developmentally oriented East Asians, most visibly over the past twenty years, have realized how important to them is the rationally based technology of Europe and America.

Pragmatic managers in the west and north, moreover, have become somewhat open to the more holistic cultural influence of the east. We are more likely, however, to halfheartedly take on board manufacturing techniques from Japan, for example, than to take on wholeheartedly the Japanese spirit that goes with it. Furthermore, whereas in the visual arts as well as in music and dance we have absorbed manifold influences from the southern hemisphere, we have only just begun to tap those southern depths in business worldwide.

In the Middle East, where our Management MBA – started within the UK – now has its second home, it is patently obvious to me how much the Arabs and the Israelis have to learn from each other, with their different western and eastern orientations. Yet this awareness has yet to become pervasive. Though there are welcome signs of a change in outlook, for the time being exclusivity rules over inclusivity. In a hair-raising recent book, *Towards the Ends of the Earth*, American journalist Robert Kaplan points out that there are many parts of the world today which are in fact physically and socially, as well as economically and ecologically, disintegrating. It would seem to me that unless and until we have equally powerful forces of integration set in place to foster unity-in-diversity, fission will supplant fusion. Nuclear explosion may well become a metaphorical – social and ecological – reality, if not also a physical one. To that extent, this book aims to make a purposeful contribution to your managerial metamorphosis, through helping you to become managerially and organizationally worldliwise. I shall now introduce you to the context in which your prospective metamorphosis is set, before exploring its worldliwise content and, finally, the all-round leadership capability it seeks to develop in you.

Wherefore? chaos to continuity – the context for metamorphosis

Conditions of metamorphosis

The setting for metamorphosis, characterizing both your personal transformation as an individual manager, and also that of your actual or potential organization, has four components. These are the four 'CMs' that form the conditions for metamorphosis underlying the subsequent management content. These four elements are the **c**umulative, **c**hange, **c**ontinuity and **c**omplementary dimensions of such a metamorphosis.

Firstly, *cumulative* metamorphosis (CM1) consists of a development trajectory from youth to maturity to be progressively scaled; *change* metamorphosis (CM2), secondly, involves your transcending the division between 'western' dissonant chaos and 'eastern' resonant harmony; *continuity* as metamorphosis (CM3), thirdly, involves your crossing the divide between 'northern' organizational exclusivity and 'southern' inclusive community; finally, *complementary* metamorphosis (CM4) involves your turning the often conflicting soft and hard edges of management into a creative tension.

CM1 – cumulative metamorphosis – scaling the developmental trajectory

The path to metamorphosis, first of all, involves a cumulative development both for you as an individual manager and for the organization in which you manage. Spread over more or less four stages, extending from youth and adulthood through to midlife and maturity, each one involves both structure-building and structure-changing phases. In other words, each stage of development along the trajectory is marked by a crisis of transition which you as a self-actualizing manager are able to resolve, or dissolve, rather than bypass.

In that context, for example, a youthful Microsoft or Bill Gates, albeit now approaching robust adulthood, are very different organizational and managerial entities from a mature Sony or Akio Morita. You need to be able, in progressively transforming yourself, to facilitate the transition from one stage to the next.

CM2 – change metamorphosis – transcending the east–west divide

The change metamorphosis straddles the east–west divide, embodied in dissonant Anglo-Saxon 'chaos', on the one hand, and resonant East Asian harmony, on the other. As an east–west manager, you, and your organization, maintain yourselves in a continually 'far-from-equilibrium' state. In psychological terms you both 'sense' and 'intuit'. In other words, you and your organization continually make a difference, or two, and then create a new resolution out a synthesis of such differences.

The most thorough exponent of this difference of business outlook today, from an economic and technological as well as a social and cultural perspective, is Britain's Charles Hampden Turner, based at the Judge Institute in Cambridge.

Together with his Dutch colleague, Fons Trompenaars,[2] he compares and contrasts what they term 'finite' western and 'infinite' eastern managerial approaches. As a master manager, therefore, you are 'wise' not only to the temporal differences and syntheses between stages of business development, but also to the spatial differences and syntheses, between diverse cultural orientations.

CM3 – continuity as metamophosis – crossing the north–south divide

The north–south axis, the third of the four conditions underlying metamorphosis, acts as the stabilizing force, complementing the dynamic east–west orientation (see figure below). The organizational north and the communal south provide what Jung terms the stabilizing 'thinking' and 'feeling' to supplement the 'dynamic' sensing and intuiting. These are the dual, and potentially opposing, as opposed to reconciling, forces of continuity. The most clearcut distinctions between north and south, presented in the economic and management literature, are based on the insights and experiences drawn from middle Italy and southern Africa. The first are introduced by the Italian American economic historians based at MIT, Piore and Sabel, illustrated in *The Second Industrial Divide*.[3] The second are presented by the South African business visionary Albert Koopman, based on the industrial democracy he created, and the book he wrote about it, entitled *Transcultural Management*.[4] Both of these place strong emphasis upon community and organization, within the enterprise and in relation to the environment without. As a master manager of such continuity, yourself, you will need to tap into these stablizing forces.

CM4 – complementary metamorphosis – promoting creative tension

Finally, the basic division between soft and hard, or what some people term 'feminine' and 'masculine', others the 'right' and the 'left' sides of the brain, and yet others 'yang' and 'yin', orientations has strong implications for management. In fact, in order to evolve from one stage of development to another, managerially or organizationally, it is necessary to embrace the two opposing dimensions. The creative tension established sets up a second context for metamorphosis. Pascale and Athos[1] have termed these the 'soft S's – superordinate goals, staff, skill and style' and 'hard S's – structure, systems and strategy' of management.

Conditions underlying metamorphosis

We now turn from the context, that is those forces underlying managerial metamorphosis, to the content, that is the domains of management you need to span in order to become a 'worldliwise' manager.

What? Global content – from competition to co-creation

Global management domains

Whereas the forces of cumulation, change, continuity and complementarity establish the overall conditions for metamorphosis, the content of such a would-be master manager's work is comprised of four general management domains, each with soft and hard edges. Moreover, set within each domain is a particular kind of managerial orientation, again both soft and hard, resulting in a spectrum of eight managerial types. These domains I have termed 'primal' (economic/anthropological), 'rational' (socio-technological), 'developmental' (bio-dynamic) and 'metaphysical' (cultural/epistemological). Encompassing all four makes you, as a manager, worldliwise. Within each of these domains organically, as in a tree (see figure below) – there are firstly basic *root* disciplines or *knowledge grounds*; secondly a *mainstem* management idea or *core concept*; thirdly *branch* theories both hard and soft relating to worldliwise *theoretical competencies*; and finally managerial *fruits* that serve as the *practical managerial capabilities* of your endeavours. Those fruits, moreover, become uniquely your own to the extent that you have recognized the knowledge grounds of management, thereby relating them to your individual search for truth, goodness or beauty – with a view to utility.

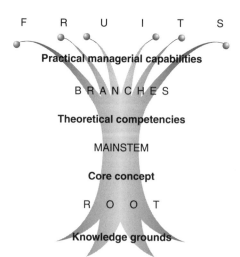

F R U I T S

Practical managerial capabilities

B R A N C H E S

Theoretical competencies

MAINSTEM

Core concept

R O O T

Knowledge grounds

The domain tree

Table 1 Global management content

Domain	Underlying discipline	Content
Primal	Economic/anthropological	Competition
Rational	Socio-technical	Coordination
Developmental	Bio-dynamic	Cooperation
Metaphysical	Cultural/epistemological	Co-creation

We now look at each of the domains and orientations in turn, in each case summarizing the underlying knowledge grounds, the core concepts, the theoretical competencies and the practical fruits.

The four domains encompass firstly the independent world of *competition* (CW1), secondly the dependable world of *coordination* (CW2), thirdly the interdependent world of *cooperation* (CW3), and finally the transcendent world of *co-creation* (CW4). Each domain, finally, has its complementary, and indeed contradictory, soft and hard attributes. We start then with the primal domain of competition.

CW1 – primal domain – economic/anthropological – competitive

	Soft	Hard
Knowledge grounds	Anthropology	Economics
Core concept	'In search of excellence'	
Branch theories	Customer care	Competitive strategy
Practical fruits	Animateur	Entrepreneur

The primal manager has a strongly commercial orientation, and competitive (CW1) outlook. We have in effect linked 'primal management' with that 'back-to-basics' movement inaugurated by California's Tom Peters[5] in the eighties. In fact this movement was a direct reaction against the supposedly ultra-rational approaches to management that had preceded it. Such a youthful, primal business approach – 'in search of excellence' – befitted small-scale enterprise, and combined some of the social orientation of the south with the economic outlook of the west.

Rooted in social anthropology on the one hand, and in political economy on the other, it has spawned many a branch theory within soft-hearted 'people'- or service-oriented management, and within hard-nosed 'enterprise'- or financially oriented, management. The managerial products of such a primal approach, that is the practical capabilities arising from it, are embodied in the typically southern people-oriented 'animateurs' and the typically western profit-oriented 'entrepreneurs'. Both are generally in their primal ascendancy between their late twenties and early thirties. We now turn from primal to rational management.

CW2 – rational domain – socio/technical – coordination

	Soft	*Hard*
Knowledge grounds	Behavioural science	Administrative science
Core concept	'Requisite Organization'	
Branch theories	Change management	Core competence
Practical fruits	Change agent	Executive

Where, as a primal manager, you have a characteristically economic and commercial outlook on business, as a so-called rational manager you are much more strongly socio-technical in your coordinated (CW2) orientation. In fact the knowledge grounds for such a managerial approach reside within the behavioural and administrative sciences, duly aligned with communications and operations technology. Such a typically northern-European manager, and oftentimes engineer, has been especially well characterized by the French Canadian management thinker Elliot Jaques.[6] Jaques' initial work on bureaucracy was succeeded by his more evolved concept of 'requisite organization'. His so-called executive leader, then, who manages such an organization, typically in his or her late thirties or early forties, has the requisite mental capacities to deal with the complexity arising. Such cognitive complexity is represented, within a 'requisite organization', through appropriate levels of stratification.

The derivative theories of such a core concept are, on the soft side 'change management', and, on the hard edge, 'core competence'. The former has been conceptualized by Sweden's Solveig Wikstrom,[7] and underpinned by networked communications technologies. The latter has been conceived by the Anglo-Saxon exponents of Japanese management, Womack and Jones,[8] and duly underpinned by integrated manufacturing processes. The corresponding managerial types, alternate fruits of such rationality, are the freedom-loving change agent, with a 'soft' perspective, and the order-seeking executive with the 'hard' one. We now turn from the rational to the developmental manager.

CW3 – developmental domain – bio/dynamic – cooperation

	Soft	*Hard*
Knowledge grounds	Ecology	Biology
Core concept	'Organizational dynamics/strategic management'	
Branch theories	Organizational learning	Emergent strategy
Practical fruits	Enabler	Adopter

As a developmental manager, whose cooperative orientation (CW3) towards business and its environment is what might be termed a 'bio-dynamic', you are well on the way towards becoming worldliwise. Characteristically eastern in your overall philosophical orientation, you will nevertheless require sufficient primal and rational strengths to function altogether holistically. Moreover, as such a manager – typically in your forties and therefore approaching midlife – you begin to move into the centre of what we have termed the global businessphere.

Not surprisingly, Ralph Stacey,[9] the seminal management thinker in this developmental arena, wrote his magnum opus *Strategic Management and Organizational Dynamics* in his mid-forties. Drawing upon ecological and biological knowledge grounds, as well on insights from physics, mathematics and psychology, his thinking was duly enriched by his prior knowledge of economics. The derivative theories here are those of organizational learning on the ecological side, where Peter Senge[10] has gained pre-eminence, and on emergent approaches to corporate planning on the biological one, where Henry Mintzberg[11] has made his mark. The managerial fruits of these developmental endeavours are the typical enabler on the one hand (Senge terms such a 'new leader' a steward, designer and teacher) and what I have termed an adopter on the other, that is a spiritually oriented manager who adopts the company faith. We now turn finally to the metaphysical manager.

CW4 – metaphysical domain – cultural / epistemological – co-creation

	Soft	Hard
Knowledge grounds	Mythology	Epistemology
Core concept	'Knowledge-creating company'	
Branch theories	Corporate culture	Creative transformation
Practical fruits	Adventurer	Visionary

To the extent that you, as a manager, have effectively evolved through the primal, rational and developmental stages of your life, into 'metaphysical' maturity, you will thereby have become truly worldliwise, and as such a co-creative (CW4) master. Such an effectively worldliwise leader will have moved into the centre of the global businessphere both within – psychologically and socially – and also without – economically and technologically. Typically in your late forties to fifties, or even in your sixties, as such a mature manager you may incline either towards physical or towards a cultural or philosophical adventure. From an organizational perspective, moreover, the point of metaphysical departure – whereby you seek after truth, goodness and beauty albeit in the context of providing utility – takes you into Ikijiro Nonaka's 'knowledge-creating company',[12] which at this metaphysical point serves as a core managerial concept.

Derivative theories lead one way towards corporate culture, including Harrison Owen's[13] work on spirit, and the other way towards 'the stories we are'.[14] The underlying knowledge grounds upon which all of this metaphysical management is based are the humanities, on the one hand, and the modern philosophy, or epistemology, on the other. We now turn from domain content, the what, to worldliwise leadership capability, the how.

How? preparatory to mastery – managerial metamorphosis

The two trajectories – from masters to mastery

In the final section of this introduction I focus on the how. Specifically, then, and based on our ten-year-long experience of maintaining and developing our Management MBA, I recommend how you can transform yourself as a manager. In essence, I compare and contrast what we have termed a transactional trajectory, focused upon the acquisition of a conventional masters, with a transformatively oriented one, geared towards the acquisition of worldliwise mastery. The first trajectory, the transactionally based 'masters' one convention-ally followed by an MBA, is the better known. Here the trajectory follows a cumulative development from pre-functional (e.g. teamworking or negotiation skills) to functional (e.g. marketing or operations management) to cross-functional (e.g. management information systems or the management of change) to general management (e.g. corporate strategy and organizational behaviour). Moreover, there are courses of instruction, backed up by coursework and projects – based on research and/or consultancy – to support these. Such a masters trajectory is in fact ill suited for our purposes here, as it is neither explicitly worldliwise nor does it serve to purposefully cultivate mastery – to which trajectory we now turn.

The transformative trajectory – from training to transformation

Preparatory training

Managerial metamorphosis incorporates, firstly, a preparatory element. This is embodied in specific *courses*, through which instruction of the *individual* takes place in the economic, technological, social and cultural aspects of management. Knowledge, skills and attitudes are acquired, with a view to their development into newly formed competencies.

Ordinary learning

Whereas training consists of putting specific information across, in an appro-priately structured way, learning consists of more systematically integrated educational activity. It involves surveying a practical problem or opportunity, formulating theoretically informed abstract hypotheses, testing the hypotheses through experimentation, and auditing the concrete results. Such so-called 'action-centred learning' is embodied in *projects*, undertaken by individuals, but set within the context of a learning set, or *group*. Your knowledge, skill and self-as-a-manager are thereby developed in predictable ways, and the performance of both you, as a manager, and of your particular department, as an organization, is improved.

Extraordinary development

A more profound development – both in your managerial role and in a product or service with which you have become associated – arises as ordinary, self-contained projects are turned into extraordinary processes of *self-organization*. Such 'self-organization' is a fluid process in which you serve to instigate, spontaneously and informally, the formation of temporary teams around issues. In fact, top managers and management educators cannot control such self-organizing *networks*. Rather, they are only able to intervene to influence the boundary conditions around them. As a developing manager, moreover, you decide who takes part in such networks and what the boundaries of their activities are. Finally, networks both operate in conflict with, and are constrained by, hierarchy.

Masterly transformation

Leadership and mastery, in cumulative conclusion, is achieved though a 'heroic' *journey*, simultaneously engaging you and your organization, whereby you turn from being an effective manager into a value-laden transformational manager,

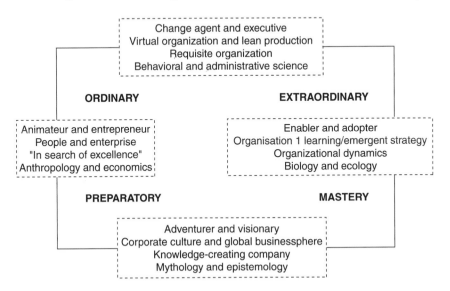

Domains and development

or knowledge creator. At the same time, the organization is turned into a *knowledge-creating company* by dint of your heroic efforts, in combination with a network of others. In the same way that such a progressive metamorphosis serves to combine the preparatory with the ordinary, the extraordinary and mastery, so the knowledge-creating company serves to transform primal, rational and developmental management into the metaphysical. In this way the whys and the wherefores, in your managerial metamorphosis, are turned into the what and the how of worldliwise leadership, as illustrated in the figure on page 15.

Postscript – the book unfolds

As shown in the contents list, there are four introductory context-setting chapters, followed by four chapters on each of the domains: chapters 5–8 on the primal domain, chapters 9–12 on the rational domain, chapters 13–16 on the developmental domain and chapters 17–20 on the metaphysical domain. Chapter 21, which is capability-oriented, concludes the text.

Part I

WHY? TOWARDS MASTERY – SETTING THE CONTEXT

1

DEVELOPING IN STAGES

From youth to maturity

Introduction

Global business development

The first of the four keys to mastery, individually and organizationally, is the capacity for cumulative development. Managers as individuals, organizations in part and as a whole, and even societies, can be seen to develop in stages. Such development, however, is by no means inevitable. To the extent that it does take place, each person or institution will undergo a succession of identity crises, as each evolves from youth through to maturity. Apple Computers, for example, at the time of writing, is going through one such crisis, as are the Eastern European countries, as they emerge from communism towards a form of capitalism. In this chapter we shall be focusing on the developmental stages underlying the international economy as a whole, on the one hand, and the individual business, on the other. The development of yourself as a manager will be reviewed in each of the respective management domains.

Both individual businesses and the international economy develop cumulatively. As this evolutionary succession takes place, there is a change in the nature and extent of differentiation and integration both within the enterprise and without. As a result, and should development ensue, a business's or economy's nature is progressively transformed. Such a progression takes place, moreover, through alternating processes of characteristically 'east–west' transition, or structure changing, and 'north–south' stabilization, or structure building. Specifically, then, and for example, whereas a successsful transition from the old world towards the new seems to have taken place in the Czech Republic, this is much less the case in Albania or Bulgaria.

Similarly, whereas Shell has historically succeeded in building a stable Anglo-Dutch organization and – to some extent – community, the Anglo-German Rover/BMW organization is still in a process of being formed. I shall start with a developmental overview, before reviewing the macro and micro perspectives.

Youthful stage 1 – economic/commercial – competition

Structure building – economic orientation

In the first developmental stage, spanning some two thousand years, business was conducted in small and isolated pockets within local regions across the globe. Contact between these regions was made through middlemen, that is through itinerant adventurers and traders. Such contact was restricted to individual and commercial dealings based on economic motives. Economic differentiation and integration was achieved through the free workings of the market-place. But trading was so limited and scattered that it hardly warranted the term international.

In fact, fully fledged international trade only began to take place in the nineteenth century, as economic and political motives began to merge. Economic trade and political ambitions intermingled as merchant adventurers such as Robert Clive of India and Cecil Rhodes in Africa, not to mention Thomas Gresham, made their weighty impact. Every time a new business or indeed social enterprise is created, such a youthful entity comes into being.

Structure changing – the emergence of cartels

International cartel arrangements, in the first half of this century, mark an extension of the in-between phase linking economic and organizational integration. This marks the transition from a vigorous and youthful international economy to a more cautious and adult one.

Adultlike stage 2 – administrative/technical – coordination

Structure building – technological orientation

Once we enter into the second stage of business and economic development, 'free' international trade is transformed. It turns into systematically coordinated multinational organization. In other words, middlemen are replaced, at least in part, by a company's own manufacturing and distribution units. Contact with indigenous peoples changes from one based on trade to another based on organization and management. Organizational differentiation and integration between parent and subsidiary, between home and host governments, now supersedes mere trading relationships. This has been very much the case in France, for example, where the administrative elite have been playing such coordinating roles for centuries.

Structure changing – towards interdependence

Between the second and third stages is another transitional period. The centrally directed multinational begins to lose its old controlling identity, by delegating

20

power and authority. But it has not yet found a new role. While perhaps wishing its internationally based managers to be 'citizens of the world', 3M, for example, remains Minnesota Mining and Manufacturing. Such a company is yet to enter wholeheartedly into the third stage of its development. Conversely, we can see that British Telecom and British Airways, for example, with their cross-Atlantic mergers amongst others, are struggling to shed their old national identity.

Midlife stage 3 – social/ecological – cooperation

Structure building – social orientation

In the third stage, multinational business is replaced by a transitional architecture. Wholly owned subsidiaries recede into the background and joint ventures become the norm. There have been a spate of joint ventures since the eighties, initially in the automobile and communications industries, and subsequently in finance and insurance. The increasing number of partnerships between small and large firms, such as IBM and Lotus, is another feature of this phase.

In fact, in this structure-building phase, cooperation replaces competition and coordination as the overriding business ethic. This is the case commercially, for example, for GEC/Alsthom, the Anglo-French engineering combine, and societally for Singapore's Economic Development Board – as we shall note in chapter 2 – vis-à-vis the multinational corporations operating in the country. Competition and coordination do not disappear, but they now play second fiddle. As a result, production-sharing arrangements become commonplace and private/public partnerships become the rule rather than the exception, especially in the Far East. Interdependent relationships therefore replace both independent and dependent ones. Therefore social differentiation and integration replaces its purely economic or technical counterpart, albeit within an ecological frame of reference. Hence the emergence of what American business consultant Jim Moore has termed an 'age of business ecosystems'.[1] Recognizing and relating to other people and things, socially and ecologically, as well as to both commercial and also organizational entities, as well as to different individuals and nationalities, becomes the greatest priority.

Structure changing – fusing together

In between the third and fourth phases there is a final transition, from the interweaving of different individuals and cultures to their genuine 'interfusion' into a global businessphere. Attention now shifts from the personal, social and economic development of particular individuals, organizations and nations to the transformation of the relations between them.

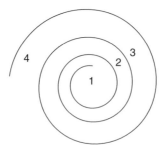

Figure 1.1 The cumulative development spiral

Mature stage 4 – cultural/epistemological – co-creation

Structure building – cultural orientation

The fourth, and most rarely attained, stage of development is represented by the truly global, that is worldliwise, corporation. Such a company not only understands and accommodates the culture of different nations but also aims to enhance each one. It aims to achieve this through a process of business and cultural co-creation stimulated by a shared vision. As such a knowledge-creating global corporation, it will be engaged in cultural differentiation and integration. Its ultimate and transcendent mission is the advancement of utility, via knowledge creation, through the pursuit of truth, goodness or beauty.

Structure changing – the never-ending spiral

A global corporation is inevitably in a state of flux, moving to and fro within itself, in between both economic, organizational, social and cultural differentiation and also integration. For business is never finished. Mature enterprises, as part of their legacy, give rise to new business births which result in youthful organizations, and the cumulative process of development repeats itself, as in a never-ending spiral (see Figure 1.1). I now want to analyse, more closely, each stage of economic development in turn.

International economic development

Youth – the advent of economics – competition reigns

Structure changing – fostering international enterprise

THE ADVENT OF MATERIAL GAIN

Accounts of barter of goods or of services among different peoples can be traced back almost as far as the record of human history. International trade, however, involves economic exchange between different nations, and accounts of such begin only with the rise of the modern nation state. That rise was paralleled by a new attitude to material gain amongst the peoples of Western Europe.

It may strike one as odd that the idea of systematic material gain is a relatively modern one. We are inclined to believe that man is an essentially acquisitive creature. Yet the idea that each individual should constantly strive to better his or her material lot was quite foreign to the great lower and middle strata in Ancient Egypt, Greece or Rome. It was also largely absent from eastern civilization and had only a scattered application throughout the Renaissance and Reformation.

In fact in Shakespeare's time, according to the American economist Robert Heilbronner, the object of life for the ordinary citizen was not to advance his or her lot, but to maintain it. Even for America's pilgrim forefathers, Heilbronner says: 'the idea that gain might be a tolerable – even a useful goal – in life, would have appeared nothing short of a doctrine of the devil'.[2] The whole world, until the sixteenth and seventeenth centuries, could not even envisage the market system. For land, labour and capital did not yet exist. It had to be invented by Adam Smith and the world's first political economists. Of course people were aware of the existence of soil, of human beings and of hand tools, but these had not yet become depersonalized economics entities.

THE PRINCIPLE OF COMPARATIVE ECONOMIC ADVANTAGE

Following in the wake of these inventions, including the concept of the market-place, was the principle of 'comparative advantage', developed in England by the economist David Ricardo. According to this principle, which will be disputed in chapter 3, 'If it takes two man days to produce a given quantity of cloth in Portugal, and one man a day to produce the same in England while it takes three man days to produce a given quantity of wine in England, and two man days in Portugal, why then Portugal should concentrate on producing wine and England on cloth'.[3] In an age of production sharing, joint venturing, and complex cross-licensing agreements, it is amazing how little our 'western' economic theory – as will be revealed in the next chapter – has advanced since Ricardo's law.

THE RISE OF THE MERCHANT ADVENTURERS

While Adam Smith and David Ricardo were developing their theories of free enterprise and of comparative advantage, the merchant adventurers were arriving on the international scene. The notion of economic gain was now entering the national agenda, most particularly in Western Europe.

Columbus, Cortés and Francis Drake were becoming not only national heroes, but also agents of economic progress. In the seventeenth and eighteenth centuries a new economic man was being thrust into the forefront. He became the stuff from which the tales of Kipling and Conrad were drawn. To start with the overriding emphasis was on gold, the emerging symbol of national power. But, by the eighteenth century, that emphasis was beginning to look a trifle naive. New schools of thought were growing up which focused on commerce as the great source of national vitality. The question to which Western European nations addressed themselves was no longer how to corner the gold market. They now looked for ways to create ever more wealth by assisting the rising class of merchant adventurers.

It was such adventurers as Robert Clive of India and Cecil Rhodes in Africa who carried out the English imperial mission. The mission was to acquire both territory and wealth for the home country. Imperial expansion brought with it the massive exploitation of raw materials to feed the industrial revolutions in Europe and America. Gold and diamonds from South Africa, cotton from India and rubber from Malaysia fuelled Britain's economic growth. In the nineteenth century most overseas business enterprises were run by venturesome entrepreneurs.

Structure building – the formation of international businesses

THE INNOVATIVE FORERUNNERS

The real forerunners of the international businesses were the scientifically based entrepreneurs who expanded out of their home base in the 1860s. One such entrepreneur was Frederick Bayer, who took a stake in an aniline plant in New York in 1865, two years after establishing his chemical plant near Cologne. Another was Alfred Nobel, the Swedish inventor of dynamite, whose company subsequently became part of ICI. In 1866 Nobel established an explosives plant in Hamburg.

Both Nobel and Bayer were pioneering innovators and entrepreneurs whose businesses were extensions of themselves. Yet they also created organizations that were to take on a life of their own. These were to become today's multinationals. Organizational management and integration would then supersede entrepreneurialism and free international trade. In 1867 the US Singer sewing machinery company built its first overseas factory in Glasgow. Singer was the original company to manufacture and to mass-market a product in basically the same form across the world. It began to specialize, standardize, centralize and establish dependent relationships with its overseas operations. It had a strong claim to be regarded as the first truly international business. No more was the romance of the man abroad to fill the pages of many a Somerset Maugham saga. Technology had changed things; suddenly, there appeared the international company which employed him, the organization that we have come to term an international business.

BUSINESS GROWTH AND EXPANSION

By the end of the nineteenth century, America had become quite prepared to challenge the older industries of Europe on its own territory. While international businesses had originated in Europe, they subsequently proliferated in America.

Each company that went in search of higher profits had its own particular reason for doing so. But there were a number of facts that influenced them all. Industrial enterprises were becoming larger, and mass production in response to mass markets was developing. The improvement in transport and communications drew the attention of manufacturers to foreign opportunities and made it possible for them to exercise control over foreign subsidiaries. They discovered that it could be cheaper to manufacture in a foreign country than to do so at home.

However, the most important reason for the growth of international companies in the last thirty years of the nineteenth century was the spread of protectionism. Nationalism was growing apace, and the First World War was on Europe's doorsteps. By 1914 the concept of the international company was well established. This was especially true of those industries, such as cars, oil, chemicals and aluminium, which are so important today. But the scale of international activity in relation to total economic activity was very small. The multinational company was yet to enter its heyday.

Structure changing – from individual enterprises to cartels

THE ADVENT OF THE GREAT CARTELS

The period of instability in the inter-war years heralded an important change in the shape of international enterprise. The period saw the emergence of the great cartels. The underlying objective was to maintain prices and profits, and to provide some mechanism whereby companies could reconcile their conflicts of interest without loss of blood. The cartels foisted stability and exclusivity on to an unstable world, increasingly dominated by industrial giants from Europe and America.

CARTELS AS TRANSITIONAL OBJECTS

However, these cartels tended to break down under stress. The companies they represented were often dominated by autocratic leaders, both in the east and the west, who lay half-way between the traditional and idiosyncratic entrepreneur and the contemporary and rational chief executive. The cartels, then, whether in Germany or in Japan, in Britain or America, were a step on the way to today's multinationals. They can be seen as both predecessors of, and successors to, the structured organization.

On the one hand their structures were brittle and their management hapha-zard, and their value system one of exploitation. On the other hand – at least to some extent – they gave their management an understanding of national differ-ences and of the need to modify business practices to take these into account. Instead of thinking primarily of supplying their home markets, and exporting surpluses, cartel managers became accustomed to approaching the problems of their industries on a world basis. They were operating, moreover, within and across all four quarters of the globe. These cartels, at least in part, and over the course of time, were superseded by the fully fledged multinationals. I say in part, though, because the developmental processes always leave 'unfinished business' behind.

Adulthood – multinational business – coordination ensues

Structure building – full-scale multinational enterprise

THE EMERGENCE OF THE MULTINATIONAL COMPANY

The period since the Second World War has seen the full realization of the powers of competitive strategy making and of structured organization on a grand scale. The period has been marked by an explosive expansion in international direct investment, which for much of the time has been rising at twice the world's GNP. The multinational company thereby became the characteristic industrial organization of the third quarter of the twentieth century.

ORGANIZATIONAL DIFFERENTIATION AND INTEGRATION

Christopher Tugendhat,[4] an English observer of the multinational scene in the fifties and sixties, who thereafter became a Euro MP, was one of the first to comment on the nature and extent of multinational enterprise.

The most striking characteristic of the modern multinational company, he said, is its central direction. However large it may be, and however many subsidiaries it may have scattered across the globe, all its operations are coordinated from the centre.

There have been variations on the centralization theme and in his book *The Multinational Man*[5] Thomas Aitken presented a more balanced view: 'Multinational arrangements', he says, 'consist of two vertical spheres; a naturally and culturally decentralized base structure designed to deal with pluralistic conditions, through strong semi-autonomous entities at the national and local levels; and, a centralized super-structure to guide and coordinate the organization as a whole on the international level'.

Whatever the precise balance, the basic model of coordination at the centre, and divisionalization at the periphery, prevailed throughout the 1950s and 1960s. Differences arose in the way that territories, product lines and management functions were allocated, but these again were mere variations on a theme. The theme began to change in the 1970s.

Midlife – transnational business – cooperative

Structure changing – the rise of joint venturing

THE INTERDEPENDENT MULTINATIONAL

During the 1960s multinationals had begun to experiment with joint ventures, especially when their hand was forced by the developing countries. Peter Drucker had already forecast in 1974 that the 'joint venture' would become increasingly important in the future. He added, at the same time: 'It is the most demanding and difficult of all tools of diversification, and the least understood'.[6] This is hardly surprising.

For the very spirit of joint venturing is as alien to the entrepreneur's competitive drive as it is foreign to the manager's analytical mind. The west and the north, therefore, have played a back-seat role in the development of transnational enterprise. In fact, initially it has been the Middle East, subsequently Japan, and most recently the Far East more generally, which have obliged multinational management to reconsider their approach. Not surprisingly, in all these eastern countries, intuition and feeling override sensing and thinking, albeit in different ways in each case.

THE EMERGENCE OF PRODUCTION SHARING

Earlier on I cited Ricardo's principle of comparative advantage as an economic basis for international trade. Today it is being overtaken by the more complex and synergistic notion of production sharing, particularly evidenced in the motor industry. Once again it is Peter Drucker who first drew our attention to it, in his book *Management in Turbulent Times*. Drucker refers to production sharing, in the late 1970s, as a vehicle for transnational integration. 'In production sharing', he says, 'the resources of the developing countries – their abundant labor for traditional jobs – are brought together with the resources of the developed countries – their management, their technology, their educated people, their markets and purchasing power.[7] He then cites several examples of this. The electronic calculator is one.

The hand-held electronic calculator may carry the name plate of a Japanese company, but that may be the only part of it that is 'Made in Japan'. The electronic chips probably come from Texas or from Silicon Valley. They may have been assembled in Malaysia, in Indonesia, or perhaps in Mexico. The casing may be the product of an Indian steel mill and of course the final product will be sold all over the world. The design, the quality control and the marketing will have been done in a highly developed country, Japan, and the labor-intensive work in developing countries.

Whereas the former has expertise readily on tap, the latter have surplus labor on hand. There is more to production sharing than comparative costs alone and

27

yet there is no acknowledged theory to explain this new pattern of international trading. For Drucker, in the 1970s, business was about to enter the stage of integrated trade, for this is what production sharing means. Yet economists and policy makers were totally unprepared, he felt, for the challenge.[8] Arguably this is still the case, twenty years later.

Drucker claims that the multinational of tomorrow will need to be organized quite differently from its predecessor. It will be organized around two focal points, technology (or design) and marketing. Instead of being a multinational corporation, he says, it will have to become a transnational confederation. The local subsidiary 'will not be a business as it has traditionally been, one that produces and markets the full range of the company's products, but only in its own country. The products it makes will be sold all over the world'.[9]

Tomorrow, Drucker says, the developing countries will matter to the multinationals as they have not mattered before. They will provide the manufacturing work. As we shall see in the next chapter, this is becoming ever more evident, for example in the case of Singapore *vis-à-vis* Indonesia. The parent company should thus become increasingly dependent on the overseas subsidiary. Top management will, for Drucker, lead an orchestra rather than an army.

Production sharing, he tells us moreover, makes high demands on design, quality control and marketing, and even higher ones on the management skills of planning, organizing, integrating and coordinating. So production sharing lies half-way between second- and third-stage thinking. There is evidence of interdependence and a need for mutual trust, but conventional management skills are still most strongly emphasized.

This is very much the case, for instance, with Ford Motors' 'Global 2000' programme for worldwide production sharing.

Peter Drucker's production sharing is a transitional influence, then, upon a new, integrated business outlook. But it still falls short of the kind of technological, economic and cultural interdependency that characterizes fully fledged industrial and organizational midlife. To take a step further we need to go and enter into the full spirit of joint venturing, as a vehicle for economic, organizational and most especially social differentiation and integration.

Structure building – joint venturing comes of age

THE SUBSTANTIATION OF JOINT VENTURING

The first global business revolution turned trading companies into international businesses, with foreign manufacturing and marketing facilities. International entrepreneurs were transformed into national and meta-national managers. Sophisticated structures and procedures took the place of intuitive deals and informal relationships. As the international businesses grew in scale and geographical diversity, they began to see themselves as multinational. However, in most instances, they entered into the true and interdependent spirit of multinationality only when their hands were forced. This was especially true, in the 1970s, when the Arabs and the Japanese both began to assert themselves as equals on the world's trading scene. They added a political to an economic imperative, obliging American and European companies to enter into joint ventures with them, if they wanted to survive. John Walmsley, an inveterate joint venturer with GKN who has spearheaded a British multinational's growth in the Middle East, has said: 'Almost without exception, the Middle East that we see today represents the product of joint business ventures'.[10]

The same picture is today emerging in China. The spate of joint ventures in the 1980s and 1990s dates back to the republic's new economic policy, reflected in the edict of July 1979: 'With a view to expanding international economic cooperation and technological exchange, the People's Republic of China permits foreign companies to incorporate themselves, within the territory of China, into joint ventures with Chinese companies, on the principle of equality and mutual benefit'.[11]

The more closely we look at today's international business scene as we approach the millennium, the more convinced I become that there is an 'invisible hand' at work. But it is not Adam Smith's. In a sense the business scene works against the 'invisible hand'. It is not self-interest exclusively, but also mutual interest inclusively, which is becoming the invisible guide. In this respect it is the Japanese who have led the way.

TECHNOLOGY AND TRANSNATIONAL INTERDEPENDENCE

The Japanese have not only taken the business world by storm in the last twenty years, but have also faced it with a fundamental dilemma. On the one hand, they, and most recently the other 'little tigers', have forced the west to become more aggressively competitive. On the other hand, they have encouraged it to become more harmoniously cooperative. Indeed, in his well-known book *Triad Power*,[12] Japan's best-known management consultant, Kenichi Ohmae, makes two key points, one spurred on by the exigencies of competition and the other by the need for cooperation. His first point is that now all major companies in America, Europe and Japan (the Triad) have to plan and implement their strategies globally. Nothing else will do. This is the new economic imperative for any large company that wants to remain competitive. In order to compete, and here lies the irony, companies need to cooperate. Ohmae's reasoning, unlike Drucker's is not founded on the comparative availability of labour on the one hand, or of management and design expertise on the other.

No, Ohmae's argument is centred upon today's technology. As the development and commercialization of new technological breakthroughs become increasingly costly, he argues, there is a threefold movement towards integration and cross-fertilization. The need for integration arises first downstream, to control interfaces with the customer; second upstream, to acquire new technologies; and third horizontally, to share complementary technologies prior to joint market exploitation.

Ohmae then cites the example of the original IBM personal computer. The interface with the customer is controlled not directly by IBM but through a group of third-party companies, such as the consumer retail experts of Sears Roebuck. IBM moved upstream, to acquire new technologies, by adopting Intel processors that originate from Hitachi. Finally, by linking up with an Epson printer, IBM shared the exploitation of the small-business market with a competitor. How odd it is, Ohmae goes on to say, that the general public holds on to the perception of Detroit fighting against Japan. For never before have the respective national car makers been so close to one another.

General Motors, for example, as the biggest of the Detroit three, in the 1980s boosted its equity in Isuzu of Japan to 34 per cent. It also had a 5 per cent share in Suzuki motors, from which it is gleaning minicar technology and for which it serves as a marketing arm in the States. That is the way companies now cooperate and mutually benefit as a result. It is only by combining forces with other people, enterprises and nations that one really gets to know others, for good or for ill. Moreover, the current wave of consortia or joint ventures is very different from the conventional merger or acquisition. For a start the thrust is more international in spirit and scope. Secondly, according to Ohmae, the consequences are different: 'The current consortia and joint ventures encourage dynamic competition; mergers tend to choke it'.[13]

To my mind it is no accident that a Japanese business consultant should have become the first to perceive the multinational arena in such explicitly interdependent terms. For all their fierce competitiveness, the East Asians, as will be described in greater detail in the next chapter, are much more attuned to reciprocity than we are in the west and north.

TECHNOLOGICAL, ECONOMIC AND SOCIAL INTEGRATION

But the times are rapidly changing. Europe, if not also America, is shedding its old, divided skin and is tentatively beginning to grow a new, more cohesive one. The European Union, poised, albeit somewhat turbulently, to enter into monetary union, has been host to a multiplicity of joint ventures in recent years. Amongst the best known are the Swiss–Swedish engineering combine Asea Brown Boveri, the Anglo-French equivalent GEC/Alsthom, and more recently the Anglo-German auto manufacturer Rover/BMW.

As we approach the year 2000, competitive product and market strategies, and the economies of scale to support them, remain critical. However, at one and the same time, technical and commercial collaboration, and the synergy that goes with it, have become enormously important. Every day in the European financial press another joint venture is announced. Both commerce and technology have become too complex for single companies and homogeneous cultures to handle. While Silicon Valley is populated by Europeans, Chinese, Indians and Americans,

Europe is inhabited by Latins, Anglo-Saxons and Teutons amongst others. Over ten years ago one of the leading influences behind the European Eureka collaborative chip-manufacturing project, Yves Stourdze, was already saying: 'Europe's technological renaissance requires the coming together of different intellectual backgrounds, nationalities and cultures'.[14] More recently, in *Light and Shadow: European-ness and Innovation*, it has been maintained that 'the pool of knowledge which is available is broadened by diversity . . . the vision to use this knowledge can be more multi-faceted in a climate of diversity, where people with differing experiences and world-views can take the same basic knowledge, interpret it in differing lights and see differing resonances'.[15]

So Europe is poised for a new phase of cooperation and integration, reaching towards monetary and perhaps ultimately political union. The third phase of its business and economic development is on hand if only the constituent enterprises and nations will rise to the challenge. Ironically they will only succeed in doing so if they manage to imbibe the interdependent outlook of the east, in order to turn their executives and change agents into corporate architects.

The global corporation – co-creation

Structure changing – from fission to fusion

TRANSITION TO MATURITY

Multinational business, then, is approaching maturity, as dependent relationships and political constraints are replaced by economic, cultural, technological and political interdependence. All of this reflects the third stage of international and business development. In the fourth, transcendent phase the focus shifts from interdependent development to physical, economic and cultural transformation. This is the phase that the countries enter into to transform themselves economically, through cultural and technological 'interfusion'.

For Michael Porter, in his review of the competitive advantage of nations: 'National differences in character and culture, far from being threatened by global competition, prove integral to success in it. Evolutionary biology stresses the role of diversity in the advancement of species. Diversity is also important to competiton. Creating diversity, finally, accelerates innovation'.[16]

All the major multinationals have at least touched this fourth stage by virtue of the size and scope of their activity. The oil companies, for example, are engaged in physical and cultural transformation whether they recognize it or not. The impact of their activities is global, to the extent that the resources and environment they transform affects the whole planet. 3M's involvement with space research hurtles the company into this transcendent domain. Shell's involvement, through its scenario-building activities, with De Clerk's South Africa, may have helped tilt it – according to Joseph Jaworski,[17] head of scenario planning in the early 1990s – Mandela's way.

Because it acknowledges its power to transform the economic and cultural fabric of the entire globe, the Bodyshop, for example, has set out its own underlying spiritual foundations,[18] rooted in ecological values. Similarly, the British-based water utility Anglian Water, influenced by the Maoris within its New Zealand-based operations, has chosen to become, there, 'guardians of the water world'. These overtly spiritual foundations, the Japan-watchers Pascale and Athos claim,[19] are singularly lacking in the west. I would argue that the main reason for this lack is not our failure to look east, but a failure to turn towards the south, and ultimately towards the centre.

Structure building – knowledge creation

FOSTERING GLOBAL UNITY

To my mind, the 'invisible hand' is leading international companies from a period of rugged independence to a stage of imposed dependence, then towards a period of mutual interdependence, followed by a glimpse of transcendence. In the process, economic, organizational, social and cultural differentiation and integration succeed one another in overlapping phases. For in the first developmental stag, economic trade is the central and limiting means of global integration. In stage two the need for organizational coordination, at a global level, arises, bringing the role of technology to the fore. Stage three marks a social process of sharing meaning, and stage four heralds a cultural era of knowledge creation.

The great historian Arnold Toynbee had great hopes of world corporations becoming the instruments of global unity.[20] Toynbee argued that the nation state as we know it is a relative newcomer to the world scene. It has spurted out of dying institutions or ancient empires – like the European nations out of the Roman state.

We are beginning to see, for the first time, multinationals such as Rover/BMW looking for opportunities of achieving unity through cultural diversity, rather than by imposing their particular brand of national uniformity. To the extent that any world corporation succeeds, it will need to accommodate the full-scale development of its physical and financial resources, its technology and organization, its people and communities, and its shared knowledge as intellectual capital. This remains to be accomplished. No truly global corporations, having developed as indicated here from a competitive and economic entity into a co-creative and cultural one, yet exists. I now want to review with you the micro perspective of the individual business.

Business and enterprise development

Having investigated the development of global business, emerging out of its origins in international trade, I now want to review the development of the global corporation, emerging out of its origins in the industrial revolution. Whereas my initial orientation was a macro one I now want to focus on business development from a micro point of view. I shall start with the youthful 'age of enterprise', encompassing both the entrepreneurial revolution and also the pioneering firm.

The stage of youth – the age of enterprise

Structure building – a commercial orientation

THE ENTREPRENEURIAL REVOLUTION

The nineteenth century brought with it an age of industrial enterprise, at a time when management was unheard of. Victorian engineers in Great Britain, railroad barons and maverick financiers in America, as well as scientifically trained entrepreneurs in Germany and Sweden, were making business history. So transport, manufacturing and commerce were transformed by heroic individuals. They had plenty of guts, and abounded in frontier spirit. Swashbuckling entrepreneurs were willing to put their money and reputation, and sometimes even their life and limb, on the line. They also had boundless enthusiasm and were able to capture the imagination of their supporters. Although the ingenious British within Europe got the whole process going, courageous Americans on the western frontiers reaped the full entrepreneurial dividends. The Americans took even bigger risks than the Europeans, operating over larger spans of territory, and by the late nineteenth century represented the true bastion of free enterprise. Europe, in the 'north', was thus eclipsed by its American, 'western' counterpart.

STARTING UP A BUSINESS

Starting up a business, like each phase of individual and organizational development, as we shall see in chapter 4, requires both hard and soft qualities – in this case, respectively, a spirit of enterprise and an affinity with people.

The entrepreneurial revolution is relived every time a person starts up a new enterprise. As anyone who has done it knows only too well, it takes lots of emotional resilience – a willingness to take personal and financial risks – as well as hard work, native wit, a capacity to improvise and enough imagination to see round corners.

Business is also about people. In fact there could be no business without people. The ability to enthuse others and to feel out a market need is indispensable, particularly within the early stages of business development.

ATTRIBUTES OF ENTREPRENEURSHIP – SOFT AND HARD

More specifically, in my book *The Roots of Excellence*[21] I identified seven particular entrepreneurial attributes, centred around finely honed business and social instincts (see Table 1.1). I have since expanded these to eight, which correspond

Table 1.1 Entrepreneurial functions and attributes

Function	Attribute
Physical	Capacity to work hard and play hard
Social	Enthusiasm and the ability to arouse it
Mental	Mental agility and quick-wittedness
Emotional	Wilful risk taking and emotional resilience
Analytical	Financial acumen and the capacity to improvise
Intuitive	Gut feel and an eye for a chance
Imaginative	Imagination enough to see around corners
Spiritual	Faith in yourself, and what you stand for

with the spectrum of managerial types[22] incorporated as the fruits of each domain within this text.

These are all innate qualities that can be acquired only through personal observation, experience and learning, as a result of living and working vigorously. There are both 'hard' thrusting qualities such as hard work, emotional resilience and financial acumen, and 'soft' binding ones such as enthusiasm, faith and gut feel. A new business requires the thrust of relentless effort, the display of mental agility, calculated risk taking and basic inventiveness. At the same time it requires the coherence created by innate warmth, improvised organization and faith in the future. The hard and soft qualities, upon which we shall amplify later, change their precise shape and form, however, as a business evolves.

Structure changing – youthful exploration to adult consolidation

THE TRANSITION FROM ENTERPRISE TO ORGANIZATION

Ironically, it is these instinctive business qualities which can prove to be the entrepreneur's downfall as his or her business expands. In other words, the very success of the business enterprise can eventually lead to its demise. Thus Ford Motors grew too big for Henry Ford to effectively handle, and Apple Computers too bureaucratic for Steve Jobs. In trying to hold on to the reins of power, both almost destroyed what they had each created. Steve Jobs, in fact, was initially eclipsed by the professional manager he recruited from Pepsi, that is John Sculley. More recently, with the departure of Sculley in his turn, the company is once more in dire straits, and Jobs has been brought in to help salvage his creation once again, albeit this time from the sidelines.

THE MANAGERIAL REVOLUTION

During the entrepreneurial revolution, guts were primary and brains were secondary! The same goes for the start-up phase of a business. During the managerial revolution, as well as in the administered phase of an organization's development, the roles are reversed. The science of management replaces the art of entrepreneurship. Brains become primary and guts secondary. Intellectual aptitudes, structures of organization and concepts of strategy, therefore, surpass purely instinctive, entrepreneurial qualities. In other words, business people and businesses – if they are to evolve – become more conscious, explicit, self-aware, scientific. Administrative and behavioural science overtake free-market economics and social anthropology. Business instinct alone is not able to cope with the advancing organizational and environmental complexity.

Although it has been American business enterprises, once they had expanded and consolidated, that have applied management theory most extensively, the theory was originally conceived in Europe. It was a German sociologist, Max Weber, who, in the late nineteenth century, developed his rational approach to organization. He called it bureaucracy. Weber's motive was healthy enough. He wanted to counteract the nepotism and corruption of his day. Healthy motives only become unhealthy when they are plucked out of their right time and place and put into the wrong ones.

Moreover, the French industrialist Henri Fayol, to whom we return in chapter 3, wrote the first book on industrial management at the turn of the century. In the 1920s, the first chairman of Imperial Chemical Industries in Britain, German-born Alfred Mond, saw his great challenge to be that of developing a true science of organization. These early ideas, hatched in the European north, subsequently came to roost in the American west, though, I would argue, never in as purely rational a form as in Germany or France.

However, the transition from business enterprise to business administration took place most wholeheartedly in American corporations, spearheaded after the war by its business schools. As the public and private organizations were growing so large, so codified principles of management seemingly had to be applied to their operation. Today, moreover, the organizational transition from enterprise to management is often acknowledged as a necessity, as an individual's

Table 1.2 Adult versus youthful attributes

Function	Youthful attribute	Adult attribute
	Business	**Business administration**
Physical	Hard work	Operations management
Social	Raw enthusiasm	Human-resource management
Mental	Mental agility	Information management
Emotional	Emotional resilience	Competitive strategy
Analytical	Financial acumen	Accounting and finance
Intuitive	Market instinct	Marketing management
Imaginative	Basic inventiveness	Research and development
Spiritual	Faith in yourself	Business ethics

transition from business studies to business administration might be, if both are to grow and prosper (see Table 1.2).

The initiating act of business is always and inescapably entrepreneurial, that is an undertaking of creativity or of innovative change by someone who pursues the belief that the inherent uncertainty of the future will turn out favourably to his or her undertaking. Successive acts to sustain the originating achievements require the formalization of repetitive procedures, to economize on the scarce entrepreneurial capacity. That requires bureaucracy.[23]

Structure building – management as a profession

STRATEGY AND STRUCTURE

In the 1950s the American business historian Alfred Chandler wrote his path-breaking book *Strategy and Structure*.[24] In it he laid the ground rules for the professional manager, illustrating how a rationally designed structure follows from a deliberately devised strategy. The company to which he referred most extensively was General Motors. It was Alfred Sloane's very success in structuring a divisionalized and functionally based organization that led to the extraordinarily successful General Motors. In its day, GM surpassed Ford because Sloane had mastered the basic principles of strategy formulation and structure formation. In a period of sustained growth and in an environment that was largely ordered and predictable, rational management won many a day. As we shall see, particularly when we come to chapter 14 on 'Strategic management and organizational dynamics', things are very different today.

Such a rational, adultlike 'north-western' approach as that adopted by GM involves a conversion of instinctive and personalized attributes into formalized and depersonalized ones. Northern formality takes over from western informality.

BUSINESS ADMINISTRATION

Hard-edged administrative formality, however, needs to be supplemented, at this rational stage of consolidation, by soft-edged participative management. Such a balance between the focus on task and relationships is quite plausible within the progressive and rationally managed organization. In fact, a 'human relations' orientation falls well within the second stage of a business's development. Such a social and psychological approach provides the soft edge, while administrative and technological thrust provides the hard one. The spectrum of managerial attributes at this 'adult' stage of development can be compared and contrasted with that of the youthful one, as shown in Table 1.2.

A rationally based orientation leads towards effective operations management, considerate human-resource management, intelligent information management, a competitive approach to business strategy, formalized accounting and financial management, coordinated marketing management, focused research and development and finally towards ethical management.

These rational aspects of business administration, incorporated in just about every MBA programme around the world, take over from hard work, innate enthusiasm, native wit, entrepreneurial flair, financial acumen, market instinct, basic inventiveness and faith in people characteristic of in most new ventures.

The subject matter of business administration, then, whether in Boston or Bangalore, follows in the footsteps of Max Weber, Henri Fayol, Alfred Mond and Alfred Sloane – the great apostles of scientific management. Yet, in the 1990s, times have again changed. The managerial revolution has been firstly – and relevant at this evolutionary point – superseded by an age perhaps of quality and empowerment heralded by the Japanese, and secondly by an age of learning and knowledge creation, heralded by the global businessphere as a whole. The degree of rigidity and impersonality created by the rational manager, from these latter perspectives, sets up dysfunctional inertia. Alienation sets in both within and without the organization. Business opportunities, human potential and product innovation are stifled. A new healing and growing force is required.

Midlife stage – the age of renewal

Structure changing

THE QUALITY REVOLUTION

As the industrialized nations evolve, so their entrepreneurial base is converted into managed organizations, if not also into a managed economy. Whilst the entrepreneurial base is still clearly apparent in the west, especially in Texas and California, the managed organizations have reached their pinnacle in the north, especially in France, Germany, Holland and Scandinavia. Much less clear, then, especially from a north-western perspective, is what happens afterwards.

J.K. Galbraith, the controversial American political economist, has maintained that a 'heightened design awareness' accompanies economic maturity. Whereas the entrepreneur concentrates on the market, thereby tapping into a source of profitability, the executive attends to the organization, thereby increasing the scope for efficiency, and the designer focuses on both the human and the physical potential, thereby tapping into the source of quality. Profit has material 'body' to it, efficiency is a product of the rational mind, and quality is the outcome not only of thought and action but also of feeling. That is one of the reasons why the Japanese, with their strong aesthetic awareness, have taken so naturally to that originally American idea of 'total quality'. Today the industrialized nations in general are going through a design revolution. Designers are coming into their own because, as societies evolve, people seek more meaning, beauty and fulfilment in their lives. Walter Teague, perhaps the greatest of America's automobile designers, was already making the point in the 1940s.[25]

FORM AND BEAUTY

For Teague, as a thing becomes perfectly adapted to the purpose for which it is made, and so approaches its ultimate form, it also advances in that power to please us which we call beauty. Use is the primary source of form. The function of a thing is its reason for existence, its justification and its end. It is a sort of life urge thrusting through a thing and determining its development. It is only by realizing its destiny, and revealing that destiny with candour and exactness, that a thing acquires significance and validlity of form. This means much more than utility, or even efficiency. It means the kind of perfected order we find in natural organisms, bound together in such precise rhythms that no part can be changed without wounding the whole. In fact, in a Japanese business context, as within a European aesthetic one, that is the essence of quality.

Structure building – process and flow

ORGANIZATION DESIGN

As the individual business evolves, and becomes more self-conscious, so entrepreneurial instinct and managerial intellect are replaced by intuitive individual and organizational development. At present most intuitive design departments, particularly those in the west, are divorced from organizational, if not business, development and as such are not yet fully evolved. Yet in the Japanese culture a whole tradition of aesthetic awareness has been converted into organizational sensitivity, as reflected in their concept of, and feeling for, harmony. For the Japanese, as should be the case at this third stage of business development, feeling (heart) is primary, and thinking (mind) as well as doing (guts) are secondary. That is why consensus forms such an important part of decision making.

QUALITY OF LIFE

Whereas the Japanese have made a major contribution towards the design of a new corporate architecture, it is the Europeans and Americans who have contributed more towards the design of new and individualized lifestyles. The notion of 'quality of life', as opposed to sheer quantity of material gain, has, in the last thirty years, begun to impinge on the managerial mind. In that context, the development of the person as a whole is allied with the development of the business and organization as a whole, towards what the American organizational psychologist Abraham Maslow has called self-actualization.[26] The self-actualized individual, moreover, is 'in tune' with the rest of society. Interestingly enough, this Maslovian perspective has been

Table 1.3 Adult and midlife attributes

Function	Adultlike attribute	Midlife attribute
	Business administration	**Corporate renewal**
Physical	Operations management	Process re-engineering
Social	Human-resource management	Service management
Mental	Information technology	Organizational learning
Emotional	Competitive strategy	Emergent strategy
Analytical	Accounting and finance	Balanced Scorecard
Intuitive	Marketing management	Environment management
Imaginative	Research and development	Technology development
Spiritual	Business ethics	Total quality

provided with an eastern touch by an Indian businessman and academic, V.S. Mahesh, based at the University of Buckingham in the UK, set in the context of services management.[27]

As the business advances, then, from its independently managed structure to its interdependently economic and social design so develelopmental replaces rational management as the guiding business force (See Table 1.3). Fluidity of process thus displaces rigidity of structure at this third stage. As interdependence supplants dependence or independence, joint ventures are replacing autonomous or wholly owned companies as the norm.

In summary, during the entrepreneurial revolution the industrialized nations advanced from economic stagnation to rapid take-off. In the same way, a new enterprise emerges from nothing at all into something commercial and tangible. The result is material wealth and economic 'body'. During the managerial revolution, planned and coordinated expansion and consolidation took place at both macro and micro levels. This kind of development is the product of a well-oiled organizational and managerial 'mind'. In the 1970s and 1980s the quality revolution, at its best, brought with it, for the first time in business and economic history, a conscious and often integrated development of people, technology and enterprise. This gave new 'heart' to the economy and to the firm, both of which may have been acquiring paralysis through analysis!

The adaptive thrust – in companies such as Canon and Rank Xerox – of intense process re-engineering, organizational learning, emergent strategy and techno-logical renewal therefore took over pride of place from operations and information technology, competitive strategy and the management of research and develop-ment. The harmonious coherence of service management, the development of a balanced scorecard, environmental management and a total quality orientation took precedence over human resources, financial and ethical management.

Yet we still have one more stage, or revolution, to go. For the problem with an emergent approach to strategy and organization is that it can become too diffuse, the alliances too loosely held, the developing individuals and enterprises too remote from one another. What is now being required is a new, transforming centre, a knowledge-creating company.

The maturity stage – the age of innovation

Structure changing – from world class to worldlywise

THE KNOWLEDGE REVOLUTION

Michael Porter, the American management guru who introduced us, in the 1980s, to competitive strategy, by the 1990s was reviewing, as we saw earlier, a nation's source of competitive advantage.[28] In doing so he concluded that neither physical nor financial resources was any longer the route to such enduring advantage. Rather it was innovation, and the continuous development of new knowledge that underpinned it, that gave an advanced economy its competitive edge. Of course, in terms of our mastery orientation here, Porter should have been talking in terms of a co-creative, rather than a competitive, advantage. Nevertheless, the Singaporean government, amongst others, has been quick to take advantage of Porter's recent insights, and to deploy his knowledge to their economic advantage. Porter, in fact, has carried on from where Peter Drucker has left off, with his concept of the knowledge worker as the key to his so-called 'post-capitalist society'.[29]

The ultimate organizational form, though, to which we shall be aspiring in this transformative context, is Nonaka's knowledge-creating company.[30] In fact this shift in orientation from land, labour, capital and enterprise to not just management, or even quality, but to knowledge, represents a fundamental shift in business and indeed human consciousness.

Indeed it represents a parallel and progressive change in focus from the respectively economic, technological and social to the cultural foundations of business. This reorientation forms part of our global economic development today. As Japan's well-known futurologist Taichi Sakaya said in the early 1990s: 'In the new society that is now forming, the life-style that will earn the most respect will be one in which the owner's conspicuous consumption of wisdom is displayed, while the products that will sell best will be those that reveal their purchaser to be a person 'in the know'.[31]

The entrepreneurial revolution in the nineteenth century, epitomized by Victorian Britain, followed a leap forward in man's acquisitive impulses. As the American economic historian Robert Heilbronner put it in *The Wordly Philosophers*, as we saw earlier, it is only in the last two hundred years that the desire for systematic material gain has entered mankind's immediate horizons. The managerial revolution, spearheaded particularly by the Americans after the war, heralded an era not only of commercial expansion and growth, but also of the advancement of technology and industry. The subsequent revolution, promoted most especially by the Japanese from the 1960s onwards, reflected a shift in orientation towards quality as opposed to mere quantity, both in physical and human terms.

Finally, the modern-day knowledge revolution developing globally in the 1990s is becoming, in the somewhat primal language of *Fortune Magazine*'s Thomas Stewart, 'the thermonuclear weapon of our time'.[32] For Stewart the new wealth of organizations, or indeed nations, is intellectual capital.

ANCIENT MYTHOLOGY AND MODERN EPISTEMOLOGY

The pursuit of knowledge is an ancient quest, stretching back most visibly, in the European tradition, to the Ancient Greeks. In fact both Socrates in antiquity and Galileo in more modern times risked their very lives in their heroic pursuit of the truth. Today, such inventive scientists as Fritjof Capra of *Tao of Physics* fame, and James Lovelock, who came up with the renowned, or indeed notorious, 'Gaia Hypothesis', have risked their lifelong reputations and livelihoods, if not, in today's more liberal environment, their very lives.

Now that such 'culture' generally – with its diffuse sources of wisdom on the one hand, and focused intellectual capital on the other – has entered into the corporate mainstream, we are witnessing a further evolutionary step in our business world. For while the great myths and artistic creations throughout the ages – whether in the east, west, north or south – have stirred the inner spirit of men and women, the great ideas and inventions have served to represent their material achievements. Corporate and national culture combined with knowledge creation therefore mark the end of the journey from physical matter (economic) towards human spirit via mind (technological) and heart (social). The same applies to business, specifically, as to our global economy and society more generally.

THE TRANSITION FROM YOUTH TO MATURITY

As business people develop their new enterprises into structured organizations, they have to undergo the sort of mental and emotional transformation that comes with difficulty to a Steve Jobs (Apple Computers) or to a Maseru Ibuka (Sony). As independent entrepreneurs, each required guts to break out of a mould, and to lead by example. Then followed the crisis of delegation. In a certain sense business entrepreneurs have to grow up from a state of childlike independence, into a state of strong dependence on others. In that respect, Ibuka's eastern cultural orientation made life easier for him than Jobs' western one. At the same time, they have to accept the adultlike responsibility of a business administrator, having others dependent on them.

Formal structure is required in place of improvisation. Mind is needed to functionally differentiate and to organizationally integrate. Once this crisis of dependence is resolved, the business can move on. However, the stage will inevitably be reached, with further growth and expansion, when the hierarchy of dependence will begin to collapse.

The increasingly turbulent and interdependent world eventually wreaks havoc upon rigidly authoritarian structures. Adult organizations have to pass into their midlife, thereby becoming reciprocating organizations within a community of interdependent technologies, functions, business ventures, or institutional partners. Sensitive harmonies are required at the front line, in place of rigid forms. Heart is needed to stimulate evolution and to foster interdependence. Yet even the adaptable, evolutionary and interdependent corporation cannot last forever. It has breadth but it lacks depth. It can evolve but it cannot continuously innovate. In order to grow up, from midlife to maturity, you need to advance from interdependence to transcendence.

Structure building – the global businesssphere

FROM VISION TO ACTION

A global corporation such as – on a small scale – the Bodyshop, based in Britain, has to transcend its personal, company or inter-organizational identity, and assume a universal one. Such a corporation has reached, at least to some extent, the fourth stage of its development. As such, Bodyshop, by way of an example, aspires towards the establishment of conditions for sustainable development by transforming traditional recipes into modern skin- and hair-care products.

In the process it draws from indigenous knowledge grounds in order to be continually creating new and contemporary products and services that serve to actualize its core value of ecological sustainability. In order to do this, its visionary leaders, the Roddicks, have to embark on a heroic journey, so as to transform their global vision into local action.

ENTERING THE GLOBAL BUSINESSSPHERE

In summary, the attributes of business transformation – as compared with renewal – again contain elements of both thrust and coherence (see Table 1.4). Thrust is provided by the energy flow, by intelligent enterprise, by strategic dynamics as well

Table 1.4 Midlife and mature attributes

Function	Midlife attribute	Mature attribute
	Corporate renewal	**Organizational knowledge creation**
Physical	Process re-engineering	Effusive human energy
Social	Service management	Organizational culture
Mental	Organizational learning	Intelligent enterprise
Emotional	Strategic dynamics	Visionary leadership
Analytical	Measuring performance	Knowledge creation
Intuitive	Crisis and renewal	Business ecosystem
Imaginative	Social innovation	Global businesssphere
Spiritual	Total quality	Spirit and transformation

as by spirit and transformation; coherence is rendered by a coherent organizational culture, a positioning at the innovative heart of a business ecosystem, and by visionary leadership set in the context of a global businessphere. Such a businessphere is set within alternately pragmatic and rational, holistic and humanistic approaches to business and management as to life as a whole.

In the final analysis, whereas commercial enterprise calls on sharply honed instinct, and managed organization on broadly based intellect, business renewal requires finely tuned insight and corporate transformation requires powerful imagination. Each of the above elements, in turn, inhabit the four domains of management with which this text will be concerned.

Conclusion

The ultimate business reality

Although business transformation apparently represents the ultimate stage of development, a final point is in fact never quite reached. Life and business involve a journey rather than a destination. All four developmental stages, like the four quarters of the globe, will be contained in some part of a continuously developing enterprise. Any major corporation will have embryonic and youthful as well as middle-aged and mature sectors within it. Parts of the organization, if not the whole of it, will also be in states of transition, in between stages. Finally, it may well be that a business needs to regress before it can progress.

Moreover, many if not most businesses – like individual people or whole soecities – stop growing in quantitative or in qualitative terms. More often than not they fail to purposefully evolve beyond adulthood, that is beyond the rationally managed organization, or beyond the MBA. In such a case they will be forced to regress to an earlier stage, in order to survive in the short to medium term. Ultimately, they will die, but it is impossible to predict how long they might endure.

Ages and stages

Over the course of the past two hundred years the global economy has passed through various ages, and stages in its development, thereby undergoing alternate periods of structure changing and structure building, as can be seen in Table 1.5.

Table 1.5 Ages and stages

Age	Domain	Structure changing	Structure building
Youth	Primal	Entrepreneurial revolution	Commercial/economic
Adult	Rational	Managerial revolution	Administrative/technical
Midlife	Developmental	Quality revolution	Social/ecological
Maturity	Metaphysical	Knowledge revolution	Cultural/epistemological

The domains of management upon which we shall be focusing, each bearing a strong relationship to the respective stages of business development, exist both within and without the individual enterprise. Each of these domains has groups of related management theories, and is inevitably culturally biased. Furthermore, within each one there are both 'softer' and 'harder' attributes.

The implication of all this is that the would-be 'master' manager must become familiar with all the stages of a business's development, with the two major cultural polarities serving to provide continuity (north–south) and change (east–west), and with the two sides of his or her brain that activate, between them, the worldliwise process. We now turn to the cultural polarities, starting with the dominant east–west.

2

TRANSCENDING THE
EAST–WEST DIVIDE

Finite and infinite games – chaos and complexity

Introduction – value creation

Value creation underlies wealth creation

The second of the keys to mastery is that of being able to manage change, embodied in the ability to combine 'western' chaos and 'eastern' harmony. This source of managerial mastery, then, involves transcending the 'east–west' divide. In so doing you captivate the dynamic value-creating forces involved in changing established structures, and thereby create wealth, that is new products and services, through new knowledge. In that respect Charles Hampden Turner, together with his Dutch colleague Fons Trompenaars, have done more than any other management thinkers not only to highlight the differences in business approach between the east (Asian tigers) and the west (Anglo-Saxons), but to illustrate how they can be dynamically combined.

Starting out from a background in psychology,[1] and having acquired his doctorate in philosophy from Harvard Business School, the Englishman Hampden Turner has worked relentlessly over the past thirty years to reveal the limited, indeed finite, nature of conventionally scientific approaches to management. He teamed up with Fons Trompenaars in the 1980s, and together they began to lead the way towards a comparative approach to management, highlighted through their work on 'the seven cultures of capitalism'.[2] At a time when the demise of communism and the corresponding triumph of capitalism were being heralded, Hampden Turner was ready to point out that there are at least seven major variations on the capitalist theme. The greatest of these variations was between east and west. Now Hampden Turner and Trompenaars have devoted a whole book[3] to describing the differences between East Asians and Anglo-Saxons. These differences are encapsulated in the alternate notions of an 'infinite' and a 'finite' game,[4] each of which embodies entirely different sets of values.

Traditionally 'western' neoclassical economics, they note to begin with, has regarded values as purely 'subjective'. Values only become objective when they register themselves as economic demand in the market-place. Hampden Turner and Trompenaars argue that, on the contrary, value creation underlies wealth creation. Cultures earn their livings, produce and develop effectively, that which their members most value. To believe that a particular task is valuable is the necessary prelude to doing it well. This process begins in values, is woven through and through with values, and constitutes much of the meaning of our lives and work. We can escape neither the richness of our values nor their poverty. Economic stagnation and chronically slow growth are rooted in failures of valuing, rooted both in religion and in science.

Valuing religion and science

Supernatural religion versus secular humanism

If mainstream religions secularize in the west, they lose popular appeal; if they evangelize, they become obsessed with single issues and intolerant excitements. East Asian philososophy and religion, by way of contrast, strives for human improvement and spiritual discipline in everyday life. In the Judaeo–Christian tradition, according to Hampden Turner and Trompenaars, moreover, it is good to have faith and it is bad to doubt. What is continually being described in the scriptures is a systematized conflict between belief and doubt, between eternal life and the everyday reminder of death. In direct contrast, the values of East Asia are largely paradigmatic, that is they describe a general approach to enquiry about the universe by trying to answer the question as to what we should assume when setting out to learn. The view taken by Asian philosophy is of a state of harmony in the universe, made up of contrasting and complementary elements.

We in the west, however, assume the world to be random and unrelated until such a time as discrete 'objects' or 'facts' reflect themselves in the mental mirrors of our dispassionate observations. We then manipulate these objects in predictable ways to establish an order amongst them. This orientation omits phenomena which do not fit the paradigm, including values.

Cartesian dualism versus the Way of Complementarity

Early on in western scientific theory there arose a schism between mind and body. The mind was the seat of the immortal soul, and was therefore to be left to the church, while accumulations of external facts were the province of scientific investigation. The dominant paradigm of East Asia, Hampden Turner and Trompenaars maintain, is 'The Way of Complementarity'. It is a framework not so much for accumulating facts but for elevating human nature. Their contention is that because cultures in East Asia have always thought this way, they are now busy weaving values together (e.g. computers grow ever more complex yet need to be 'user friendly'). Meanwhile, westerners pile one value on top of another, a heap of 'goods' (good things) 'added' to each other.

The implication for westerners, therefore, is that values are things, which is equivalent to seeing the world as composed of particles. The probability of getting trapped in adversarialism is obviously much higher if values are conceived as solid things, rocks of righteousness or colliding billiard balls. While waves can harmonize, solid missile-like objects cannot. The concept of harmony requires members of a culture to be different, yet create from those differences aesthetic wholes. If values are wave-forms then it follows that these are mirror-images of each other. This means that no culture is wholly strange to us. Where cultures differ is in the relative salience they give to one or another complementarity. Hence Anglo-Saxon cultures extol individuals more than communities. East Asian 'tigers' extol communities more than individuals.

To visit such cultures, according to Hampden Turner, therefore, is to discover your own 'lost values'. What we find in China, Japan and East Asia is our own world turned upside-down. For example, it makes as much sense to say – with Adam Smith – that pursuit of individual self-interest leads to customers being served and the public being benefited, as it does to say the opposite – that serving customers and seeking to benefit the public will lead to satisfying individual self-interests.

Valuing pioneering versus development

Early versus late industrializers

As a result, the experience of cultures which have pioneered capitalism is very different from the experience of those which have 'come from behind' to catch up. Hampden Turner and Trompenaars summarize their differences as follows.

	Early industrializers	Late Industrializers
Development strategy	Innovate piecemeal	Follow selectively
Role of government	Seen as ignorant about technology and foolish in business	Seen as informed about technology trends
Type of intervention	After the fact to regulate and reform – referee	Before the fact to manage and facilitate growth – coach
Educational policies	Stress on pure knowledge which is subsequently applied	Stress on successful technologies and industrial processes
Fundamental orientation	Competitive individualism	Co-operative communitarianism

	Early industrializers	*Late Industrializers*
Labour relations	Poor, because wages come under pressure when others catch up	Good, because wages increase steadily as nation catches up
Development philosophy	*Laissez-faire*: no one knows who will succeed, so don't pick winners	Managed competition: we do know what succeeds, so we pick the best teachers

Finite and infinite games

The authors' fundamental thesis, then, is that Anglo-American and East Asian capitalisms contain varying blends of competing and cooperating. These correspond with what they call finite and infinite games. Finite games are separate 'things' or episodes with no necessary connections. Infinite games are joined together like harmonized waves. Each is the mirror-image of the other. In finite games you compete, the better to cooperate. In infinite games you cooperate better to compete, but because cooperating is foremost, every game is one in an infinite series joined to the Way itself. We now turn to their more detailed argument concerning those factors serving to differentiate the 'finite' outlook of the west from the 'infinite' orientation of the east.

West versus east

Finite and infinite games

Winning versus improving the game

In the finite game, for Hampden Turner and Trompenaars, two allegedly serpentine forces struggle to be uppermost. Progress comes when losing contestants become winning ones.

This means that the more competitive will drive out the less so, the tough will exclude the tender, the efficient will displace the inefficient, and all contestants, lured by the fear of defeat, will work harder. Valuable resources, land, labour and capital, pass from the incompetent into the hands of the competent. And this, of course, benefits customers.

The characteristics of the infinite game can be so defined as to include many finite episodes along the way. You can continuously improve the game by drawing intelligent conclusions from who won and who lost successive rounds.

Finite game	*Infinite game*
Purpose is to win	Purpose is to improve the game
Improves through fittest surviving	Improves through game evolving
Winners exclude losers	Winners teach losers better plays
Winner takes all	Winning widely shared
Aims are identical	Aims are diverse
Relative simplicity	Relative complexity
Rules fixed in advance	Rules changed by agreement
Rules resemble debating contests	Rules resemble grammar of original utterances
Compete for mature markets	Grow new markets
Short-term decisive contest	Long-term generative process

You can knock out losers from one or more of these rounds, then invite them back to teach them better plays. Winning can be widely shared if knowledge from winner-take-all episodes is widely acknowledged and widely distributed. The long term includes many short-term events and contests whose outcomes informed all players. In the finite game, therefore, who wins and who loses is the whole point of playing in the first place. The purpose of the infinite game in contrast is to improve the Way (Tao), including such industrial processes as the 'way' of automobiles, the 'way' of electronics, and the 'way' of desalination. Moreover, almost no traditional Japanese 'ways' are spectator sports. Judo, bushido and aikido are forms of spiritual mastery, personal improvement, heightened discipline and infinitely expanded consciousness. The purpose is to improve plays, to perfect the game itself.

Improving through the fittest surviving versus the game evolving

We must not ignore the fact, Hampden Turner and Trompenaars assert, that the capitalism of finite game playing involves improvement. This comes about by the familiar neo-Darwinist process of the fittest surviving and forcing out the weak. This is very much to the advantage of consumers, because they will be served only by the best. The genius of capitalism, then, is that resources are channelled selectively to where the talent is. China's switch to open markets, in recent years, has thereby unleashed a whirlwind. But is this the only way, much less the best way, that economies improve? There is surely another source of improvement; for Hampden Turner it is the evolution and improvement of the game itself. The problem with the Darwinist metaphor is the assumption that the unit of survival is the individual, whereas in the reality of today, which is somewhat different from entrepreneurial yesterday, the units of survival are the individuals-in-the-game-being-played. It is technologies and whole industries which survive, informed by human heads and hearts.

The game is not a static institution, but improves and co-evolves with the players. Better games, infinitely improving, are what transforms an economy and leads to fast growth. Who wins and who loses are of minor importance compared with the development of products and services themselves. If we focus on the infinite improvement of the game itself, Hampden Turner and Trompenaars maintain, the better players will recommend themselves.

Winner takes all versus winning widely shared

At the same time, and as a direct result, they believe that to remain competitive parasitic 'losers' must cost less. The problem, of course, is that while we have knocked such losers out of finite games, we have not eliminated them from society. They are still huddled on the sidelines, sheltering in cardboard boxes and generally confronting us with their helplessness and hopelessness, not to mention the costs of welfare. With infinite games, losers are not so much eliminated or knocked out of the workplace as invited to learn from winners. There is no right to ignorance in a complexifying world. A feature of all tiger economies therefore is a vigorous domestic competition and an unwillingness to reduce the number of contestants, who are often 'down' but seldom 'out', duly supported by cross-shareholding by customers, suppliers and banks.

So rather than being eliminated from the game, contestants keep playing and keep learning how to improve the game. It helps to improve the game in fact if there are many players, and a greater diversity from which better ideas and new plays can arise, to be learned by all players. In contrast, finite games tend towards fewer players in which one or two dominate. This brings regulation and litigation in its wake.

In fact, there are many problems with the winner-take-all finite game playing: a vast number are immobilized by the hope, not the likelihood, of winning. Their aspirations are inevitably dashed. Their efforts are misdirected, their genuine talents are under-rewarded and obscured in the darkness around the spotlights. This skews national resources and celebrates inequalities. It reduces the number of, say, electrical engineers and magnifies ambitions to become millionaire barristers, playing finite games. Where, on the other hand, business is an infinite game, 'winners' are any or all of those whose participation, suggestions, contributions and commitments were incorporated into the larger game. Mitsubishi, for example, reported over the course of the 1980s an amazing twenty thousand implemented suggestions per year, which realized 'requisite variety' from the increasingly complex task in hand.

Relative simplicity versus relative complexity

In fact, while it is crucial to a finite game that contestants have the identical aim, namely to win and to wrest profits from rival players, the infinite game draws its strength from the complementarity of diverse aims. The latter outlook stems from ancient traditions in the east which seek unity amid diversity, and hence growing complexity.

Playing the market, similarly, requires a massive reduction in the subtlety and complexity of the companies being traded. Reduced to trading in simple commodities, measurable in quantities only, traders' minds run like rats in straight lines and non-communicating pathways. It may be 'smart' to make a killing in the financial markets, Hampden Turner and Trompenaars point out, but it is wise to put yourself at the places where streams of knowledge cross-fertilize and complexity reigns. It is only when you realize that possibilities are infinite that you are strategically best placed. Such possibilities are precluded by the verbal cut and thrust of the 'western' adversarial political and economic system. Britain's mother of parliaments, our two authors assert, was the first to substitute words for swords, but the use of words as swords has lingered on ever since.

The finite game is enshrined in Westminster, Washington, Canberra and Ottawa at the legislative pinnacle of these societies. The rules are to ensure that the confrontation is fair, that each side gets equal time to fire sound-bites at the other. Nothing as complex or boring as a possible solution sullies the entertainment. Indeed the only solution sought is the victory of one side and its deliberately polarized ideas. But this is not the only form, or the best form, which rules can take. Nor do rules have to be apart from content. They can be embedded within it. When we speak to each other in grammatical sentences these obey rules, yet they may be original to the speaker, even to that society. What applies to spoken sentences applies also to the ways products and services are created, developed, produced, refined and distributed. All such processes are lawful. All are elements of an infinite game. The rules within the process of creation are not restraints upon a shouting match, but ways of reconciling values so as to create a more attractive synthesis of values. What is being sought after is the process of origination itself and this will vary with the disciplines being fused. It is perhaps not surprising, Hampden Turner and Trompenaars maintain, that infinite games are preferred by cultures which dislike confrontation, prefer conversation to debate, are shy and respond indirectly to questions and believe in the values of harmony. This includes China, Japan, Indonesia, Thailand and most of the economies managed by the Chinese. In the west we tend to regard anything less than a clash of public wills as undemocratic. This limits our possibilities for growth.

Short-term contests versus long-term processes

The finite game, our two authors maintain, has an affinity for mature markets, in which products and services are well on their way to becoming commodities. In this view the market is a piece of machinery, hence the 'market mechanism', which becomes the impersonal arbiter of those playing the game, taking away resources from some contestants and allocating them to others. In contrast, infinite game players see the market as Us not It, as something we are making between us as a gift to customers. Such attitudes are typical in new fast-growing markets. If a market is an Us not an It, such a market is no longer an aggregate of isolated episodes. Rather, the market is in part our own passionate commitment to what we have wrought, a new way of engaging customers, our own dedications writ large.

Within this finite game, moreover, lie the origins of our much-lamented short-termism among western economies. The quarterly or half-yearly report to shareholders has to please Wall Street or the City, if major reductions in share price are not to occur. Long-term profitability is valued only if it consists of regular increments of short-term profitability. Those who manage assets or large mutual funds are hired and remunerated for anticipating short-term finite 'plays'. If they inform themselves of thousands of short-term exigencies they will move money out of companies making losing plays into those making winning ones, and the average performance of their share portfolios will beat those of rival asset managers. You get in fast and out fast. Every smart move is a finite game.

What makes infinite games different from finite ones is a logical joining of different plays, which transcends the making of money. Such logic includes the science and technology of the developing industry, the social process of getting the products to the people, and the learning necessary for people to use the product properly. There may be intervals of low returns as the larger system is assembled. Pay-back may be years away where a whole new game is being designed. What you need is investors who know, care, and will wait for their returns. Indeed, cross-shareholding, common among Asia's tiger economies, means that customers, contractors, suppliers, banks, townships and joint-venture partners may all own shares in each other's corporations and may have long-term interest in their prosperity and growth. This brings us onto the knowledge-based economy.

Knowledge as a perpetual feast: beyond scarcity

Knowledge relationships are infinite games

Britons, North Americans and Australians – in Hampden Turner's and Trompe-naars' eyes – tend to see knowledge as something inside the heads of hunted individuals. Such individuals, moreover, are recruited from skill markets, not groomed as an organizational or national infrastructure deliberately nurtured and enriched.

If our minds are therefore perceived in terms of 'markets' rather than as combinations of values, the authors maintain, then value will fight value within westerners' divided souls. If public service bureaucracies create 'internal markets', they maintain, every department gets into a finite game with every other, rather than saving lives or serving the public with improved knowledge. If wealth is thought of as goods, literally 'good things', then these will always will be scarce, will always use up the world's finite resources. But it is equally legitimate and much more conducive to good national morale to see wealth as streams of knowledge, capable of informing products and services, whose intelligence can tap into renewable energy sources such as sunlight. This, our authors have found from their distinct combination of empirical research and reflective experience, is the viewpoint of the Pacific Rim and much of East Asia, which is duly lodged in a diffusely oriented strategy of so-called 'knowledge intensification'.

The strategy of knowledge intensification

'Western' managers, centred on specific goods and action, tend to say, 'What is the bottom line? How much profit will this product earn?' 'Eastern' managers, oriented towards diffuse knowledge and learning tend to say, 'What will making this product teach us, our suppliers, distributors, customers, and the nation? What more might we discover while developing and supplying it? What new opportunities will open up?' Accordingly, what really creates wealth is thinking diffusely, while also identifying important specifics, that is knowledge-which-is-also-profitable. Japanese and Chinese cultures, Hampden Turner asserts, have from their very beginnings upheld knowledge, learning and the elevation of the human spirit. In the Confucian tradition, the leader is both sage and teacher, the master of the infinite game. The right to rule is based on superior knowledge, the right conduct of the leader includes the duty to impart knowledge and organize learning, and this is still true today. Between 1960 and 1985, Japan, Singapore, Hong Kong and Taiwan had gained market share in industries with high knowledge intensity, while losing it in industries with low knowledge intensity. These four 'little tigers', especially, were deliberately running down the simple products they made and switching human and capital resources to industries of higher complexity. In direct contrast, the USA, Britain, France and Germany were either not upgrading their knowledge intensities or, in the case of the USA, increasing its share of relatively simple products.

For example, when Goh Chok Tong, Singapore's Minister of Trade and Industry, presented his budget in the early 1980s, he announced that the replacement of labour intensity with knowledge intensity had become the challenge of the new decade. Textiles, shoes and furniture – as he saw it – would run into import barriers everywhere. Singapore therefore had to leap to a higher level, that of a modern industrial economy mastering complex tasks, based upon science, technology, skills and knowledge. The search was now on for high-wage, high-knowledge industries including semi-conductors, integrated circuits, computers, speciality chemicals and pharmaceuticals as well as industrial electronic equipment.

Singapore's Economic Development Board (EDB) had thereby become a 'business architect'. As such it was able to broker relationships, provide or obtain financing, manage the industrial park, find joint-venture partners. It was involved, moreover, in setting up the requisite technology and providing what the then president, Lee Kuan Yew, called the 'software' or mental programming to industrialize. More recently, in the 1990s, Singapore has launched the International Hub 2000 programme, aimed at turning the nation into the intellectual and strategic headquarters of the burgeoning regional economies. The governments of Singapore, Japan and Malaysia, then, are not so much picking winners as picking teachers. They are not, for example, favouring one company over another in precision engineering. Rather they are favouring precision engineering per se. They are saying that these processes will educate the whole economic infrastructure. What the tiger economies have decided, in effect, is that $1,000 worth of potato or casino chips are not worth as much to culture as a similar amount of pentium chips. For the enhanced intelligence of pentium-chip making has ramifications for all subsequent games. What looks to us in the west like a series of one-off contests is for tiger economies successive rungs in a knowledge ladder by which they ascend to infinite heights. Provided markets accept both simple and complex products, there is greater potential value within the complex products.

In fact, processes involved in making and using these, Hampden Turner and Trompenaars point out, are educative of all concerned. Moreover, the pursuit of such learning, they maintain, may bring more freedom in its wake than beating the drum for human rights. It was always wrong to exploit workers, but as the world complexifies it becomes uneconomic and in fact plain stupid. Indeed within such a knowledge-intensified context, the traditional theory of the firm set within the context of a level playing field, as Michael Porter has latterly pointed out,[5] loses its effective power, and hence its realistic appeal.

Catalysing development: beyond the level playing field

Catalysts and clusters

Free-for-all competition, just like first-past-the-post democratic elections, and indeed trial by jury, are all versions of those 'level playing fields' which are much loved by Anglo-Saxon cultures. Financial markets are also examples of the same. All publically quoted companies vie with each other to make returns to shareholders. Those who most succeed get most to invest. These rules are allegedly neutral, value-free, meritocratic and governed by timeless economic laws. But what if such games, Hampden Turner and Trompenaars ask, are not separate episodes of win-lose conflict? What if games form clusters, so that victory in one makes for victory in a second? If these victories help generate another, then what is the secret of their connections?

Clusters in fact help to explain why films are made in Hollywood, currency swaps take place in the City of London, flowers are bought and sold in Spenger and Aalsmeer in Holland. It is not 'efficient' to have such a huge proportion of the world's currencies exchanged in that one City square mile, but it is essential for learning within the cluster. Clusters, moreover, are not only a historical phenomenon; they can also be created, though more easily in some cultural contexts than in others. For finite game players find the consensus required in clustering very difficult and frustrating to achieve. So, when they do combine, it is often as allies in a finite game against third parties.

If East Asian Singapore goes too far in building a participative consensus which excludes those who declare an opposition to that process, then western Anglo-Saxons surely go too far in staging colourful contests from which intelligent, participative consensus building is entirely absent.

Singapore is less democratic in its toleration of outright opposition and media attacks on its leaders, but it is more democratic in its struggles to create negotiated consensus and intelligent participation amongst its citizens and employees. And there is no doubt, Hampden Turner and Trompenaars maintain, that negotiated consensus does more for economic growth than rhetorical battles.

Creating clusters – unity in diversity

Clusters, moreover, are in the end not just clusters of economic units, but clusters of ideas which reinforce each other and radiate larger meaning. Visions are realizable through the clustering of ideas. Clustering industries is in every way consistent with the logic of community, the patterns of complementarity and the aesthetics of ebb and flow. Western approaches to creativity, on the other hand, tend to focus upon the heads of lone geniuses in which divine sparks fly. East Asian approaches, conversely, steer professions and disciplines into conjunction and cross-fertilization, wherein ideas are likely to fuse and hybridize. It is a similar pattern to the individualistic western version, but conducted at a social level. Precision engineering, for example, is not simply a cluster in its own right, it is a crucial ingredient in the modernization of all complex manufacturing, and clusters with industry after industry.

There is a clear difference, therefore, between western and 'tiger' approaches to government intervention. In western economies where state initiatives are permitted, these are all product- or project-specific. The Tennesse Valley Authority in America, Concorde or Ariane in Europe, all had specific objectives. They were high risk in the sense that they visibly succeeded or failed. All efforts converge on a single aim. You win or you lose. But the interventions by tiger economies are quite different.

Initiatives are aimed at improving 'seminal' technologies in which a great many businesses need to be successful. The metaphors are biological, 'rice of industry', 'blood of business', 'food chain', 'seed corn' and 'technology trees'. In such 'seminal' interventions clusters beget clusters; machine tools, robots and semi-conductors procreate successive generations of new products. Products have knowledge 'genes' which are passed on from one generation to the next. A consensus orientation, ultimately, is vital to the building of clusters, in which victory in one game contributes to victories in clusters of games or one infinite game. These are typically joined by horizontal technologies which act as catalysts.

Targeting a technology common to a cluster develops the entire group. Clustering also greatly increases the chance of fortuitous and creative connections, combining competition with cooperation.

'Co-opetition': beyond competitiveness

Competing cooperatively to learn

From the beginning of industrialization, the competitive ethos used by the west to explain and justify its success has posed a dilemma for East Asia. These nations and other emerging economies of the region are overwhelmingly communitarian and cooperative in their cultural values. So East Asians are now learning to compete in a way that improves their communities. This combination, which we call co-opetition, may prove far more powerful than the pure competition advocated by the west. The logic of cooperative competing uses competition to discover which of several solutions, processes or products are best, and then shares these among all the players so that play improves overall, and the game itself evolves. Under this logic, competing is both play and learning. By comparing many rival efforts and ideas you differentiate the very best. By swiftly disseminating best practices you incorporate this vital knowledge, so that all players benefit.

Pure competition dis-engages the knowledge economy

The problem with what Hampden Turner and Trompenaars term 'promiscuous' competitiveness is that the whole world is seen as competing with you. Yet in fact scores, perhaps hundreds, of business activities do not compete with yours so much as complement yours. In East Asia as in France, examinations are for entry into elite institutions, in contrast with the Anglo-Saxon world, where, for example, you exit educational institutions with an individual rank order. Once you are part of the group, attempts to distinguish yourself from colleagues cease. You are a *todai* (top-school) graduate, your destiny is to add lustre to the group. It is the same in France. You do not ask the graduate of the grande école how they ranked. It is enough that they were admitted and graduated. The vitality of connecting self to society, in that 'eastern' context, is that each one of us dies but the school, the corporation, the society continues through its products and processes, as do our genes and the 'genes' of knowledge we are able to pass on. This difference in orientation between 'east' and 'west' is further illustrated, in institutional terms, by what Japanese American William Ouchi[6] termed the co-opetitive 'M-form' and competitive 'H-form' organizations.

The H-form (holding company) is the traditional conglomerate, with a financial holding company. Such an entity acquires a portfolio of companies in different industries, and manages them through an 'internal market', with most investment funds going to those with the highest returns. This, for Hampden Turner and Trompenaars, of course, is a finite game, with every business unit competing with every other for finite funds. This H-form misses out, therefore, on the opportunity to cluster and cross-fertilize technologies. Its leaders are largely accountants and lawyers with scant knowledge of the scattered technologies within the portfolio, but astute about what all those portfolios share – money. Typically the businesses are low in knowledge intensity, something that can be managed at a distance without involvement. In contrast, the M-form corporation groups its divisions around one central core of developing technologies which all divisions co-operate to enhance. They compete in selling the different applications of these technologies, for example watches, calculators, organizers. It follows, in this case, that decentralized competing is the derivative of centralized cooperation and feeds back profits to sustain the process.

The leaders of M-forms, typically scientists, engineers and inventors, share a knowledge of the corporation's core competence. Its logic is less of money than of science and technology. This development of core competence, moreover, is an infinite game. It is usually characterized by what Ouchi calls a 'clan' culture of enthusiasts for the potential of their technology, be it micro-electronics or metal ceramics. In contrast, the H-form has a market culture, flexible and fast in its optimum allocations, but also superficial, abstract and overly quantitative. It cannot grasp the density of interconnections, cannot see the new emerging.

A good way of finding out whether a culture is really more cooperative or more competitive, Hampden Turner maintains, is to see how it behaves in a crisis when thrown back on basic values. While the Japanese do have elaborate contingency plans to save the cooperative group of employees, the first act of an American or British company in trouble is to shed labour. The dream of an infinite game thereby shatters into tiny pieces at the first sign of trouble, as we look for people to eject from the game to save ourselves. An 'inner-directed' as opposed to an 'outer-directed' orientation, as we shall see, prevails. This 'rational' outlook, whether embodied in 'total quality' or in 'business process re-engineering', affects the approach to product, as much as to organization, development.

Cycles of return: beyond reasoning

Western inner direction versus East Asian outer direction

Almost nothing is as precious to the western Enlightenment as are our reasoning powers. Reason is typically contrasted with instinct, imagination, faith and desire – all of them intellectually untrustworthy. We are exhorted to look to our reason and eschew emotion. Enlightenment reason, according to Hampden Turner and Trompenaars, rested on the specific premise that an individual's goals and intentions should be deliberately planned, calculated and implemented, so that consequences logically follow. 'I think therefore I am', said René Descartes. Our two authors call this orientation 'inner direction'. In fact, the value common to all celebrations of reason is that the human actor should be 'in the driver's seat'.

The destinies of managers in East Asian cultures are often decided elsewhere, that is outside of their inner-directed selves. What therefore works, for them, is seizing upon 'inner-directed' technologies, originating in the west, and refining these for Asian and western markets, via an 'outer-directed' customer orientation. Losers in such a society are those who clamour to get their inner-directed way and so create, outwardly, disharmony everywhere. It is the willingness, therefore, to connect your aims to other people's, to react to their suggestions in an outer-directed mode, which creates harmony. As such it is the joining of game to game which creates infinite games. As the environment of business fills up with players, contestants and complementary businesses, every move becomes a reaction to every other move, so that more outer-directedness is required as businesses complexify. Such thinking, in terms of apposite approaches and time coordinations that will connect and relate you to others in a continuous, infinite process of aesthetic wholeness, is, for Hampden Turner, an outer-directed mode. This involves thinking more often in circles than in straight lines.

Thinking in lines of reduction – thinking in amplifying circles

Americans, accordingly, use feedback to reduce deviance from their original sovereign intentions. They remain inner-directed like missiles homing in on a chosen target. The Japanese, conversely, may use feedback to amplify deviances towards the sovereign intentions of their customers. They assume that customers will want something different from what the company originally intended to supply, and that such differences must be discovered and catered for. There may be learning loops in both cultures, but while one narrows, the second broadens, while one regards any deviance as 'error', the second regards it as legitimate diversity of demand. The Singapore economy, according to our two authors, therefore, has been built almost entirely upon outer-directed reactions to the initiatives of others. So while multinationals (MNEs) provide the text, Singapore provides the context, while MNEs 'did their own thing', these 'things' converged into clusters of mutual assistance and cross-hybridization. It is like conducting a huge orchestra so that there is harmony among the international players of various instruments. No wonder the Economic Development Board (EDB) refers to itself as a Knowledge Arbitrageur,[7] a Catalyst, a Vision Sharer and Information Hub. It is the top management sounding board to whom the world's mightiest corporations bring their ideas and plans to be finely fitted together. There is more to business, and to economic development, than establishing a level playing field, creating an enterprising environment, or enhancing competitiveness.

Self-worth and economic worth: beyond achievement

Aligning people with needs

The finite games a person, or indeed a whole society, has played may give us access to their individual or economic track records, but not to their personal or national sense of purpose. People are rewarded according to how much they are appreciated in the open society. It is a form of natural justice, harnessing the initiatives of individuals to the requirements of corporations and the demands of markets. Achievement is pragmatism applied to commerce. Such finite games are certainly adequate for a thrilling calendar of sporting fixtures, with our gazes focused on victory and averted from the vanquished, but they are only half of what it takes to build a modern economy and grow rather than shrink in world stature.

Achieving what has been deemed to be important

What is important for Hampden Turner and Trompenaars, in combining eastern and western outlooks, is the capacity to first choose your values, technologies and industries and then achieve these goals. In other words, you need some form of ascription of value to escape from the finite games into an infinite game. Conversely, where achievement is defined by the relative prominence of successful contestants, then markets become the sole arbiters of what is true and beautiful. We speak of 'selling' our proposition to others, or of 'buying in' to a new policy. In fact moral majorities which have struck America periodically supposedly represent desperate yearnings to reach beyond the subjectivism of markets to something higher, infinite and transcendent.

You can only create an infinite game, in other words, if you first agree on what is valuable and then set out to achieve this. Such an infinite game as played out by most Asian tigers reads as follows. Values *ascribed* to the developmental state and to the learning society are superordinate goals by which you inspire encourage and motivate all citizens to *achieve* such aims so as to fulfil these. This is a different perspective from the classically *laissez-faire*-based western one.

Natural versus learned advantages

It has long been the endeavour of Anglo-Saxon economists to keep their 'science' free of values. To that end the nineteenth-century English economist Ricardo proposed that nations specialized in different products, not so much because they valued them, but because of their having a natural advantage in producing them. Hence Britain would use its damp meadowland to raise sheep and produce wool, while Portugal should utilize its sunny slopes to grow grapes and produce port wine. What this theory does not explain, though, is why Britain prospered mightily in the eighteenth and nineteenth centuries and Portugal did not.

Such theories of 'natural advantage' have had little attraction to East Asian economies, beginning with Japan, because they had virtually no such advantages. All they really had was people, lots of them, and so they set them to the task of learning. Learned, not natural, advantages have therefore been the secret of the tiger economies. It was also the secret of the United Kingdom's industrial revolution, but the British invented a different explanation and lost the thread. Such a thread follows the argument that rising markets, at least according to Hampden Turner and Trompenaars, create knowledge more slowly and less certainly than rising knowledge creates markets. You cannot grow fast if highly skilled employees are not abundant and hence relatively cheap, and if consumers are not educated enough to use your products. By putting achievement ahead of knowledge, we expect knowing to be pulled in achievement's wake. Therefore, our two authors maintain, we have it back to front. It is knowledge that adds value to achieving.

If you put learning first as an ascribed value, then people will use it to achieve, and the more knowledge and skill that is around the more they will use. Knowledge-intensive products will arise because it is boring and unfulfilling to do anything less. Moreover, the workplace will be where you learn and grow, as opposed to the western concept of learning at school in order to achieve in the workplace, and buying smarter people when you need them via 'headhunters'.

Knowledge surpluses rather than scarcities also affect the design and implementation of new technologies. In Japan technologies are used to upgrade worker skills. There is so much skill that technology depends upon being able to use it. First, value is ascribed to health, education and social responsibility, and achievement follows, not the other way around. Knowledge is therefore an infinite game spread by affection and other close relationships. To see in it only pre-match training for competing achievers shrinks its value to a fraction of the whole. Cultures thinking in this way are in grave danger of falling behind.

Another vital reason for ascribing status to people before they achieve is that human potential precedes achievement. Achieving is a prophecy that fulfils itself and that prophecy must ascribe status to all actors in the economy in order for the achievements to be generated. Moreover, within a learning environment the leaders are the coaches and mentors of those that achieve, not achievers themselves, although they may have achieved earlier. Such employees' value lies less in their latest achievements and more in the breadth and versatility of their capability to achieve. Singapore is now following Switzerland and Japan in skills-deepening programmes. The idea is to train workers in the theoretical base which joins their old jobs to their new ones. In this way any changes they must make have one coherent meaning, an underlying theme of continuity. Such a continuity arises out of a respect for age, and tradition, just so long as both are being continually renewed.

Seniority, legacy and renewal

Respect for age and seniority, Hampden Turner and Trompenaars stress, is much more a feature of Chinese and Japanese culture than of an Anglo-Saxon one. Promoting by seniority, in East Asia therefore, creates a system in which top people can create an environment for achievement, a culture of excellence, without having to prove or achieve themselves. They can listen, encourage, guide, advise and manage values, while their subordinates can consummate those values by achieving them. Steady promotion by age – based on qualities of humility, modesty and judgement – does not prevent executives competing, rather it ensures they compete in their contributions rather than in gaining personal rewards.

The achievement system provides a useful pretext for ridding the company of non-achievers. It allows the supervisor to attribute successes or failures to particular subordinates, as opposed to attributing them to his or her relationship to those subordinates and the culture of his or her workplace. In 'firing' the person, the supervisor only appears to have rid him- or herself of the problem, which is often right there in his or her office. If it is difficult to get rid of people, you are more likely to invest in their training and development. Dumping losers prevents you from learning how you might have helped them to win. We have all heard by now of midlife crisis. It is often a crisis of meaning, a confrontation with the futility of winning the finite game for promotion. You have reached the summit of your ambition only to experience a profound anti-climax, a spiritual vacuum. This helps us to explain why the better American multinationals, Motorola and Ford for example, have begun to ask their senior officers, what is your legacy? What do you seek to leave behind you, as a lasting gift to your corporation, to your customers and to your country? The form this legacy takes is the creation of values, ideas, vision and a sense of mission which other people will consummate after you have gone.

Motorola's response to the 2020 vision statement of the Malaysian government, cited by Hampden Turner and Trompenaars, is remarkable in such legacy terms. For the company has created joint institutes with the University of Malaysia, has led to the co-founding of the Penang Skills Centre, has made the R & D centre of Land Mobile Products the design HQ of Motorola's worldwide operations, and has improved the quality of locally developed and designed products 150 times over – integrating in the process all its manufacturing technology through information technology. Employing over 12,000 people in Malaysia, Motorola accounted for 10 per cent of the value of the country's manufactured exports in 1991. Moreover, the company, for example, organizes visits to orphanages and old people's homes, sustains and donates to local schools and libraries, and constructs children's playgrounds, in order to foster social and cultural as well as technological and economic renewal. To all of these together Motorola ascribes value, and it is helping both Malaysia as a whole and itself in the process.

What is worth achieving?

Hampden Turner and Trompenaars maintain, then, that there is a natural tendency for countries coming from behind economically to ask themselves 'Which technologies should we adopt? Which among this variety of tools is worth studying and using? What will our culture express with such tools?' In this way, developing countries ascribe status to a business activity and then set forth to achieve it. Achievement remains essential, but as a vindication of values already indicated. Superordinate goals which reconcile many sectional interests are the form which value ascriptions take. They give a larger meaning to all economic activities and allow citizens to dedicate themselves to a transcendent cause. Knowledge, moreover, for Hampden Turner and Trompenaars, is the medium in which novel achievements are expressed.

In the context of a finite game, the expense of a college education may pay back to the achieving individual too little for it to compete successfully with alternative uses of the time taken. Conversely, within the context of an infinite game, because knowledge is the ascribed value of society, it self-generates among its members, and all achievements become thereby more complex, scarce and valuable. When you reach retirement, moreover, in individualistic western countries, even the triumph of getting to the top of your 'game' rings somewhat hollow. You look down from the edifice you climbed to see only your personal replacements, your individual retirement, your finite lifetime. Conversely, in East Asian economies you see genuine and lasting value in the vision and legacy you leave behind with those whose potential growth and learning you nurtured, and whose achievements you made possible. These are set altogether in the possible context, finally, of one amongst many lives to come hereafter, stretching beyond a single life contract!

Dynamic prosperity: beyond contract compliance

Contracts as finite, relationships as infinite

If we ask what makes our western finite games so fragmented, so easily insulated from larger meanings, the answer for Hampden Turner and Trompenaars is compliance with contracts. We 'westerners' typically use contracts to define, to 'put an end to' business activities, so that we conceive of these as separate games and finite episodes. Contracts, the two authors argue, force foreigners to play our game, by our rules. In a very real sense, they say, we use contract law as a defence against anxiety. East Asia, for example, presents us with so much perplexity or ambiguity that the impact they have may overwhelm us. As a result, it is difficult to control such 'foreigners', but it is possible to control the games we play with them, by stipulating all the possible moves.

However, such defences are erected at a severe cost to our opportunities to prosper and compete. In most of East Asia the relationship comes before the contract. Where changing circumstances render contract terms onerous to one or both parties, let the terms be changed. The mutual relationship which made the contract initially takes precedence over the terms negotiated. After all, a relationship is of potentially infinite duration. Where you mingle your genes or products you are forever joined through the next generation of offspring. Contracts are mere milestones, recordings of your progress along the way, joint understandings reached at finite moments of time. It follows that the infinite game which is your developing relationship will define, and if necessary re-define, all contracts between you.

The finite game of contract-terms-before-relationships sees good relationships as the product of contract compliance, of 'keeping your word'. 'Your word is your bond.' Unfortunately such literal compliance becomes a weapon of finite game playing. By enforcing your 'foreign' partner and potential opponent to play by your rules, on your terms, in your way, you wrest advantage from him by legally or morally enforcing contract terms. But in the infinite game it is your relationship that wins. Each partner ensures that all contracts are complied with by going beyond the contract to a process of mutual enrichment, wherein escalating favours are reciprocated, relationships deepen and performance improves. Like bannisters on stairs, as Hampden Turner and Trompenaars vividly portray, contracts are to be gripped only in emergencies. Far more important is the growing satisfaction of both parties, and the capacity of their relationship to learn and accumulate information.

Contracts are the floor – reciprocity is the ceiling

Most contracts among major Japanese, and some tiger, corporations, then, are used to make a minimal floor, below which the contract has been breached. Standards specified are the springboard. From this springboard the supplier or contractor is expected to gain higher elevation after each try. Going beyond contracts is therefore a moral rather than a legal act. Relationships are renewed and maintained by feelings of indebtedness. The problem with carefully specified contracts, in fact, is that you get what is due to you, and that is all. Contracts are closed systems. Relationships, but not contracts, are wide open to infinite possibilities. A consequence of such relationships being open is that these are flexible and can change as situations around them change. But contracts, being closed systems, are brittle. Circumstances change but contracts insist upon compliance with logic that no longer applies. In most cases these changes elevate the fortunes of one party, while depressing those of another. A finite game breaks out which ruins the relationship.

A characteristic of contracts, moreover, is the accurate, signed reports they give of what both parties promised to do. There it is in writing. In contrast, relationships are all about rapport, the enjoyment of another's presence. Reporters fail to relate, while rapporters try to protect their relationship from 'the truth'. But, and this is crucial, rapport can, like relationships, include tough reports. Any hope of influencing change needs a toughness about the predicament you face together combined with a tenderness about your mutually intense relationships. This is the stage when *tatamae* – surface politeness and etiquette – gives way to *honne* – the sharing of deep feelings.

Western cultures, moreover, especially English-speaking ones, prefer the individual to articulate clear and precise ideas. The clarification takes place in the mind before speaking. East Asian cultures, for the most part, prefer more vague and tentative statements, clarified through dialogue and relationships. In other words, meanings and precise formulations are negotiated. It is considered ungraceful and uncouth to confront other people with completed and pre-clarified propositions of your own, so that in effect you shove these down their throats. While westerners are trying to build a solid edifice out of agreed pieces, like laying bricks, the Japanese are inviting you to jointly mould a lump of soft clay, into an aesthetic and elegant shape, going back to parts westerners thought had been agreed hours ago and modifying their shape.

Beyond contract compliance

Hampden Turner and Trompenaars argue that, overall, contracts have the effect of chopping relationships into finite episodes, each independent of the other. While for westerners the contract terms are the end point, for easterners they are the starting point. While contracts were close, brittle and frozen in time, relationships are open to new ideas, flexible in the face of new environments.

The infinite games preferred in East Asia start with vague, ambiguous and tacit knowledge learned from customers and colleagues. This becomes more precise, more clear, more refined, better articulated selling propositions as a result of dialogue. Instead of seeking consensus on the value of the contract, the two parties look for congruence between two quite different needs, which through dynamic reciprocity can deliver ever more value. Latent, tacit and vague ideas are exchanged between confidantes in a process of mutual refinement, so that finished and clearly defined products can emerge, with excellent prospects of pleasing customers. The traditional western corporation states that individuals learn, thereby becoming like 'units of intelligence'. Yet knowledge is stored in relationships. A learning organization resembles a fractal super-brain, a brain of brains with neural connections.

No wonder Japanese auto producers average 30 suggestions per worker, 23 of which are implemented, whereas in the US the average is 1.3, of which 0.7 are implemented. In contrast to inclusive relationships, contracts are exclusive, excluding all issues save those deemed relevant to the finite contest.

One of the commonest accusations, finally, made against the East Asian tigers is 'predatory' pricing. This would be the right word if we were playing finite games. But 'sacrificial' is the better description of those trying to set an infinite game in motion. Suppose the customer knows all too well the cost to you of the sacrificial price, and decides to save you from the consequences of your generosity by quadrupling his or her order? Such is the value of reciprocity. People who have made themselves dependent on other people's gratitude and kindness establish close bonds of trust. If we save each other's economic lives we are blood brothers, partners for ever, infinite players. We now turn from the differing perceptions of social space, pertaining to east and west, to equally varied perspectives on physical time.

Designing with time: beyond time and motion

Finite sequences, infinite circles

Clock time has always had a powerful grip on the western imagination. Newton, on the one hand, conceived of the cosmos as a celestial clock, wound up by God and left for the faithful to discover. Eastern philosophies, on the other hand, have conceived of a cycle of eternal return, a seasonal Tao of shifting day and night, summer and winter. Time in fact plays a crucial part in the history of western industrialism. It was America's Frederick Taylor who developed time and motion study. This in turn gave rise to scientific management and to Fordism. Work was 'machine timed'. Mass manufacturing geared to the mass market was spectacularly successful in lowering production costs.

With tasks reduced to a few simple hand motions, workers could be trained in hours. However, by the 1980s, international competition put an end to this western dominance as cheap labour came into play. A sequence, or a straight line, is necessarily finite. You compete in a race and pass the winning post. But a circle never ends. If you make a line into an arc and join two arcs you get a circle, and infinite games go round and round forever. The same principle applies in the workplace or factory. While it is obviously better to complete jobs in the fastest possible time, this is only half the battle. The faster such sequences, the greater the challenge to co-ordinate them. Nor is sheer speed the answer if this keeps workers stupid, divided and cheap. 'Making a quick buck' may not be conducive to the development of complex products, built to last. The race against time is a popular motif through western cultures. Time wins. People and their values lose. And, according to Hamden Turner and Trompenaars, inevitably these failures lead to re-engineering. In contrast, the inifinite game works by synchronization. Processes are run in parallel. To do this requires synchronous approaches.

If the future is aimed at the development of knowledge and the elaboration of core competence, you can no more afford to stop investing than to stop thinking. After all, the country, the corporation, the community and the family all survive your own death. Your savings not only transcend your own life, but in Buddhist religion could facilitate and enrich your re-birth. Long-term orientations are also involved in making 'remote connections' over time. For example, the current standards of public education are crucially important to the effectiveness of the skill-intensive economy thirty to forty years hence. In contrast, Hampden Turner asserts, Britain's public education sector is restricted by the fact that the elite educate their children privately. In California, moreover, as of 1995, spending on prisons and crime fighting overtook spending on education for the first time in the history of the state.

Customization, flexible manufacturing and short runs

If the Americans invented ever faster motions in ever less time, then the Japanese brought to this just-in-time synchronization. Stockpiles of inventory, hitherto, had become the universal symbol of poor coordination. Led by Taichi Ohno of Toyota, Japanese industry declared war on such excess inventories, thereby exposing uncoordinated workings. The activities of the whole plant needed fine-tuning. Work now resembled a choreographed dance. Suppliers clubs proliferated, exchanging information, sharing training activities, and coordinating delivery schedules as well as ensuring compatibility of parts.

The need for such careful synchronization rises as customization increases and shorter production runs become necessary. American inspired high-speed, standardized mass production is in general decline among wealthy economies because its long runs are typically suited to simpler goods, and lower-wage economies have captured these markets. The shorter the run, the more tool changes are necessary, the more specialized components need to be ordered, and the greater becomes the demand for lightning synchronization. The flexible manufacturing that results, which was first developed by Toyota in the 1950s, qualifies the economies of scale with so-called economies of scope. The line moves as fast as it ever did, but combinations of different components reach the line, meaning that every car is customized.

Planning for hybridization and fusion

In the west, products, like profit centres, make individual contributions to the 'bottom line'. It is all immaculately logical and sequential. But cultures which think synchronically need to consider that products are like families. Each such product may be thought of as carrying knowledge 'genes'. Joined with the genes of a product partner, and passed onto the next generation of products, these serve to develop the core competencies of the company. Just as families turn outwards to strangers to avoid the incest taboo, so products cross-fertilize with different products to procreate offspring. Two finite game players join together in the infinite game of creation, which develops more like a spiral than a straight line.

In fact we have now more or less convinced ourselves even in the west that planning, in the form of straight-line forecasting, is a pretty hazardous process. We still do it because the only alternative would be to appear to drift. Synchronous planning, as conducted by Singapore's EDB in conjunction with MIT in America, has instead steered corporations towards hybridization and fusion. Rather than saying 'We plan to produce this specific product by this specific date', synchronous plans cross-fertilize technologies and businesses with high predispositions to 'mate' and then wait for something to happen. For example, the area of 'mechatronics' – a fusion of mechanical with electrical engineering – is highly developed in Japan and has also been taken up in Singapore, Korea, Malaysia and Taiwan.

While most western thinkers attribute creativity to the interaction of single ideas within one mind, Hampden Turner and Trompenaars maintain, the Japanese view creativity as the interaction of many ideas within a team, especially where its membership is cross-disciplinary. Hence, for example, the bullet-train was created by locomotive engineers working with aircraft engineers who were unemployed because the Japanese aircraft industry had been dismantled by the occupation government after the war. The EDB today has a cluster development fund as well as joint training initiatives where partners are required to 'showcase' their latest equipment. Synchronicity is everywhere. Pull, as opposed to push, strategies are now entering into common parlance in the context of product development.

Pull and push strategies: beyond time and motion

'Time to market' has become a major preoccupation of business strategists. Generally speaking, in the west, a company with faster 'cycles' from product conception to product delivery will win most business. It is conceived again as a finite game with speed the essence of victory. Amongst 43 nations surveyed by our two authors, 4 Asian tigers – Hong Kong, Taiwan, Japan and Singapore – were amongst the top 5 when it came to 'time to market', with New Zealand as the fifth! These are all characterized by 'pull' rather than 'push' strategies. In other words, rather than scheduling tightly, and engaging in progress chasing, they count backwards from the time the customer wants the product, and synchronize the time of the rendezvous. Just-in-time is not objective but inter-subjective. Speed is only half of it. Synchronicity is the rest.

In fact the psychology of long-termism versus short-termism depends on whether past, present and future are seen as objective increments passing in sequence (short term) or as overlapping ideas with which to design your strategy (long term). You are more likely to save, domestically, if the 'past' and the 'future' is with you in the same room to deliberate with the 'present'. Moreover, as the more developed economies encounter complexity, more customization and short runs are required, and hence more synchronization. How fast you move is therefore nothing like as important as how smartly you design activities in parallel processes. The finite game implies that the economies of scope, together with variety, flexibility, customization and short runs are sacrificed to the economies of scale, with standardized mass manufacturing in long runs. The infinite game, conversely, implies that with feeder lines converging at synchronized intervals, variety, scope and customization among the products assembled can be combined with the fast movement of the final assembly line.

Similarly, within the context of a finite game, product lines which lose money or make insufficient money tend to get beaten by winning products. By way of contrast, within the context of an infinite game, by combining products into families and cross-fertilizing them, new lines and rapid developments take place which will 'win'. Such 'symbiosis is a form of co-operative competing that extols the Life Principle, as opposed to the west's vision of the Universal Mechanism, otherwise known as modernism. Symbiosis, then, is post-modernist. Symbiosis grows from oppositions among cultivated sensibilities. It moves beyond quantities to ever new qualities of combination'.[8]

Conclusion – value integration

The double helix and the cross

In the final analysis, for Hampden Turner and Trompenaars, it is critical to reach beyond east–west rivalries, to explore the processes of development itself, and how human beings supply each other with what they value.

For we are not going to create wealth successfully, they maintain, unless we put into the goods we make and the services we provide all the knowledge, values and commitments at our command. Modern competitive conditions demand of us nothing less. The issue to be addressed therefore is not that east is right and west is wrong. Were this so, the west would not have jumped off so early or got so far ahead. Nations such as Singapore have learnt assiduously from the west. What accelerates economic development is reconciling opposites, for example individuals with groups, narrow and broad criteria, achieving that to which value has been ascribed. However, currently the East Asians are learning much faster from us than we are from them. Knowing that they were behind in the east, they studied us, in the west. Knowing we were ahead, we 'westerners' first established colonies, our two authors assert, then patronized 'foreigners', and now we lecture them!

If the pioneer economies of the west are to learn from East Asia, it must be in our own way, based on our own strengths. If East Asians can start with communitariansim, and learn from the west how to make that community responsive to every individual through democratic means, then North America and Europe can start with their own individualism and learn from East Asians how to better form groups, teams and communities in the workplace and in civic society. All great cultures, east and west, are treasure troves of contrasting ideas and traditions. There is a great variety of individualism in western societies. For example, Dutch and Scandinavian individualism puts far more stress on individual responsibility to others than do Anglo-Saxons. New England Puritans were highly individualistic but still formed tight, worshipful communities. English Quakers doffed their hats to no man, gave women unequalled rights, formed small groups linked into networks, contributing massively to the industrial revolution.

You can start with the finite game playing, but as the coming of death concentrates your mind, you search for more infinite meanings. Competition that never moves beyond finite plays, in fact, is what has earned western business people their reputation for philistinism, and has made business writing so impoverished. We have to learn how to create wealth, Hampden Turner and Trompenaars maintain, without inflicting so much damage on each other. Because, moreover, losers are so expensive – a quarter of a million dollars for each child sent to a secure unit in the US – cultures with fewer losers will prevail economically and morally.

In the great struggle of theoretical physics in the twentieth century we find complementarity at the base of our hardest discipline. In biology we find a double helix, clockwise and anti-clockwise winding past each other. Parliamentary debate allows you to fight but to do so peacefully. All this is a marvellously contrived synthesis of contrasting values. It is upon such masterfull integration that all great cultures depend. The continuous improvement of Deming, the cluster development ideas of Porter, Senge's 'fifth discipline' originated concepts the East Asians now use.

**Knowledge-intensive
strategy**

Generate more *diffuse*
knowledge as as to
create . . .

more scarcity, more
specific profits, with
which to . . .

**Cluster-development
strategy**

Catalysis and horizontal
strategies promote . . .

the *survival* of the
"fittingest" joined
by . . .

Co-opetition strategy

Competing which is friendly
and non-traumatic leads
to . . .

Co-operating based
on the victorious idea
shared by all to
sponsor

**Continuous-improvement
strategy**

Inner-directed data and
information from juniors
allows . . .

Outer-directed senior
staff to integrate this
knowledge and
elicit . . .

**Strategic superordinate
goals**

Value being *ascribed* to
the key aims of the
learning society . . .

motivates citizens to
achieve such aims, so
as to fulfil the . . .

**Making relationships
more valuable**

Contracts with *universal*,
legal obligations are texts
within

the context of
particular relationships
whose warmth
cements . . .

Designing with time

Faster delivery of products
and accelerated *sequences*
are abetted by . . .

lightning
synchronization of
parallel processes
which facilitate . . .

Figure 2.1 How the values of East Asia are transforming business

To cross cultures, finally, is to discover the unknown self within our own beings. The cross bars symbolize our rival fanaticism, from which we are redeemed when infinite meanings are created from finite conflicts. This reconciliation heals shattered minds and grows value systems. The infinite game is as much Jewish or Christian as it is Taoist or Buddhist. In fact it is a metaphor for a part of the double helix. Hampden Turner and Trompenaars borrow consciously from the life science of development in order to argue for the development of values. They suspect that the so-called market mechanism is closer to an organism and that economics would be less dismal if it had modelled itself on something alive and growing. For, they maintain, we grow by differentiating ourselves (finitely), and integrating ourselves (infinitely). All cultures everywhere are laboriously trying to spiral upwards, sometimes gaining, sometimes slipping back. There is a never-ending search for the next integrity and the expansion of meanings which such integrity brings. (See Figure 2.1.)

3

CROSSING THE NORTH–SOUTH DIVIDE

The stabilizing forces – community and bureaucracy

Introduction

The third of our four sources of mastery – following upon both cumulative development and also the capacity to manage change – is the ability to provide continuity, inclusive of community and organization. So while we may be captivated by the east–west polarity as representing the dynamic field of change, we cannot afford to ignore the stabilizing field of continuity. For straddling this north–south divide is bureaucracy and community. Both horizontal and vertical fields, moreover, as can be seen in Figure 3.1, are characterized by both positive attributes (shown in bold type) and negative attributes (shown in italics).

Hitherto, within the field of business and economics, the power and influence of the organized north has eclipsed that of the communal south. While, for the moment then, there is no southern economic force to match the power of America (west), parts of Europe (north), or Japan (east), we cannot merely write off southern Europe specifically, and Africa and Latin America generally, not to mention the Middle East in between.

We shall begin by focusing in between north and south, in a European context, upon middle Italy, in relation to which two Italian American economic historians based at MIT, Piore and Sabel, have made a vital contribution. Thereafter we provide a more profoundly southern perspective on this north–south tension, set within the overall context of an industrial democracy established by a remarkable business visionary in South Africa, Albert Koopman. Finally, I want to set both Piore and Sabel's and Koopman's work within the broader context of Bernard Lievegoed's 'worldliwise' business model. Hopefully, then, this variety of approach, north–south, will make up for the comparative lack of focus, when compared with Hampden Turner's discussion of east–west orientation. We start then with Piore and Sabel's *Second Industrial Divide*.

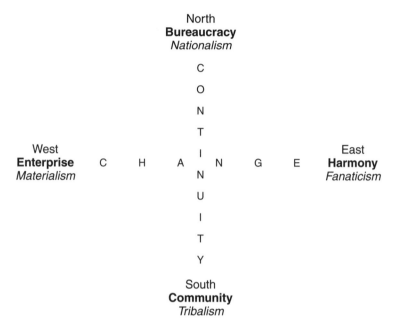

Figure 3.1 The global businessphere

The second industrial divide

Craft versus mass production

In 1984 Piore and Sabel, two professors of economic history at MIT in Boston, wrote their seminal work *The Second Industrial Divide*. Their claim is that the relative deterioration in economic performance in America in the 1980s was due to the fact that its industrial development was founded on mass production (in our terms, north-western). They argue, therefore, that the technologies and operating procedures of most modern corporations, together with the forms of labour-market control defended by many labour movements, must change, to become, in our terms, more south-eastern.

Similarly the instruments of macro-economic control developed by bureaucrats, administrators and economists in the welfare states, and the rules of the international monetary and trading systems established immediately after the Second World War, must be radically altered. 'All must be modified, perhaps even discarded, if the chronic economic diseases of our time are to be cured'.[1]

In their view, then, the first industrial divide came in the nineteenth century. At that time the emergence of (north-western) mass-production technologies, initially in Great Britain and then in the United States, limited the growth of less rigid south-eastern manufacturing technologies, which existed primarily in various regions of Europe. These less rigid manufacturing technologies were craft systems. In the most advanced ones skilled workers used sophisticated general-purpose machinery to turn out a wide and constantly changing assortment of goods for large, but constantly shifting, markets.

In fact mass production has, Piore and Sabel maintain, always necessitated its mirror-image, craft production. During the high noon of mass production, craft production was used by firms operating in markets too narrow and fluctuating to repay the specialized use of resources of mass production. Craft production supplied luxury goods and experimental products. It supplied the specialized equipment used in mass production, and the standardized goods for which the demand was too unstable to make the use of dedicated equipment profitable. Craft production thus appeared either as a residual category, taking up the markets rejected by mass production, or as a limit on the pace of the introduction of mass production. Yet, in the 1990s, such 'reborne'[2] craft production heralded, for Piore and Sabel, the 'second industrial divide'. In our terms, moreover, this represents a renewal of a source of continuity, that is a traditionally craft-based form of production.

Integrated producers, in the 1980s and 1990s, then, tailored their set-ups to exploit possible combinations of craft and mass production. Computerized process-control equipment, for example, allows firms to regulate the carbon content of steel more precisely, and to add a sequence of different alloys without interrupting the flow of production. New factories were being designed to manufacture a diversity of products, using a wide range of starting materials. The institutional environment required to support them, as we shall see, was very different from the one required to support mass production.

Community and organization

Three support systems, according to Piore and Sabel, can be distinguished for encouraging such a north–south recombination through innovation. These were municipalism, welfare capitalism or paternalism, and an entrepreneurial use of kin relations that they call 'familiasm'. Any given industry might move from one system to another as it adopted new technologies and entered new markets. Municipalism, firstly and historically, involved guaranteeing the mobility of resources, by protecting the firms against paralysing shocks from the market, and by providing access to skills and knowledge that the firms lacked. Welfare capitalism, secondly, involved the industrialists in creating an extraordinary network of social institutions. There were schools for mechanized weaving and spinning, an Ecole Supérieure de Commerce in France, a savings society, and a society for maternity care. Familiasm, finally, the *système Motte* (named after Alfred Motte of Roubaix, France), was to pair each family member who had come of age with an experienced technician from one of the family's firms. These two were provided with start-up capital, after which they established together a company that specialized in one of the phases of production that was still needed. Contemporary versions of each of these support systems are most likely to be found in middle Italy, and to a lesser extent in southern Germany.

73

The role of impannatore

Middle Italy's textile industry is a particularly suitable case for reviewing a recombination of community and organization. The most mature of the mature industries is textiles. Between 1966 and 1976 employment in the Western European textile industry was declining, by about 25% in France and West Germany and by more than 35% in Great Britain. But employment in Pratese textiles remained steady and exports boomed. Prato's success rested on two factors: a long-term shift from standardized to fashionable products, and a corresponding re-organization of production. This involved a shift from large integrated mills to technologically sophisticated shops, specializing in various phases of production. With constant experimentation on the finishing of cloth, the Pratese achieved a variety of textures and finishes that gave products 'born poor' the appearance of luxury.

While these small shops were springing up, then, they needed to be formed into a network. To combine them into a flexible production system became, as of the late 1950s, the function of the *impannatore*, a descendant of the early modern *Verleger* (putter-outer). The *impannatore* became a designer, responsible for shaping and responding to fashion, as well as being responsible for organizing production, also urging firms to experiment with materials and processes. 'More significantly, the local banks, the trade unions, and artists and industrialists' associations collaborated in a vast project. They began to devise computer based technologies to increase the flexibility of the links among the firms, as well as the efficiency of each production unit. The expectation was that technology could be suited to the region's vocation as a collective specialist rather than adapting regional structures to the technology used in advanced mass production firms'.[3]

Four coincident factors were crucial in the Italian case. These included firstly the Italian *extended family*, secondly the view of *artisan work* as a distinct type of economic activity, thirdly the existence of *merchant traditions* connecting the Italian provinces to world markets, and finally the fact that municipal and regional *governments* were often *allied to* the *labour* movement, thereby helping to create the infrastructure that the firms required but could not themselves provide. The story of Prato textiles can be retold, in Italy, for many industries. There is the mini steel mill of Brescia; the ceramic building-materials industry of Sassuolo; the high-fashion silk industry of Como; the farm-machine industry of Reggio Emilia; and the special-machinery and motorbike industry of Bologna. That is why middle Italy has today taken the lead in Europe, in reversing the trend towards mass production, introducing in its stead so called 'flexible specialization'.

Flexible specialization – economy and society

Piore and Sabel, in introducing us to the concept of flexible specialization, cite past examples of regional conglomeration in Italy and in Germany, in France and in Spain. Each of the industrial districts therein was composed of a core of more-or-less-equal small enterprises bound in a complex web of competition and cooperation. Trade associations, unions, guilds, purchasing cooperatives and cooperative marketing all prevailed. But no single institution formally linked the productive units. The cohesion of the industry rested on a sense of community – ethnic, political or religious.

Flexible specialization, Piore and Sabel therefore maintain, works by violating one of the key assumptions of classical political economy, that the economy is separate from society. Markets and hierarchies are the two categories that dominate contemporary theory and practical reflexion in the organization of industry.

Both presuppose the firm to be an independent entity. In market models, the firm is linked by exchange relations to other units. In hierarchy models, it is so autonomous as almost to constitute an industry itself. By contrast, in flexible specialization it is hard to tell where social community (southern) ends and where economic organization (northern) begins. Among the ironies of the resurgence of craft production is that its deployment of modern technology depends on its reinvigoration of affiliations that are associated with the pre-industrial past.

Flexible specialization, then, requires a fusion of competition and cooperation that cannot occur in the market model, where economy is distinct from society and firms are independent competitive units. By contrast, within a system of flexible specialization, firms depend on one another for the sharing of skills, technical knowledge, information on opportunities and information on standards. 'Structure shades into infrastructure, competition into cooperation and economy into society'.[4] Interestingly enough, according to Piore and Sabel, large firms in mature industries, such as IBM, are trying to transform themselves from self-contained corporate communities into organizational centres of industrial districts. They are doing so by moving towards just-in-time production systems, which blur the distinction between inside and outside suppliers, while encouraging the spatial concentration of production.

Despite their large size, the modern 'solar' and workshop firms frequently treat external suppliers as collaborators. Subcontractors retain considerable autonomy; and unlike the mass producer, the solar firm depends on subcontractors for advice in solving design and production problems. These firms are large and central enough to their respective industries to supply internally many of the services that in a regional conglomeration would be supplied by the community. But firms in this category often cooperate with community institutions, for example in research, education and welfare.

In mass production the central problem is stabilizing and extending the market. Once this is done, the corporation as a self contained unit has the interest and capacity to advance the division of labour through the simplification of tasks. This requires the creation of special-purpose machines, thereby lowering production costs and setting the stage for further growth. In a system of flexible specialization, by contrast, the problem of organizing innovation just begins with the creation of a market. Because its product only appeals to a limited number of customers, there is no presumption that cuts in production costs will substantially increase the market. In fact, the very fluidity of the resources that makes the system flexible paradoxically also makes it necessary to create institutions that facilitate cooperation.

Mass production's entire division of labour routinizes and therefore, for Piore and Sabel, trivializes work to a degree that often degrades the people who perform it. By contrast, flexible specialization is predicated on cooperation. Moreover, the frequent changes in the production process put a premium on craft skills. Thus the production worker's intellectual participation in the work process is enhanced, and his or her role revitalized. Furthermore, craft production depends on solidarity and communitarianism. Production workers must be so broadly skilled that they can shift rapidly from one job to another; even more important, they must be able to collaborate with designers to solve the problems that inevitably arise in execution. Such craft workers are bred, not born. Moreover, the formation of their identity as persons is bound up firstly with their admittance into a group of workers, and secondly with their mastery of productive knowledge. We now turn from middle Italy to southern Africa, where the socio-political emphasis is even stronger than in the southern European context.

Having versus being

Going north – through west and south

A remarkable African entrepreneur and visionary, Albert Koopman, has devoted his life to turning the north–south force field into one of creative tension as opposed to endemic conflict. During the course of the 1980s, he created Africa's first viable worker democracy, and in the process developed a management ethos that straddled the north–south divide. As such it is both profoundly rooted in 'southern' community and society, as well as strongly imbedded in 'northern' bureaucracy and democracy. His company, Cashbuild, with its thousand-strong workforce supplying building materials across southern Africa, has not only survived the country's prolonged depression during the last days of apartheid better than most, but even prospered then, and continues to do so now.

Albert Koopman is a member of South Africa's Africaaner – a mix of Hollander and African – community, and the best way to convey his communal southern essence, set against a northern organizational backdrop, is to allow him to tell his story,[5] starting from when he was a teenager.

The Cashbuild story

I entered life as a moral fighter

I was raised as a street fighter. My mother died when I was 13 and my father lived in Mozambique, 1,240 miles from me. Set free at a very early age, I had to learn to survive. That meant dealing with people, including people who had hang-ups, and people who wanted to do me in for what I believed. The one thing that I learnt as a result was that I was going to enter my life as a clean, moral fighter, someone who sterilized his bicycle chains before he entered the fight of interpersonal relationships.

Unlike the animals with claws and teeth, God gave me his supreme gifts: choice and intellect. Making use of these two gifts I was able to observe my fellow-man going about his daily activities and make his life more meaningful. From this I acquired my moral purpose. The story you are about to hear is one of my personal experience in an African context, through my involvement as the Chief Executive of a Cash and Carry Building Material Merchant in South Africa. It is a story of success and many failures, a story of victories and sadnesses in my attempt to create an excellent company in a somewhat turbulent society (to put it mildly). It is the story of how a white (northern) man in Africa became a White African (southern). It is the story of how I combined the rationality of the First World with the humanity of the Third.

First World and Third World initially failed to meet

Cashbuild was started as a wholesaler in 1978 and became a very successful business in a short space of time. Situated predominantly in the rural areas of South Africa and focusing on the black housing market, our staff complement consisted of 84% black, 13% white and 3% Indian. However, by mid-1982, with 12 outlets, profits started sliding. Everything 'northern' was in place – systems, procedures, technology, combined with a booming market – but something was going wrong and I did not know enough about the south, at that point, to recognize where to start looking. We embraced our cardinal principles of giving value to our customers, being innovative, adaptable and totally committed to the business as well as having efficient organizational structures, but obviously something was changing and we did not know what it was. Our hierarchy was well displayed on the walls of all our outlets, everyone was placed in neat little boxes with prescribed job descriptions and functions, and no one was achieving our objectives as had been laid out! I came to the conclusion that we had a lot of trained men but no actual committed soldiers.

It was clear that our organizational structure was autocratic, as was my own personal management style. We had to change, but how? What if people started seeing me as soft, when I became more participative and democratic? What about the chaos that might occur during the period of transition?

Well there was no other way to do it at the time but by MBFA – Managing by Fumbling Around. There was no alternative but to plunge in at the deep end and to risk my neck and possibly be forced to say 'I'm sorry' for my original way of doing things. I immediately commissioned an attitude survey and found that pro-company feelings, to the tune of 89% in 1980, had slipped to 74% in 1982.

Typical remarks of the predominantly white, first-world (northern) management team about the majority of our third-world (southern) workforce were 'there's no way one can train them; they're too badly educated'; 'they simply won't open up as people and talk about their aspirations, needs and fears because of cultural barriers'; 'none of them understands our business and they simply don't care'. Remarks about myself were even more demeaning. 'You're pompous, ego-centric, and very distant from what's happening at the coalface.'

Uncovering the Divine Will of Africa

Key questions went through my mind. Why do the workers actually work? What is their social or Divine Will? What went wrong in Cashbuild with respect to capital and labour? What were we actually trying to achieve as a business organism? How do we bring together the rights of people, their spiritually based humanity and the economic process as represented in the workplace? Subsequently I conducted a succession of brainstorming sessions to uncover the purpose of Cashbuild's existence. It soon became clear to us that one purpose existed in management's head and another in the workers'.

Management up north was pulling one way and the people down south another. There was no transcendent purpose linking one with the other.

Meanwhile, in the course of participating in these workshops over a period of six months, it became clear to me that active listening and intensive interaction between people made each aware of the other's spirit. Day in day out I was confronted with people's vitality, their reasons for being, and their creativity. I became aware that there was a spirit or soul that lay deep within each person which needed awakening. However, our current Cashbuild organization was patently incapable of releasing it. North was north and south was south and never the twain did meet!

Typically, a chief executive, after fighting like hell to get to the top, goes into hybernation once he gets there and forgets his leadership role. In order to enrich his own existence he all too often forgets his responsibility to benefit his followers. Until this point I had become just such a self-centred person. Perhaps now, though, I had begun to see the light. It was time to nail our new colours to the Cashbuild mast.

Establishing our cardinal principles

Arising out of 3,000 issues that came to our attention through the brainstorming sessions, we drew up a set of cardinal principles emerging out of the inter-dependent relationships that existed between customer, employee, company, competitor and motivation. (See Figure 3.2.)

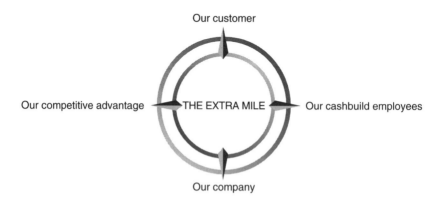

Figure 3.2 Cashbuild's cardinal principles

We realized, at the same time, that the 'northern' principles would have to embrace the 'southern' spirit of every employee, so they were spelled out as follows:

- we recognize that the marketing process of getting goods from supplier to customer is the concern of every employee and that we have to liberate him/her to achieve this
- we want to strive for quality service through people and keep our system as balanced as possible through on-the-job training, motivation through better supervision, self measurement and statistical control rather than boss control, giving people a say over their workplace
- we recognize that quality service and total productivity will only come if we rediscover the spirit of man within the workplace, providing job enrichment by changing the work people do
- people need to belong to and identify with the company's cause; customers must be satisfied through committed people

At every workshop session which followed we probed all the obstacles which stood in the way of our following our cardinal principles. No stone was left unturned and over a period of a year we listened to why people worked, with whom they preferred to work, and what they saw would be the design of the perfect workplace. After spending extended periods of time living amongst our black employees, experiencing life within their communities, and consulting with them directly, I found I had to review my whole understanding of the people I employed, as well as how they saw their relationship with our business and with its philosophy. The degree to which aspects of indigenous 'southern' culture were to become 'spiritualized' in the workplace was to depend on the type of 'northern' organization imposed upon the individual, including the degree to which the organization would allow expression of these elements.

Turning our thinking about people upside-down

I was therefore forced to seek a way in which we could spell out and determine our objective common interest in the production of commodities – customer service (southern) – to replace capital's pure interest in increasing profits (western). Lots of meetings, small-group activities, discussion groups and open two-way communications had to form as much of the way we ran our business as did the work itself. Everything had to be focused upon the common interest of creating wealth and fostering an understanding amongst workers that the correct management of capital benefits the organization as a whole. This correct management, in turn, could only occur if the worker was democratically involved in contributing towards the overall success of the organization. I visualized that in this manner so-called capitalist exploitation (of the 'southern' community) would no longer be able to exist.

We had to turn our thinking about people upside-down and look at our business totally differently. The perception of capitalist exploitation at Cashbuild had to be changed.

This change needed to be achieved not merely through some superficial 'western' programme of empowerment, but through an active 'northern' restructuring of the hierarchy, to liberate the work ethic. We had to design an organization that was truly free so that the cooperation between all individuals in fact became its own sustainable social form. We needed a social form that could accommodate the 'western' freedom to be enterprising, as well as harnessing the 'southern' spiritual consciousness of all our employees. Enter our CARE philosophy – Cashbuild's Aspirations with Regard to Excellence.

Care philosophy

In essence the CARE philosophy sought to bring about a balancing of power within the organization. At that stage, in 1982, authority was vested in management (but no power) and power lay with the unions (but no authority). Firstly, we built in mechanisms for the protection of individual rights *vis-à-vis* the organization, through a 'northern' code of conduct. Secondly, CARE groups were formed to give expression to the 'southern' spiritual consciousness of individuals, serving as a vehicle for discussion of issues affecting their working life. Groups were formed at five levels – general labourers, semi-skilled personnel, junior, middle and senior managers – each with their own majority-elected president. Thirdly, these groups were to engage with the economic process, sharing information about efficiency and productivity, and learning about as well as influencing the company's wealth creating process.

A CARE philosophy designed by the people for the people spelled out how our workplace should be regulated, and set out the rules of the business game. Some of the salient points were:

- a commitment to joint decision making at all levels, with everyone playing their part in finding solutions to problems
- an open and free culture with everyone in the organization having access to any line manager
- a team consisting of different races, sexes and cultural creeds, none of which were to be discriminated against
- a belief in the 'Extra Mile' concept (see Figure 3.2) both for the organization and for the individual

After the philosophy has been translated into seven languages and a little booklet given to each and every employee to read, we felt we could start moving into the future. Our view towards people changed dramatically as we recognized that:

- each employee had his/her own rights, will to work, and wanted some control over his/her destiny
- we needed to understand the cross-cultural complexities of our workplace through continuous ineraction
- the company would place no limits on human growth

They told it like it was

Whilst our CARE horizon extended over five years, I found after only eighteen months that resistance to change had become an insurmountable obstacle. Although we had begun to find that people actually cared for the company, and were starting to find such meaning and purpose in their work that productivity was considerably enhanced, the euphoria was short lived. After many consultative workshops we decided to have a major get together to assess our performance so far. As the management team, our ears fell off – they told it like it was!

'Mr Koopman, I would like to resign as President because my fellow men see me as siding with management; they're no longer carrying out my instructions.'

'I have no power. Although my people voted me in I cannot get my manager to act on their requests. He simply is not interested.'

'The company has cheated us for so long. Why is it suddenly changing? We don't believe in it.'

'My manager told me the other day that he sees me as a threat and will not cooperate with me.'

'We don't trust our manager. He is prejudiced against blacks.'

'What happens to my family if I die.'

The advent of VENTURECOM

It was time to look at the whole situation again. We were sure that our belief in raising spiritual consciousness was valid, but we could now see our employees expressing their 'southern' social selves as apart from the 'western' economic process. While they were perceiving their labour power as intimately associated with themselves as human beings, they still saw the company as viewing their labour content as part of the production–distribution–consumption process. They were being treated as commodities. Our CARE structures, as representatively democratic, were still separating management and worker. What they were crying out for was for 'northern' participatory democracy, thereby integrating their 'western' economic and 'southern' social selves, so as to relieve labour power of its commodity character. It dawned upon me as a result that:

- no one can demand productivity from anyone, but I can create a climate within which social man is willingly productive
- I cannot manage people, only things, but I can create a climate within which people take responsibility and manage themselves
- one cannot demand quality from people, but I can create conditions at work through which quality work is a product of pride in workmanship

We thought these new conditions would help to create the human face which I had been looking for earlier. Exploitative capitalism demands quotas, productivity and quality, all as part of a commodity outlook on life. People remain part of the production–distribution–consumption process, without their spiritual work or social ethos being recognized. The protagonists of class consciousness, meanwhile, became a rallying point in the name of social justice, without actually giving expression to the human face. We promptly decided at Cashbuild to pursue our own course, dividing control of the business into soft variables (enterprise and labour) and hard ones (capital and land). A convention of some two hundred workers was held and the ground rules were established:

- respect human dignity and individual freedom of speech
- allow everyone to have access to company results and performance standards
- give everyone a role in developing company policy
- improve the quality of life of all employees outside the work sphere through active community involvement

Views and feelings just poured out of the hearts of the workers for the first time. The basis for removing barriers ('isms') between capital and labour was still the CARE groups, but this time around we were talking team – total team, only us.

This was our company. It was proposed that a governing body of five people be constituted to each outlet – the VENTURECOM – with each person being democratically elected to hold a portfolio, save for the manager who was appointed to the Operations Portfolio, based on his or her expertise. This portfolio was concerned with the 'hard' variables whereas the Safety, Labour, Merchandise and Quality of Work-Life portfolios were the 'soft' ones. Moreover, each of these managers was continually assessed by lower levels in the hierarchy. The subsequent newspaper headlines – 'Cashbuild – the company where workers have the right to dismiss their managers' – frightened the hell out of the capitalist fraternity. Yet precisely because that right existed within the workforce we never needed to use it. In fact this Cashbuild VENTURECOM system was socialistic (northern bureaucracy/southern community) in that it reinstated distributive justice and offered security against destitution. It was likewise capitalistic (western chaos/eastern harmony) to the extent that individual expression was given its due reward, and group development its due recognition. Our system thus gave expression to the work ethic and also to the enterprising spirit of people.

Reviewing my learning curve

As newly appointed Managing Director, back in 1982, I had first begun to realize that the internal workings of the organization were simply not matching up with external demands. Profits were going down. To me, power had been a thing, a toy. My 'western' nature was individualistic and competitive. I was the only person existing in the world. I saw coercion as the way to get things done. So when I confronted the results of our attitude survey I was inevitably confused. At the end of a protracted period of soul searching, I began to realize that I had been using power and the 'ism' through which it had to be executed in pursuit of the protection of my class. In a sense I was still a product of the industrial society, and my 'western' self had forgotten that there was actually no such thing as the means of production.

There were only people who actually work machines in order to produce. Without the 'southern' people, the machines and the factories would stand still. Without the effort of 'western' enterprise, there would be no progress in humanity. Here was my key to change.

I could now see that if I recognized and restored the dignity and pride of the workforce I could achieve a new human spirit that would drive the enterprise for the betterment of all. I would therefore be able to change, not by losing my individual competitive value system, but by finding 'southern' solidarity as Managing Director with all the people in the organization. To do this I had to go 'north'! This entailed in effect, at a technical level:

- taking Cashbuild employees on a journey, strengthening their relationships with management
- turning all employees into stakeholders of the organization
- aggressively addressing the distributive aspect of the business, through profit sharing, in the ultimate interest of the business, its workers and their families

- promoting excellence of quality and productivity, within the organization, and fostering a communal climate for its achievement

At the structural level I had to restore meaning into people's lives, by constructing a code of ethics around which people could be rallied for the common purpose. This entailed developing:

- a superordinate goal for the enterprise through the people themselves – bottom up
- a philosophy of social justice and equality
- pride and dignity within every employee

I found later that this last point was in fact the spark for all endeavours, and took precedence over any of the other technical systems, rewards, or structures we introduced. It reflected, in fact, the Divine Will of Cashbuild which in its turn manifested the parallel will of the communities which the company represented. It reflected the difference between competitive, north-western 'having', and cooperative 'south-eastern' being. (See Figure 3.3.)

HAVING MODE   **Individual**   **Competitive**

Self-reliant/rational	Individual	Wealth and
Individual	control	status
Self-interest		
Reward/punishment base	Own	Accumulate
Management-oriented		
Directive style	Goals and deadlines	
Production concern		
	Demanding	

The more I have,
the more I am

BEING MODE   **Group**   **Cooperative**

Cooperative/Emotive	Sharing	Giving
Collective		
Community interest	Team	Dignity/
Recognition/rejection	cooperation	respect
Leadership-oriented		
Participative style	Sacrificing	
People concern		
	Vision/Faith	

I am, therefore,
the more I give

Figure 3.3 Modes of life

The African work group

In my ten years of experience at Cashbuild, then, I had observed that the African work group regarded their fellows primarily in terms of 'southern' morals and emotions rather than in terms of their 'northern' roles and functions. Traditionally, blacks have emerged through the spoken word. Wisdoms were carried forward in the form of metaphors and stories as opposed to the written word, which preserved information for western cultures. So 'southerners' will tend to think aurally and emotionally, which is why they would think aloud and use continuous discussion as the main part of their reasoning process. The traditional *indaba* (place of discourse) of such cultures had, at its base moreover, the removal of all dissent before the group could proceed. (See Table 3.1.)

Table 3.1 Competitive versus communal cultures

Individual competitive	*Group communal*
Profit for me is derived from self interest	Profit for me is a vote of confidence my society gives me for service rendered to that society
I am exclusive from my fellow man	I am mutually inclusive
I prefer to be a self actualized person	I prefer to be a social man
The more I have the more I am	I am, therefore, the more I am prepared to share and give
I demand productivity from people	I prefer to create a climate in which people will be willingly more productive
I am an aggressive kind of a person	I am a receptive kind of a person
I look you in the eye and challenge you	I bow my head and show you respect
My concern is for production	My concern is for people

The African work group therefore has to clear dissent by engaging interactively with the morality of an issue. Thus performance is valued less for its own sake than for the sake of the group. The Divine Will of Africa, then, reflected in the 'southern' work groups that I came across at Cashbuild, is hidden between the lines of the following passages:

- Africa shows a strong reverence for ancestors and other departed relatives who are believed to be able to affect the living.
- Africa sees that the principle of age is an important source of wisdom.
- Africa places a high value on ceremony and ritual in many aspects of social life.
- Africa attaches great importance to group life and to social harmony, thereby placing a high premium on consensus in group endeavours.
- Africa is extremely social through its spontaneity of self expression and ease of communication, thereby regarding correctness of speech as a prerequsite for social standing.
- Africa can forgive and forget very readily because of its great capacity for reconciliation.

Managing transition

Albert Koopman left Cashbuild in 1987 to help form ITISA – Interdependence and Transformation in Southern Africa – a participatively oriented management consultancy. His successor as chief executive was Gerard Haumant, Albert's long-standing associate in Cashbuild, a Frenchman with a chemical-engineering background on the one hand, and a radical orientation on the other.

Not surprisingly, Haumant, while honouring the southern foundations of the organization, gradually reinforced the systematic, northern influence.

By 1994, Cashbuild had 72 outlets of which 56 were in South Africa and 16 in surrounding African countries. Company turnover had reached the equivalent of some one hundred million US dollars, while remaining a significantly profitable undertaking. The CARE groups and VENTURECOMS were still well in place and every year all the management together with employee representatives would gather together for three days, for a 'Great Indaba'. The issues discussed would range from wage and salary increases to housing loan schemes, combined with major strategic issues, the agenda for it being compiled from one year prior to the great meeting.

> The objective is that by the time the Great Indaba comes, everybody in the company has had a say and all the Venturecomm representatives who will be attending have a record of how each branch member feels about the issues raised in the Indaba document. All proposals are voted after extensive debate and decisions are taken as positive if there is a 75% majority.[6]

A day in the life of the branch

The lifeblood of Cashbuild, in the 1980s as well as in the 1990s, is the branch operation. This is described by consultant and researcher Elton Bondi, for a Wednesday morning in 1995, at the Thaban'Chu branch nearby an African township.

> Employees could best be described as highly aggressive towards the competitor, and many showed a profound knowledge of Cashbuild's bulk buying power. I was truly amazed by the level of business understanding and high degree of loyalty demonstrated by employees wearing overalls who packed corrugated iron most of the day. The second overall impression was that of relaxed humour. One feels, in fact, like an outsider to a tight family unit, who share their own customs and values. Most employees went about their work in a cheery manner with much shouting and laughing to each other across the yard.[7]

The communal southern spirit of Cashbuild obviously lives on, together with the practice of value sharing that takes place through the northern CARE groups, the VENTURECOMS and the Great Indaba. Interestingly enough, Koopman had to migrate northwards, that is to create newly bureaucratic and democratic organizational vehicles, before he could integrate the western spirit of enterprise with the southern spirit of community. In fact for the past ten years, since he handed over the reigns at Cashbuild, Koopman has been trying to instil his unique philosophy, and practice, into other companies in southern Africa and recently in north America.

Interdependence and transformation

Value sharing

Together with his colleagues at ITISA (Interdependence and Transformation in Southern Africa), then, Koopman has been attempting to spread his brand of African humanism across business enterprises. The underlying approach involves sharing value to add value. Most notably, moreover, within ITISA's southern context – as differentiated from east, west and north – politics cannot be separated from economics. Therein lies the primal southern force of unity. 'The three interrelated facets of society, namely authority, economy and community, form an interdependent whole. If they are in open interaction with one another it is called a democracy'.[8] Whereas the *authority* pole stands for the rationality of the north, and the *community* pole for the humanism of the south, the *economy* represents a force of pragmatic integration. In business, Koopman maintains, the equivalent of the economy is creating and keeping customers through adequate performance. If, for whatever reasons, the relationship between northern authority (management and shareholders) and the southern community (employees and trade unions) breaks down, then the organization's western economy (performance to create and keep customers) will suffer.

Authority, community and economy

The combination of these three, then, forms not only the politics of society and the sociology of organizations but also the dynamics of business. Each of these elements, moreover, is built into the fabric of the enterprise politically and authoritatively through the institutionalization of justice and dignity; socially and communally through communication; and economically and commercially through wealth creation.

> We understand that communication is the sharing of meaning of our stated objectives . . . Each employee has the right to remain informed on matters affecting his life . . . As teamwork is the seed of human accomplishment, and participation the sap of human growth, so justice

and freedom are the combined and moral fruits of human endeavour. We share a mutual respect, in common purpose and respect for our diversities of interest, applied through a principle of non-violation of each other's rights, individual against individual, individual against company, labour against capital, white against black, man against woman, management against worker, or the reciprocal of any of these.

We invest money to buy plant, put up buildings, purchase materials, and pay running expenses. The wealth created, however, is not driven by self interest, but rather serves as a reward and vote of confidence in us by society, for the services we render to that society. We understand that our wealth creation process will only only remain paramount if individuals are able to retain a wealth creating consciousness. Freedom to create wealth through a freeing of spirit will be our ultimate drive. For we realize that it is only through wealth creation that we remain free.[9]

In the final analysis, as we can see, Koopman combines 'northern' authority and 'southern' community with 'western' economy, so that only 'eastern' epistemology is missing.

There is, moreover, a clear difference between what he calls the 'having mode' of the north-west, encompassing individual wealth and control, wealth and status, goals and deadlines, and secondly the south-eastern 'being mode', of sharing, giving, team cooperation, dignity and respect and sacrificing. (See Figure 3.3.)

Interestingly enough, in fact, Koopman's insights, drawn from the meeting of his own southern African experiences with his originally northern, and subsequently western colonial, heritage, are replicated, and in fact further extended, by a man who shared Koopman's Dutch heritage – Holland's leading management thinker, the late Bernard Lievegoed. Lievegoed's business model serves, as we shall see, as the only radical departure from the French Henri Fayol original to stand the test of time conceptually.

Managing the developing business

North-western business administration

The way we conventionally describe business activity today, within for example a standard MBA programme, remains circumscribed by what we have termed western and northern perspectives. In the early 1920s the French engineer and administrator Henri Fayol[10] divided business into:

- *technical* activities, including production and what he termed 'adaptation'
- *commercial* activities, including buying, selling and exchange
- *financial* activities, involving both a search for and also the optimum use of capital

- *accounting* activities, including stocktaking, costing, the preparation of balance sheets and statistics
- *security* activities, so-called, actually including the protection of property and persons
- *managerial* activities, including – as we have seen – planning and organizing, command, coordination and control

Little has changed in seventy years, save the fact that information technology has made its mark, and human-resource management has come of age. Within the Anglo-Saxon world, therefore, and in Koopman's terms, the emphasis on 'having' (western) and on 'ruling' (northern) has supplanted 'becoming' (eastern) and 'being' (southern).

Bernard Lievegoed has been Holland's most advanced management thinker. As an organizational psychologist, who founded a worldwide management consultancy in the 1970s – the Nationale Pedagogic Institute (NPI) – he had on the one hand an affinity with the east, through his philosophical connections with Austria's philosopher and mystic Rudolph Steiner in the 1920s, and on the other hand a link with the developing world, having been born in Indonesia. He also had the capacity to conceive of an institution, and to bring it into being.

Global business development

Lievegoed conceived of a business organization as developing in three stages, as opposed to the four that we have proposed. In the first pioneering stage, as per Tom Peters, the acquisitive (western) entrepreneur is commercially driven, buying and selling within a market-oriented enterprise. In the second differentiated stage, as per Henri Fayol, the rule- and role-bound manager (northern) is functionally driven – producing and marketing, financing and staffing – within a hierarchically controlled organization. The third and most developed 'global' stage, championed by Lievegoed and portrayed as a 'clover leaf' (see Figure 3.4),[11] was quite

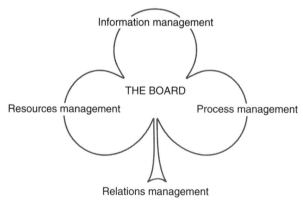

Figure 3.4 The clover-leaf organization

		West HAVING	**East** BECOMING
North	RULING	Resources management	Information management
South	BEING	Relations management	Process management

Figure 3.5 Worldlywise modes of organization

different. For the duly integrated functions are characterized by him as resources and information management, on the one hand, and process and relations management, on the other. Interestingly enough, and in many ways, they bring together a 'western' and 'eastern' – resources versus process – management with a 'northern' and 'southern' – information versus relations – management.

Relations management – south/west

Firstly, 'southern style' relations management, for Lievegoed, incorporates external and internal relations. External relations encompass not only conventionally based marketing activities, but also relations with suppliers and distributors, with business partners and with the community at large. Internal relations, at one and the same time, incorporate conventionally based employee relations as well as more comprehensive organizational democracy. It is best undertaken, as can be seen in Figure 3.5, in the 'being' and 'having' modes, linking southern communality with western enterprise.

Information management – north/east

Secondly, and at the integrated stage of Lievegoed's developing business, information management has grown quantitatively and qualitatively to such a degree that it warrants a completely separate subsystem. Its function is to distribute information in a form which is useful for everybody as regards content, frequency and intelligibility. As such it will need to be closely integrated, as we shall see, with resource management, with the process flow and with the management of internal and external relations. Thereby information management combines 'ruling' and 'becoming', that is a regulatory and developmental orientation.

Resources management – north/west

'Western style' resources, thirdly, of many kinds, need to be managed – in order, as we can see below, to make possible the process flow, which is determined in turn by external relations. The procurement, management and disposal of these physical, economic and human resources at the right place, in the right amounts and also at the right time comprise this third subsystem of the enterprise. As such it combines the 'having' – acquiring – and the 'ruling' – regulating – modes.

Process management – south/east

'Eastern style' process management, finally, is involved in the orchestration of physical, financial and informative flows, through which organizational subsystems are linked together. People, in that process context, are horizontally work-oriented within the process flow. Only the 'hardware' of technical requirements and the 'software' of social requirements, in combination, can together guarantee a truly integrated process flow. Such a flow is best facilitated by a combining of 'being', that is expressive and experiential, and 'becoming', that is purposive and developmental modes.

Conclusion

Mastering management, and in the process becoming worldliwise, requires you to travel around the globe, in thought if not also in action. The compass you will need to take along, to guide you, contains the standard east–west and north–south axes. At an individual managerial level, drawing upon Jung's typology, this is represented in both your perceptual orientation – either sensing (western) or intuiting (eastern) – and in your judgmental outlook – either thinking (north) or feeling (south). At a business or institutional level, secondly, it is reflected either in the management of change – through resource exploitation or process innovation – or else in the management of continuity – through conserving information or through nurturing relationships – as can be seen in Figure 3.6.

Overall, then, you need to maintain and develop the creative tension between change and continuity. Each is embodied in our respective east–west and north–south axes. Within each of the four different worlds, moreover, there are both

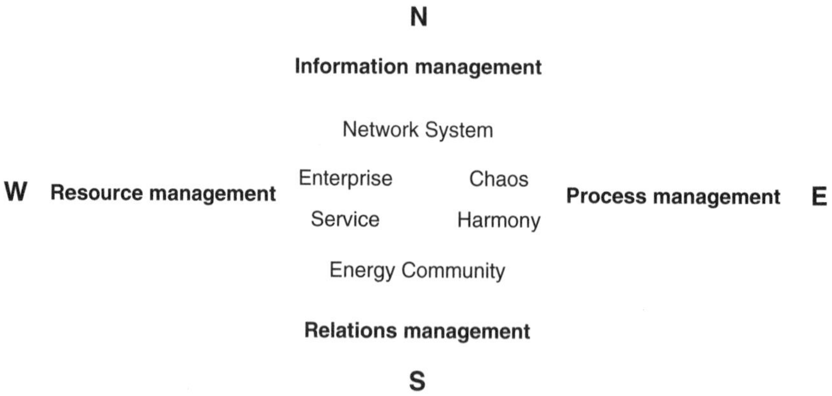

N

Information management

Network System

W   Resource management   Enterprise   Chaos

Service   Harmony   **Process management   E**

Energy Community

Relations management

S

Figure 3.6 The organizational compass

hard and soft edges. Along the west–east axis, firstly therefore, you need to combine (western) enterprise with service, on the one hand, and (eastern) chaos with harmony, on the other. Along the north–south axis, secondly you need on the one hand to combine network and system (northern) and on the other hand to combine energy and community (southern).

As we can see, then, each facet of organization, set within the global busines-sphere, comprises both hard and soft elements. Socially these are the physical energy and social community that underlies relations management, and culturally they are the chaos and harmony that make up process management. Technolo-gically, information management is made up of orderly systems and freestanding networks, while economically, resources management puts enterprise into service. This brings us on to chapter 4, where we review the power of complementarity in management, that is the fourth and final source of mastery.

4

THE SOFT AND HARD EDGES
OF MANAGEMENT
Promoting complementarity

Introduction

The 'soft' and 'hard' Ss

The fourth and final part of management mastery, following upon cumulative development, change and continuity management, is the cultivation of complementarity, that is between the soft and hard aspects of management. In the early 1980s the well-known firm of business consultants McKinsey's introduced us to the 'soft' and 'hard' edges of management. Having gone to Japan in search of excellence, Pascale and Athos,[1] two McKinsey-based Americans, discovered that it was the unique blend of soft and hard qualities that enabled the Japanese managers to be successful. They subsequently concluded, as did Peters and Waterman, who wrote *In Search of Excellence*,[2] that the best American companies follow the same pattern. Their managers combine soft qualities – skills, staff, shared values and style – with hard ones – structure, systems and strategy.

From yang competition to yin cooperation

The need to combine soft attributes with hard is of fundamental importance to us, as prospective worldiwise managers, at each point of our developmental trajectory, and within each of the domains of management. To that extent I am at one with my American colleagues. However, for the purposes of this text, the division between soft and hard qualities that they have developed is inadequate. For it tends to be managerially *ad hoc*, rather than being rooted in substantive philosophical thinking. I have chosen, rather, the Ancient Chinese source of wisdom as a basis for such division, that is the distinction between 'yin' and 'yang'. In case this particular source of distinction fails to make the point clearly enough, I have drawn – subsequently – on the division between the right and left sides of the brain.

This physiological difference has recently captured the imagination of neurologists, psychologists and managers alike, especially over the last ten years. Thirdly, and finally, I have related the soft and hard edges of management to cooperation and competition, respectively.

Yin and yang

Principles of complementarity

Yin and yang philosophy

All great philosophical or managerial disputes, for American social philosopher Alan Watts,[3] can be reduced to an argument between two parties. The one party is tough-minded, rigorous and precise, and likes to stress differences and divisions between things. The other is tender-minded, romantic, likes wide generalizations and grand syntheses, and stresses underlying unities.

The first group thus prefers the idea that particles rather than waves are the ultimate constituents of matter, while the second prefers the concept of waves. The first favours structuring organizations according to hierarchies kept in place by rigorous control and discipline, while the second inclines towards the underlying unity of all things, and the spontaneous capacity of people to know what is right for them.

The yin and yang of organizations

An American management thinker resident in Britain, Nancy Foy, wrote a book in 1980 entitled *The Yin and Yang of Organizations*.[4] As a management consultant with IBM, and as an astute observer of organizational life, she became particularly interested in the complementary between the so-called yin/soft and yang/hard forces. She presents us with a series of yin–yang opposites, as shown in Table 4.1.

Table 4.1 Complementary features of organizations

Yin	Yang	Yin	Yang
Feeling	Thinking	Applied knowledge	Knowledge itself
Relationships	Individuals	Oral tradition	Modern science
Myths	Models	Rituals	Games
Comprehensive	Analytic	Non-disciplinary	Disciplinary
Cooperation	Competition	Pleasure	Accomplishment
Intuition	Action	Diffuse awareness	Focused awareness
Mediator	Inventor	Relaxation	Determination
Consequence	Result	Maintenance	Construction
Community	Hierarchy	Space	Time
Unity	Polarity	Integration	Differentiation
Nourisher	Fertilizer	Spontaneous	Planned

Foy emphasized, then, that organizations need to secure a balance between competition and cooperation, between diffused and focused market awareness, between informal traditions and formal practices – to mention just a few of the important managerial complementarities. Should they not achieve some such balance, she argued, they would be doomed to fail.

Masculine and feminine

Yin–yang philosophy, which receives some affirmation from both modern physics and analytical psychology, maintains that there are two overall principles, the masculine and the feminine, inherent in all phenomena and responsible, by their interactions, for the emergence and dissolution of all things. 'Masculine' and 'feminine' principles, moreover, do not correspond directly with male and female. A woman may have strong masculine traits and a man strong feminine ones. Yin and yang describe a world in which people and things, structures and processes, make up different expressions of a continuum, rather than irreconcilable opposites.

Management, like humanity at large, can only reveal itself in its essential wholeness when yin and yang are brought into conscious contact with one another.

The laws of change

Chaos and order

Human (or managerial) consciousness, then, has the possibility of finding wholeness if it learns to recognize the principles of development inherent in the changes of yin and yang. This involves a gradual evolution, moving cyclically from chaos to order, from integration to differention. It is a development in which an organization and its environment are divided into yin and yang by the active, separating energy of yang, which, in turn, calls forth its polar opposite, the feminine principle. The opposing and yet complementary relationship of the two principles leads to their increasing polarization, but not, if the laws of change follow their course, to their irreconcilable alienation.

The so-called laws of change or development will be investigated much more thoroughly, and more specifically, in the context of each of the developing managers (chapters 8, 12, 16 and 20). In fact they lead to the progressive evolution of our so-called primal, rational, developmental and metaphysical management through cumulative changes in the composition of yin and yang. 'The yin–yang views civilization as a systematic and progressive development from simple, undifferentiated beginnings, towards a complex structure. The task of the sage is to understand the way in which change operates, and to learn to recognize moments of germination, maturity and decay'.[5] Such change arises, according to

Britain's Sukie Colegrave, within an evolving organization and environment, through the interaction of masculine and feminine principles.

The masculine principle behind change

The birth and development of the masculine principle, for social philosopher Colegrave, revolutionizes humanity's experience of itself and of the world. 'Instead of participating in the rhythms of nature, being contained and regulated by her laws, a drive emerges, drawing upon the assumption that people, not nature, should be primarily responsible for organizing life'.[6]

The masculine principle, then, in the form in which it developed in Ancient China, offered the elite a liberation from their previous bondage to nature. It provided them with a way of understanding the world instead of being enslaved by it, of directing and planning their own lives instead of being the unwitting participants in nature's designs. It also offered them the chance of discovering their own individuality instead of being compelled by the collective impulses of the group. Through the masculine principle, people through the ages have acquired the hitherto unknown possibility of deliberately creating organizations, and whole societies, according to their own conceptions of morality and achievement, order and justice.

The masculine principle not only helps us to differentiate the world in which we live, to discriminate between the different aspects of man and nature, organization and environment, thereby to classify and to order, it also leads us to an experience, as people and as managers, of our essential individuality. For Colegrave 'it gives us the certainty that we stand utterly alone in this world, unsupported by personal relationships'.[7] It brings the extraordinary and alarming knowledge that we can look to no one and no thing other than ourselves for directions and answers. An awakening of the masculine principle is therefore essential for a person, a manager, an organization or even a nation if each is to acquire a sense of individual identity, and the ability to discriminate. However, if a manager relies too much on either the masculine or the feminine principle, he or she loses it. One principle can only be continually explored and developed in relation to the other.

The feminine principle behind change

An awareness of the feminine principle is valuable to all stages of the development of the masculine. But at the beginning, in the birth of an organization or whole society, its importance is likely to be less significant. For at this early stage the need is to acquire personal independence from the communal whole. However, once sufficient independence from the primal whole has been achieved, individuals, organizations and societies need the complementary influence of the feminine if they are to avoid despotism and psychological impoverishment. Whereas the masculine approach to business involves, for example, exploiting opportunities, the feminine approach is different. It involves conceiving an idea, waltzing around it, lovingly participating in it, and letting it grow quietly from within until it is ready to be born into the world. It is a way of submitting to an evolving process rather than deliberately achieving fame or fortune through an effort of the will.

The feminine is, in fact, a bridging influence. It bridges the individual and the external worlds, one department and another, the conscious and subconscious minds, corporate strategy and corporate culture. In this capacity it acts as an agent of renewal and transformation. Without it we ossify. Whereas the masculine principle promotes an objective relationship which characterizes, for example, hard-headed western approach to total quality management, the feminine principle encourages an experience of qualitative unity between person and product. This is in fact a feature of the Japanese approach to quality circles, where subjective involvement with a product is all important. Solitary, disciplined effort to master a skill, moreover, or to conquer a technical or political problem, is a masculine strength.

Such an approach allows such 'masculine' managers to be 'objective', cool and rational. They have been taught, admittedly more so in some cultures than in others, from an early age to shut off their feelings, so that their connections to other people are often weak, as are the bridges between the emotional and intellectual hemispheres of their minds. The feminine orientation, again subject to cultural differences, has a different texture. The surface is thickly woven with connections, love and friendship ties, family links, often a hypersensitivity to their own and others' feelings. These form a web of loyalties that, according to the well-known American author Gail Sheahy,[8] most women put before rules or abstract principles.

Masculine and feminine principles

Ultimately, any healthy manager or organization needs to balance masculine principles with feminine ones if their organization is to develop and prosper. In fact the very emergence of the feminine approach to management – whose salient characteristics are those of recognizing and helping to create relationships, between either people or things, of being receptive and recognizing harmony – depends on a prior differentiation by the masculine principle of organizational and commercial activities. We cannot receive, integrate and harmonize – economically, technologically or culturally – before discovering separate products, people or activities, both in the outside environment and within our own organizations.

The feminine consciousness, then, does not deny the existence of the differentiated world; on the contrary, it could not exist without it. But it does assert that the separation between people and things is not the only reality. Rather, in these terms, there is another way of seeing, one which perceives the unity between the differences, and focuses on the relationships between things rather than on their separate identities.

Instead of seeing ourselves and our organizations as ways of separating us from the world, the feminine principle sees them as means through which we are joined to the world. To understand things, a tree for example, we need the masculine consciousness to help us focus on the constituent parts of the tree, its trunk, branches, roots and leaves, to see everything which distinguishes the tree from both ourselves and the rest of nature. We need the feminine to reveal the inner qualities of the tree, its strength, its life force, and to understand the relationship between its parts, how its branches stretch out, gradually tapering off into leaves, until they intermingle and finally disappear into the air. 'Explored through the feminine principle, the tree ceases to appear as something separate from both ourselves and from the universe, and becomes an expression of general principles at work throughout the human and natural worlds. Through the feminine in us it is possible to discover and experience the tree in ourselves and ourselves in the tree'.[9]

It does not take too great a stretch of the imagination to substitute 'organization' for 'tree' and, thereby, manager for horticulturalist. In such a context we can, I hope, easily see the complementary demands that masculine and feminine principles place upon us. The two sets of attributes, moreover, are not at all dissimilar from those associated with the two sides of the brain.

Left brain – right brain

The complementary functioning of the mind

During the 1960s, particularly in the United States, extensive research was being undertaken by both neurologists and psychologists into what came to be called 'the two sides of the brain'. What they were discovering was that the right side of the brain, controlling the left side of the body, and the left side of the brain, controlling the right side, yielded very different behaviour.

A direct link between yin and yang and the complementary functioning of the human mind was made by the Austrian physicist Fritjof Capra, who – in the 1970s – published his best-selling book *The Tao of Physics*.[10] Capra was the first person to make direct links between modern quantum physics and the philosophical traditions of the east. As such he revealed that the analytical and the intuitive are complementary modes of functioning of the human mind. Analytical thinking is linear, focused and structured. It belongs to the realm of the intellect, whose function is to discriminate, measure and categorize. Thus analytical knowledge tends to be fragmented. Intuitive knowledge, on the other hand, is based on a direct, non-intellectual experience of reality, arising in an expanded state of awareness. It tends to be synthesizing, holistic and non-linear. From this it is apparent that analytically based knowledge is likely to generate self-centred or yang activity, whereas intuitive wisdom is the basis of ecological, or yin, wisdom.[11]

Table 4.2 Two modes of consciousness

Left brain	Right brain	Left brain	Right brain
Day	Night	Focal	Diffuse
Intellectual	Sensuous	Creative	Receptive
Active	Sensitive	Masculine	Feminine
Explicit	Tacit	Light	Dark
Sequential	Simultaneous	Verbal	Spatial
Argument	Experience	Time	Eternity
Intellectual	Intuitive	Causal	Acausal

The psychology of consciousness

By the 1970s these findings had begun to enter the theory and practice of management, particularly via the work on 'mindmaps' developed by the Australian guru on learning processes Tony Buzzan.[12] However, the leading authority on this emerging so-called psychology of 'consciousness' was the American depth psychologist Robert Ornstein. For Ornstein, there are two modes of knowing, those of argument and experience.[13] They are complementary to one another; neither is reducible to the other, and their simultaneous working may be incompatible. One mode is verbal and analytical, sequential in operation, orderly; the other is intuitive, diffuse in operation, less logical and neat, a mode we in the west devalue. Ornstein compared and contrasted his 'two modes of knowledge' (see Table 4.2) and yielded results that largely parallel those of Nancy Foy (see Table 4.1).

The left side of the brain, represented by the right hand, is the 'masculine' and aggressive side that wants to control, to determine what is, to decide what is right. The right side, represented by the left hand, is the 'feminine' and sensitive side that wants to respond, to adapt to what is, and to recognize what is right. Entrepreneurs who desire to exploit markets, and executives who want to control people and information, have highly developed left brains. Managers who run successful cooperatives, and project coordinators who are highly responsive to change, need to have strongly developed right brains. But when power and sensitivity are working in coordination, there is wholeness.

The right brain, then, 'tunes' information, the left brain 'sifts' through it. The left brain deals with the past, matching the experience of this moment to earlier experience, trying to categorize it; the right brain responds to the unknown. We confine much of our conscious awareness, in the north and west, to the aspect of brain function that reduces things to parts. And we sabotage our only strategy for finding meaning, according to social forecaster Marilyn Ferguson,[14] because the left brain is habitually cutting off conflict from the right, thereby also cutting off its ability to see the whole. Without the benefit of a scalpel, she says, we perform split-brain surgery on ourselves. We isolate heart and mind.

Cut off from the fantasy, dreams, intuitions and holistic processes of the right brain, the left is sterile. And the right brain, cut off from integration with its organizing partner, keeps cycling its emotional recharge. As our organizations and environments become more complex, Ferguson argues therefore, we need whole-brain understanding as we never needed it before: 'the right brain to innovate, sense, dream up, and envision; the left to test, analyse, check out, build constructs and support for the new order'.[15] Yin and yang, right brain and left brain, reflect two similar sets of complementary, managerial activities. There is one more similar set of opposites, though, and that is 'cooperation' coupled with co-creation versus 'competition' aligned with coordination.

Competition versus cooperation

The signs of our times

Until the 1970s the best companies, at least in the west, sought after cooperative practices within the enterprise and competitive advantage without. However, times have changed. In recent years companies such as IBM, ICL, Siemens and Eriksson have been stimulating internal competition, as well as cooperation, and external cooperation, as well as competition. Business life is no longer simple. In all walks of life people, organizations and whole societies seek an appropriate balance between competition and cooperation. However, it is much easier to find business texts on competitive strategies than on cooperative ones. 'Aggressive, competitive behavior alone would make life impossible. Even the most ambitious, goal-oriented individuals need sympathetic support, human contact, and times of carefree spontaneity and relaxation'.[16]

The need to balance competition and cooperation has been better documented in biological and ecological studies than in management science, as we shall see in chapter 13. However, one individual who has brought the two together is the Dutchman Roel Van Duyn. Van Duyn, a municipal councillor in Holland in the 1960s, had a vision of a Utopian society in which competition and cooperation would be in a state of economic, political and social balance. He and his collea-gues set up a Dutch 'Freestate' with 12 ministries paralleling the existing govern-ment. Homes, creches, schools and health-food shops were established. All over Europe similar groups were set up until the movement withered away in the sober 1970s.

Creativity and destructiveness

Van Duyn concluded that there is a special reciprocal relationship between competition and cooperation. On the one hand, he saw this relationship as a form of mutual aid. Competitive aggression fulfils the repellent functions which cooperation, because it attracts, cannot fulfil. So while the one pushes competitors out of the market-place the other attracts customers to the company's products or services. On the other hand, cooperation, through its capacity for organization, can enhance the strength of the self-same competitiveness. 'The urge to cooperate induces zebras to form intimidating groups, and it is this that makes their aggression towards the leopard so effective'.[17] When 'masculine' competitiveness and 'feminine' cooperation complement one another,[18] we have creativity. When they overrule one another, we have destructiveness. For example, in the pioneering days of the American computer-chip makers, internal collaboration and external competition were in a state of healthy balance. Each company was stimulated to produce more for a growth market. However, with the advent of fierce Japanese competition it was not enough for these same 'chip' makers to compete, individually, against a foe that was accustomed to collaborating with its own government.

So, in 1986, the American companies began to collaborate with each other and with their government, externally, as well as their staff working together, internally. That particular strategy, though, was short-lived. It went too much against the western cultural grain. Instead we have seen, as business consultant James Moore has so insightfully charted, the emergence in the 1990s, of new-style business ecosystems. Intel, the pre-eminent US chip maker, is amongst the leaders within these.

> Intel's Architecture Labs are now promoting an open framework for investment, that is a framework that invites others to bring their innovation to the personal computer platform. The framework is particularly valuable in making a place for smaller, highly creative companies. Intel's aim is to help coordinate the investments of others, rather than try to make these investments by themselves. Overall, and in that respect, Intel had added dramatic ecosystemwide scope to its leadership activities. Once the concept caught on, ideas sprang up all over the place. They talked about themselves as chip heads willing to learn, that is, as managers starting out with a semi-conductor industry orientation learning to become ambassadors to a larger, more diverse community of companies around them.[19]

For some social philosophers in the 1990s, including America's Riane Eisler, this re-emergence of co-evolution, as exhibited by Intel here, forms part of a broader historical pattern. Within this pattern she sees a return to the 'partnership' model – based on linking rather than ranking – that existed in the earliest stages of human civilization, after a long period in which the 'dominator' model prevailed, whereby one half of humanity was ranked superior to the other.

From domination to partnership

For Eisler,[20] then, the formative stages of mankind's development, following the explosive birth of our expanding universe, were contained within the binary elements of matter and energy. During the next great phase change – the emergence of life – nucleic acids and proteins combined into a variety of forms. Then a new set of binary elements required for survival were introduced: male and female. Spanning a period of several million years, the first human emergence phase marks the beginning of the co-evolutionary age. It entails a transformation from one living system to another, from hominid to human. And it marks another fundamental transformation, from living systems that may at best select among given realities to a new form of life with the capacity to create new realities. It is also during this early phase of our development that we see the emergence of the first human-made tools and artifacts, including the most fundamental of the conceptual tools, language. The second phase change, the agrarian age of co-creation with macroscopic organic matter, was the first technological milestone in human culture, from the harvesting of food, through the use of human-made technologies, to our co-creation with nature of natural resources. The third phase change, the machine age, involving co-creation with macroscopic non-organic matter, comprises a shift from the use of hands and tools for the production of material objects to the creation out of non-organic matter of a new order of technics: machines.

This major technological expansion led in turn to a still greater expansion of human, physical and mental powers through the emergence of modern science, and the resultant far greater complexity in human ideological and social structures.

The fourth major technological phase, the electronic/nuclear age of co-creation with microscopic non-organic matter is the shift that occurred only a few decades ago. This represented a shift from the use of human brains to process information to the creation of electronic brains, as well as the co-creation of sources of energy rivalled only by the sun. The fourth phase has led, in turn, to the emergence of a new scientific paradigm focusing on interconnections and process. This phase takes us into a world that is, through human-made technologies, Eisler maintains, inextricably linked into one interdependent system, whereby the partnership model returns.

Conclusion

From modernism to post-modernism

A similar view to Eisler's is expressed by yet another American philosopher, Richard Tarnas, who for many years ran the Essalen Institute in Monterey, California. In his philosophical primer, *Passion of the Western Mind*, Tarnas – reviewing the history of western civilization – concludes that we have reached a specific turning point as we approach the millennium, which he identifies with 'postmodernism'. It is within the context of such a turning point, in fact, that this book is located.

Postmodernity, for Tarnas, involves an appreciation of the plasticity and constant change of reality and knowledge. It maintains that no single a priori thought system – in our terms, primal or rational, developmental or metaphysical – should govern belief or investigation.

It involves, moreover, a recognition that human knowledge is subjectively determined by a multitude of factors, including gender orientation, and a belief that all truths and assumptions must therefore be continually subjected to direct testing. Thus the search for the truth, whether for mankind in general or for management in particular, must be tolerant of ambiguity and pluralism.

According to Tarnas, postmodern thought has, moreover, encouraged a vigorous rejection of western 'canon', long defined and privileged by a more or less exclusively male, white elite of European heritage. It has encouraged a flexibility and cross-fertilization, reflected in the widespread practice of open 'conversation' between different understandings, joined, and affected, by a multitude of cultural perspectives from outside the west. 'All gather now on the intellectual stage as if for some kind of climactic synthesis'.[21]

The postmodern collapse of universal meaning, then, has been countered by an emerging awareness of the individual's – in our context, manager's – self-responsibility and self-transformation in his or her response to life. The personal and organizational challenge, therefore, is to engage that world view which brings forth the most valuable, life-enhancing consequences. Major theoretical interventions such as chaos and complexity theory, as we shall see, have pointed towards new possibilities. The more complexly conscious and ideologically unconstrained the individual or society, the more free is the choice of worlds, the more profound his, her or its participation in reality.

The complementarity shift

The western intellectual tradition, ultimately for Tarnas, has been produced and canonized almost entirely by men, and informed mainly by male perspectives.

The 'man' of the western tradition has constantly striven to differentiate himself from and control the context out of which he emerged. He became visible in the west's patriarchal religion from Judaism, in its rationalist philosophy from Greece, and in its objectivist science from modern Europe. To manifest this the 'western' masculine mind has repressed the feminine more distinctly than has been the case in the east and the south. Therefore, the crisis of modern man, for Tarnas, is an essentially masculine one, so that the resolution already occurring is reflected in the tremendous emergence of the feminine, in the deepening recognition of the value and necessity of partnership, pluralism and the interplay of many perspectives. As Jung prophesied, an epochal shift is taking place in the contemporary psyche, a reconcilliation between the two great masculine and feminine polarities. These polarities, in their turn, underlie the four philosophical domains – primal and rational, developmental and metaphysical. These, as we have seen, underpin our journey to mastery, drawing upon a worldliwise orientation.

Complementarity in management

The complementary and parallel sets of principles of cooperation and competition, domination and partnership, right brain and left brain, 'femininity' and 'masculinity', yin and yang, have a very important part to play in this global management text. For they form a demarcation line between so-called 'soft' and 'hard' orientations, at each step of the domain-based, managerial way. Moreover, and in general terms as we have indicated, the south and the east display their soft edges more fully than the north and the west, and the north and the west exhibit their hard edges more fully than the south and the east. Finally, the yin–yang symbol of wholeness reflects the paradoxical nature of softness and hardness. In every hard edge there is at least a touch of softness and in every soft edge there is at least a touch of hardness. In the next chapter we turn to the roots of our first, 'primal' domain, lodged in 'hard' economics and 'soft' anthropology.

Part II

WHAT? GLOBAL MANAGEMENT – ESTABLISHING THE CONTENT

5

PRIMAL ROOTS – CULTURE
AND ECONOMICS

Introduction

Market economy and cultural anthropology

Primal roots

Having provided you with a global perspective on management devcelopment through cultural diversity, we now turn to the primal domain generally, and to its roots specifically. The primal roots of management, lodged in fact relatively close to the surface, lie on the one hand in economics, and in Adam Smith's 'market economy'. Through the 'market', resources are allocated and controlled. Deeper down within the historical soil, and on the other hand, the primal roots reach cultural anthropology, inside primordial, Stone Age communities. Through such 'culture', physical and human nature is cultivated and values are exchanged and shared. The human being also evolves a sense of place.

Oikos

Hundreds of thousands of years ago our ancestors, the ape men, lived out in the wild as nomads, barely able to communicate with their fellows, or to settle in one place. Then, some 10,000 years ago, Neolithic men and women began to settle in one home, one place, one *oikos*, to use the Greek term. At this dawn of history, a village society had emerged in which life seemed to be unified by a communal disposition towards work, and its products. Nomadic bands of hunter-gatherers had begun to develop a crude system of horticulture, and had settled down in small villages, where they engaged in mixed farming. Although both hunter and gatherer had their parts to play, the one killing and trapping animals and the other cultivating the land, social life began to acquire distinctly 'matricental' qualities.

The first settled communities, then, under their primal, Neolithic management, began to shift their prime focus from the male hunter to the female food gatherer. Woman's foraging activities helped awaken in humanity an acute sense of place, of *oikos*. Her stake in society was different from that of the male. It was more domestic, more pacifying and more caring. The primal roots of management

107

are to be found, therefore, not in the armies and churches of antiquity, but in the first settled villages, in our original *oikos*. The modern term 'economics', in fact, owes its origins to this Greek word for place.

Economic and cultural transformation

The hunter becomes an entrepreneur

It was not until the seventeenth and eighteenth centuries that economics was transformed, and gradually lost its homely connection. It was at this point that primal management took a strong turn towards the hunter, and gave birth to the modern 'entrepreneur'. Thus the entrepreneur, and his business enterprise, visibly evolved from primal, hunting origins.

The subsequent entrepreneurial tradition has lived on since the eighteenth century, and has even gained renewed force, in recent times, within business and the community. In the 1980s in fact, for the first time, it was brought into the conventional managerial fold, and even given a new title, 'intrapreneuring'. The original 'hunting' image, moreover, stretching back to Neolithic times, still retains much of its primal force and identity, most especially within the west.

The gatherer reappeared in Marxian guise

The communal tradition, on the other hand, has undergone an ironic transformation. The gatherer has been thrust out of classical economics, despite the original *oikos*. She reappeared in the nineteenth century, in Marxian guise. By this point, of course, the gatherer was sitting outside of, and in opposition to, business, rather than within it. In the twentieth century this resulted in both Russian and Chinese revolutions. The stage was then set for a conflict between 'capitalism' and 'socialism' that eclipsed the gatherer role within business. Therefore when the 'behavioural sciences' were introduced into management they lacked the basic, instinctive thrust that entrepreneurship carried. Inevitably as a result, 'human relations' got pushed into the commercial sidelines, that is until the 'soft' side of Japanese management began to make itself apparent. However, we are now jumping the gun. Let me return to anthropology and to economics, from whence management came.

The gatherer's role and evolution

From 'economizing' to 'substantive' economics

Karl Polanyi[1] was an unusual mix of anthropologist and economist who took a particular interest in the way economics became transformed over the course of thousands of years. Economics, for Polanyi, had two meanings. The first, 'formal' meaning related to the 'economizing' function, that is to the allocation of scarce resources. It ties in with the manager's survival role. The second, 'substantive' meaning, pointed to the elemental fact that human beings, like all other living creatures, cannot exist for any length of time without a physical and social environment that sustains them. This second perspective ties in with the manager as nurturer and communicator.

It is this second, often neglected, definition that brings the gatherer into the foreground. Its substantive connotations are derived from man's dependence for his livelihood upon nature and upon his fellows. It draws from primal origins within matricentric, Neolithic communities. The American social ecologist Murray Bookchin characterizes such horticultural communities as 'procreative in their relationship with the natural world, touching the earth and changing it, but with a grace, delicacy and feeling that may be regarded as nature's own harvest'.[2]

The social and economic imagery of that primordial time, therefore, was oriented more towards the procreator than towards the creator, emerging from the domestic hearth rather than the camp fire, and with cultural traits associated with mother rather than with father. The role of 'gatherer' as collector, grower, carrier and maker of useful things superseded that of hunter. In contemporary terms, shared values surpass autonomy and entrepreneurship as a guiding, primal ethic.

Subsistence communities

Of course the substantive economy of 10,000 years ago still exists today, in so-called 'subsistence' communities. One such community which I happen to know well has been formed, over the centuries, by the Shona peoples of Zimbabwe. While, as the country develops, traditional and modern forms become increasingly juxtaposed, a 'substantive' economy still exists within substantial parts of the society.

Wealth, therefore, is not a personal matter for the indigenous Shona, even today. It is not a man's own possession which he can will as he pleases. It belongs to the family group and its use is restricted and bound up with marriage and family life.

Shona villagers extol the virtues of solidarity, fraternity and equality. The chief, his councillors and his headmen are thus expected to set an example by not living differently from the rest of the people. They must avoid creating the impression that he is superior to others.

In his or her traditional background, therefore, no Shona man or woman works alone or independently; all are geared towards dependence. They have to learn that an individual is part of a society that depends for its smooth working on the control of its wants. Without such self-abnegation there would be insufficient food for the whole community.[3]

In a traditional community, then, the economic process is embedded in the extended 'kinship' relations. The communal setting formalizes the situation, and the shared values, out of which organized economic activities spring. What there is of production and distribution of goods and services is therefore embedded within the overall communal and 'corporate culture'. As we have seen in chapters 2 and 3, in fact, such a commmunal tradition lives on within both generically southern and also more generally far-eastern business enterprises.

From self-sufficiency to reciprocity

Indeed the substantive view of economics, as embedded within the norms and values of the community at large, continued to be held for thousands of years. Aristotle, in Ancient Greece, saw the role of barter in society to be that of returning society to self-sufficiency rather than that of securing profit or gain. He saw the need to set rates of exchange, through law and custom, in such a way that the natural friendliness that prevails amongst members of a community is maintained. At the same time he likened the labour process not to a form of production, but to one of reproduction, not to an act of fabrication, but to one of procreation.

In feudal times, moreover, in Western Europe, even though the famous open-field system was indeed organized around individually formed narrow strips, this strip farming necessarily involved such close coordination of planting and harvesting between cultivators of adjacent strips that the peasantry normally shared its ploughs, draft animals and implements. The reciprocity involved reinforced archaic communal traditions, and, with them, the gatherer's role. In fourteenth-century England, therefore, technology was still deeply embedded in society. Every village had its masons, carpenters, spinners, smiths and millers, each of whom was bound to his fellow craftsmen through a guild. Home and occupation were still closely intertwined, as were family and working life. A self-contained economic world had not yet lifted itself outside of the social context. The very idea of personal gain was foreign to social and religious thought, at least for most people, during the Middle Ages.

Whereas the concept of personal gain was blasphemous, the broader notion that a general struggle for gain might actually bind a community together would have been considered to be little short of madness. There was a reason for this supposed blindness. Land, labour and capital – the basic agents of production which the market system allocates – did not yet exist. They did not enter the gatherer's vocabulary, just as they are falling out of post-industrial favour today. Land, labour and capital in the sense of soil, human beings and tools are of course co-existent with society itself. But these same entities as impersonal, dehumanized agents of production had not yet been conceived of as such, almost in the same way as they are becoming the 'lesser evolved' factors of production in our knowledge-based economies.

The hunter's role and evolution

The advent of self-interest

Over the course of the seventeenth and eighteenth centuries all that morality changed, paving the way for the transformation of the hunter of old into the new entrepreneur. The gatherer was left very much behind. She became, until only very recently, the proverbial housewife. What forces, then, could have been sufficiently powerful to smash a comfortable and established world, and institute in its place this new unwanted society? There was no single massive cause. The new way of life grew inside the old like a butterfly inside a chrysalis, and when the stir was strong enough it burst the old structure asunder.

It was not great events, single adventures, individual laws or powerful personalities which brought about the economic revolution. It was a process of internal growth. First there was the gradual emergence of national political units in Europe, the isolated existence of early feudalism giving way to centralized monarchies. With the growth of monarchies came the growth of national spirit; in turn this meant royal patronage for favoured industries. A second great current of change was to be found in the emergence of Protestantism. The Protestant leaders paved the way for an amalgamation of spiritual and temporal life. Acquisitiveness became a recognized virtue, not immediately for one's private enjoyment, but for the greater glory of God. From here it was only a step to the identification of riches with spiritual excellence, and of rich men with saintly ones. Perhaps most important of all in the pervasiveness of its effect was a rise in scientific curiosity. The pre-capitalist era saw the birth of the printing press, the paper mill, the windmill, the map and a host of other inventions. Experimentation and innovation were looked on for the first time with a fresh eye.[4]

Self-interest in the market-place

Whereas the role of gatherer had been left behind in the economic history books, by the eighteenth century, the hunter of old was gaining a new lease of life. With the birth of 'economic man' came the entrepreneur, hunting for economic and financial, rather than for natural and physical, gain. Whereas the Neolithic hunter had made his 'killings' on the open plain, the new entrepreneur made his particular ones on the open market! The problem of survival, in the eighteenth century, was to be solved not by groups of men of physical prowess, bound by community and custom, but by the free action of profit-seeking individuals bound together only by the market.

Moreover, the idea of personal gain that underpinned it became so firmly rooted that it was soon assumed to be an omnipresent attitude. The idea, though, needed a binding philosophy. That philosophy came, in 1776, in the form of Adam Smith's *Inquiry into the Wealth of Nations*.[5] Dr Smith, a Scot and Professor of

Moral Philosophy, a slight man who had more than a slight tendency to be absent-minded, turned traditional society on its head. Instead of focusing on the community, within which the individual is contained, Smith focused on the individual, around whom society revolves.

Adam Smith concluded that through his famous and 'invisible hand' the private interests and passions of men are led in the direction 'which is most agreeable to the interests of society'. The 'gatherer' has therefore become 'invisible'; her role has been overtaken by that of the impersonal market. She becomes a non-entity. The entrepreneur's role gathers pace. Adam Smith demonstrates to us that the drive of 'individual self-interest', within an environment of similarly motivated individuals, will result in healthy competition.

He then further illustrates how competition will result in the provision of those goods that society wants, in the quantities that society desires, and at the prices that society is prepared to pay. 'It is not from the benevolence of the butcher, the brewer or the baker that we expect our dinner', says Smith, 'but from their regard to their self interest. We address ourselves, not to their humanity, but to their self-love, and never talk to them of our necessities, but of their advantages'.[6]

Self-interest therefore replaces social interest as the primal force. A primal motive is retained, through its powerfully instinctive nature, but the direction of such a motive is fundamentally changed. The directive and controlling side of primal management, instinctively expressed, takes over from the communicative and nurturing one. This imbalance, over time, is destined to lead towards the 'ugly face of capitalism', rearing its nasty head particularly noticeably, for example, in the former Soviet Union in the late 1990s.

Yet such self-interest is only half of Smith's picture. The other half is represented by competition. For each man, out to do his best for himself with no thought of social cost, is faced with a flock of similarly motivated individuals who are in exactly the same boat. Thus a man who permits his self-interest to run away with itself will find that competitors have slipped in to take his trade away. The trouble with Smith's argument, of course, is that he relies on one hunter to scare the other away. There is no gatherer in place to create a balance. The result, historically speaking, has been the rise of socialism, of communism, and of workers' movements around the globe, each of which has attempted to alter the 'capitalist' imbalance. The problem was that they in turn became imbalanced, overturned by a 'pseudo-scientific socialism', so that in the 1990s we witnessed the demise of communism.

Today, then, to a large extent because of the 'soft' primal influence from Japan, both 'hard' and 'soft' attributes of management, as we saw in chapter 4, have been brought firmly within the ambit of a capitalism that now assumes different forms. In time, inevitably in my opinion, such a monolithic notion of 'capitalism' will itself dissolve, and will be resolved in more definitively contrasting forms. However, we are not yet quite ready for it.

The emergence of the entrepreneur

The art of primal management, then, as we shall soon see, is to maintain an effective balance between hunting and gathering. In other words, both enterprise and community must have their proper place. Ironically, although Adam Smith introduced us to the entrepreneur as the creator of the Wealth of Nations, neither Smith nor his successors amongst the classical economists gave us much insight into this entrepreneur's character. In fact the first of the political economists to do so properly was Joseph Schumpeter.

Schumpeter was an Austrian, born in the second half of the nineteenth century, who spent much of his life in America. In *The Theory of Economic Development* Schumpeter portrayed the entrepreneur as a man of courage and instinct, a truly primal hero. For it was the entrepreneur's will and intuition rather than his formalized knowledge and skill that made him successful.

More specifically, Schumpeter identified three leading attributes of enterprising man. These three attributes incorporated the desire for a private kingdom, a will to conquer, and joyful creativity.

Attributes of entrepreneurship

First of all there is the dream and the will to found a private kingdom. What may be attained by industrial or commercial success is the nearest approach to medieval lordship possible to modern man. Its fascination is specially strong for those people who have no other chance of achieving social distinction. Then there is the impulse to conquer: the impulse to fight, to prove oneself superior to others, to succeed for the sake of success itself, not for the sake of the fruits of success. Finally, there is the joy of creating, of getting things done, or simply of exercising one's energy and ingenuity.[7] This third set of motives is the most directly anti-hedonist of the three.

In his theory of economic development, Schumpeter not only saw the entrepreneur to be an innovative and disruptive force, but also acknowledged that such a person played an important part within a large organization as well as within a small one. Schumpeter therefore sowed early seeds for the subsequent emergence of the 'intrapreneur'. Finally, Joseph Schumpeter equated enterprise with development, both of these set under the guise of the carrying out of new combinations. Such new combinations could involve firstly the introduction of a new good, that is one with which consumers are not yet familiar; or secondly of a new quality of good; thirdly the introduction of a new method of production, that is one not yet tested by expeience in the branch of manufacture concerned; fourthly the opening of a new market; fifthly the conquest of a new source of supply of raw materials or half-manufactured goods; and finally the carrying out of a new form of industrial organization.

Conclusion

The new primal wave

In the sixty years since Schumpeter wrote *The Theory of Economic Development*, primal management had been largely eclipsed by, particularly, rational management in some guise or another. However, in the 1980s the search for primal 'excellence', in a contemporary context, began in earnest. *In Search of Excellence* by Peters and Waterman is in fact a modern updating of primal management, both 'soft' and 'hard'. As we shall see in chapter 7, the two Americans have resurrected both hunter and gatherer in modern garb, and given their respective qualities equal weight and influence.

The need for character balance

Despite their efforts, though, we still find ourselves bereft of character balance at this primal stage. For while the entrepreneur or intrapreneur is alive and well, his 'gatherer' counterpart remains somewhat characterless. He or she has 'soft' qualities, but has no name to call his or her own. In my own work I have borrowed from the French and come up with the word 'animateur' to give modern substance to the gatherer of old. Such an 'animateur' is the person who brings life to a community, who fosters group spirit, and who animates people in a communal setting. He or she shares with the entrepreneur enthusiasm and flair; where they differ is in their relative individualism and competitiveness, as Albert Koopman has intimated.

Primal management, over the course of the past decade or two, has come into its own so as to ward off the prospects of 'paralysis by analysis'. It also serves as a reminder that basic human qualities, both soft and hard, remain vitally important, in business in particular, and have served mankind, in general, for many thousands of years.

What we must not forget as we go out 'in search of excellence', and indeed liberation, is that the soft and communal values are as important as the hard and individual ones, and that primal management initiates, rather than culminates in, the managerial debate. While all managers – primal, rational, developmental and metaphysical – control and direct, on the one hand, and communicate and cultivate, on the other, the primal species do so in a particular way. Their approach is basic, instinctive, immediate, as we shall see in the next chapter when we turn to Peters and Waterman, and attend to their 'excellent' primal thesis, duly supplemented by Tom Peters over the course of the subsequent fifteen years.

6

PASSION FOR EXCELLENCE

The primal mainstem

Introduction

Enterprise and shared values

In the 1980s, and to a lesser degree in the 1990s, management has simultaneously undergone a regression and a progression. For on the one hand management has 'regressed' back to its primal origins; on the other hand it has progressed through, and beyond, its supposedly analytical straight-jacket. The prime instigator of this 'back to basics' movement has been Tom Peters, a highly energetic and dynamic American based in California. Initially going out 'in search of excellence' with his McKinsey colleague Bob Waterman, Peters established a new wave of management thinking that very quickly became vogue in both Europe and America. Peters' 'new' wave represented, at one and the same time, a return to primal, hunter-gatherer instincts and a reinstatement of the American enterprising-communal spirit. The personalized, hunter instinct, firstly then, was resurrected in the form of 'winning':

> The message that comes through so poignantly in the studies we reviewed is that we [Americans] like to think of ourselves as winners. The lesson that the excellent companies have to teach us is that there is no reason why we can't design systems that continually reinforce this notion.[1]

The communal, gatherer instinct, secondly then, initially resurrected by Peters in the form of 'shared values', ultimately secured the upper hand in his second book, written with Nancy Austin, *A Passion for Excellence*.

> Let us suppose that we were asked for one all purpose bit of advice for management, one truth that we were able to distill from the excellent company research. We might be tempted to reply, figure out your value system, decide what the company stands for. What does your enterprise do that gives everyone most pride?[2]

115

What Peters has done, of course, in his pursuit of excellence, is to figure out his country's primal, or instinctive, value system. He has therefore rediscovered what America most basically stands for, including the approach to management and enterprise that gives Americans most pride. For that rediscovery we have the Japanese to thank, for edging American business out of what Peters deemed an evolutionary and analytical cul de sac. In other words, the Japanese threat forced American business, and its management, to rethink its whole approach. The rational orientation that it had adopted, largely under the influence of such central European *émigrés* as Peter Drucker, was being called into question. Something new was now being put in its place, something much more Anglo-Saxon in scope and form.

From the search for excellence to liberation management

In fact, for all Peters' subsequent refutations of his initial findings – in the wake of the demise of many a company hitherto termed 'excellent' – his theoretical framework has remained substantively the same. His two major works in the 1990s, that is *Thriving on Chaos* and *Liberation Management*, are mere variations on his 'excellent' theme. Indeed, Tom Peters, and the Tom Peters group, have maintained their influence in the 1990s through the sheer force of Peters' primal personality rather than through any major new insights he has provided over the past decade. Let me therefore elaborate on 'excellence', its origins and development, thereby revealing the mainstem of what I have termed primal management.

In search of excellence

The seven Ss

The American search for a new approach to management was spurred on by the accelerating Japanese competition in the mid-1970s. At the time the rational approach advanced by the Teutonic stream of American management thinkers – to which I allude in chapter 9 – held sway over the purer Anglo-Saxons, people such as Peters and Waterman. A search was therefore instigated by McKinsey's, the highly reputable American business consultants, and by Richard Pascale and Anthony Athos. Pascale and Athos, who subsequently wrote *The Art of Japanese Management*,[3] concluded that the Japanese had managed to combine so-called soft and hard approaches to management more successfully than most American companies had done.

They subsequently developed the 'seven Ss' framework, still popular today, some fifteen years later. Shown in Figure 6.1, it incorporates four soft elements (in brackets), as well as three hard elements. Strategy, structure and systems comprised the 'cold triangle', so revered by business schools, and rationally oriented managers. Skills, staff, style and – most importantly for Peters – shared values,

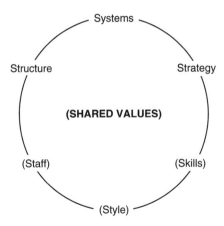

Figure 6.1 The seven Ss of management

made up the 'warm' and softer side. Japanese companies, it appeared, were uniquely adept at both.

However, Pascale and Athos then discovered that the best American companies, like their Japanese counterparts, combined soft and hard, warm and cold, attributes. Peters and Waterman, focusing on America rather than Japan, continued on from where Pascale and Athos left off, placing less emphasis on conceptual sophistication and more on finding home truths.

Back to basics

Primal attributes

The seven Ss framework, as far as Peters and Waterman were concerned, enabled them to say:

> All that stuff you have been dismissing for so long as the intractable, irrational, intuitive and informal organization can be managed . . . Not only are you foolish to ignore it, but here's a way to think about it.[4]

However, the two Americans still felt at the time that McKinsey's had only scratched the surface of, particularly, the softer sides of management. More work needed to be done. So in 1979 they chose 75 highly regarded American companies and searched for reasons for their excellence in performance and reputation.

Their research showed, more clearly than could have been hoped, that the excellent companies were, above all, brilliant on the basics. Tools did not substitute for smart thinking. Intellect did not overpower wisdom. Analysis did not impede action. Rather, these companies worked hard to 'keep things simple in a complex world'.[5] We can now investigate what the companies did, and how.

The primal mainstem

Peters and Waterman identified a set of core attributes that characterize their excellent companies. It is these basic attributes which have since displaced the conventional and analytical wisdom in many a 'progressive' manager in America and Europe in the 1980s and, to a lesser extent, in the 1990s. As we can see from Figure 6.2, their characteristics (for example 'bias for action') – both soft and hard – are much more basic, or primal, in language and tone than those of Pascale and Athos (for example 'systems'). The so-called 'hard and cold triangle' – strategy, system and structure – amongst the seven Ss were displaced by more distinctly 'western', more basic and tangible, as well as more primal and entrepreneurial, virtues:

- strategy – autonomy and entrepreneurship; stick to the knitting
- systems – bias for action
- structure – lean staff, simple form; loose–tight organization

Similarly the soft and 'warm' attributes of staff, skills, style and shared values have also been suitably displaced:

- staff and skills – productivity through people
- style – close to the customer
- superordinate goals – shared values

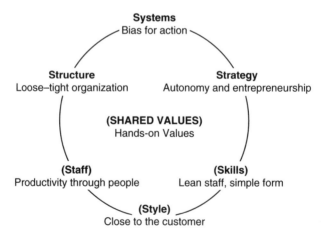

Figure 6.2 Primal attributes

The 'hard' primal forces

Strategy — autonomy and entrepreneurship

The central character in 'hard' pursuit of excellence is the winner, the champion, or the individual that has since been termed the 'intrapreneur', that is an entrepreneur within an established organization. This instinctively driven 'primal manager' thereby displaces his or her analytical counterpart as the 'go-ahead' business's linchpin.

THE CHAMPION

This product or process 'champion' embodies such presence, immediacy, heroism and ingenuity that this person can be associated with the primal hunter and entrepreneur. He or she merely transfers these attributes from the traditional hunting ground into an organizational context, albeit a favourable one such as 3M in America, where his or her approach is welcomed rather than ridiculed or ignored. Such a champion, for Peters, is not a blue-sky dreamer, or an intellectual giant, but he or she is the pragmatic one who grabs hold of a theoretical construct and bullheadedly pushes it to fruition.

CHAMPIONING SYSTEMS

More specifically, then, all the activity and apparent confusion Peters and Waterman observed within their excellent companies revolved around 'fired up champions', and around making sure that the potential innovator, or champion, comes forward, grows and flourishes, even to the extent of 'indulging in a little madness'. An average 'non-excellent' company is unable to cope with the irrationality, the egotism and the impatience of such a characteristic champion. So he or she never gets hired, or if the individual does pass through the recruitment barrier, he or she is made to feel uncomfortable for ever after.

The excellent and innovative companies, by way of contrast, have the appropriate support systems for this entrepreneurial character.

Three primary roles are required in order, to foster innovation. There is first the product champion him or herself, cranky and fanatical. He or she is supported by an 'executive champion' and a 'godfather'. The executive has been through the lengthy process of husbanding, and has learnt how to shield an embryonic product from organizational negativity. The godfather is typically an aging leader who provides a role model for championing. For champions are pioneers, and pioneers get shot at.

The companies that get the most from champions have rich support networks for them. In particular their systems are designed to 'leak' so that scrounging champions can get something done. Whereas rational managers sort things out by rules and procedures, primal ones use internal competition as a basis for selection. In other words, the fittest, rather than the most reasonable, survive.

In excellent companies, moreover, there are two attributes of communication that seem to foster innovation and enterprise – informality and intensity. Both encourage looseness (freewheeling) and tightness (peer pressure). Finally, a special feature of the success-oriented, positive and innovating environment is a substantial tolerance for failure. Specifically, champions do not automatically emerge. They emerge at companies such as 3M because history and numerous supports encourage them to, nurture them through trying times, celebrate their successes, and nurse them through occasional failures.

Within an 'innovative' company such as 3M or Microsoft or Virgin, therefore, the champion, the supportive executive and the venture team are at the heart of the process. Moreover, according to Peters, they succeed – when they do succeed – because:

> heroes abound; the value system focusses on scrounging; it is okay to fail; there is an orientation towards nichemanship and close contact with the customer. There is a well understood process of taking small manageable steps; intense, informal communications are the norm; the physical setting provides plenty of sites for innovation; the organizational structure is highly accommodating of 3M style innovation; and the absence of planning and paperwork is conspicuous, as is the internal competition.[6]

STICK TO THE KNITTING

Peters and Waterman want little to do with such rationally managerial devices as 'strategic intent' or 'core competence'. For them it is the individual who drives the organization and shared values that make it cohere. It is as simple as that. They reduce 'corporate strategy', therefore, to its simplest terms. Companies, they say, must 'stick to the knitting'. While individuals should be encouraged to champion a wide range of ideas, the organization itself should be circumspect. In other words, businesses which branch out to only a limited extent, and thus 'stick very close to their knitting', out-perform others. 3M, which has diversified around a single knowledge base, coating and bonding technology, is a good case in point. When in fact the primal manager strays too far afield, he loses his 'feel'. Such instinctive hunting (exploiting opportunities) or gathering (nurturing champions) feel can be trusted, whereas a business concept, abstract and abstruse, is inevitably suspect. We now turn from primal strategy to primal systems.

Primal systems – bias for action

ON THE MOVE

In the same way that abstract business concepts are suspect, for Tom Peters learning divorced from action is unreal. The best systems are therefore those which are always moving, and always changing. Just like the hunter and his prey, they are seldom still.

Such a bias for action involves organizational fluidity as well as constant technological, commercial and social experimentation.

ORGANIZATIONAL FLUIDITY

In rapidly changing times, bureaucracy, and its static procedures, are insufficient. An 'adhocracy' is needed, that is an organizational mechanism to deal with all the new and emerging issues that fall in between the bureaucratic cracks, that lie across its unchanging divisions. 'Chunking' for Peters and Waterman means breaking things up to facilitate organizational fluidity and to encourage action. The resulting, action-oriented bits and pieces come in many guises, as teams, as quality circles, as task forces, as project groups.

Such small and temporary groups are the building blocks of excellent companies. Yet they hardly appear at all in the formal organization charts. Temporary task forces of this kind usually have ten or fewer people attached to them; their duration is limited; membership is always voluntary; documentation is informal and scant.

EXPERIMENTING ORGANIZATIONS

'Do it, fix it, try it' is the favourite axiom of Peters and Waterman. Getting on with things, especially in the face of complexity, simply comes down to doing something. Primal management is therefore involved, unstintingly, in a process of basic – if not scientific – experimentation. The most important and visible outcropping of the action bias in the so-called 'excellent' companies is their willingness to try things out, to experiment. Sheer numbers of experiments are critical ingredients for success through experimentation. The key difference between successful and unsuccessful oil-exploration companies, for example, in the opinion of Peters and Waterman, is the sheer volume of drilling each has accomplished.

Experimentation, then, acts as a form of cheap learning for most of the excellent companies, usually proving less costly – and more useful – than sophisticated planning or market research. Management therefore has to be tolerant of leaky systems, it has to accept mistakes, support bootlegging, and roll with unexpected changes. Fluidity, chunking and experimentation are facilitated by such simplified systems. Proctor and Gamble, for example, are famous for their one-page-only memoranda.

In summary, and according to Peters and Waterman, there is no more important trait amongst excellent companies than an action orientation: 'Ready. Fire. Aim. Learn from your tries. That's enough'.[7]

Primal structure – lean staff, simple form

Peters and Waterman show positive uninterest in organizational form, particularly if it smacks of complexity. As far as they are concerned, the less formal the organization, and the simpler the structure, the better. In that sense they reflect, to a tee, the attitudes and behaviour of an entrepreneur. In the excellent companies such as Microsoft or Virgin, therefore, small in almost every case is beautiful. In the small unit, maintains Peters, the motivated and highly productive employee, in communication and in competition with his or her peers, out-produces the worker in big facilities time and again. Small, quality, excitement and autonomy belong to the same side of the coin. The point about smallness, in fact, is that it induces manageability and, above all, commitment. More importantly, if the divisions are small enough, the individual still counts, and can stand out. Virtually all the growth that the two Americans found in the excellent companies had been internally generated, starting small – and home-grown. The few acquisitions followed a simple rule. They were small businesses that could be readily assimilated, and, if there was subsequent failure, the company could write or sell off the acquisition without incurring financial damage.

The 'structure of the 1980s', for them, responded to the need for efficiency around the basics by retaining a lean, but stable, form; responding to the need for innovation by having an entrepreneurial focus; responding to the need to avoid calcification by creating a habit-breaking structure. The composite and resulting form contained 'three pillars' of structure and strategy, as shown in Figure 6.3.

We now turn from the 'cold triangle', in Pascale and Athos's terms, to the 'warm' one.

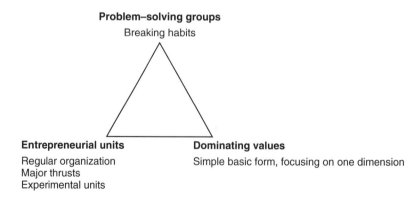

Figure 6.3 The excellent structure

The 'soft' primal attributes

Shared values

Peters and Waterman were much more interested in 'shared values', as a means of coordinating individual activity, than in organizational structures. They were particularly struck, during their researches, by the attention paid, in their supposedly excellent companies, to 'corporate culture'. Shared values, within such a cohesive culture, formed the glue that bound individuals together. Clarifying the value system, they maintained therefore, and breathing life into it, are the greatest contributions a leader can make.

Moreover, the sort of values an excellent company might espouse needed to be narrow in scope, including just a few basic values and beliefs, that is a belief in:

- being the best
- the nuts and bolts of doing the job well
- the importance of people as individuals
- superior quality and service
- most members of the organization being able to innovate
- the importance of informality to enhance contact
- the explicit importance of economic growth and profit

Once again Peters and Waterman affirm their orientation towards basic, visible, Anglo-Saxon values. In focusing on 'hands-on, value-driven' leadership, they also reflect the importance of personifying such values up front. Values and beliefs are not relegated to mere statements of intent. They must be reflected, and exemplified, in everyday behaviour. This will become even clearer when we turn to *A Passion for Excellence*. Before we do so, however, we need to investigate those two crucial and soft attributes of primal management: productivity through people and closeness to the customer.

Productivity through people

Peters and Waterman's book appeared some fifty years after the first social scientists, as we saw in chapter 5, had begun to focus on 'people in organizations'. However, by the 1980s, 'human relations' in business enterprises had become first 'personnel' and subsequently 'human-resources management'. Analytical managers had taken over where their less formal predecessors had left off. True to overall form, then, our two Americans were going back to basics, and treating people as people!

> Treat people as people. Treat them as partners; treat them with dignity; treat them with respect. Treat them – not capital spending and automation – as the primary source of productivity gains. Respect the

individual. Give people control over their destinies. Turn the average Joe and Jane into winners. Accentuate the positive. Insist that people stick out.[8]

Peters and Waterman went on to advocate that companies measure performance regularly, and purposefully, through peer review rather than through complicated and formalized control systems. They should participate with the individual in setting high performance standards. Moreover, such a true people orientation requires a language to go with it. Words and phrases such as family feeling, open door, and management by wandering around, show people in the organization that the orientation is 'bone deep'. Indeed a business should be viewed as an extended family. Companies such as Hewlett Packard and Bodyshop become a community centre for employees, as opposed to just a place of work.

From their primal perspective, then, companies should avoid any rigidly followed chain of command. They should make informality the norm, ensure that top management is constantly in touch with all employees, leaving open doors, establishing open plan and open workspaces. Moreover, it is important to socialize incoming managers, teach people the corporate values through role models, through heroes, and through stories. Hewlett Packard, for example, one of the select band of 'excellent' American companies cited in the 1980s which have remained so today, even systematically collect 'HP Way stories' via a suggestion box, to revitalize the existing stock of corporate tales. Finally, information should be shared widely so that people know quickly whether or not a job is getting done, and who is doing it well or poorly. As such, peer comparison rather than the chain of command becomes the basis for such information and evaluation.

So excellent companies, according to Peters and Waterman, have a deeply ingrained philosophy that says, in effect, respect the individual, make people winners, let them stand out, treat people as adults. Thus the primal manager's attitude to people is distinctive. He or she is concerned with both the person and the task, in the context of individual and commercial achievement. Moreover, his or her attitude to people inside the company is very similar to his orientation towards those without.

Close to the customer

A distinguishing feature of the primal manager, and one which links him or her closely to the entrepreneur, is a closeness to both customers and employees. It is as if both emerge out of the same mind-set. Closeness to the customer, as far as the excellent companies are concerned, involves an obsession with four things: service, quality, nichemanship and listening. The obsession with service, then, according to Peters and Waterman, lies at the heart of excellent company attitudes and operations. Whether they are involved with metal binding, high technology or hamburgers, all these enterprises have defined themselves as service businesses, in which all of their staff become involved. The real barriers to market entry, therefore, lie not in the costs of investment in plant and equipment but in the investment cost of developing and maintaining quality. This quality orientation, the search for excellence revealed, is the critical one, that is the people-capital tied up in ironclad traditions of service, reliability and quality.

Nichemanship, moreover, involves learning about a particular sector of the market, test marketing and solving problems for the potential buyers within it, getting in early and stretching the price to reflect the newly added value to the customer, and being prepared to get out when the niche becomes saturated.

Finally, the excellent companies are not only better on service, quality, reliability and finding a niche, but they are also better listeners. That is the other half of the close-to-the-customer equation. The fact that these companies are so strong on quality and service comes, in large measure, from paying attention to what the customer wants. They listen, they invite their customers into the company, they become partners with them.

In their search for excellence, then, Peters and Waterman came up with a powerful array of soft and hard attributes that characterized the best-run American companies. These attributes were all basic, colloquial, primal to business in America. They were more like instinctive home truths than sophisticated business concepts. As such they took American business in the 1980s by storm, instilling it with a new sense of vigour and pride at a time when its fortunes were waning. Drawing on the hunting instincts of action and competition, and the gathering instincts of community and intimacy, Peters and Waterman regressed to business basics. The 'hard' drive to act and to win ('ready, fire, aim!') led the way, but was closely followed by the 'soft' attachment to people and to shared values. We now turn from Peters' search for excellence, together with Bob Waterman, to his passion for excellence, shared with Nancy Austin, that is before he moves onto even more 'eccentric' ground.

From excellence to liberation

The passion for excellence – business as a show

In Peters' second book, *A Passion for Excellence*, which came out in the mid-1980s, he reversed the priorities. The soft attachment to people, albeit in a primal sense, took precedence over the hard desire to win. Not surprisingly, Peters' co-author, on this occasion, was a woman, Nancy Austin. Moreover, in this impassioned work, the primal nature of their management orientation became even more apparent.

Peters and Austin, then, becoming even truer to primal form, decided to simplify even further. Instead of eight fundamental attributes, they now reduced them to only two, irrespective of the size or the orientation of the institution.

> In the public or private sector, in big business or small, observe that there are only two ways to create and sustain superior performance

over the long haul. First, take exceptional care over your customer via superior service and quality. Secondly, constantly innovate. That's it. Obviously, the two courses of action do not constitute all that's needed. Sound financial controls are essential. Solid planning is not a luxury but a necessity. Nonetheless these factors are seldom, if ever, the basis for lasting distinction. That is, financial control is vital, but one does not sell financial control, one sells a quality product or service.[9]

In fact, and in the final analysis, Peters almost reduces business and management to one attribute, and that is 'people', as innovation becomes absorbed by and through them. Such people are activated by a leadership that is required to link up people and innovation. Such leadership draws on two main elements: management by walkabout – the technology of the obvious – and an enriched concept of coaching. As a result, leadership, in effect, becomes a form of show business. It involves enthusiasm, cheerleading, love, trust, verve, passion, obsession, the use of symbols as well as out-and-out drama. In fact, as far as Peters and Austin are concerned, the whole of business becomes a show. Such a 'show business', in the late 1980s, became a recipe for chaos!

Thriving on chaos – handbook for a management revolution

The world turned upside-down

As we turned from the competitive 1980s into the turbulent 1990s, Tom Peters began to change not so much his underlying tune, but some of the basic notes.

As the threat of Japanese competition began not so much to recede as to become the norm, so the 'thriving on chaos' began to take precedence over competitiveness per se. Tom Peters' approach, moreover, remaining true to primal form, was to anticipate the chaos that would ensue, not in the rational or developmental vein that Margaret Wheatley and Ralph Stacey (see chapters 13 and 14 below) have since entered into, but with 'gut feel'.

> Most fundamentally the times demand that flexibility and love of change replace our longstanding penchant for mass production and mass markets, based as it is on a relatively predictable environment now vanished . . . Chaos and uncertainty are (will be) market opportunities for the wise; capitalizing on fleeting market anomalies will be the successful business' greatest accomplishment. It is with that mindset that we must proceed.[10]

Peters then supplies five different, though related, recipes for dealing with a 'world turned upside-down'. In each case, though, supplying a touch of added sophistication, he provides a guiding premise, strategies and tactics, and an overall orientation.

NICHEMANSHIP

The first recipe, *creating total customer responsiveness*, follows on from being close to the customer in his 'excellence' days. Whereas the guiding premise here is the need to specialize, to differentiate, to fill a niche, the overall orientation for the firm is that of launching a customer revolution. Basic value-adding strategies range from providing top quality and superior service to achieving extraordinary responsiveness – nationally and internationally – to ultimately being unique.

SMALL STARTS

The second recipe for *pursuing fast-paced innovation* again follows from the orientation towards innovation reflected in Peters' passion for excellence.

The guiding premise this time is that companies should invest in applications-oriented small starts, and the overall orientation of the firm, therefore, is to create the corporate capacity for innovation. The key strategies involved are to pursue product or service development in teams, to encourage pilots of everything, to become obsessed with competitors, and to make word-of-mouth marketing pervasive.

Finally, the management tactics involved are those of supporting committed champions, as well as being more tolerant of failure, while both modelling innovation qualitatively and setting goals for it quantitatively.

INVOLVE EVERYONE

In advocating, thirdly, that companies *achieve flexibility by empowering people*, Peters follows on from where 'productivity through people' left off. The guiding premise involved here is to involve everyone in everything, while the overall orientation is towards the use of self-managed teams. The support factors are those of listening and celebration, of heavy investment in recruitment and training, and of providing both incentive payments and also employement guarantees to everyone. The tactical moves are to simplify organizational structures, to revitalize the middle manger's role and to remove bureaucratic inhibitors of flexibility.

MASTER PARADOX

In learning, fourthly, to love change, the new leadership's guiding premise is that of *mastering paradox*, which purportedly receives renewed emphasis from Peters, and yet in effect remains barely visible, because of the primal overlay. The overall orientation is in fact towards creating a sense of urgency, whereby everyone is evaluated according to their love of change. While the leadership 'tools for establishing direction' are those of developing an inspiring vision, managing by example and practising visible management, the means of empowering people are those of listening, delegating, and pursuing horizontal management.

MEASURE WHAT'S IMPORTANT

Finally, with a view to 'thriving on chaos', Peters provides us with a recipe for *building systems for a world turned upside-down*. While the guiding premise is that of measuring what is important, the overall orientation is towards a combination of so-called 'total integrity' with the setting of conservative goals. The strategy to be pursued in this context is one of decentralizing information, authority and strategic planning and revamping the major control tools accordingly.

From thriving on chaos to liberation management

Tom Peters' most recent piece of serious work is his massive tome *Liberation Management*.[11] As is the case with *Thriving on Chaos*, Peters' primal message, first revealed to us through his researches into 'excellence', remains pretty much the same. People and enterprise, albeit ever more firmly ensconced in a 'world turned upside-down', remain central to his primal aspirations. Get these basics right, he says, and all these will follow.

Within his massive liberatory tome, littered with practical examples of companies 'turning the world upside-down', Peters shifts his orientation, somewhat, from 'excellence' to 'fashion'! Subtitling his book 'Necessary Disorganization for the Nanosecond Nineties', he reinforces his new stand, that 'there are no excellent companies', and thereby, duly chastened, proposed that 'flexibility', along with fashion, be the watchword of the 1990s.

The dominant influence of fashion comes about in a world where lifecycles of computers and microprocessors have shrunk from years to months. All this means that we have to engage even more intimately with customers than before. The idea of fashion, moreover, Peters confesses, unnerves traditional managers.

> It demands liberation, everyone exhibiting bravery and bravura, pursuing breathtaking failure as assiduously as success . . . fashion also connotes liberation in another sense. To offer a barrage of customized solutions to fleeting customer problems requires quick-change artistry within our product lines, and calls forth the pirate and the gambler in us all. It cries out for the wholesale exercise of the human imagination. In short, as the service sector grows and the service component of manufacturing comes to dominate, every one of us is in the 'brainware' business.[12]

In fact, the one – and perhaps only – substantive change in emphasis over the ten-year period separating *In Search of Excellence* from *Liberation Management* is towards knowledge – its generation and deployment – within business. Ironically therefore, in reorienting business towards 'brainware', as the seat of reason, Peters may be signalling his own primal demise!

Conclusion

A passion for excellence

Peters, Waterman and Austin during the 1980s and 1990s have established the core of what I have termed 'primal management' and what they call 'back to basics'. Although they are by no means the first to adopt this raw, immediate, tangible approach to the management of people and things, they have certainly been the most comprehensive in their primal approach. *In Search of Excellence*, and the eight basic attributes that emerged from it, brought management in the 1980s thoroughly back, to basics. Rational and scientific management was virtually thrown out of the window and any differences between small or large, young or old, public or private, organizations were largely dismissed.

Enterprise, under the guise of autonomy and entrepreneurship, and community, reflected in shared values, reinstated the 'American dream' within a corporate context.

A Passion for Excellence, although longer and somewhat less readable than its predecessor, in fact represented a distillation of Peters' previous work. *Thriving on Chaos* established some link, albeit a rather tenuous one, with the emergent ideas on chaos and complexity, and *Liberation Management* provided lots more tangible examples of 'primal management' at work than had previously been the case. Finally, Peters' most recent books *Wow*[13] and the *Tom Peters' Seminar*[14] provide icing on the back-to-basic cake. In fact there is now even a biography of Tom Peters[15] to set the seal on the influence he has had on management in the last quarter of this century.

What emerges, set in the context of people and enterprise, is fundamentally two, and only two things. Successful companies constantly innovate by caring for their customers, and are led by active individuals who are also natural coaches. Moreover people are people, not personnel, customers are customers, not markets, and quality, which unites the two, is homespun America. Quality is not a technique. It is about care, passion, eye contact and gut reaction. We now turn from the primal mainstem to its branches, firstly the 'hard' ones, Michael Porter's competitive strategy and Robert Kaplan's performance measurement, and secondly the 'soft' one, Sandra Vandermerwe's care for the customer and service management. Whereas the one is focused upon adding value the other is oriented towards sharing it.

7

STRATEGY, PERFORMANCE AND VALUE

The primal branches

Introduction

Hunter and gatherer

The hunter and gatherer in modern guise, as we indicated in chapter 5, appear as the 'primal' entrepreneur and animateur. Until very recently, moreover, the former has eclipsed the latter. This has partly been due to the predominance of men over women in management thought and practice, and partly due to the pre-eminence of western over northern, eastern and southern managerial orientations. In the last five years, in particular though, the balance has begun to be redressed, in no small measure due to the efforts of Tom Peters, with his 'primal' passion for people, combined with the rise of firstly Japan in the east, and secondly South Africa and Brazil in the south, as sources of 'primal' management thinking. In the mean time the hunting instinct has remained strong, as reflected recently in the renewed emphasis upon competitive strategy and performance measurement. Whereas the hunter in the final analysis 'adds value', the gatherer in effect 'shares value'.

Adding and sharing value

One of Britain's best-known business economists, John Kay, who recently became Dean of Oxford University's new business school, wrote a book in the mid-1990s that immediately touched a chord in this country. The title was *Foundations of Corporate Success*, and the theme was how business strategies add value. Firms, for Kay, add value by developing distinctive contracts and relationships with various stakeholders. Such relationships are then financially accounted for, in typically 'western' fashion, in the firm's added-value statement. For John Kay, then:

> The added value of a firm is the difference between the market value of its output and the cost of its inputs. Adding value, in this sense, is the central purpose of business activity. A commercial organization that

adds no value – whose output is worth no more than the value of its inputs in alternative uses – has no long term rationale for its existence.[1]

Such a 'western' primal/rational orientation can be compared and contrasted with a 'southern' primal/metaphysical one. One of the new South Africa's favoured business sons, as we have already seen in chapter 3, is Albert Koopman of Cashbuild fame. The consulting company that Koopman helped to form, after handing the management of Cashbuild onto his successor, was ITISA (Interdependence and Transformation in South Africa). Within it, he and his colleagues originated an approach to business called 'value sharing', which is very differently oriented from John Kay's value adding:

> A key question for building a value is to ask 'why should this association exist?' People will always have different interests. However if we concretize the spiritual relationship between us in the form of a value we could have a beacon to live by in order to manage conflict constructively. In this context we will have found unity in diversity and we will actually be valuing each other's difference.[2]

In this chapter, therefore, John Kay and Albert Koopman having set the initial scene, we shall be drawing upon the more coherently focused works of a cast of three illustrious characters, two 'westerners' and one 'southerner'. Westerners Michael Porter and Robert Kaplan, at Harvard Business School, focus upon the 'hard' related fields of competitive strategy and performance measurement. Southerner Sandra Vandermerwe, meanwhile, focuses on caring for the customer specifically, and on service management more generally, set in the 'soft' context of 'creating value through services'.

Specifically, then, and in the process, the subject matter of strategy, often considered to be 'the capstone' course within an MBA curriculum, is divided up among its primal, rational, developmental and metaphysical orientations, starting with competitive strategy. Similarly, the so-called 'management of organizations' is represented four times over, starting with service and value. We begin with 'adding value' (hard), before going on to 'sharing value' (soft).

Adding value – competitive strategy and performance measurement

Porter's competitive strategy

An Anglo-Saxon thoroughbred

Michael Porter, the modern-day strategy guru based at Harvard, whose pathbreaking books on competitive strategy[3] and on competitive advantage[4] appeared in the early 1980s, is the first of the strategic thinkers that we consider in this text.

For his approach is the most concertedly 'primal' in the 'hard' sense, to the extent that the discipline underlying it is economic, its institutional orientation is competitive, and its managerial outlook is aggressive-defensive. Porter, in fact, to some degree like Peters, reacted in the early 1980s against the hitherto more thoroughly rational approaches to corporate strategy and long-range planning. For these had been vigorously adopted in the 1960s and 1970s by American business academics of central European origin, most particularly the highly cerebral Igor Ansoff, the inimitable Peter Drucker, and the highly analytical George Steiner. On the other hand, Porter, again like Peters, is an Anglo-Saxon thoroughbred. As such he has combined a tough-minded analytical approach with an aggressively primal one, initially for hunters only!

Enterprise and environment – defend and attack

Every firm competing in an industry, Porter maintains, has a competitive strategy, whether explicit or implicit. In other words, this strategy may have been developed explicitly through a planning process or it may have evolved implicitly through the activities of the various functional departments of the firm. The essence of formulating competitive strategy, for Porter therefore, involves relating a company to its environment, albeit primarily to an economic rather than a social, technological or cultural one. For the key aspect of the firm's environment is the industry or industries in which it competes. The goal of competitive strategy, as a result, is to find a position in the industry where the company can best defend itself against these forces or influence them in its favour. This approach, for example, would be typical of the strategy taken in the mid-1990s by the 'western'-oriented conservative party in Britain towards the European Community.

In an evolutionary way, then, Porter adapts the conventional wisdom on corporate strategy formulation to his own competitive orientation. The central thrust of Porter's instincts and analyses lies therefore in his 'competitive forces'. These he divides into the commitment to compete, the forces driving industrial competition, the components of competitor analysis and the generic competitive strategies themselves. We shall now consider each of these in turn.

The commitment to compete – aimed at deterrence

Without the basic commitment to compete, as far as Porter is concerned, there is no point whatsoever in entering into a strategic arena. Analysis in itself, for Porter – with his primal 'hunter' orientation – without the instinctive drive to compete to win, is sterile. There are three major types of commitment, then, each designed to achieve a type of 'deterrence'.

Firstly, there is the commitment that the firm is unequivocally sticking with a move that it is making. Secondly, there is the commitment that the firm will retaliate and continue to retaliate if a competitor makes certain moves. Thirdly, Porter cites the commitment that the firm will take no action or forgo an action.

Figure 7.1 Forces driving competition

Perhaps the single most important concept in planning and executing offensive or defensive competitive moves, for Porter, is this concept of commitment. Commitment can guarantee the likelihood, speed, and vigour of retaliation to offensive moves, and can be the cornerstone of defensive strategy. Establishing such commitment, moreover, is essentially a form of committing the firm's resources and intentions unequivocally.

The forces driving competition

An effective competitive strategy, for Michael Porter, involves taking offensive or defensive action in order to create a defendable position against a number of competitive forces. These are laid out in Figure 7.1, embodying Porter's now-famous 'five forces'.

Such a strategy broadly involves three alternative points of emphasis, that is on positioning, influencing or anticipating.

Firstly, then, it involves positioning the firm so that its capabilities provide the best defence against the existing array of five competitive forces. Secondly, it entails influencing the balance of the five forces through strategic moves, thereby improving the firm's relative position. Ultimately, moreover, it involves anticipating shifts in the factors underlying the five forces and responding to them. Thereby change is exploited by choosing a strategy appropriate to the new competitive balance before the competitors realize it.

Components of competitor analysis

Porter's primal instincts are finely tuned to 'competitive response', which therefore makes up a key element of his overall competitive strategy. Such instincts need to address the following questions:

- What drives the competitor? What is the competitor doing?
  And what can he do?
- Is the competitor satisfied with his current position?
  What likely moves will he make? Where is he vulnerable?
  What will provoke the most adverse reaction?
- What are the strengths and weaknesses of the firm *vis-à-vis* its competitors?

Porter, ultimately, is best known both for his 'five forces', as seen above, and for his generic strategies, as outlined below.

Generic competitive strategies

In the final analysis, Porter cites three generic strategies, and only three, for attaining competitive advantage:

1   Overall *cost leadership* requires the aggressive construction of cost-efficient, usually large-scale facilities; the vigorous pursuit of arising cost reductions; tight cost and overhead control; and cost minimization in areas such as research and development, advertising, after sales service, and so on.
2   Aggressive product or service *differentiation* provides insulation against competitive rivalry because of the brand loyalty of customers, and results in a lower sensitivity to price. It also leads to an increase in profit margins, because the customer is willing to pay a price premium. This avoids the necessity of adopting a low-cost position. Finally, the resulting customer loyalty, and the need for a competitor to provide uniqueness, creates significant entry barriers.
3   The *focus* orientation rests on the premise that the firm is able to serve its narrow market more effectively or efficiently than competitors who are competing more broadly. This form of strategy has also been termed by Porter and by Peters as 'nichemanship'.

A vigorous debate has since ensued, amongst management academics and practitioners, as to whether or not it is possible to simultaneously pursue cost leadership and differentiation. The point is that such a 'both/and' position is much more readily accessible, as we shall see, within the developmental domain than within the 'either/or' primal or even within the rational domain.

The competitive advantage of nations

As we can see, then, Porter adopts very much the role of the hunter and the hunted, albeit with a Harvard overlay of analytical prowess, in his approach to competitive strategy. As such he accurately reflects the attitudes and perceptions of most economic and political analysts and practitioners in the 'western' world, who see the international business arena as a global battlefield.

At the same time, it is important at least to point out that as Porter has matured, advancing in the 1990s from his own youth and adulthood towards midlife, his tone has somewhat softened, and indeed broadened. In fact his knowledge grounds shift somewhat, from economics to evolutionary biology, from Adam Smith to Charles Darwin! In his most recent tome, *The Competitive Advantage of Nations*, his emphasis shifts from the individual firm to the 'industry cluster'.

This heralds something of a move away from primal independence and natural selection, to a more developmental orientation towards interdependence and species diversity. Moreover, and in the final analysis, Porter now argues that competitive advantage, at a national level, stems from culturally and technologic-ally based continuous innovation, in industry clusters, as opposed to merely individually and economically oriented wealth creation.

> Competitive advantage emerges from close working relationships between world-class suppliers and the industry. The exchange of R & D and joint problem solving lead to faster and more efficient solutions. The pace of industry innovation is accelerated . . . Once a cluster forms, the whole group of industries becomes mutually supporting. Benefits flow forward, backward and horizontally. Information flows freely and innovations diffuse; people and ideas combine in new ways, as in Silicon Valley . . . Aggressive rivalry in one industry tends to spread to others in the cluster, through the exercise of bargaining power, spin offs, and related diversification by established firms . . . Nations gain an important national advantage where national attributes are supportive of intracluster interchange. As clusters develop, resources flow toward them and away from isolated, less productive industries. The more firms are exposed to international competition the more pronounced the clustering . . . Finally mechanisms that facilitate inter-change within clusters are generally strongest in Japan, in Sweden, and in middle Italy, while being weakest in the UK and the US.[5]

Interestingly enough, Porter was recently appointed as an adviser to Singapore's Economic Development Board. While seemingly holding on, then, to his youth-fully based primal instincts, he has latterly, in midlife, opened out to the more developmental and even metaphysical influences of society and culture, evolu-tionary biology and knowledge creation. In the same way, the mature Robert Kaplan, also based now at Harvard Business School, while retaining a primal focus on 'the bottom line' has at the same time spread his measurement wings, towards a 'balanced scorecard'.

The balanced scorecard

Relevance lost and regained

Robert Kaplan, former Dean of Carnegie Mellon's business school in the US, and his colleague Thomas Johnson at Portland State, first rose to fame in the second half of the 1980s, when they published *Relevance Lost: the Rise and Fall of Management Accounting*.[6] Their argument was that management accountants, in their striving for rationality in the period after the war, had lost touch with the 'primal' reality of people and things. Moreover, in his subsequent treatise, *Relevance Regained*, Johnson put the case for a more 'real' or indeed 'primal' way forward:

The difference between the typically American approach to business – optimizing costs and maximizing profits within constraints – and our approach here, that of continuously removing constraints to profitably satisfy customer wants, is the difference between success and failure in an economy where the customer is in charge of the marketplace and the work force must be in charge of processes . . . Management information's true function, today then, must be to help companies respond to the real imperatives of global competition – responsiveness and flexibility. Responsiveness is achieved by building relationships that lead to satisfied customers, suppliers, and employees. Flexibility is achieved by reducing output variation in processes, thus eliminating delays and excesses caused by variation. These imperatives are achieved by companies that empower employees to solve problems and to improve constantly the output of processes.[7]

Robert Kaplan, now based at Harvard, with a new colleague – the business consultant David Norton – has continued from where his old colleague Thomas Johnson left off, to produce the Kaplan–Norton 'balanced scorecard'.

Measurement and management in the information age

The financial reporting process, Kaplan and Norton maintain, remains anchored to a purely 'rational' accounting model developed centuries ago for an environment of arms-length transactions between independent entities. This venerable financial-accounting model is still being used by information-age companies as they attempt to build internal assets and capabilities, and to forge linkages and strategic alliances with external parties. Ideally this financial-accounting model should have been expanded to incorporate a company's intangible and intellectual assets. These comprise high-quality products and services, motivated and skilled employees, responsive and predictable internal processes, and satisfied and loyal customers. The collision between the irresistible force to build long-range competitive capabilities and the immovable object of the historical cost-accounting model has created a new synthesis: the 'balanced scorecard'[8] (see Figure 7.2).

Information-age companies, Kaplan and Norton maintain, will succeed by investing in and managing their intellectual assets. Financial specialization must be integrated into customer-based business processes. Mass production and service delivery of standard products and services must be replaced by flexible, responsive, and high-quality delivery of innovative products and services. These need to be individualized to targeted customer segments. Innovation and improvement of products, services and processes will then be generated by reskilled employees, superior information technology and aligned organizational procedures.

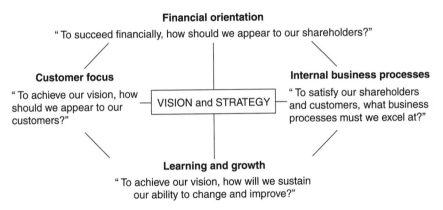

Financial orientation

" To succeed financially, how should we appear to our shareholders?"

Customer focus

" To achieve our vision, how should we appear to our customers?"

VISION and STRATEGY

Internal business processes

" To satisfy our shareholders and customers, what business processes must we excel at?"

Learning and growth

" To achieve our vision, how will we sustain our ability to change and improve?"

Figure 7.2 The balanced scorecard

Why does business need a balanced scorecard?

THE OVERALL PERSPECTIVE

Why then does business need a balanced scorecard, that is a statement of account that differs from the conventional, rationally based management accounts? To begin with, Kaplan asserts, as indeed does Peters: 'Measurement matters – if you can't measure it you can't manage it'. Unfortunately, Kaplan adds at this point, many organizations espouse strategies about customer relationships, core competencies and organizational capabilities while motivating and measuring performance with only financial measures. The balanced scorecard, in contrast, retains financial measurement as a critical summary of managerial and business performance, but highlights a more general and integrated set of measurements that link current customer, internal process, employee, and system performance to long-term financial success. As such, from a measurement perspective, it goes 'back to basics', albeit now in the context of a so-called 'process'-oriented approach to the inner workings of the business. Inevitably, as 'rational' managers are pressured to deliver consistent and excellent short-term financial performance, trade-offs are made that limit the search for investments in growth opportunities.

Even worse, for Kaplan and Norton, the pressure for short-term financial performance can cause companies to reduce spending on new-product development, process improvements, human-resource development, information technology, databases, and systems as well as customer and market development. Over such a short run, the financial-accounting model reports these spending cut-backs as increases in reported income. This applies even when the reductions have cannibalized a company's stock of assets, and as a result severely constrained its capabilities for creating future economic value. The financial measures, for Kaplan and Norton, tell some, but not all, of the story about past actions and they fail to provide adequate guidance for the actions to be taken today, and the day after, to create future financial value. Hence the need for a balanced scorecard, recording financial, customer-related, operational and employee-related performance.

THE BALANCED PERSPECTIVE

The *financial perspective*, firstly then, typically relates to profitability – measured, for example, by operating income, return on capital employed or, more recently, economic value added. The *customer perspective* typically relates to customer satisfaction, consumer retention, customer profitability and market share in targeted segments. The *internal-business-process perspective* focuses on the 'processes' of delivering today's products and services to today's customers. They attempt to control and improve existing operations that represent the short wave of value creation. But the drivers of long-term financial success may require an organization to create entirely new products and services that will meet the emerging needs of current and future customers. The *learning-and-growth perspective*, finally, therefore identifies the infrastructure that the organization must build to create long-term growth and improvement. Business has to invest in reskilling employees, enhancing information technology and systems, and aligning organizational procedures and routines.

MEASURING BUSINESS STRATEGY

Thus a properly constructed balanced scorecard, for Kaplan and Norton, should tell the story of the business unit's strategy. It should identify and make explicit the sequence of hypotheses about the cause-and-effect relationships between outcome measures and performance drivers of those outcomes. A comprehensive system of measurement, as indicated in Table 7.1, must specify how improvements in operations, customer services, and new products and services link to improved financial performance through higher sales, greater operating margins, faster asset turnover, and reduced operating expenses.

We now turn, with Kaplan and Norton, to each of these four perspectives in turn.

Table 7.1 Generic measures

Perspective	Attribute
Financial	Return on investment and economic valued added
Customer	Satisfaction, retention and market share
Internal	Quality, response time, cost, and new products
Learning and growth	Employee satisfaction and information-system availability

The financial perspective

The scorecard should tell the story of strategy, starting with the long-term financial objectives. Then these need to be linked into the sequence of actions that must be taken with financial processes, customers, internal processes, and finally employees and systems, to deliver the desired long-term economic performance.

Financial objectives for businesses in each of three stages, Kaplan and Norton maintain, are quite different. In the *growth* stage they will emphasize sales growth – in new markets and to new customers and from new products and services – maintaining adequate spending levels for product and process development, systems, employee capabilities, and establishment of new marketing, sales and distribution channels. Secondly, financial objectives in the *sustain* stage will emphasize traditional financial measurements. These include return on capital employed, operating income and gross margin. Investment projects for businesses in this category will be evaluated by standard, discounted cash flow, capital budgeting analyses. The financial objectives, finally, in the *harvest* stage will stress cash flow. The goal is to maximize the cash that can be returned to the company from investments made in the past.

Customer perspective

OVERALL MEASURES

In the customer perspective of the balanced scorecard, companies identify the customer and market segments in which they have chosen to compete. These segments represent the sources that will deliver the revenue component of the company's financial objectives. The customer perspective enables companies to align their core customer outcome measures – satisfaction, loyalty, retention, acquisition – to targeted customers and market segments. It also enables them to identify and measure, explicitly, the value propositions they will deliver to targeted customers and market segements. The value propositions represent the drivers, the lead indicators, for the core customer outcome measures.

In general, existing and potential customers are not homogeneous. They have different preferences and value the attributes of the product or service differently.

A strategy formulation process, using in-depth market research, should reveal the different market or customer segments, and their preferences along dimensions such as price, quality, functionality, image, relationship and service. The company's strategy can then be defined by those customer and market segments that it chooses to target. The balanced scorecard, moreover, as a description of a company's strategy, should identify the customer objectives in each targeted segment.

139

Figure 7.3 Core measures of customer focus

GENERIC MEASURES AND PERFORMANCE DRIVERS

Kaplan and Norton have found that companies generally select two sets of measures for their customer perspective. The first set – the core measurement group – is generic, while the second set represents performance drivers. They start with the first set, as revealed in Figure 7.3.

The second set of measures represent the performance drivers – differentiators – of the customer outcomes. They answer the question: 'What must the company deliver to its customers to achieve high degrees of satisfaction, retention, acquisition and eventually market share?' The performance-driver measures capture the value propositions that the company will attempt to deliver to its targeted customer and market segments. Such customer value propositions represent the attributes that supplying companies provide, through their products and services, to create loyalty and satisfaction in targeted customer segments.

The value proposition is the key concept for understanding the drivers of the core measurements of satisfaction, acquisition, retention, and market share. There are three dimensions to it. *Product and service attributes* encompass the functionality of the product/service, its price and its quality. The *customer relationship* dimension includes the response and delivery time dimension, and how the customer feels about purchasing from the company. The *image and reputation* dimension finally reflects the intangible factors that attract a customer to a company.

Internal-business-process perspective

For the internal-business-process perspective, according to Kaplan and Norton, managers identify the processes that are most critical for achieving customer and shareholder objectives. Most organizations' existing performance-measurement systems focus on improving existing operating processes. In the balanced score-card, they recommend that managers define a complete internal-process value chain that starts with the innovation process – identifying current and future customers' needs and developing new solutions for these needs – proceeds through the operations process – delivering existing products and services to existing customers – and ends with post-sale service.

> Think of the innovation process as the long wave of value creation in which companies first identify and nurture new markets, new customers, and the emerging and latent needs of existing customers. Then, continuing in this

long wave of value creation and growth, companies design amd develop the new products and services that enable them to reach the new markets and customers. The operations process, in contrast, represents the short wave of value creation, that is delivering existing products and services to existing customers.[9]

Learning-and-growth perspective

LONG-TERM ORIENTATION

The fourth and final perspective on the balanced scorecard involves objectives and measures to drive organizational learning and growth. The objectives established in the financial, customer and internal-business-process perspectives identify where the organization must excel to achieve breakthrough performance. The objectives in the learning-and-growth perspective provide the infrastructure to enable ambitious objectives in the other three perspectives to be achieved. Kaplan and Norton's experience, in building balanced scorecards across a wide variety of service and manufacturing organizations, has revealed three principal capabilities for the learning-and-growth perspective.

EMPLOYEE CAPABILITIES

Kaplan has found that most companies use employee objectives drawn from a common core of three outcome measurements, as shown in Figure 7.4

Companies typically measure *employee satisfaction* with an annual survey, including the following characteristic elements:

- involvement with decisions
- recognition for doing a good job
- access to sufficient information to do the job well
- encouragement to use initiative and to be creative
- support level from staff functions
- overall satisfaction with the company

Long-term, loyal employees carry the values of the organization, knowledge of organizational processes, and sensitivity to the needs of customers. *Employee retention* is generally measured by the percentage of key staff turnover. *Employee*

Figure 7.4 Employee scorecard

productivity is an outcome measure of the aggregate impact from enhancing employee skills and morale, innovation, improving internal processes, and satisfying customers.

SITUATION-SPECIFIC DRIVERS

Once companies have chosen measures for the core employee measurement group – satisfaction, retention and productivity – they should then identify the situation-specific drivers in the learning-and-growth perspective. Kaplan and Norton have found that such drivers tend to be drawn from three critical enablers – reskilling the workforce, information-systems capabilities, and alignment.

Specifically, then, and firstly, many organizations building balanced scorecards are undergoing radical change. Their employees must take on dramatically new responsibilities if the business is to achieve its customer and internal-business-process objectives. A strategic *job-coverage ration* tracks the proportion of employees qualified for certain strategic jobs relative to organizational need. Secondly, moreover, if employees are to be effective in today's competitive environment they need excellent information on customers, on internal business processes, and on the financial consequences of their decisions. Several companies have developed, Kaplan maintains, a means of assessing current availability of *information relative to anticipated needs*.

Finally, even skilled employees, provided with superb accces to information, will not contribute to organizational success if they are not motivated to act in the best interests of an organization, or if they are not given freedom to make decisions and take actions.

Thus the third of the enablers for learning and growth focuses on the *organizational climate* for employee motivation and initiative. One widely used measure of motivation is the number of suggesions per employee, which can be supplemented by the number of measures implemented. Organizations can also look for improvements, say in quality, time, or performance, for specific internal and customer processes.

Telling the whole story

REVEALING CAUSE–EFFECT

Ultimately, for Kaplan and Norton, balanced scorecards need to be more than a mixture of 15–25 financial and non-financial measures grouped into four perspectives. The scorecard should tell the story of a business unit's strategy. This story is told by linking outcome and performance-driver measures together via a series of cause–effect relationships. The outcome measures tend to be lagging indicators. They signal the ultimate objectives of the strategy and whether near-term efforts have led to desirable outcomes. The performance-driver measures are leading indicators, which signal to all organizational participants what they should be doing today to create value in the future. The best such balanced scorecards, for Kaplan, will tell the story of the strategy so well that it can be inferred by the collection of objectives and measures and the linkages between them.

So much for performance measurement, which together with competitive strategy represents the 'hard' primal edge of management. At the same time, there is some overlap between the primal and the rational, and even the developmental, orientation, both for Kaplan and for the mature Porter. It is just that the overall flavour, as we shall see with Vandermerwe, remains 'primal'.

In other words, it deals with the business basics. Whereas for Porter this is based on commitment, set in the context of competitive rivalry, for Kaplan it is oriented toward measurement, set in the context of – on the one hand – financial and operational, and – on the other hand – employee and customer perspectives. It is important to bear in mind, then, that the primal orientation to people and things – customers, employees and internal processes – albeit with a broadened base of information, remains in the foreground. We now turn from the hard end of adding value through competitive performance, to the softer edge of sharing value through customer care and service management. In the process, the stage set moves from America to southern Africa and to Europe.

Value sharing – customer care and service management

From tin soldiers to Russian dolls

From male to female

Sandra Vandermerwe grew up in South Africa in the 1960s, and developed a formidable reputation as a consultant in marketing and business development. As such she was both a hunter and a gatherer. On becoming a business academic, she moved to Europe and joined the International Management Institute in Geneva, which was being run by a great Chilean humanist, Juan Rada, before most recently joining Imperial College in London.

It was firstly no accident that Vandermerwe's book on creating added value through services was given the title *From Tin Soldiers to Russian Dolls*. In fact she was signalling, as Shoshana Zuboff at Harvard (see chapter 11) has also done, a move from a masculine to a feminine orientation, as well as from a military to a civilian set of management metaphors.

It is secondly no accident that Sandra Vandermerwe, like Shoshana Zuboff and Solveig Wikstrom (see also chapter 11), is one of that growing breed of influential female management writers. Let me now share with you Vandermerwe's basic thesis, which starts out with customers being at the centre of business gravity,

Table 7.2 Customer focus

'Hard' industrial	'Soft' contemporary
Produce volumes for firm	Offer value to customers
Start with producer and work forwards	Start with end-user and work backwards
Compete in closed, protective environments	Collaborate in open, interdependent systems
Emphasize internal productivity	Focus on utility for customers
Pursue economies of scale for firm	Obtain optimization of scale–scope for total system
Choose mass or specialized markets	Markets consist of generic, targeted, individual components
Machines add value	Man (or woman) adds value

rather than with Porter's competitive advantage or Kaplan's performance measurement.

From competitive performance to customer care

For Vandermerwe, while it is of course important to take the competition into account, that should not come first in formulating a strategy. First comes painstaking attention to the needs of customers. First comes close analysis of a company's real degrees of freedom in responding to these.

First comes the willingness to rethink, fundamentally, what products are and what they do, and how best to organize the business system that designs, builds and markets them.

> Only when corporations see products and services from the outside-in, can they really understand what should be happening from the inside-out.[10]

Vandermerwe, as we can see from Table 7.2, consistently compares and contrasts a 'hard' industrial with, in our terms, a 'soft' contemporary orientation to business, starting with customer focus. She then turns from customer focus, specifically, to an approach to doing business, more generally, drawing upon her own experience of living with indigenous peoples.

From making things well to doing things better

Whether Aborigine or Amazonian, Hopi or Hottentot, tribal people have one common feature, she says, that is objects are described in terms of what they do, not in terms of what they are. A tree, for example, is described as a source of nourishment and protection. A room is where people live and work.

Table 7.3 From products and services to total solutions

Industrial ('Hard' Noun)	Contemporary ('Soft' Verb)
Bearings	Trouble-free operations
Animal feed	Productive pig farming
Insurance	Risk protection (industrial)
	Lifetime investment (personal)
Dyestuffs	Risk-free dyeing
Air trip	Total travel management
Carpet fibre	Floor-covering enhancement

The point of differentiation, in business then, has shifted from the material to the immaterial – from making and moving 'things' to the value-added services which could provide customers with the ability to 'do' things better (see Table 7.3).

The gadgets, bells and whistles so loved in the 1960s and 1970s lost their lustre by the mid-1980s. Customers wanted, according to Vandermerwe, functionality, not instead of, but in addition to, everything else. Rather than buying just the product or the service, they wanted the solutions these goods could provide. In business-to-business markets, relationships could no longer centre around official buyers and sellers, as links had become much more multi-faceted, operating on different levels between buying and consuming organizations. In fact the roles of the buyer and the salesperson have oftentimes changed to become brokers between producers and users, rather than just negotiators.

Customer decisions are being based increasingly on applied performance rather than industry specification. Such customers are therefore keener on the application potential and the interconnectivity of systems than in buying an assortment of bits and pieces from various suppliers, hoping to fit and operate

Table 7.4 From products to services

'Hard' industrial	'Soft' contemporary
Goods or services conforming to industry standards	Applied performance of goods and services
Compatibility of products, parts and components bought	Interconnectivity of working system
Buyers dealing with technical salespeople	Multi-level links with various specialists
Curative features after the event	Preventative maintenance throughout use
Being on time according to schedule	Responding instantly and just in time (JIT)
People there if and when needed	People present and accessible to all, and at any time
Updated offerings and new features	Ongoing support and potential for improvement
Variety in range and depth of offering	Multi-choice and flexible menus
Firms conscientious in their business	Firms easy to do business with

Table 7.5 The evolution of marketing

Stage	Contents	Object	Market
1 Stick to core	Core products or services	Volume	Generic
2 Augment core	Core products and services plus value-added services	Volume Value	Generic Targeted
3 Extend core	Solution modules products/ services	Volume Value Results	Generic Targeted Individual

them together. The real value for customers today, therefore, comes not from the core of the good but from how well it serves their purpose. By and large, anyone can produce and distribute the material 'things' well enough. Competitive strength for a corporation – be it large or small, in the traditional manufacturing or service sector – comes from the capability of making things work for customers. (See Table 7.4.) This leads us on from adding value to sharing it.

The evolution of marketing and services

From adding value to sharing value

Vandermerwe's service-oriented perspective, in fact, represents an overall shift in marketing orientation from 'hard' analysis and interpretation to 'soft' empathy and understanding. In many ways, therefore, she and other kindred spirits, that is people such as southern African Albert Koopman, on the one hand, and an Indian colleague of mine based at Buckingham University's School of Service Management, V.S. Mahesh,[11] on the other, are continuing where marketing academics such as Philip Kotler left off. She has effectively charted the way in which the marketing of products and services has evolved, towards the new millennium (see Table 7.5). Stage 1, that is *sticking to the core* in the 1950s and 1960s, involved concentrating on doing better what you do best – stick to the knitting – a vigorous pursuit of mass production and distribution. Stage 2, that is *augmenting the core* in the 1980s and early 1990s, combined the advantages generated by volume sales with the provision of value specific to the needs of particular customer segments – adding finance, transporation, insurance and JIT delivery.

The third, and most advanced, stage, involving *extending the core*, incorporates enhancing the firm's ability to identify, package and deliver value-added service capabilities. Products and services are thereby transformed into solutions for customers.

In effect, as we approach the year 2000, products and services are being transformed into composites of 'goods', inclusive of the basic products and service, combined with support facilities, information and know-how, as shown in Figure 7.5.

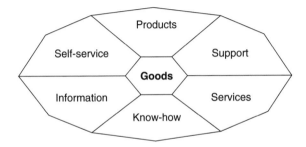

Figure 7.5 The product/service bundle

Why and how, then, has this move from a transactional to a relational orientation come about?

Marketing and services towards the millennium

PRE-INDUSTRIAL TO INDUSTRIAL

In the craftsman-like days of the pre-industrial era, Vandermerwe writes, firms were close to their customers by definition. Between buyers and sellers an open channel existed, and relationships were close and personal. In the industrial era, thereafter, customer relationships suffered as the more pressing concerns of producing voluminously and affordably for the masses took hold. By the 1990s, however, a more systemic approach had begun to appear.

What really hit home was the realization that no individual firm in a distribution chain could single-handedly accomplish total customer satisfaction. Nor could any supplier of products or services delegate totally its relationship with end-users to intermediaries. Put differently, Vandermerwe asserts, if businesses could learn to collaborate, they would be able to achieve more jointly than any one firm or industry could achieve on its own.

FROM TRANSACTIONAL TO RELATIONAL

If one traces the relationship between producers and consumers in some kind of historical framework, it is clear that over the last few decades the gap between them has gradually narrowed. By and large, relationships were mostly 'transactional' in the 1960s, assigned to professional salespeople who were expected to sell as much and as many 'things' as possible. A more 'relational' approach began to catch on in the 1970s when marketing began seeking a better understanding of markets and strategies to satisfy customers more fully. What the experts were now proposing was that corporations analyse their customers more rigorously and thereby get a better reading of their needs.

Management had left the delicate job of customers to a single function, which happened to be marketing. Yet it was impossible for any one function to handle

147

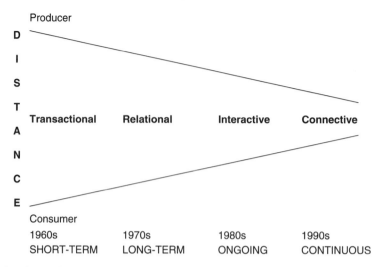

Figure 7.6 Stages in customer relationships

this alone because, as people such as Peters and Austin began to stress, a focus on customers is an attitude rather than a task, a state of mind as opposed to a functional responsibility. For most industries, the importance of customers as long-term assets only really began to take root in the late 1980s. Observers were now advocating so-called 'interactive' relationships, specifically demanding stronger, ongoing bonds between a company and its customers, more apt responses in tune with contemporary values. By then the services school had made management more acutely aware that, certainly when it came to the intangible aspects of business, customers and firms could not be separate because they were part of the same process.

FROM RELATIONAL TO CONNECTIVE

A new orthodoxy (see Figure 7.6) began to surface in the 1980s. It had a different kind of nuance, based on relationships being more 'connective', that is doing things not only for, but also with, customers. Partnering between a firm and its customers entered the general management vocabulary. It implied collaboration. In such connective relationships, such partnering takes place at various levels, leading to greater empowerment.

Moreover, each of the stages described above has different skills associated with it, which build upon one another, with connective relationships therefore requiring all four. Specifically, then, if transactional skills are not up to scratch, sales are compromised. If relations are not solid, market position will be in jeopardy. If the interactive side of a relationship is lacking, bonding will be impossible to achieve. And finally if the connections – be they physical, psychological or electronic – are not made, according to Vandermerwe, firms cannot hope to sustain long-term customer satisfaction.

Adding value by sharing value

Today, then, according to Vandermerwe, any firm which confines itself to one activity in the customer's total experience, especially if it is in isolation from the rest of the distribution chain, must risk eventually becoming a commodity supplier and having competitors gnaw away at its markets. The service ethos means establishing relationships with customers that start sooner, last longer and cover more ground. The same amount of effort and resources now goes into the pre-purchase, purchase and post-purchase services as went into making and selling things before. Above all, a firm must be there for its customers, visible and accessible throughout the activity cycle, so as to influence and activate important decisions and facilitate results. What we are talking of, in organic terms, is something that more closely resembles 'whole brain' activity rather than either 'left' or 'right'. What this leads to, according to Vandermerwe, is service-intensive networks.

Building service-intensive networks

From organizational functions to service activities

High-value enterprises, according to Vandermerwe, think in terms of activities, not functions. The corporation is seen as a series of these activities, instead of a series of layers. Structures are designed based on the processes needed to create value for customers over the period of their experience. Preoccupation with upstream and downstream switches into concern for what goes on instream – within the inter-functional and inter-company spaces which form the service-delivery process. Instead of people being cramped inside vertical silos, dealing in categories of 'things', those with relevant skills come together from various parts of the network and, through their webs of professional and social relationships, disseminate know-how and services about things. The multi-disciplinary groupings of people become 'partners' devoted to projects and processes. In their synergy and synchrony lies the key to a firm's success or failure, setting new criteria for organizational design.

With value enhancement for customers as the core business concern, building the capabilities to enhance value, rather than acquiring hard assets, becomes management's major preoccupation. For therein lies the firm's differential advantage. In theory, any part of the customer-delivery process can be outsourced if it can be done more quickly, cheaply or better somewhere else. Corporations need to choose partners well, favouring firms or individuals who uphold the same customer ideals, and from whom synergies can be extracted to augment the strength of the network as a whole.

The 'soft' side of know(ing) how

By the dawn of the 1990s a great deal had been said and done to make sure that the corporation would no longer be sufficient unto itself. Increasingly, corporations have become more reliant on brain skills and the interconnections among people. It is here that companies are discovering their chief source of market power, or their most dangerous restraining factor. The organization was often a place of accumulating machines, muscles and matter. More and more frequently, it is a way of bringing together individuals and ideas to either create the immaterial value that adds to what machines can do or, alternatively, do what machines can never do. This involves making these roles harmonious – including how they fit and belong into the overall organizational scheme of things – a theme which, for Vandermerwe, is bound to run throughout the decade. Managers will need to learn better ways to capture the know(ing) of individuals and teams, to make both their individual and collective learning part of the institution's competitiveness. Those in charge of contemporary corporations will have to harness the immaterial soft assets within their firms with the same sense of urgency that they formerly used to accumulate the hard. They will have to build 'capability portfolios' as professionally as they previously did 'product portfolios'.

The employee as partner

The strong sense of mutual identity and reciprocity between Japanese organizations and the individuals who work in them can in many ways be seen as a spirit of partnering, making them distinctly different from conventional western firms. In the Japanese language, the words 'worker' and 'employee' don't exist – everyone is a *sha-in*, or a 'member' of the organization (see Table 7.6).

Increasingly, some European countries – most notably Germany, Switzerland, the Benelux, Scandinavia (especially Sweden) and, to some extent, France – have instilled a stronger sense of collegiality within their firms, as have many of the East

Table 7.6 From worker to member

'Hard' industrial	'Soft' services
Work responsibility limited to what can and must be done	Employee free to be co-responsible for results
Workers must do things harder and smarter	Employees must learn creative ways of doing things
Management sees labour as a cost	Management sees the employee as a contributor
Worker's input is manager's primary aim	Outcome for customer and for organization a shared goal
People expected to obey without question	Employees empowered to figure out own solutions

Asian countries. For Vandermerwe, having a balance between the soft and hard is altogether essential in making a service network a living entity rather than an advanced organogram. While methods, procedures and process engineering lead to productivity, it is often the soft skills which enable the parts of the network to function as a whole. While an eye for detail is essential for producing results for customers, so too is the creativity to translate situations into customer-satisfying opportunities:

- enhancements for core *good*s frequently need an intuitive feel for where the market might be going
- the *product*s to deliver services have to be anticipated based on reflection and on envisioning future trends
- effective *service*s depend on the empathy and sociability of people so that relationships can have a long lifespan
- true *support* systems are those which are intuitive about customer reactions, and create harmonious environments and social networking
- *information* must be turned into relevant solutions using both interpretive and creative skills, insights rather than just data
- *know-how* is having a superior ability to read the environment differently and to combine wisdom with the technicalities of know(ing) what, how, for whom

Conclusion

Making 'hard' tin soldiers into 'soft' Russian dolls

Before and throughout the pre-mass-production days of the nineteenth century, people had to know how to make the entire object when they undertook something. Their working life, working day or what they did at work had not yet been segmented into bits. When the assembly line appeared, so too did the careful division of work into tasks. From the factory workers to the supervisors and managers who controlled them, this had become the firmly entrenched norm by the 1950s. These 'organization men' strove to climb the corporate ladders and skyscrapers which were the symbols of achievement. No mingling of a person's work and life were tolerated. To succeed was to conform; anything that smacked of individualism was rejected as going against the corporate grain.

Knowledge workers today (see Table 7.7), Vandermerwe argues, are neither able nor willing to make sharp distinctions between their personal and professional lives. Similarly, the commercial and social aspects of their work lives are not clearly delineable. Essentially what they want is a better balance than the last generation, unwilling to play the obedient cog in a huge corporate wheel. Unlike industrial days, individual differences no longer run counter to corporate goals. Rather, they give it versatility and resilience. Instead of their colleagues from different parts of the organization being potential competitors and adversaries with whom they may have previously collided and contended, they are now part

Table 7.7 From tin soldiers to Russian dolls

'Hard' industrial	'Soft' contemporary
People are dependent on the organization – their development is a means to an end	People are part of an organization – development is an end in itself
People occupy one job at a time, where they can be controlled	People involved in several jobs, belong everywhere
The organizational way of doing things is valued	Behaviour that is valued suits the role at the time
Relationships amongst employees are fixed, creating stability	Relationships are entrenched and temporary, making the firm tenacious and adaptable

of the same customer-serving process, accumulating and transferring know-how, both within the organization and without.

From competitive strategy to national advantage

Interestingly enough, finally, whereas Porter and Vandermerwe start out at opposite ends of the primal continuum, they end up meeting somewhere in the middle. For Porter, in reviewing the competitive advantage of nations, ultimately found that competitive advantage grows fundamentally out of improvement, innovation and change. Firms gain advantage over international rivals because they perceive a new basis for competing, or find a new and better means to compete in old ways.

Competitive advantage, moreover, involves the entire value system, that is the entire array of activities involved in a product's creation and use, encompassing the value chains of the firm, suppliers, channels and buyers. For Porter, as for Vandermerwe, such competitive advantage frequently comes from perceiving new ways to configure and manage the entire value system. As such, moreover, both Porter and Vandermerwe are merging together primal and developmental perspectives as their outlooks mature. We now turn from branches to fruits, from American Michael Porter to American Bill Gates, and from South African Sandra Vandermerwe to Brazilian Ricardo Semler.

8

ENTREPRENEUR AND ANIMATEUR

The primal fruits

Introduction

Factors impinging on the individual manager

In each of the four sections on the 'fruits' of management, I will be aiming to help you identify and develop your individual, managerial potential over the course of your lifespan. In the process I shall be exposing you to eight prominent real-life managers, as role models from all around the globe, who have developed their personal and managerial individualities. These are Microsoft's Bill Gates (entrepreneur) from the US and Semco's Ricardo Semler (animateur) from Brazil in this chapter; Trumpf's Dr Liebinger (executive) from Germany and F International's Mrs 'Steve' Shirley (change agent) from the UK (chapter 12); the Centre for Leadership's Joseph Jaworski (enabler), again from the US and Honda's Fujisawa (adopter) from Japan (chapter 16); Virgin's Richard Branson (adventurer), again from the UK, and Quantum Fund's George Soros (innovater) from Hungary (chapter 20). At the same time, in focusing on you, as an individual manager, I am exhibiting cultural bias towards the north and west. I therefore owe some of you in the south and east an apology, though the fact that this book is written in English already makes such bias inevitable. Before I embark on this individual orientation, however, let me emphasize that your managerial style and orientation will be influenced by four major factors, as can be seen in Figure 8.1, other than your own individuality.

In other words, the national and ethnic culture of your birth and residence; the particular organization and industry in which you are working; your professional background and affiliation, and the age as well as degree of maturity that you have reached, will each have an important bearing on your managerial self.

However, in this section of this text, I shall be placing special emphasis on the development of your individuality over the course of your life cycle. As a result, I shall be focusing on your maturation, as it unfolds through your youth, adulthood, midlife and maturity, set within each of the four domains, on the one hand, and leaning towards a 'soft' or a 'hard' orientation in each case, on the other.

Figure 8.1 Factors impinging on management style

The process of individuation

Structure building and structure changing

Although you each have a different path to forge, or to follow, each of you will be crossed by somewhat predictable demands at particular stages of your life. In other words, if you choose to open yourself to life, and to personal growth, you will progressively round out your managerial personality, but still operating from a unique and individual base. There is a natural cycle of development, then, that applies to all individual managers, at least in an approximate way. In fact, if you are to 'mature' as an adult, in the best sense of the word, you need to develop, roughly speaking, through what American psychotherapist Daniel Levinson[1] has characterized as four major phases. These in fact correspond with our four domains, that is primal youth, rational adulthood, developmental midlife and metaphysically oriented maturity.

Moreover, as we noted in our first chapter, these phases can also be associated with stages of business and economic development. Finally, each such stage, both for the individual and for the institution, has a structure-building (hard) and a structure-changing (soft) phase to it, that is if growth and development are to ensue.

Unfortunately, however, most of us – as managers, organizations or societies – fail to realize our full maturational potential, because the successive crises of identity involved in moving from one stage to another prove too much to bear. In other words, to the extent that you evolve from primal to rational, so you have to discard much of your youthful identity; to the extent that you develop from rational to developmental, so you need to successfully negotiate your 'midlife crisis'; ultimately, and to the extent that you evolve from a developmental to a metaphysical way of being, so you will need to ground yourself in perennial wisdom, thus letting go of much of your hitherto established individual identity. In the final analysis, moreover, should you become a master manager, thereby assuming worldly wisdom, you will need to cross from south and west to north and east, so as to be able to finally gravitate towards your centre.

Exploration phase – primal youth

In your youth, from your late teens to late twenties, you need to explore, to experiment and to take risks – just like the pioneering enterprise. This is the time to find a new job or start a new business. To the extent that you are willing and able to move on, moreover, you will need to round out some rough and sharp edges, thereby becoming more empathetic to others.

Consolidation phase – rational adulthood

In your young adulthood you need to settle down into more of a routine, to establish yourself and to specialize. Thus in the period between your late twenties and thirties you can model yourself on the conventionally, and bureaucratically managed, organization. As such you evolve from a narrowly based job, product or service into a more broadly based role. To the extent that you are able to move on, morever, you need to be able to discard some of your depth and rigidity of focus, and assume a greater breadth and flexibility of outlook.

Renewal phase – developmental midlife

Then as you enter midlife, in your forties, you have to renew yourself, that is to uncover and release those parts of your managerial self which have hitherto lain dormant. As a characteristically extroverted manager, for example, you now turn inwards, not only towards your own core, but toward the core competence of your organization. As such you 'adopt the faith', embodying what your organization stands for, not in the sense of 'blind faith', but with renewed conviction in what your product or service is ultimately about. You become involved in the conscious development of yourself, of other people, or of products or markets in the broadest sense. To the extent that you are able to move on, more often than not, you need to help yourself by helping others to develop in one capacity or another.

Individuation phase – metaphysically based maturity

Finally, as you mature, you tap the true centre of your – and your organization's as well as your society's – being. In the process you become, for the first time, your true self, thereby realizing your youthful dream. To the extent that you are ready to move on, that is yourself through others and others through yourself, then you will have come to embody the combination of tradition and continuity (age) with modernity and change (youth).

Growing worldlywise – managerial fruits

Inhibitors to development

As has been indicated throughout this text, management theory and practice occupy four distinct, though necessarily overlapping, domains. Each moreover can be divided into alternately softer and harder realms of thought, feeling and action. Thus we have a total of eight subdomains. For each I have identified an archetypal managerial character that serves to embody our 'managerial fruits'. Each one is, alas, seldom 'actualized' to the point of full ripening, because of our reluctance to respond to the full-scale agonies and ecstasies of an authentic journey to mastery.

The specific factors that inhibit so-called individuation, from an organizational perspective, are:

- lack of awareness, individually and culturally
- poor management recruitment
- inappropriate reward systems
- inadequate training and development

as well as the overall personal, organizational and cultural inhibitions that foster these inadequacies. In the four chapters on 'managerial fruits', spread respectively over the four domains, our intention is to help you – as an individual, as a company or as a society – to overcome these limitations, in both theory and practice.

Modelling individuation

A HERO AND HEROINE IN EACH DOMAIN

For each of the four management domains, there is both a soft and a hard individual subdomain. This is summarized in Table 8.1. Furthermore, you may choose to use the Spectral Management Inventory (SMTI), to recognize your managerial self.[2] Remember that, as an individual manager, you are capable of inhabiting more than one domain at any one time. The cast of prominent characters we have cited, while epitomizing one particular subdomain, will be occupying at least three or four others. In fact, the more versatile you become, the more able you will be to switch between one domain and another. Interestingly enough, as and if you grow and develop, within any one domain, you will inevitably broaden, as well as deepen, your abilities. However, you are likely to remain most at home within one of the four domains, be it primal, rational, developmental or metaphysical.

I shall now investigate each of these domains, and individual subdomains, in turn. In each case I shall invite you, for yourself or on behalf of your colleagues or employees, to discover:

- what kind of individual manager you are
- how to recruit people like yourself
- what rewards you seek
- how you develop your managerial individuality

Table 8.1 Domains of self-as-manager

Domain	Managerial type		Personal quality		Managerial attribute	
	'Hard'	'Soft'	'Hard'	'Soft'	'Hard'	'Soft'
PRIMAL	Entrepreneur	Animateur	Dynamic	Enthusiastic	Enterprise	Shared values
RATIONAL	Executive	Change agent	Authoritative	Flexible	Hierarchy	Network
DEVELOPMENT	Enabler	Adopter	Magnetic	Humble	Potential	Spirit
METAPHYSICAL	Innovator	Adventurer	Charismatic	Active	Vision	Energy

In each case I shall also be providing a role model from different corners of the globe. I begin, in this chapter, with the two primal individuals, the entrepreneur and the animateur. Inevitably, of course, some of you may be some combination of the two, and the role models we draw upon, Bill Gates from the US and Ricardo Semler from Brazil, are certainly a composite of many colours, even though their primary orientations, are, respectively, entrepreneur and animateur.

The 'hard' primal manager – the 'western' entrepreneur

Are you an entrepreneur/'intrapreneur'?

As such a 'hard' primal manager, you:

- are a marginal operator, establishing an edge
- are, by birth or by choice, marginal to the establishment
- seek to find your niche rather than to fill a role
- are a risk taker, taking chances
- believe that the future will turn out in your favour
- enjoy taking calculated risks
- are an opportunist, spotting chances
- see the creation of customers as fundamental to you
- expand outwards, like an amoeba, and then fill the spaces
- are a wheeler-dealer, making chances
- negotiate, creating a system of exchange and transaction
- by scheming, create profitable combinations out of people
- are an achiever, securing results
- bring your desired future into being
- are competitive, determined and persistent
- are a gamesman who enjoys winning
- respond to work and life as a battle, or as a game
- maintain control by making the first moves
- are powerful, influencing people
- seek, defend and increase your power base
- get into a position where you can dictate the moves
- are a champion, committing yourself
- personally identify with an idea and vigorously promote it
- combine self-interest with commitment to your product

The qualities of the business entrepreneur, or corporate 'intrapreneur', are to a large extent instinctive and therefore difficult to cultivate. However, through appropriate challenges and support, mentorship and coaching, you can develop entrepreneurially within an organization, as Peters and Waterman have revealed, if you have the innate tendencies in the first place.

Your negative, or 'shadow', characteristics, finally, are manifested in an overly territorial, materialistic, exploitative, manipulative and imperialistic outlook and orientation, which is indeed often associated with the adverse side of the 'west'.

Do companies recruit entrepreneurs?

As an entrepreneur, or intrapreneur, you are therefore marginal to the establishment; a risk taker, an opportunist, a wheeler-dealer, an achiever, a gamesman, a powerful person and a product champion.

Most people believe that no self-respecting entrepreneur will join a large organization. That is only a half-truth. After all it may take a prospective entrepreneur like you many years before you are ready to take the plunge. Moreover, there are many shades of entrepreneurship. Some of you entrepreneurs may find that the balance of risk and security offered by an autonomously structured organization is more acceptable to you than a business of your own. Moreover, and paradoxically, managers with at least a touch of this entrepreneurial, power-seeking character are innately respected within a 'western' Anglo-Saxon world. Within a go-ahead company such as Microsoft or Virgin there will inevitably be a number of opportunities for entrepreneurs who can recognize and exploit a main chance. The areas in which entrepreneurship is particularly encouraged are merchandizing, sales and customer services, new ventures, and in the general management of rapidly changing products in highly competitive markets.

How are entrepreneurs rewarded?

Entrepreneurs are not motivated to climb up the corporate ladder in the conventional way. In fact the naturally entrepreneurial path is circuitous rather than direct. As part of your wheeling and dealing, as an entrepreneur or intrapreneur, you need to be able to step sideways, or move in a zigzag path, rather than stick to the straight and narrow.

As such a 'hard' primal manager, you love to overcome obstacles and to take calculated and emotionally thrilling risks. Your life and work-style are full of ups and downs, and of mistakes from which you are able to learn. Each new territory lost or gained is a landmark in your dramatic journey.

As an entrepreneur you need to be given the rope either to hang yourself or to climb commercial mountains. You need capital both as a form of outward recognition and as a means to acquire personal freedom. You want to achieve the targets that you have set yourself and to be rewarded directly and financially for your accomplishments. The entrepreneurial sector of the business you need to work for will not only offer you scope for financial gain, but it will also encourage new ventures within which you can take an equity stake. Such new or joint ventures are the lifeblood of Microsoft in Seattle, where Bill Gates has developed as a super-entrepreneur over the past two decades. In fact Gates at Microsoft alongside Jack Welch of GEC – as respective entrepreneur and intrapreneur in the

1990s – has become a business icon in America, in the same vein as Steve Jobs of Apple Computers and Lee Iacocca of Chrysler Motors in the 1980s.

The developing entrepreneur – Bill Gates – Microsoft

Let us now hear Bill Gates' unfolding, entrepreneurial story, albeit very much in brief, as told firstly by him in *The Road Ahead*,[3] and secondly by Philip Rosenzweig, Professor of International Management at International Management Development (IMD).[4] Whereas the extracts from Gates himself cover the years of youthful exploration and adultlike consolidation, Rosenzweig's analysis applies to ongoing business development. For Bill Gates, now in his forties, is entering his own period of renewal, in midlife. We start, then, with Gates' period of youthful exploration.

Youthful exploration – trader/entrepreneur

I wrote my first software programme when I was thirteen years old. It was for playing tic-tac-toe. The computer I used was large and cumbersome, and absolutely compelling. I realized later that part of the appeal must have been that here was an enormous expensive machine and we, the kids, could control it. We were too young to drive or do any of the other things adults could have fun at, but we could give this big machine orders and it would always obey. To this day it thrills me to know that if I can get the programme right it will always work perfectly, every time, just the way I told it to.

My parents paid my tuition at Lakeside high school and gave me money for books, but I had to pay my own computer time bills. This is what drove me to the commercial side of the software business. I needed money to buy access. A bunch of us, including Paul Allen, got entry-level software programming jobs in the summers. One summer day in 1972, when I was sixteen and Paul was nineteen he showed me a ten-paragraph article buried on page 143 of *Electronics* magazine. It announced that a young company called Intel had released a microprocessor chip they named the 8008. A microprocessor is a simple chip that contains the whole brain of a computer. I realized that this first microprocessor was very limited, but he was sure that the chips would get more powerful. This insight of Paul's was the cornerstone of all that we did together later, including the founding of Microsoft. Once I started at Harvard University a year later Paul and I had realized that computer hardware, which had once been scarce, would soon be readily available, and that people would soon find all kinds of new applications for computing if it was cheap. Then software would be the key to delivering on the full potential of these machines.

While we thought that the Japanese and IBM would likely produce most of the hardware, we believed we could come up with new and innovative software. In 1975 we naively decided to start a company, to put on a show in the barn! After five sleepless weeks our BASIC was written and the world's first microprocessor software company was born. In time we named it Microsoft.

By 1977, at the age of 21, I had dropped out of Harvard – temporarily I thought – to pursue the business of business. Apple, Commodore and Radio Shack had by then entered the personal computer business, and we provided them with the

BASIC software. While, for our first three years in business, most of the other professionals at Microsoft focused soley on the technical work, I did most of the sales, finance and marketing as well as some of the code writing.

Each time I succeeded in selling BASIC to a computer company, I got a little more confident. Although we were successfully selling our software to US hardware companies, by 1979 almost half our business was coming from Japan, thanks to an extraordinary guy named Kazuhiko (Kay) Nishi. He too was a college student on leave, because of his passion for personal computers. We were kindred spirits, and, having heard of Microsoft, he happened to walk into my life. For the next 8 years he seized every opportunity for Microsoft to do business in Japan. At the same time, in 1979, Microsoft moved from Albuquerque in New Mexico to Seattle in the west coast's Washington State.

Adultlike consolidation – enterprising manager

At this point I needed help running the business, and turned to my old Harvard pal, Steve Bullmer, who had worked as an associate product manager at Proctor and Gamble. Microsoft's goal, at this point, was to write and supply software for most personal computers without getting directly involved in making or selling computer hardware. We licensed our software at extremely low prices because we believed money could be made betting on volume. We'd adapt a programming language, moreover, to each machine that came on the market. Our strategy worked. Along the way Microsoft BASIC became an industry standard. Even IBM decided to license the operating system of the PC it was developing from us, rather than create the software itself. Working with their design team, we encouraged them to use a 16–bit microprocessor chip, as we could see that the move from 8 to 16 bits would take the personal computer from the hobbyist toy to high-volume business. We could see that, with its reputation and its decision to employ an open design that other companies could copy, IBM had a real chance to create a new, broad standard in personal computing, and we wanted to be part of it. So we took on the operating system challenge. We hired in a top engineer from another Seattle company, Tim Patterson, who became the father of MS-DOS, the Microsoft Disk Operating System.

IBM then became our first licensee. Their personal computer hit the market in 1981. It was an immediate triumph. We practically gave away our software to them to create strategic value. Our goal was not to make money directly from IBM but to profit from licensing MS-DOS to computer companies who wanted to offer machines more or less compatible with the IBM PC. This put Microsoft in the business of licensing operating system software to the computer industry. In fact Microsoft operating systems are offered today by over 1,000 different manufacturers, which gives customers an immense range of choices and options.

In 1992, over a decade since IBM's first PC had been launched, the joint development of a second operating standard with Microsoft, OS/2, was stopped. Thousands of people years were wasted. The success of Windows, in the meanwhile, was a long time in coming. For most of the 1980s many people had written it off because it required any computer running it to have lots of expensive memory. It took many years of persistence, a very long-term approach, to make Windows a success. Today's main challenge for us is making Windows the best way to gain access to the Internet. Three-dimensional graphics are becoming important, and when speech and handwriting recognition becomes accurate enough, these innovations will cause another big change in operating systems.

We now turn from Bill Gates' own description of Microsoft's development to that provided by Philip Rosenzweig, while he was Associate Professor of International Business at Harvard.

Midlife renewal – business development

Microsoft, as the world's leading producer of computer software products, has become a legend in its time. Fundamental to Microsoft's success, moreover, has been its ability to attract, select and develop talented individuals. As Bill Gates said: 'We're in the intellectual property business'. From the company's earliest days, in effect, the constant need to develop new and better products made hiring top talent, as well as quickly bringing their individual contributions on-line, a top priority. 'We've always had the most aggressive approach of any software company in finding people with top IQ's and bringing them in. We also pushed to the absolute limit the people we brought in from overseas. Finally, we designed a development methodology that could make use of different individual's talents.'

Hiring and developing talented individuals was, in fact, critical but not sufficient for Microsoft. They needed not only to develop such people but also to place them in circumstances where each would excel. As such Microsoft has tried to retain the feel of a small firm, with an informal atmosphere, but an intensely competitive one.

'The Microsoft style is pretty aggressive', remarked one manager. 'People jump on each other all the time. But it's not personal. It's a challenging, aggressive style.' So stories abound of combative meetings and 'yelling matches' between groups of software developers, each advocating new features for coming products.

Critical e-mail messages, often sarcastic or sharp in tone, are known around the company as 'flame mail'. The overall tone, then, is not only informal but also profoundly pragmatic and achievement oriented. All that ultimately matters is that the Microsoft products should work, and work well.

To reinforce such an achievement orientation, moreover, Microsoft's compensation policy has continued to emphasize employee participation in the company's fortunes. In addition to salaries, which remain somewhat below industry levels, new employees receive a sizeable stock grant. The company's philosophy of personal responsibility is further emphasized, in fact, by a management accounting system which fosters visibility and accountability. All revenues and costs, identified by product and by sales channel, are fed into a single, consolidated ledger. This database is then exploded into many profit and loss statements, each focusing on a particular business unit, marketing channel or geographical area. Actual sales and expense figures can be reviewed on-line, resulting in high visibility and individual accountability. Profitability is not the province of someone in HQ, but the responsibility of everyone. As a software developer, in fact, revealed: 'one of the reasons our products are so successful is that everybody takes responsibility for them. You own this thing; you make it great; you're responsible for it . . . Your input is taken seriously. It doesn't matter what level you're at or where you are, you compete like hell for the business.'

In the final analysis, for Gates, success is based on deploying individual talent within the organization. 'Once you let mediocre people into the organization, particuarly at very high levels, that's going to replicate itself and you won't be a world class organization any more.' This is a lesson Microsoft may have learnt from IBM in its prime, one which also differentiates the individualistic and entrepreneurial 'westerners' from their group oriented Japanese competitors.

How do you develop as an entrepreneur, or intrapreneur?

As an entrepreneur or intrapreneur like Bill Gates, then, you do not develop, managerially, by going on formal training courses. You need to set or, rather, be set, challenging personal and business targets to which to respond. You also need to be provided with coaches and mentors who can not only live up to your entrepreneurial expectations, but also supersede them.

Trader-entrepreneur

Your dream is to be rich and powerful! In your youth you are likely to find the most opportunities in sales or marketing, or else in championing a particular product or service in any one of the other functions. Travel to far-flung places and rewards directly related to your achievements are likely to enhance your performance, as an itinerant salesman, market trader and budding entrepreneur.

Enterprising manager

In your adulthood you should have the opportunity of managing a profit centre of semi-autonomous function in your own particular way. Challenge needs now to be accompanied, as it was for Bill Gates, by growing territory and responsibility, as an entrepreneurial manager.

Business developer

In midlife – in your forties – the entrepreneurs among you, like Bill Gates, should be broadening your terms of reference. Instead of being preoccupied only by money and markets you should also be widening your field of concern to encompass, to a much greater extent, the development of people and the business as a whole. This is a natural time for you to enter a development function, therefore, without losing your marketing or financial touch. Such a role would also and naturally serve to broaden the base of a personnel or R & D department, with you as a business developer.

Embodying the spirit of enterprise

Finally, as you fully mature, in your fifties and sixties (Gates has not yet reached such a point), you might become involved in an organizational transformation, through which the re-creation of the company, its culture and its overall direction may be achieved. This is a role that Bill Gates may play at Microsoft during the next millennium, as he becomes his ultimate and managerial self, thereby embodying the spirit of enterprise.

So much then for the entrepreneur, in his or her own company, or for the intrapreneur, within someone else's organization. He or she represents the 'hard' side of primal management, and as such the archetypal 'westerner'. However, if you are be successful over the long term, like Bill Gates, you need to open up to other management domains – rational in adulthood, developmental in midlife and metaphysical in maturity. While you retain your fundamental and, in this case, 'hard' primal identity, you therefore progressively round out, as you grow and develop. This will only happen in this instance, however, if you are open at the outset to the soft, as well as to the hard, attributes of primal management. That leads us on to the 'animateur'.

The 'soft' primal manager – the 'southern' animateur

Entrepreneur and animateur

The entrepreneur and animateur, like the hunter and gatherer of old, are the formative primal couple. As one rounded person, or as a management duo, they spearhead the youthful phase of a business's development. More often than not it is the entrepreneur who takes the hunting lead, and the animateur – in the background – who provides the nurturing 'family' support. Marks and Spencer in Britain, Albert Koopman and Gerard Haumant in South Africa, the late Gianni Versace and his sister Donatella in Italy, are just three of many cases in point.

However, in recent years, as more and more women have set up in business, we find instances where the animateur in fact takes the nurturing lead, and the hunter entrepreneur plays the back-up role. An example of this, in the UK, is the Bodyshop, where Anita Roddick is in the foregound and her husband Gordon is in the wings. The role of the animateur, a term I have borrowed from the French, has also been brought in to recent focus as a result of the growing interest in corporate culture. Let me now investigate, with you, who the animateur is, and how she or he is recruited, rewarded and developed.

Are you an animateur?

As such a 'soft' primal manager, you:

- operate informally, making personal contacts
- establish a strongly cohesive, informal organization

- create ways and means of keeping in constant touch
- establish rituals and ceremonies, uniting people
- hold 'revivalist' meetings, especially for salespeople
- establish rituals to protect staff from fear of the unknown
- establish a 'family feeling', in which everyone partakes
- ensure that the needs of individuals serve those of the tribe
- become like a mother to your business children
- are an animateur, activating people's social lives
- provide access to an active and creative group life
- widen people's horizons and enlarge their social circle
- create a corporate culture, thereby sharing values
- create heroes who pass on your primary corporate values
- make sure that formative corporate legends live on
- embody the spirit of the community
- become a 'mother earth' figure
- ensure the business becomes identified with the community

As an animateur, then, you are not a cartoonist, but, in the original sense the word, a person who animates individuals and groups within a particular locality. You accomplish this not only through your own charm and enthusiasm but also by drawing on your organizational and cultural heritage.

The negative or 'shadow' side of your personality, however, is manifested in your overly 'tribal' outlook, oriented towards 'us and them' specifically, or in nepotism or even corrupt practices generally. Such practices are often associated with the 'south' in Africa, Asia, Europe or Latin America.

Do organizations recruit animateurs?

As an animateur, then, you operate informally, you establish rituals and ceremonies, you create a family feeling, you activate people's social lives, you create a corporate culture and you come to embody community spirit. Animateurs are more likely to be found, and indeed respected, in Italy rather than in Britain, in Ireland rather than in England, in 'black' South Africa or New Zealand rather than amongst the 'whites', and generally more amongst women than men. However, there will be many exceptions to these very generalized rules, and you may well be one of them. In functional terms, animateurs are most likely to be found amongst the salesforce, amongst the secretarial staff, or amidst those of you in personnel or in operations who are seen to be natural and gregarious 'people people'. In fact, in Britain at the present time, with the growing emphasis on 'customer care', animateurs are in ever-increasing demand. Anglian Water, British Airways and British Telecom are just three examples of companies which have rapidly developed their emphasis on service.

Moreover, in the world at large, as the importance of the 'services sector' increases (see previous chapter), so the role of animateurs will become ever more significant, that is if they are encouraged to develop themselves.

How are animateurs rewarded?

As an animateur you seek out a social circle to which to belong, whether or not it is entirely of your own making. The last thing you want is to be promoted into a position of isolation from your familiar friends, colleagues and workmates, and from the product or service which matters to you. However, if you are ambitious and are encouraged to grow, you will need progressively to broaden your circle of contacts. As an animateur you will be intent on bringing your practical and social skills to bear on situations, and you will be frustrated if prevented from doing so. You therefore need to be recognized for your skill, whether as a skilled craftsman or for your innate social skills.

You are rewarded, though, not so much by individual recognition, but by recognition of your group of skilled workers, whether as joiners or linguists, in which you may have become a leading influence. In fact, the reason that cooperative enterprises are more widespread in Italy or Spain than in Britain or Scandinavia is because of the gregarious, Mediterranean influence. Cooperative activity, in its inherent nature if not necessarily in its legally constituted form, comes naturally to the animateur. Rewards for cooperative achievement are therefore welcomed.

The developing animateur – Ricardo Semler – Semco

Natural business

In the same way that Bill Gates is a folk hero in the 'west' generally, and in North America more specifically, so Ricardo Semler is such a folk hero in the 'south' generally, and in Latin America more specifically. Whereas Gates is your archetypal 'western' entrepreneur, Semler, while certainly being somewhat entrepreneurially oriented, is more typical of the 'southern' animateur, not unlike Albert Koopman in South Africa. Again, we shall let him tell his own story, drawn from his own best-selling book entitled *Maverick*.[5] As we shall see, this rather remarkable man has grown up fast, approaching his midlife renewal some ten years before some of us lesser mortals!

Every Wednesday afternoon dozens of men and women file through the front gate on their way to a third-floor meeting room in Semco, the company I lead in Sao Paulo, Brazil. The guard at the entrance has been expecting them. For years now, executives from such companies as IBM, General Motors, Mercedes-Benz and Siemens have been making an unlikely pilgrimage to our nondescript industrial complex on the outskirts of the city. Semco manufactures an impressively varied roster of products, including pumps that can empty an oil tanker at night and dishwashers capable of scrubbing 4000 plates an hour. But it's not what Semco makes that has executives and management experts the world over waiting months for a chance to tour our plants and offices. It's the way people of Semco make it.

When I took over from my father 12 years ago, it was a traditional company in every respect, with a pyramidical structure and a rule for every contingency. But today, our factory workers sometimes set their own production quotas and even come in on their own time to meet them, without prodding from management or overtime pay. They help redesign the products they make and formulate the marketing plans. Their bosses, for their own parts, can run our business units with extraordinary freedom. They even set their salaries, with no strings. Then again everyone will know what they are, since all information at Semco is openly discussed. For truly big decisions, like buying another company, everyone gets a vote. Everybody moreover, even top managers, stands over photocopiers, types letters. It's all part of running a natural business.

Youthful exploration – a people person

I always wanted my father, who started our family business, to enjoy the money he made. He never did. He was always worrying. Late in life, after his cancer had been diagnosed, he would walk through the park after radiation therapy and tell my mother that he had never really noticed the flowers and the ducks before. It took him 73 years and a terminal illness to make him see the small but fascinating details of life. The secret of life, in fact, is to enjoy the passing of time.

When I was a teenager, my father would take the family on a long European holiday at the end of each year. For him it was half-skiing, half business. I remember we would always have dinner in the hotel restaurant. There was a sign on the wall on which room numbers would flash, indicating a phone call. Our room number appeared constantly. No matter how far dad was from the office he coudn't leave it. He wanted to know everything, and could not delegate any-thing. Father had a stroke, caused by cancer of the liver, while on a ship off the Italian coast in 1985. It was the first time he had been on a long cruise. He thought he was finally removed enough from the business to be out of touch for a while.

In the late 1960s the military dictators who ran Brazil had decided the country needed a ship-building industry. My father, who had emigrated from Austria to Brazil as a young man, sensing an opportunity, took on two British pump manufacturers as partners, and Semco became a major supplier of marine pumps in Brazil. When I was 16 I took a summer job in Semco's purchasing department, but afterwards went back to my first love, the guitar, and my despairing father considered selling out. Soon enough, though, I discovered the depressingly narrow range of my musical abilities. Given my father's desire for a successor and my previous stint as a snack-stand mogul, business seemed a sensible aspiration.

My first experiences in the executive suite distressed me. Everyone was as starched as their shirts. For my first few years in the company I struggled to survive, as did the business. I started to diversify our product line, got rid of the stuffy dress code, as well as some of our most stuffy managers. Life and business was a continuous struggle, and the only way I kept my sanity was to take off over the week-ends to have a good time. There had to be a better way to live and to work than this. I wanted our people to have more contact with each other. I wanted less clutter. I wanted fewer levels. I wanted more flexibility. I wanted a new shape for our organization.

Adultlike consolidation – people manager

In the autumn of 1988 my soon-to-be wife, Sofia, and I rented a house for two weeks in the Caribbean. I brought along a small library – Thomas Mann's *Death in Venice*, Machiavelli's *The Prince*, Alex Haley's *Autobiography of Malcolm X*, and a collection of poems by e.e. cummings. Watching the clear, gentle Caribbean waves, it suddenly seemed so obvious. Why not replace the pyramid with something more fluid – a circle. A pyramid is rigid and constraining. A circle is filled with possibilities. So pyramids would be contained within them. We began sketching it out on the sand. Sofia and I would find sticks and draw. Back in Sao Paolo I continued to refine the idea. A small, innermost circle, including me, would enclose a team of half a dozen people called counsellors. The second circle would enclose the seven to ten leaders of Semco's business leaders and be called partners. The last, immense circle would hold virtually everyone else at Semco. They would be called associates. Triangles would then be scattered around the last big circle, each enclosing a single person we would call a coordinator. There would be six to twelve such triangles for each business unit.

Although doubters and sceptics abounded when I first drew my circles, even the most cynical observers were astonished to find that things were better off once we got rid of the pyramid and all its rungs and roles. Traffic jams were becoming rare. Semco was moving at the speed limit. Based on our new philosophies and policies Semco now boasted one of the highest growth rates in Brazil. Sales, which had been $4 million a year for decades, had swelled to $35 million, and in just a few years we went from one to six factories and from 100 to 830 employees. Semco was now number 1 or 2 in every one of its markets. A Semco employee told a magazine – 'the company has become a paradise to work in and nobody wants to leave'.

It's enough to go to your head. So the age of 28, I decided it was time to write my memoirs. So Sofia and I headed for the mountains. For nine days I wrote furiously. It all came gushing out, years of experimentation and craziness, frustration and joy. I drove down from the mountains with 750 handwritten pages I called 'Turning the Tables', which became Brazil's best-selling non-fiction book ever.

Midlife renewal – corporate animateur

Nothing is harder work than democracy, I keep telling myself. I don't remember the last time I made a corporate decision alone, nor can I count all the times I've been voted down.

With Semco now restructured in a way that made it much less vulnerable to the economy, I decided to eliminate another level of our hierarchy: mine. So now I'm just another counsellor. My job hasn't changed – I try to make things change, just like a catalyst. I lobby for what I believe in. I step in when I believe I can do some good. I attend meetings only when I'm invited, which is about once every two or three weeks. Otherwise they're on their own. The truth is the company hardly needs me now in their day-to-day operations. And the ideas Semco is built on aren't my own either. They flow from the company culture. It's really not my company any more. I am not Semco. Semco is Semco. Not even my death will change these circumstances, since outstanding shares in Semco will be handed onto a foundation, which will be managed by a board including employees and outsiders, but not family members.

What then do I do with the rest of my time? I write a weekly newspaper column. I talk about Semco to business groups around the world. I am interested in politics. I watch a minimum of three movies a week, buy the recordings of Billie Holliday and Philip Glass, take piano, cooking, golf and Chinese lessons, and also read fifty books a year. I believe I have turned Semco into the most sought-after workplace I know. I have created a foundation to provide opportunities for poor Brazilians. I am five-sixths of the way towards speaking six languages fluently. I travel incessantly, taking balloon trips in Kenya, scuba diving in the Seychelles, crossing the Sahara and floating down the Nile.

One of the biggest misconceptions about modern man is that he is somehow different from his ancestors. Man has always lived in tribes and I daresay always will. Whether these groups are ethnic, religious, political or vocational, they are our anchors. People derive their identity from companies too, wearing Mitsubishi or Motorola like a surname. And within companies they can belong to sub-tribes, each with its own norms and dress conduct. Companies must be redesigned to let tribes be. They must develop systems based on co-existence, not on some unattainable ideal of harmony. Different tribes will never fully integrate.

As Ricardo Semler approaches his nominal midlife he is in fact voicing the opinions of someone entering maturity, reaching for the depths of his 'southern' self and society, seeking a profound sense of 'tribal' continuity, while his primal counterpart Bill Gates is fostering ever more change. For Semler, then:

> The issue of tribal co-existence is, I believe, critical for survival in modern times. Up until now it has been easy enough for the First World to keep its distance from the Third World and view the Southern Hemisphere as very far away. But technology is drawing everyone and every place closer together. Like lava from a huge volcano, tribes are moving towards areas where the standard of living is higher. In a few decades all that will be left of the First World will be a few ghettos of the super rich, islands of luxury surrounded by misery. There will be a lot of Cairo in Paris, Mexico in Colorado, and Syria in Switzerland. And as the Third World makes its glacial movement north, it will leave behind places like Somalia, Bangladesh, and the Ivory Coast, which will become an even more abject Fourth World.

Most companies, Semler argues, are unprepared for this new world order. Moreover, if they are to respond in a way that accords with Semler's 'southern' humanism, they should:

> forget socialism, capitalism, just-in-time deliveries, salary surveys, and the rest of it, and concentrate on building organizations that accomplish the most difficult of all challenges; to make people look forward to coming to work in the morning.

As a fellow southerner, Semler's words are music to my ears. My own search, to become worldliwise as a management educator, was first instigated when, at the tender age of seven, I used to walk down the factory floor of our family business in Zimbabwe, where nobody ever smiled. I resolved there and then to pursue my own humble path towards enabling people 'to look forward to coming to work in the morning'.

How do you develop as an animateur?

People person

In your youth you will welcome the opportunity of meeting lots of warmhearted people, and of working with people and things which you really care about. Like Ricardo Semler you are more of a 'natural' than a professional manager. Indeed, for Semler, professionalism came later when he sent himself off to Harvard. You learn best from people with whom you feel a natural rapport. Because Ricardo did not have that rapport with his father, he learnt virtually nothing from him. Any training programmes you go on therefore have to be fun and friendly if these courses are to achieve the desired effect. Your dream is to be happy, and to make others so.

People manager

As you enter adulthood, in your thirties, you need to substantiate the base of your activities and relationships, thereby becoming a skilled operator in commercial and social, as well as technical, terms. Having a supportive coach and an admired mentor is particularly important for you at this stage. Ricardo Semler drew on his tried and trusted Human Resources Manager in that respect.

Corporate animateur

In midlife you need to broaden out even further, beyond the relatively limited circle of sales, production or personnel activity in which you might have been working. A natural development is from production or sales to regional, divisional or company animateur. You will need to become more involved with consciously creating a corporate culture, rather than with just instinctively generating a family feeling.

Though your enthusiasm and charm, rather than your dynamism or authority, will still remain to the fore, more of these latter qualities will begin to come out. Moreover, you will begin to acquire a reflective capacity that was not in evidence before. Finally, as you approach maturity, you develop the potential to create a new and powerful culture in your organization, as indeed Ricardo Semler has done. Such a corporate culture may be more in tune with the times than the one you inherited. You, in your turn, as you mellow and become more philosophical, will come to embody the spirit of community.

Conclusion

'West' meets 'south'

So we can see the way in which you, as entrepreneur and animateur, embodying 'west' and 'south' – sensing and feeling – within the 'global businessphere', build up the base of your business. Enterprising cells and a cohesive culture are now in place. Autonomy and entrepreneurship, combined with shared values, are your joint creation. The net result is a profitable and growing business – in itself or within an existing organization – as well as contented customers and employees. In a functional context it is sales, rather than marketing, the product or service rather than operations, people rather than human resources, and money rather than finance, which are the primal preoccupations.

Developing yourself as a primal manager

However, as you develop towards maturity, the scope, if not the essential nature, of your managerial role changes. It becomes more broadly based and more deeply founded. In other words, you absorb, if you open yourself to growth and development, some of the rational, developmental and metaphysical attributes that characterize others around you. In effect, while product is paramount, more rationally based notions of product standards and more developmental notions of quality do begin to have their place. Although sales remain primary, design and marketing assume important secondary, rational and developmental functions. Similarly, while it is basically people that count, rationally based human-resource management and even the metaphysically oriented corporate culture have their supportive roles to play. Finally, while profit is all-important, profitability and productivity have their rational part to play, and excellence its developmental one, in the evolving, primal whole.

In sum, the primal essence is retained, but its shape and form is broadened and deepened over time. As a result, Peters and Waterman go out 'in search of excellence' rather than in pursuit of fame and fortune. The enterprising and materially prolific 'west' is enriched by the communal and naturally abundant 'south', rather than the one exploiting, or being corrupted by, the other. While Ricardo Semler argues that 'tribal co-existence' is the key to our global survival, Bill Gates is joining up with Boeing to build and launch hundreds of satellites in order to create 'an Internet in the sky that will put every mud hut in Africa and every igloo in the arctic on the information superhighway'.[6] Undoubtedly Semler and Gates need each other, as entrepreneurial and animateurial supremos, but they also need a cast of our other six characters. We now turn, to begin with, from the primal domain to the rational one.

Primal and rational management

A developing business, in fact, needs more than its primal and instinctive duo. The bigger and more complex the business the greater the need for the executive and for the change agent, whether within manufacturing or marketing, finance or human resources, management services or general management. While it is viable and sufficient for you as an individual manager, or for a nationally based company, to round out primally, if you and it develop internationally, you both have to acquire 'new cultural spots'. Such 'spots' will need to be more northern and eastern rather than western or southern in orientation. Moreover, and in any case, in order to grow into the other three domains, you have to understand their inner nature. So we now turn, in chapter 9, to the knowledge grounds that underlie the two inhabitants of the rational management domain.

9

RATIONAL ROOTS –
ADMINISTRATIVE AND
BEHAVIOURAL SCIENCE

Introduction

The classical management heritage

The roots of management, as we have seen, reach down to the primal hunter-gatherer communities. Management of this basic kind is still to be found in trading communities in developing societies, as well as on market stalls and in households throughout the world. It also characterizes the newly emerging business enterprise, whether one created by an animateur such as Ricardo Semler or by an entrepreneur such as Bill Gates.

The problem, of course, with primal management is that it is generally implicit rather than explicit, subconscious rather than conscious, felt and acted upon rather than thought out, and based on oral rather than literary traditions. In Nonaka's terms, primal management is thus based upon tacit rather than explicit knowledge. Therefore, despite the primacy of its existence, it is not recognized by the conventional, literary based wisdom.

Conventional management texts, then, locate the origins of management in other, more explicitly codifiable, 'civilized' quarters. In most cases its origins are drawn from the civil, religious and military administrators of ancient civilizations, chiefly in China, Babylon, Egypt and Rome. The oldest known military treatise, in fact, is the product of the Chinese general Sun Tzu, around the sixth century BC. He wrote of marshalling the army into subdivisions, or gradations of ranks amongst officers, and of using gongs, flags and signal fires for communications.

In Ancient Mesopotamia, flourishing around 3000 BC, the temples developed an early concept of a corporation, or a group of temples under a common body of management. The 'rule of ten', for example, in the span of management, is an Ancient Egyptian practice. Excavations also revealed distinct dress for managers and workers amongst the Ancient Egyptians. The Romans, in their turn, had a genius for order, and the military autocracy ran the empire with an iron hand. Moreover, in the early Middle Ages, the leaders of the Roman Church perceived the need to convey policies, procedures, doctrine and authority to its minions.

The scientific origins of management

Frederick Taylor and Mary Parker Follett

Management, as a rationally based science, has much more recent origins, and it is with these roots that we shall be more concerned here. Because this more recent management heritage is firmly linked with business enterprise, it is more accessible to us and provides more digestible food for thought. These more contemporary and scientifically based roots, then, draw from two major sources. The first one, now strongly entrenched within business, taps into the physical sciences, especially engineering in the latter part of the nineteenth century. The second, and the more shallow-rooted within business, taps into social sciences, particularly in the early part of the twentieth century.

In this chapter, therefore, I want to draw on the two traditions, one focused on the physical sciences and the other on the social. The two key figures that will be represented are both American: Frederick Taylor, an industrial engineer at the turn of the century, and Mary Parker Follett, a social philosopher who was most influential during the 1930s. Whereas Taylor was an Anglo-Saxon strongly influenced by Adam Smith, Parker Follett was very much influenced by Hegelian, that is Germanic, philosophy.

The socio-technical balance

Both Taylor and Parker Follett were very formidable and – in their time – influential characters. However, the subsequent influence of Taylor has been much greater than that of Parker Follett, who has only been rediscovered[1] in very recent years. The reason for this, at least in America and Western Europe, is that the 'hard' analytical side of rational management has pervaded the entirety of business, whereas the 'soft' and integrative side has either been restricted to the 'personnel' function, or else submerged within a poorly conceptualized 'general management'.

As we saw in chapter 2, moreover, this imbalance in the conduct of business, in the western and indeed northern quarters of the businessphere, has been one of the main reasons why America and Europe have lost out to the Asian tigers in the global market-place. For Japanese and Singaporean management in particular, as Hampden Turner has described, has more successfully blended soft and hard qualities in finance and technology, as well as in personnel and organization. In the interests of overall balance, I give equal historical weight to the social as to the technical roots of rational management.

Hierarchy and network

The hunter and gatherer are now upgraded into the 'hierarch' (technical/administrative) and the 'networker' (social/behavioural). For both, thought and reason take precedence over feeling and instinct. However, whereas the former is particularly good at dividing things – analytical cut and thrust – the latter is especially adept at putting them together – integrative appreciation and coordination. Similarly, whereas the hierarch is oriented towards order and organization, into which the individual must be fitted, the networker is geared towards cohesive interpersonal relationships, around which the organization must be fitted.

For the classical and hierarchically oriented business 'executive', then, the organization rationally serves the impersonal individual interests of the employee, the customer and the shareholder. For the contemporary and network-oriented 'change-agent', it serves the social needs of a diversity of parties, each with their own particular group interests.

Individualistic versus group values

The individualistically oriented technical/administrative (north-western) and group-oriented social/behavioural (south-eastern) ethics are like superordinate values for management. The individualistic ethic is rooted in liberalism, the Protestant ethic, and the American frontier. The group ethic has grown as a dominant current in social thought during the twentieth century because of increased human interdependence.[2] Interdependency requires a social philosophy directed towards collaboration and solidarity rather than competition and conflict. The reference point of the social ethic is the collective nature of man. The social ethic affirms the value of human collaboration and social solidarity. Individual satisfactions are seen to result from participation in a social environment. In contrast, the individualistic ethic starts with the person as the ultimate source of individual and social values. The atomistic person, acting intelligently in pursuit of his or her own self-interest, will eventually contribute the most to the good of the group.[3] Let me now review, in turn, the knowledge grounds for 'hard' and 'soft' rationally based tradition. In the next three chapters I shall identify the mainstem, branches and fruits of rational management, both administrative/technical and behavioural/social, that have developed in more recent times.

The 'hard' technical/administrative tradition

The visible hand

Before introducing you to the founding father of so-called 'scientific management', I want to describe to you, via the eminent business historian, Alfred Chandler,[4] the economic and industrial conditions under which Frederick Taylor rose to prominence. The market forces through which primal enterprise

175

emerged in the eighteenth and nineteenth centuries had been benevolently guided, or so it seemed to Adam Smith, by a remarkably 'invisible hand'. Of course, for the rational and scientific mind, such invisibility is anathema. Smith's theory lacked scientific and demonstrable proof. Alfred Chandler, a contemporary Harvard-based apostle of the rationally managed organization, has referred to the 'visible hand' that made its appearance, in America, in the late nineteenth century.

Through Chandler's so called 'visible hand', modern business enterprise took the place of market mechanisms in coordinating the activities of the economy and allocating its resources. In many economic sectors, the visible hand of management replaced what Adam Smith referred to as the invisible hand of market forces. The market remained the generator of demand for goods and services, but modern business enterprise took over the functions of coordinating flows of goods through existing processes of production and distribution, and of allocating funds and personnel for the future. As modern business enterprise acquired functions hitherto carried out by the market, it became the most powerful institution in the American economy and its managers the most influential group of economic decision makers.

The new captains of industry

As large-scale enterprise began to take over from small-scale production and distribution in the latter part of the nineteenth century, the newly qualified engineers were on hand to take on the role of the critical actors in industrialization. Their self-image was one of men (rather than women) who made things work, who avoided any waste of time, capital and labour. They also saw themselves as the mediators in the struggle between capital and labour, and were convinced that the best of their profession, men who combined a scientific with a business orientation, were the ideal captains of industry. As engineers, finally, they were heavily affected by their 'mechanistic' view of people and life.

Daniel McCallum, one of the first such engineers to write on management matters in the mid-nineteenth century, was railroad superintendent of the Erie Line. His mechanistic view of a living organism was indicative of the engineer's

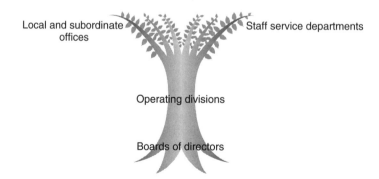

Local and subordinate offices

Staff service departments

Operating divisions

Boards of directors

Figure 9.1 Formal organization tree

approach. In fact, McCallum developed a formal organization chart that took the form of a most unnatural tree, yet one which remains familiar in large-scale bureaucracies to this day. Such a tree, somewhat different from the more organically derived one that underlines this text, depicted the lines of authority and responsibility, the division of labour amongst operating units, and the reporting lines for communication and control. (See Figure 9.1.)

The roots of the tree, then, represented the board of directors and the president; the trunk was the operating divisions; the branches were the staff service departments; the leaves were the various local freight and ticket forwarding offices, and subordinate offices. Adherence to formal lines of authority was to be absolute.[5]

The emerging science of management in the west

McCallum reflected the prevailing managerial wisdom of the day, in the same way that he represents the more mechanistically inclined of our executives today. Indeed, because management in the new factories and railroads relied heavily on the engineer's advice, it is not coincidental that their associations were the first to examine and write about management problems. The American Society of Mechanical Engineers, founded in 1880, became the first active proponent, in that country, of the search for a systematic, scientifically based management. Of course, in Western Europe, and most particularly in France, this search had begun – admittedly somewhat haphazardly as we shall see – some two hundred years before. In the early part of the twentieth century, moreover, this scientific work was to culminate, as we saw in chapter 3, in the insights of that great Frenchman, Fayol.

The evolution of management science in the north

At the call of a minister of France's Louis XIV, physicists and engineers in the second half of the seventeenth century made the first experimental researches into 'human work'. A short time afterwards, the French Academy of Sciences invited all its scientists to study the activities of the workmen in their workshops, with a view to improving their work-rate. De La Hire (1640–1718) investigated the relationship between the physical strength of the worker and his weight, and concluded that sloping boards were the most rational and effective way to elevate heavy loads.[6]

Amontons (1663–1705) subsequently conducted experiments on the comparative work-rate of men and horses, and methodically collected data on both, on a daily basis. In a book entitled *Architecture hydraulique* (Paris, 1750), Belidor, moreover, a military engineer, studied the problems and opportunities involved in separating planning from performance, in the course of preparing for a military campaign. Dublin, a Professor of Mechanics, noted in 1829 that 'whereas a huge effort toward perfecting machinery had been made, very little had been done towards perfecting workmen'.[7] He therefore initiated a campaign for rational methods of work analysis in industry.

Efficiency and productivity

Frederick Taylor joined the American Society of Mechanical Engineers (ASME) in 1880, against this backdrop of early scientific investigation into work and organization. Daniel Wren has put Taylor's scientific management into perspective:

> On the technical side, Taylor's scientific approach sought to analyse existing practices, study them for standardization and improvement, and rationalize resource utilization. On the human side, Taylor sought to attain the highest degree of individual performance improvement, and financial reward, through such visible and determinable measures as fatigue reduction, scientific selection, matching men's (rather than women's) abilities to jobs, and incentive schemes.[8]

The concept of increased productivity became the lodestar of modern work in the late nineteenth century, replacing such concepts as morality, expiation of sin, individual self-realization, aesthetic fulfilment and community well-being, which, singly or together, had defined and guided work in other epochs. Efficiency, with which Taylor's name is primarily associated, has come to mean that particular 'efficiency' which can be expressed in measurable, quantifiable terms.[9] This intention was borne out by a speech Taylor gave to ASME at the turn of the century:

> I do welcome the opportunity of speaking upon the far broader subject, of which the art of cutting metals and the proper use of machines is but one of the small elements, namely, the great opportunity as well as the duty, which lies before us as engineers of taking such steps as will result in a very material increase of output if every man and every machine in their manufacturing establishments is significantly upgraded. It gives us the opportunity at this time to give the men what they want most – higher wages, shorter hours, better working conditions; and, on the other hand, to give the companies what they need most – a lower labour cost, so that they may be able more successfully to compete at home and abroad.[10]

Principles of scientific management

In a nutshell, then, Taylor's principles of scientific management were directed at increasing productivity, for the benefit of both worker and management, by:

- breaking the work process into the smallest possible components
- fitting jobs into structures that clearly emphasize the duties and boundaries of each job, rather than its part in the total

- wherever possible, using individual, financial incentives, thereby gearing pay to output
- subtracting skill and responsibility from the job to make them functions of management

Taylor's scientific management principles were derived from many years of his own meticulous observations of the work process, of the interface between man and machine, and of the interaction between management and worker. His structured observations led him to make two major conclusions about the process of scientific management. First, the manager's job was to provide planned and authoritative direction, including training, while the worker's responsibility – in his own best interests – was to follow the lead he had been individually given. Similarly, he maintained, the efficient teacher gives a class definite tasks to learn.

In that respect, for Taylor, all of us are grown-up children, and the average workman will work with the greatest satisfaction, both to himself and to his employer, when he is given each day a definite task which he is to perform in a given time. This also furnishes the workman with a clear-cut standard by which he can throughout the day measure his own progress, and the accomplishment of which affords him the greatest satisfaction.[11]

Secondly, Taylor concluded, individual responsibilities and relationships were much more productive than group ones. It is in that respect that he clearly set himself apart from those social scientists who were to follow him in their own different 'soft' approach to rational management. For Taylor, though, it was his so-called 'rabble hypothesis' that underlined his 'scientific' worldview:

> A careful analysis has demonstrated the fact that when workmen are herded together in gangs, each man becomes far less efficient than when his personal ambition is stimulated, that when they work in gangs their individual efficiency falls almost invariably down to or below the level of the worst men in the gang; and that they are all pulled down instead of being elevated by being herded together.[12]

From administrative to behavioural sciences

It is in direct reaction to Fredrick Taylor's so-called 'rabble hypothesis' that Elton Mayo, the first and most prominent of the emerging behavioural scientists before the war, nailed his colours to the new 'behavioural' or 'social' mast. We shall see what he had to say very shortly. Before we move on to that other, social side of the rational manager's coin, though, we need to make some concluding comments – on the 'scientific manager's' behalf. We have deliberately focused on Frederick Taylor, at this point, because he has presented the 'hard' side of rational management in its purest, traditional form.

As you will see when we come to consider Elliot Jaques in the next chapter, there is a greater breadth to the 'hard', rational argument than has been indicated so far. Moreover, and in more recent times, this 'hard scientific' argument has shifted away from that of the traditional civil and mechanical engineers to the contemporary electronically oriented ones.

The most pre-eminent of these has been the German American Norbert Wiener,[13] who is said to have invented 'Cybernetics', that is the science of communication and control. Cybernetics incorporates standard setting, measurement systems and the negative-feedback or learning loops that fall in between. This scientific discipline in fact emerged after the last war, when experts in mathematics, communications theory and engineering, social and medical science combined skills and insights to create machines with the adaptive capacities of organisms. The core insight emerging from this early work was that the ability of a system to engage in self-regulating behaviour depended upon processes of information exchange involving negative feedback. Such negative feedback loops involve error detection and correction automatically, so that movements in one direction initiate compensating movements in the opposite direction. Such a system, moreover, may be both social and technical, 'soft' and 'hard' in its nature.

The 'soft' social/behavioural tradition

The call for a new deal

The advent of social man

Within its organizational and cultural context, scientific management, at the turn of the century, found its basis – as the gospel of efficiency – in the economic necessities of running a large-scale business.

It also secured social sanction through the belief in free and unfettered enterprise, and political sanction, in Europe and America, through the widespread concern for national productivity in a competitive market-place. The 1930s era of 'social man' was an age in which individual hopes had been dashed on the reefs of economic misfortune, and during which political beliefs were undergoing dramatic shifts. While in Europe the new socialist parties were being formed, or consolidated, in America a 'New Deal' was soon to be announced. The trigger for it was, of course, the Great Depression.

Psychological depression – the Great Crash

The Great Crash of 1929 found the winter of its discontent in earlier days. The 1920s saw a wave of business consolidations. American productive capacity began to outrun its ability to consume. A scramble for size to gain efficiencies of scale led to more consolidations. The public wanted a piece of this dynamic growth. An orgy of speculation led to Black Friday, 24 October 1929. On that day $30 billion was wiped off the market. By 1933, 30 per cent of the nation's workers were without jobs. Gone was the optimism of prosperity and promise; the old guideposts had apparently failed as 'rags to riches' became the midnight pumpkin. Perhaps it was not the economic depression but the psychological one which left the lasting imprint on our forefathers.[14]

The human problems of industrial civilization

In 1933 the Australian-born Harvard professor and social psychologist Elton Mayo published a book appropriately entitled *The Human Problems of an Industrial Civilisation*.[15] In it he vehemently rejected Taylor's 'rabble hypothesis' (see above). Rather, he lamented the passing of that form of social solidarity that characterized traditional societies, and to which Ricardo Semler poignantly alluded in the previous chapter.

The factory system and the process of industrialization, Mayo said, had destroyed this community feeling through its widespread division of labour. Increased social and physical mobility and the growth of organizations had led towards increasing impersonality. The result was growing rootlessness, loss of identity, and social discontinuity. In essence, social invention had not kept up with the technical inventions of industrial change.

The advent of the social sciences

Mayo's solution, that is his social invention, was not to abandon a scientific approach to management, but to turn it in a new direction. In fact, Mayo had himself drawn on a scientific tradition, not rooted in physical science or engineering, but in the emerging discipline of sociology. There were three 'giants of sociological theory' emerging in Europe during the latter part of the nineteenth century: the German Max Weber, the Frenchman Emile Durkheim and the Italian Vilfredo Pareto.

Durkheim divided society into two primary types, 'mechanical' and 'organic'. This typology was destined to recur at regular intervals in the evolution of management thought. Durkheim identified Adam Smith's approach, which drew on abstract market mechanisms, as mechanistic. His own approach, as a sociologist – who substituted the group for the individual as a source of values – was organic. Mayo continued where Durkheim left off, always adopting a thoroughly scientific approach to his work. In fact his best-known and epoch-making Hawthorne experiments were set up in a thoroughly scientific manner. In that methodological context, Mayo quotes – with obvious approval – a medical scientist of his immediate acquaintance, Laurence Henderson:

> In the complex business of living, as in medicine, both theory and practice are necessary conditions of understanding. First is needed, persistent, intelligent, responsible, unremitting labour in the sick room, not in the library. Second is required accurate observation of things and events, guided by judgement borne of familiarity and experience of the salient and recurrent phenomena, and their classification

and methodical exploitation. Third, is needed the construction of a theory, not a philosophical theory, but a useful walking stick to help on the way. All this may be summed up in this way. A physician (or a social scientist) must have, first, intimate, habitual, intuitive familiarity with things; secondly, systematic knowledge of things; and thirdly, an effective way of thinking about things.[16]

As a result of his systematic research at the Western Electric relay room (the Hawthorne experiments), Mayo concluded that the group rather than the individual was the fundamental building block of organizational life:

> Management in any continuously successful plant is not related to single workers, but always to working groups.[17]

The 'new administrator' that Mayo subsequently sought out would be able to restore opportunities for human collaboration in work and in life, by recognizing and then fulfilling people's need for social solidarity. Unlike the 'primal animateur', however, such a contemporary 'agent of change' would be trained for his or her role – particularly in listening and counselling skills – and, in his or her own managerial turn, would act as a skilled social scientist. For all his pioneering insight, however, Mayo was not the person to fully develop the role and operating context of this new, group-oriented administrator. That was left to his colleague at Harvard – not in fact at the Business School but in the School of Government – Mary Parker Follett, one of the few women to make their historical mark on management theory, albeit from the socio-political wings.

The new basis of managerial authority

Democracy and management

Mary Parker Follett, who rose to pre-eminence in America in the 1920s and 1930s, started out in life as a political scientist.[18] As a democrat, in the truest sense, she wanted to bring a 'new psychology of individuality-in-community' into public awareness. In that respect, Parker Follett was already sewing the seeds of a wholly developmental, as well as a 'soft' rational, orientation to management.

As a social and political analyst, moreover, Parker Follett – like Elton Mayo – focused on the power of the group. Her analysis of the group, though, is much more far-reaching than Mayo's. In fact it is so penetrating, and indeed radical for the time, that it had got substantially lost, until it was recovered initially by Pauline Graham[19] within the UK, and subsequently by the Harvard Business School.[20] Pauline Graham had been a senior manager at the John Lewis Partnership, one of the most prominent retailing and co-operative enterprises in Britain. For Parker Follett:

> By my new psychology I mean partly that group psychology which is
> receiving more attention and gaining more influence every day, and
> partly I mean simply that feeling out for a new conception of modes of
> association which we do see in law, economics, ethics, politics, and
> indeed in every department of thought. It is a short way of saying
> that we are now looking at things not as entities but in relation.[21]

Immediately we can see the broad sweep of Parker Follett's analysis, and synthesis.
She is combining psychological, social and political insight into one, grand design.
She is playing the role of a new style 'gatherer', that is coming from a conscious
and intellectual rather than from a subconscious and instinctive perspective. She
also extends her reference point, with no great difficulty, from a socio-political to a
commercial and industrial context:

> The business world is never again to be directed by individual intelli-
> gences, but by intelligences interacting and ceaselessly influencing one
> another. Every mental act of the big businessman is entirely different
> from the mental acts of the man of his predecessors, continuing to
> manage their own competitive businesses. There is of course competi-
> tion between our large firms, but the cooperation between them is
> coming to occupy a larger and larger relative place.[22]

These might have appeared to be, in the 1920s if not currently in 'the age of
business ecosystems' (see chapter 13), the words of a romantic idealist. However,
what is noteworthy is the real influence Parker Follett had on practising business
people and community leaders of her day. She had a particular affinity with a
group of business leaders and management consultants in Great Britain, of whom
Seebohm Rowntree, a captain of industry, and Lyndall Urwick, a leading business
consultant, were the most prominent. Her analysis was certainly a compelling one,
coming, as it did, in the trouble-torn years between the wars, and just before the
Great Depression. As always, she combined economics and politics with psychology and sociology.

> Our political life is stagnating, capital and labour are virtually at war,
> the nations of Europe are at each other's throats – because we have not
> yet learnt to live together. The twentieth century must find a new
> principle of association. Crowd philosophy, crowd patriotism, crowd
> government must go. The herd is no longer sufficient to enfold us.
> Group organization is to be the new method in politics, the basis of our
> future industrial system, the foundation of international order. Group
> organization will create the new world we are blindly feeling after, for
> creative force comes from the group, creative power is evolved through
> the activity of group life.[23]

The great American psychologist William James was a contemporary of Parker Follett's. While he maintained that a human being is a complex of 'many selves in one', she saw society as a complex of groups, all of which together made up a social whole. Within the group process was contained the secret of collective life, the key to democracy, the master lesson for every individual to learn, and the chief hope for the political, social and international life of the future. What, more specifically then, is this extraordinary group process, in which Mary Parker Follett had so much faith?

Follett's group process

The key to unlock Parker Follett's group process is the human craving for totality, or for wholeness. Democracy, for her, is not a spreading out and an extension of suffrage. That is merely its external aspect. It is rather a drawing together.

> It is the imperative call for the lacking part of the self. Democracy is the finding, then, of the one will to which the will of every single man and woman must contribute. We have an instinct for democracy because we have an instinct for wholeness. The human being, then, craves totality. This craving is in fact the motor of social progress. The process of getting and growing is not one of adding more and more to ourselves, but one of offering more and more of ourselves.[24]

We can see again, then, that Parker Follett is interweaving rationalism with holism and thereby serving as a key transitional influence, in leading from the one to the other. For her, therefore, contribution, not appropriation, is the law of growth. What our special contribution is, as individuals, is for each of us to discover. The definition of individuality must therefore be, finding one's place on the whole.

> One's place gives you the individual; the whole gives you the society. The connecting agency is the small, adaptable group. If I fail to make my individual contribution to the group, the whole of society suffers.[25]

As early as the 1920s, Parker Follett wrote:

> the individual is being submerged, smothered, choked by the crowd fallacy, the herd theory. Free him from these, release his energies, and he will work out, together with all other free men and women, quick, flexible, constantly changing group forms, which shall respond sensitively to every need.[26]

Parker Follett, as we have seen, had a gift with words, which was one of the reasons why she was so influential in political as well as business circles:

Imitation is for the shirkers, like mindedness for the comfort lovers, unifying for the creators. The unifying now demanded of us is that which is brought about by the enlargement of each by the inflowing of every other. Then I go forth a new creature. But to where do I go forth? Always to a new group, to a new society. There is no end to the process. A new being springs forth from every fresh contact. My nature opens up to a thousand influences. I feel continuous new births.[27]

Integration not compromise

What Parker Follett had to say, then, had very direct implications, not only at a philosophical level, but also at a practical business level. In fact the whole of 'industrial relations', as conventionally practised, cut completely across her convictions, and her understanding of constructive human behaviour. As far as Parker Follett is concerned, whoever advocates compromise – which is the stuff of everyday negotiations – abandons the individual. Individuals have to give up part of themselves in order that some action might take place. The integrity of the individual can only be preserved through integration. If you believe in compromise, you see the individual as static. So what is integration? Integration is a qualitative adjustment, whereas compromise is a quantitative one.

In the former there is a change in the ideas and their orientations; in the latter there is mere barter of opposed 'rights of way'. In a compromise situation the underlying conflict continues. Compromise, then, is on the same plane as fighting. Integration, on the other hand, involves, first, the discovery of difference, and, second, the unifying of apparent opposites. After all, we attain unity only through variety. Differences must be integrated rather than annihilated or absorbed. Every difference that is swept up into a bigger conception feeds and enriches society; every difference which is ignored feeds on society – or on a business – and eventually corrupts it. Heterogeneity, not homogeneity, makes for unity. The higher the degree of business or social organization, the more it is based on a wide variety across its members.

Friendship and sympathy

The deep and lasting friendship, therefore, is one capable of recognizing and dealing with all the fundamental differences that must exist between any two individuals, one capable therefore of such an enrichment of our personalities that together we shall mount to new heights of understanding and endeavour. Pleasant little glows of feeling can never be fanned into the fire which becomes the driving force of progress. Sympathy is a whole feeling; it is a recognition of oneness.

Suppose six manufacturers, Parker Follett asserts, meet to discuss some form of union. What these people need most is not altruistic feelings, but a consciousness of themselves as a new unit, and a realization of the needs of that unit. True sympathy, therefore, is not a vague sentiment they bring with them. It springs from their very meeting, to become, in its turn, a vital factor in the meeting.

The law of the situation

Amongst all this wealth of Parker Follett's group analysis and integration, only a very small amount has been picked up and assimilated by management posterity. I find this extraordinary, especially given Parker Follett's powers of communication during her lifetime. She was apparently able to communicate easily with business people and politicians, psychologists and community workers alike. Parker Follett evidently practised what she preached.

When I began my career as a management educator, I can clearly remember my senior colleagues mentioning Parker Follett in passing, with an intriguing mixture of superficiality and awe. The one crucial aspect of her thinking which was picked up by Peter Drucker, as documented by Wren, was her 'law of the situation'.

> In all forms of life, from interpersonal relations to the handling of interpersonal disputes, power over has to be reduced, and obedience has to be shifted to the law of the situation.[28]

The basis for such integration is what Parker Follet called a 'circular response'. By this she meant a process based on the opportunity for each party to influence the other, and through open interaction, over a period of time, 'power with' could be obtained. For labour and management it would come through an open disclosure of costs, prices and market situations, or even of profits and losses, as practised by Semler's Semco. In international diplomacy it would involve open disclosure, rather than a withholding of the facts. Parker Follett thought that 'final authority' was in fact an illusion, based on a false premise of power; authority for her accrued in the situation, not in the person or his or her position. Responsibility was inherent in the job or function, and was cumulative in the sense that it entailed a seam of responsibilities in a system of cross-relationships. For Drucker, as indeed for Jaques, such a 'law of the situation' accords very well with their position, which is that task, (rationally derived) rather than personality (primally projected), should rule the management roost.

Conclusion

The two-way stretch

In tapping the roots of rational management, and thereby uncovering its knowledge grounds, I have been necessarily selective. For the entirety of the generally acknowledged management tradition lies within this rational realm. Management historians, such as Daniel Wren, have devoted complete books to the subject, whereas I have restricted myself to a chapter. At the same time I have purposefully attempted to cover the purest 'hard' and 'soft' extremes of rational management, those of Taylor and Parker Follett. All too often, in management texts, a cluster of historical streams are presented, with inadequate reference to their very fundamental differences. On the one hand, for example, Frederick Taylor is portrayed as much more of a humanist than one might have imagined; on the other hand, Mary Parker Follett's seminal work is bypassed or substantially watered down. Equally undesirable is the tendency to stereotype management thinkers according to one's ideological preferences. In my view, both Taylor (as well as the other 'hard' rationalists such as Fayol and Chandler) and Parker Follett (and the other 'soft' rationalists such as Mayo and Likert) have had vital roles to play in the evolution of management thought and practice.

Where I agree absolutely with Parker Follett, is that if we try to hide the real differences, or select one side rather than another for ideological reasons, we will make poor theorists and bad knowledge creators. In fact, I would argue that the recurring and usually sterile debate over generalist versus specialist management is plagued by a lack of clear differences.

We management educators and consultants are usually unwilling, or unable, to provide the generalist with the kind of integrative framework he or she needs, and that Parker Follett has developed. As a result, we have nothing that genuinely contrasts with the more narrowly based but more penetratingly analytical frameworks used by the specialist. In the same way, if we put the primal operators on a pedestal, as Peters and Waterman have done, or alternatively the rational managers, as we shall see with Jaques, both will inevitably fall off. One without the other, like the soft qualities without the hard, will lose its balance.

The rational way forward

Let me now introduce you to Elliot Jaques, who has had such an all-pervasive influence on rational management, and has achieved as unique a balance between the hard and soft approaches as anyone. After we have had a chance to properly review Jaques' rationally based mainstem, we shall then move on to the vital management branches, both 'hard' and 'soft'. While the former are most formidably embodied in Jones and Womack's 'lean thinking' and Hamel and Pralahad's notion of 'core competence', we shall certainly be visting total quality management and business process re-engineering in passing. While the latter is most significantly represented by Solveig Wikstrom's *Knowledge and Value*, and by Shoshana Zuboff's 'Informating' processes, we shall be visiting quality circles and virtual organizations along the rational way.

10

REQUISITE ORGANIZATION
The mainstem of rational management

Introduction

By far the most respected of all the management gurus is the redoubtable Peter Drucker. Drucker, moreover, as a central European (northern) émigré to America (western) has strong, rationally based credentials. He has perhaps done more to advance the cause of management, as an administrative and as a social science, than anyone else this century. However, Drucker lacks a coherent theory of management and organization. In fact, his concept of management seems to have been forever changing over the course of the fifty years during which he has been writing. In fact, the management theorist who has the most consistently rationally based theory of 'requisite organization'[1] is the French Canadian Elliot Jaques.

Bureaucracy in management and organization

Requisite bureaucracy

The argument that Jaques has consistently pursued[2] over the past twenty years is that, contrary to general opinion, bureaucracies *per se* are neither centralizing nor localizing powers, neither humanizing nor dehumanizing. They are dependent instutions, social instruments, taking their initial objectives and characteristics from the associations which employ them. The bureaucracies that dehumanize are those which have outgrown their organization structure or have never had an adequate structure, or are too rigidly controlled from the centre.

Some types of structure facilitate normal relationships between individuals, making it easy for them to link into immediate social relationships, with feelings of trust and confidence. Jaques calls such structures 'requisite' or socially connecting. They are 'requisite' in the sense of being called for in the nature of things, including human nature. They are socially connecting in the sense of linking people to their society, and giving them a hold upon it.

Other types of structure make it difficult or impossible for individuals to have normal relationships of confidence or trust. They force social interactions into a mould, calling for forms of behaviour which arouse suspicion, envy, hostile rivalry and anxiety, and put breaks on social relationships. Mutually antagonistic groups and societies form. Jaques calls such institutions 'anti-requisite' or 'alienating'. They run counter to normal human nature, and split individuals off from their society. His rationally based bureaucracy is different.

Bureaucracy in industrial society

Ubiquitous organization

Until the onset of the industrial revolution, the bureaucratic hierarchy, Jaques maintains, was almost exclusively confined to the governmental and religious sectors of society. One of the outstanding features of twentieth-century industrial socities, therefore, is the concentration of nearly all the working population into employment in bureaucratic organizations for a wage or salary. There is little purpose in arguing in favour of this process of bureaucratization, according to Jaques, or even decrying it, for bureaucracy is merely the instrument of a deeper social process. The simple fact is that if we decide to proceed with the development of industrialized societies, then bureaucracies on a large scale are here to stay.

Fortunately for mankind, he says, the progress of civilization does not depend on changing the nature of people; there is more than enough goodness in human nature to make a better society possible. If further progress is to be made, it will be because of the discovery and creation of more humane institutions. The well or ill functioning of an institution is not just a matter of 'personalities'. Its primary source lies buried in the structure of the organization itself. Because, then, bureaucratic institutions are ubiquitous in industrial society, their possible organizational form is a matter of importance to the establishment of a good society. Such institutions have their characteristic role relationships.

Role and social structure

The concepts of role relationships and social structure are central to Jaques' argument. The design of institutions is the theme, and functional roles and role relationships are the building blocks of which the institutions are to be constructed. In a most general sense, a role may be defined as a knot in a social net of role relationships. A role stands not on its own feet but in relation to other roles with a connection between them. Role relationships thus constitute a field within which behaviour occurs. The persons occupying the roles are part of the total field. Roles, finally, are, firstly, noted for their detachability from the person who occupies them; secondly, they are permanent.

There are two main levels at which Jaques' concept of social structure may be used. The first level is the system of connected roles. The observable, concrete relations may be termed the surface structure. The second meaning applies to underlying systems or wholes which can give explanatory meaning to the world of observation. Unlike the pragmatically based approach to organization and management, which is focused upon personality shaping role, Jaques' rational outlook is focused on role shaping personality. Role, in its turn, is shaped by function.

Social justice and bureaucratic employment

Freedom and discretion

According to Jaques, the functioning of social institutions depends on more than having the right individuals. It is based, to begin with, on having the right social structures. As far as bureaucratic systems are concerned, then, it is impossible to describe or define what is meant by the right person, until the nature of the task has been defined, and the organization designed and constructed to enable the work to be done. Different situations therefore require different sorts of leadership.

The need for managerial leadership, of any kind, is a reflection of the fact that the employment relationship is 'requisitely' a social exchange. It is not just a matter, therefore, of the manager saying 'Do this, it's what you're paid for!' Rather, for Jaques it is requisitely a matter of his saying:

> I want this task done and I am assigning it to you; I am accountable for assessing the outcome, and for keeping a running appraisal of your competence; if you do well, I shall arrange for you to be rewarded within the limits of the resources allocated to me, and I shall also see to it that you are considered by those higher up for advancement; I believe that I will act justly towards you, but if you feel that I do not then you have access to an appeal procedure. You must finally adhere to the rules and regulations that bind us both, but within those limits you have the freedom to exercise your own discretion in carrying out tasks without undue interference from me.[3]

Employees in such a 'requisite' bureaucracy, moreover, have their rights.

The rights of the individual

There are four basic rights, according to Jaques, that must requisitely be taken for granted if bureaucracy is to be humane and creative.

They involve the right to employment and opportunity; the right to participation in the control of policy changes in the employing organization; the right to equitable reward; and the right to individual appeal against decisions which are felt to be unfair or unjust.

The technical problem of an enlightened society is to create a production technology which is not only economic but which provides a balance of work roles. These ought to be suited to the spread of talent and ability of the population at any given time. Unemployment is 'non-requisite' for the insecurity it brings, and the wastage of human capacity it entails. Requisite procedures and the avoidance of societal imbalance call for a continually bouyant economy and full employment. Socialist planning made this possible – but the cost was the loss of opportunity for individual entrepreneurial initiatives and risk. Capitalist societies gain the freedom for more or less individual enterprise, but manipulate the employment situation. The requisite solution requires getting the best of both worlds.

The functioning of bureaucratic systems

The three operational tasks

The translation of the objects of an enterprise into actual work, for Jaques, requires the assigning of specific tasks to be carried out by employees of the enterprise. Tasks that are directly concerned with the objects and operational activities of the enterprise are termed operational tasks. They can be distinguished from all other types of task concerned with supporting and facilitating the discharge of the operational tasks. These are referred to as support tasks. Operational tasks are those which constitute the content of the business transactions, both public and private. The three major operational tasks are the development of goods and services (D); provision of these (M); and their sale (S).

All three are necessary to constitute a full operational transaction. 'D' exchanges energy in the form of new knowledge and ideas; 'M' exchanges energy in the form of raw material brought in and services delivered; 'S' exchanges energy in the form of active negotiation with the client and market environment. It is essential that these systems should be organized in terms of these operational transactions.

Vertical and horizontal relationships

The widespread desire, as Jaques sees it, to get rid of the bureaucratic hierarchy because it is allegedly autocratic, finds expression, he says, in the continual search, as Parker Follett illustrated, for more 'democratic' or more 'organic' forms of work organization. Each new group structure, be it autonomous work group or matrix structure, is thereby hailed as a victory for cooperative over bureaucratic organization, signalling the imminent demise of bureaucracy.

In fact, Jaques argues, these are simply various arrangements of laterally related roles into working groups. As such they are exceedingly important in their own right, being essential components of effectively functioning bureaucratic systems. So-called functionally autonomous work groups, for example, in his terms, are stratum-1 groups of workers encouraged by their stratum-2 section manager to work together in a collateral relationship. Similarly, groups put together, in matrix fashion, for special projects form integral parts of the functioning of bureaucratic systems. Managers or co-managers remain accountable for the performance of their subordinates. Such performance varies, according to the organizational strata involved.

'Requisite' management and organization

Organizational strata

Bureaucracies are hierarchical systems, but, for Jaques, these are hierarchies with a difference. They contain a range of different levels, reflected in different levels of work. Jaques' definition of level of work is given in the form of a measuring instrument based upon the maximum time-span during which people are required to exercise discretion.

> Evidence suggests, as a first proposition, that there is a universally distributed depth structure of levels of bureaucratic organization, whereby natural lines of stratification exist at 3-month, 12-month, 2-year, 5-year, 10-year and even higher levels still.
>
> The second proposition is that the existence of the stratified depth-structure of bureaucratic hierarchies is the reflection in social organization of the existence of discontinuity and stratification in the nature of human capacity. The capacity is referred to as work-capacity, which is further analysed in terms of a person's level of abstraction. A multi-modal distribution of capacity is postulated. The third proposition is that the rate of growth of the work-capacity of individuals follows predictable paths. Maturational shifts in the quality of an individual's capacity occur as he moves across the boundary from one level of abstraction to another.[4]

Layers of complexity

What Jaques postulates, then, is the existence of a universal bureaucratic depth structure, composed of organizational strata with boundaries at levels of work represented by time-spans of 3 months to 20 years. These strata are real in the geological sense, with observable boundaries and discontinuity.

They are not mere shadings and gradations. Requisite organization of bureaucracy must be designed accordingly. In other words, strata of organization need to be built up that are 'requisite' for the complexity of the task in hand. The complexity of a task lies in the number, variety, rate of change and degree of interweaving of the variables involved in it. Jaques identifies seven such levels, or strata, of organization:

1 These are *concrete* shop or office floor-level *activities*, requiring a person to proceed along a prescribed linear path, getting continual feedback in order to do so – for example, drilling holes with a jack hammer, typing a letter.

2 These kinds of tasks are found at first line managerial level; the individual

must anticipate potential problems through *accumulating* significant *data* – for example, design a new jig for a machining process, working out the design as the job proceeds.

3   Increasingly complex situations require *alternative plans* to be constructed before starting out, one to be chosen and serially progressed to completion. This involves heading a project team, for example, to create a new software programe, having initially to select between alternatives with varying times, costs, specifications.

4   These comprise a number of *interacting programmes* which need to be planned and progressed in relation to each other. Trade-offs must be made between tasks to make progress along the composite route. New venturing, for instance, requires a combination of overlapping product development, market analysis, product engineering and commercial assessment, with mutual adjustment along the way.

5   These are the kinds of tasks faced by presidents of strategic business units in large corporations. Practical on-the-spot judgements must be used to deal with a field of *ambiguous conceptual variables*, and to make decisions envisaging second- and third-order consequences. This involves driving half a dozen critical tasks to achieve a seven-year plan, continually picking up important areas of impact and likely consequences of change, keeping profitability at a reasonable level while maintaining customer goodwill, high employee morale, and a growing asset base.

6   At this level executives must build up a picture of likely critical events worldwide. This entails international networking to accumulate information about *potentially significant developments* that could affect the business and its business units, forestalling adverse events and sustaining a friendly environment for corporate trade.

7   At this level CEO's work out *strategic alternatives for worldwide operation*, using complex conceptual information concerned with culture, values and the business of nations and international trade well into the twenty-first century.

Because, in the final analysis, each category of task complexity has a corresponding category of cognitive complexity in human beings, complexity in work can be matched with complexity in people in the same organizational layer. These propositions, then, can be applied not only to the design of organizational structure for bureaucracies but also to coping with changes in these systems induced by the developing capacities of their employees. If the propositions are valid and reliable, Jaques argues, they will show that the relationship between bureaucracy and individuality is not an unresolveable conflict to be softened by uncomfortable compromise. Rather it is a dilemma which can be dealt with by creative interaction between social institution and individual.

'Requisite' executive leadership

Effective leadership

Effective leadership for rationally minded Jaques is indistinguishable from 'requisite' management. It demands four straightforward and basic conditions.[5] First, a person must have the necessary competence to carry the particular role, including strongly valuing it. Second, that person must be free from any severely debilitating psychological characteristics that interfere with interpersonal relationships. Third, the organizational conditions must be requisite, that is conforming to the properties of hierarchical organizations and human nature. Fourth, each person must be encouraged to use his or her natural style, namely to allow the full and free expression of his or her natural self.

Powers of cognition

Central to Jaques' concept of 'requisite' management is the manager's powers of cognition. In that sense, Jaques is a direct disciple of the well-known Swiss child psychologist Jean Piaget. However, he is also concerned with values, knowledge and skill, wisdom and temperament. Ever inclined to use mathemetical formulae, Jaques proposes the following equation:[6]

CURRENT ACTUAL CAPACITY (CAC) = $f \{CP.V.K/S.Wi.(-T)\}$, where:

- CP = cognitive capacity, that is mastery of complexity
- V = values, interests, priorities
- K/S = skilled use of relevant knowledge
- Wi = wisdom about people and things
- $(-T)$ = the absence of serious personality/temperament defects

The concept of cognitive processing, for Jaques then, lies at the heart of any possibility of understanding the nature of competence at work. Cognitive processes are the mental processes by means of which a person is able to organize information to make it available for doing work. This processing enables the individual to deal with information complexity. When a person's cognitive processing is up to the complexity, he or she is comfortable. Cognitive power is the potential strength of cognitive processes in a person, and is therefore the maximum level of task complexity that someone can handle at any given point in his or her development. Just as we find that the greater a person's cognitive power the greater is the mass of information that can be coped with, so we find that the greater the person's cognitive power the longer is that person's time horizon.

Not only do cognitive processes come in greater or lesser degrees of complexity, but they proceed in discontinuous jumps. Each of these steps is characterized by a change in the very nature of the cognitive process, just as materials change in state from chrystalline to vapour as they are heated. A fundamental point is that as we mature we progress through developmental stages, moving from one type of cognitive processing to the next more complex type. But there is more to management, for Jaques, than cognition.

Values – knowledge – wisdom – temperament

Jaques' experience is that everyone will put their best effort into doing what they value. People, he says, are spontaneously energetic with respect to things that interest them. The issue is not to encourage output by incentives but to provide conditions in which the work itself has its inherent value. Such work allows the individual to release and direct his or her energy and imagination into the work.

We learn, according to Jaques, from our experience, from teaching and from practice. We store our learning in the forms of knowledge and skill in the use and application of that knowledge. By knowledge we refer to objective facts, including procedures, which can be stated in words, formulae, models or other symbols that one can learn. By 'skill' Jaques refers to the application of facts and procedures that have been learnt through practice to the point that they can be used without thinking.

Finally, action without sound theory, Jaques believes, can be counter-productive. Unsound theories distort our experience, narrow our vision, and leave us none the wiser about the effects of our actions on others. Action without sound theory is folly. Wisdom can be developed in people, especially by good mentoring by a more senior person.

For rationally minded Jaques, though, in the final analysis, focus upon personality traits is misguided. Emotional make up has little effect upon the person's in-role leadership work, unless these qualities are at unacceptable or abnormal extremes. 'Our argument is that the personality variable figures in managerial leadership in a negative rather than a positive way'.[7] Take note, within this objectively rational world view, of the mistrust of raw, subjective personality.

Many people would argue that it is precisely by understanding and attending to the special emotional needs and personality styles of each individual that a 'leader' can best motivate a follower. But that can result in the 'difficult' personalities getting special attention as compared with their more collaborative colleagues. This is not, for Jaques, what managerial hierachies should be about. Managerial hierarchies are not seller–buyer situations, nor families. It is simply not acceptable, Jaques argues, for individuals to behave in ways that are disruptive of working relationships. At the same time, people are in need of development.

Fostering the development of individuals

Mentoring and coaching

The development of individuals, then, involves taking note of the rate of growth of their potential and trying to provide work opportunities consistent with it.

Secondly, and in addition, they should be given the opportunity to consider their values, gain the necessary skilled knowledge, reinforce their wisdom, and take the necessary steps to get rid of any seriously abnormal personality quirks they might have. Mentoring, in relation to the former, is the process whereby a manager-once-removed (MoR) helps the individual understand his or her potential and how it might be applied to achieve full career and organizational growth. There are four major approaches to development.

Coaching is the process through which a manager helps subordinates to understand the full range of their roles and then points out the subordinates' strengths and weaknesses. Teaching involves the imparting of knowledge to individuals by lectures, discussion and practice. Training is a process of helping individuals to develop or enhance their skill in the use of knowledge through practice, either on the job or in a learning simulation. Developing skill enables individuals to use their knowledge in problem-solving activities without having to think, thus freeing up discretion and judgement.

Career progress and level of aspiration

Whereas an individual's aspiration towards equilibrium between work capacity and level of work is absolute, that between level of work and payment is relative. In the case of pay, each person's aspirations appear to be geared to a sense of fairness of economic reward relative to others. In the case of work, however, each person's level of aspiration is geared to his or her deepest feelings of reality and freedom.

The construction of adequate grading and progression systems, therefore, is an essential mechanism for making individual freedom real. For if an individual's level of work in time-span terms is shorter than his or her time-span capacity, the individual will be deprived of the opportunity to test his or her capacity at full stretch. He or she will therefore be unable to maintain his or her relationship with reality over as wide a spectrum as possible. Conversely, if the level of work is longer than his or her current work capacity, the person's freedom will be destroyed. His or her relationship to reality will be disorganized, and his or her deepest anxieties aroused. Notwithstanding all of this, individuals and organizations are always in a state of flux.

Conclusion

Growth of bureaucratic systems

Bureaucratic systems, for Jaques, are internally live and changing, as the occupants of the systems join, develop, change and leave. There is a continual ebb and flow, with stable periods, and critical change periods. At the same time, different parts of the system change at different rates, as do the individual members of these parts of the system.

It is precisely by identifying such differences in individuals that a society can accomplish two important social ends. First, it can arrange social procedures to make it possible for everyone to gain a level of work and career consistent with their work capacity. Second, it can bring political power and legislative control to bear to ensure that bureaucracy is managed in a manner consistent with the political outlook of the society. Thus whether or not bureaucratic organization would lead to economic elitism would be a political decision.

Size of organization, Jaques maintains, tends to be regarded as a function of size of market, the nature of the economy, the type of technology and other such external factors. They are necessary but not sufficient. For Jaques, ultimately, the distribution of sizes of bureaucracy will be determined by the distribution in level of work-capacity of those available to manage the bureaucracies. There is a kind of Archimedes principle at work whereby bureaucratic systems grow to the level of work capacity of their chief executives. Conversely, chief executives stimulate bureaucratic systems to grow to the level consistent with their work capacity. In citing the existence of up to seven strata of organization, preconditioned by executive work capacity, Jaques is following in the structural footsteps of Piaget.

Evolving strata of organization

As the strata of operation ascend, from the concreteness of the operational world to the abstraction of general management, the total field is available now to the manager only in conceptual form. It appears

> in histograms of performance, drawings of product families and other such conceptual models. He must now have that sense of security in his abilities to let go to some extent of the concrete outside world, and to rely upon an interplay between data of immediate experience and data culled from mental constructs. The manager or administrator must learn how to work from an office, not in complete detachment but with sufficiently frequent contact with the various parts of his domain to keep lively examples in mind of the activity of the situation he is dealing with in abstracto.[8]

Elliot Jaques, in the final analysis, stands firmly on the foundations of French structural functionalism. Within his general theory of bureaucracy he is pursuing the 'quest for mind', that perennial concern of the rationalist philosophers, in an organizational context. In so doing he takes bureaucracy out of its mechanistic confines, and gives it an organic facelift. He also, with his developmental outlook on organizational strata, moves the managerial debate towards the developmental orientation, to which we shall turn in chapter 14. Before then, however, we need to review the rationally based branches, and fruits, both 'hard' and 'soft'.

11

CORE COMPETENCE AND CHANGE MANAGEMENT

The rational management branches

Introduction

Rational approaches to management, as you would expect, continue to proliferate in the halls of business academia. However, whereas when I did my MBA at Harvard in the late 1960s, long-range planning and human behaviour in organizations appealed most particularly to my rationally oriented mind, towards the turn of this century the intellectual ground has shifted: concepts of 'core competence' and 'strategic intent', on the one hand, and those of 'informating organizations' and 'value networks', on the other, have taken on from where traditionally oriented corporate strategy and organizational behaviour have left off.

Similarly, amongst practical managers, whereas in the 1960s and 1970s, such functional areas as operations and marketing, financial and human-resource management were uppermost in their minds, in the 1980s and 1990s the ground has shifted towards total quality (TQ), business process re-engineering (BPR) and lean production, on the one hand, and towards quality circles, 'informated' systems or virtual organizations on the other. Such a reorientation represents a modern-day reinterpretation of what people such as Frederick Taylor and Mary Parker Follett had to say to us at the beginning of the twentieth century. I shall start then by reviewing the 'hard' rational branches, incorporating TQ, BPR, lean production and strategic intent. I shall then turn over to the 'soft' branches, that is to quality circles, informated systems and virtual organizations. We shall start with that evergreen, total quality management.

The 'hard' rational branches

From scientific management to total quality

TQ is to the second half of the twentieth century, in many ways, what 'scientific management' was to the first half.

That might seem an odd thing to say, given the supposedly rounded nature of the total quality orientation. In fact the overall quality movement stems from a very broad church, to some of whom we shall be paying homage when we come to consider the 'soft' branches of rational management.

However, the strongest influence on TQ, which has since given rise to so-called 'BS5750' or 'ISO9000' administrative quality standards around the world, has been America's Philip Crosby. For Crosby, the American TQ guru, 'quality means conformance to standards'.[1] To serve such a purpose, he established a quality improvement programme, involving 14 elements:

- *Management commitment* – helping management to recognize they must be personally committed to raising the level of visibility for quality
- installing a *quality improvement team* – the tools to do the job are brought together in one team
- instituting *quality measurement* – formalizing the measurement system strengthens the inspection and test function
- *Cost of quality evaluation* – a measurement of quality management performance is established
- fostering *quality awareness* – communications get employees in the habit of talking positively about quality
- taking *corrective action* – the habit of identifying problems and correcting them is beginning
- implementing a *zero defects programme* – preparing for implementation ensures the goals of the programme will be supported
- undertaking *supervisor training* – a formal orientation with all levels of management prior to implementation
- regularizing a *zero defects day* – making a 'day' of ZD commitment provides an emphasis and a long-lasting memory
- *Goal setting* – helps teams to learn to think in terms of meeting goals and accomplishing specific tasks
- *Error cause removal* – people know that their problems can be heard and answered
- *Recognition* – genuine recognition of performance is something people really appreciate
- *Quality councils* – these councils are the best source of information on the status of the programme
- and finally, do it over again – *repetition* makes the programme perpetual, and it thereby becomes ingrained into the organization

Such an overall TQ approach is accompanied by a raft of rationally based techniques ranging from methods of statistically based quality control, to so-called 'fishbone' diagrams, Pareto curves and so on, as can be seen in Table 11.1.

Frederick Taylor, in fact, would be delighted with what his successors have come up with, half a century after he departed from the scene. However, during the course of the 1990s, even TQ has been overtaken by another, modern-day variation on the Taylorite theme, that is 'business process re-engineering'.

Table 11.1 Total quality management techniques

Elementary statistical methods
1 Pareto chart
2 Cause-and-effect diagram
3 Stratification
4 Check sheet
5 Histogram
6 Scatter diagram
7 Graph and control chart

Intermediate methods
1 Theory of sampling surveys
2 Statistical sampling inspection
3 Methods of making statisitcal estimates and tests
4 Methods of utilizing sensory tests
5 Methods of design of experiments

Advanced methods
1 Advanced methods of design experiments
2 Multivariate analysis
3 Methods of operations research

From total quality to business process re-engineering

BPR, so-called, is in fact a 'western' reinterpretation of the 'eastern' process-oriented *kaizen* (continuous improvement) approach. One of the leading proponents of *Kaizen*, Japan's Massaki Imai, has argued:

> If asked to name the most important difference between Japanese and Western management concepts, I would unhesitatingly say Kaizen and its process way of thinking versus the West's innovation and results oriented thinking.[2]

Whereas in the west, then, for Imai, cross-functional problems are often seen in terms of conflict resolution between, say, production and marketing or sales and accounting, *Kaizen* strategy has enabled Japanese management to take a systematic and collaborative approach to cross-functional problem solving. In fact such *Kaizen* is an umbrella concept to cover a range of typically Japanese measures all coming under the banner of 'process thinking'. These include just-in-time, productivity and quality improvements, and a zero defects orientation.

Business process re-engineering, at face value, is the western counterpart to *Kaizen*, whereby 'processes' supplant functions, and a horizontal customer-facing orientation transcends a vertical, silo-laden mentality. Ostensibly, it represents the antithesis of what Adam Smith and Frederck Taylor, between them, had to say about the organization of work. For the two American re-engineering gurus Hammer and Champy, therefore:

The core message is this. It is no longer necessary or desirable for companies to organize their work around Adam Smith's division of labour. Task oriented jobs in today's world of customers, competition, and change are obsolete. Instead, companies must organize around the process . . . We define a business process as a collection of activities that takes one or more kind of input and creates an output that is of value to the customer. Reengineering must therefore focus on redesigning a fundamental business process, not on departments or other organizational units . . . Adam Smith argued that people work most efficiently when they have only one easily understood task to perform.

Simple tasks, though, demand complex processes to knit them all together, and for two hundred years companies have accepted the inconvenience, inefficiencies, and costs associated with complex processes in order to reap the benefits of simple tasks. In reengineering we stand the industrial model on its head. We say that in order to meet the contemporary demands of quality, service, flexibility and low cost, processes must be kept simple. This need for simplicity has enormous consequences for how processes are designed and organizations shaped.[3]

In effect, BPR has promised much, shifting the emphasis from rigid and sharply differentiated structures to flexible and loosely connected processes. The trouble is, all too often though, the same 'keep-it-simple' north-western mind-set is employed to turn the old function into a new process, so that the one becomes little different from the other. For a more authentic, perhaps 'northern', interpretation of the Japanese way, we turn to James Womack and Dan Jones, famed for their book that shocked the American motor industry. Substantively based on Honda, Nissan and Toyota, it was called *The Machine that Changed the World*.[4] Their more recent work, *Lean Thinking: Banish Waste and Create Wealth in your Organization*,[5] extends the message they have been conveying to the manufacturing and distribution industries around the world. The core concept they draw on is that of *muda*.

From BPR to lean thinking

Dealing with muda

Muda in Japanese means 'waste', specifically any human activity which absorbs resources but creates no value: mistakes which require rectification, production of items no one wants so that inventories and remaindered goods pile up, processing steps which are not actually needed, movement of employees and transport of goods from one place to another without any purpose, groups of people in a downstream activity standing around waiting because an upstream activity has not delivered on time, and goods and services which do not meet the needs of the customer.

In short, lean thinking is 'lean' because it provides a way to do more with less.

And in striking contrast – in Womack and Jones' view – with what they consider to be the recent craze for process re-engineering, it provides a way to create new work rather than simply destroying jobs in the name of efficiency.

The immediate needs of the shareholder and the financial mind-set of the senior managers, for Womack and Jones, have taken precedence over the day-to-day realities of specifying and creating value for the customer. These are conventionally inhibited by *muda*:

> The value stream is the set of all the specific actions required to bring a specific product (whether a good, a service, or increasingly a combination of the two) through the three critical management tasks of any business: the *problem solving* task running from concept through detailed design and engineering to production launch, the *information management* task running from order taking to detailed scheduling to delivery, and the *physical transformation* task proceeding from raw material to finished product in the hands of the consumer . . . almost always exposes enormous, indeed staggering amounts of 'muda'.[6]

Once value has been precisely specified, the two authors maintain, the remaining value-creating steps flow. Things work better, moreover, when you focus on the product and its needs, rather than the organization or the equipment, so that all activities needed to design, order and provide a product occur in continuous flow. The most obvious problem, though, is that flow thinking is counter-intuitive. Re-engineers, as a result, have not gone far enough conceptually. In other words, they are still dealing with disconnected and aggregated nominal 'processes' rather than with the entire flow of value-creating activities for specific products. In addition, Womack and Jones lament, they often stop at the boundaries of the firm paying the fees, rather than looking at the entire value stream.

The lean alternative is to redefine the work of functions, departments and firms so that they can make a positive contribution to value creation, and to speak to the real needs of employees at every point along the stream so it is actually in their interest to make value flow. When you make what the customer wants, when they want it, you can throw away the sales forecast and simply make what the customer actually needs. You can let the customer pull products from you rather than push them, often unwanted, onto them. As organizations begin to accurately specify value, identify the entire value stream, make the value-creating steps for specific products flow continuously, let customer pull value from the enterprise, it seems that something very odd begins to happen. It dawns on those involved that there is no end to the process of reducing effort, time, space, cost and mistakes while offering a product which is ever more nearly what the customer actually wants.

> Conventional wisdom on economic growth focussed on the new technologies, and on training people for them. But most of the world, at any one time, is a brownfield of traditional activities performed in traditional

ways. New technologies and augmented human growth may generate growth over the long term, but only lean thinking has the demonstrated power to produce green shoots of growth all across the landscape within a few years.[7]

The steps to lean production

OFFERING VALUE

Why is it so hard to start at the right place, to correctly define value? Partly, our two authors maintain, because most producers want to make what they are already making, and partly because many customers only know how to ask for some variant of what they are already getting. They simply start in the wrong place and end up at the wrong destination.

Then, when providers or customers do decide to rethink value, they often fall back on simple formulae – lower cost, increased product variety through customization, instant delivery – rather than jointly analysing value and challenging old definitions to see what's really needed.

THE VALUE STREAM

To identify a value stream, you need to map out every action required to design, order and make a specific product and sort these into three categories: (1) those which actually create value as perceived by the customer; (2) those which create no value but are currently required by the product-development, order-filling, or production systems; (3) those actions which do not create value as perceived by the customer and which can be eliminated immediately.

MAKING VALUE FLOW

How do you make value flow? The first step for Womack and Jones, once value is defined and the entire value system is identified, is to focus on the actual object – the specific design, the specific order, and the product itself – and never let it out of sight from beginning to completion. The second step, which makes the first step possible, is to ignore the traditional boundaries of jobs, careers, functions and firms to form a lean enterprise removing all impediments to the continuous flow of the product or the product family. The third step is to rethink specific work practices and tools to eliminate backflows, scrap, and stoppages of all kinds so that the design, order, and production of the specific product can proceed continuously. The lean enterprise, moreover, groups the product manager, the parts buyer, the manufacturing engineer and the production scheduler in the team area immediately next to the actual production equipment and in close contact with the product and the tool engineers in the nearby design area dedicated to that product family.

The old-fashioned and destructive distinction between the office (where people work with their minds) and the plant (where people work with their hands) is eliminated.

> We're often struck that in the old world of mass production, the factory workforce really had no need to talk to each other. The isolated workers simply donned their ear protection and shut out the world. In the lean enterprise, however, the workforce on the plant floor need to constantly talk to solve production problems and implement improvements in the process. What's more they need to have their professional staff right by their side and everyone needs to see the status of the entire production system.[8]

To get continuous-flow systems to flow, every machine and every worker must be completely 'capable'. This means that the production team must be cross-skilled in every task. Employees and machines must also be taught to monitor their own work through *poka-yoke* or mistake proofing. Everyone involved must be able to see and understand every aspect of the operation and its status at all times. The end objective of flow thinking is to totally eliminate all stoppages in an entire production process and not to rest in the area of tool design until this has been achieved. To achieve this good, the work in each step is very carefully balanced with the work in every other step so that everyone is working to the same cycle time.

THE 'PULL' FACTOR

Pull, in its simplest terms, for Womack and Jones, means that no one upstream should produce a good or service until the customer downstream asks for it. At every step they have noted, in a 'lean production' context, the need for managers to see the value stream, to see the flow of value, to see value being pulled by the customer. The final form of seeing, moreover, is to bring perfection into clear view so the objective of improvement is visible and real to the whole enterpise.

A channel for the stream – a valley for the channel

For Womack and Jones, then, as lean enterprises are created to channel the value stream, it becomes apparent that the traditional functions should not perform most of their traditional tasks. Engineering, for example, should not engineer, in the sense of performing routine engineering on a product. Quality should not conduct detailed audits. These are all tasks for dedicated product teams, dealing with issues of the present. What functions should do is think about the future. Product engineering should work on new technologies that will permit products to do new things for the user and develop new methods and materials. Purchasing should identify the suppliers the firm will work with over the long term. Every function should provide a 'home' to employees with a given technical specialization, including production workers, to systematize current knowledge and teach it. The functions' other job would be to search for new knowledge and summarize it in a form that could be taught.

> We can now think of functions as the hills and mountains forming the valley for the value stream. Their knowledge washes down to those working alongside the stream to create value and speed its flow. If functions then create a valley for the stream flowing past and through many firms, what purpose does the firm itself serve? Firms provide the link between streams. They are the means of crossing from one valley to the next in order to make maximum use of the technologies and capabilities accumulated by each of the firm's technical functions. They also provide the means of shifting resources from value streams that no longer need them to other streams that do. From this it follows that most firms will want to participate in multiple value streams.[9]

Therefore, the great challenge for westerners, Womack and Jones maintain, is to overcome their 'every firm for itself' individualism in which each organization along the value stream optimizes its own stretch while suboptimizing the whole. This tendency of Anglo-Saxon management is exacerbated by the industrial finance system, which asks each firm to optimize its short-term performance but ignores the value of the whole.

For no shares of a whole value stream are traded in the market. The solution, Womack and Jones believe, lies with management, working together with other firms. The German challenge, moreover, for our two authors, is in many ways the reverse of the Anglo-Saxon one. The idea of cooperation between assembler and supplier is well established and the industrial finance system understands and encourages this. However, workers in German firms show a clear discomfort with horizontal teamwork of the sort needed to operate lean enterprises. Lean production supplants the traditional *Meister* hierarchy of command. The Japanese challenge, finally, is quite different. What is seemingly most problematic is the role of vertical functions – which accumulate knowledge, teach it, and push it ahead – in a society based on horizontal levelling. What is also problematic is the relocation of production near to the customer in a society which very much wants to stay at home.

From lean thinking to core competence

From re-engineering to strategic intent

Whereas Womack and Jones have focused on the internal environment of a business and its associated enterprises, Gary Hamel at the London Business School and C.K. Pralahad at Michigan Sate University have oriented themselves towards the business in its external environment. Moreover, unlike Michael Porter, for whom outward-looking competitive strategy is key, for Hamel and Pralahad,[10] inward-looking core competence is central to their strategic argument. For these two authors, in fact, any company that succeeds in restructuring and re-engineering, but fails to create the markets of the future, will find itself on a treadmill, trying to keep one step head of the steadily declining margins and profits of yesterday's businesses.

> Reengineering aims to root out needless work and get every process in the company pointed in the direction of customer satisfaction, reduced cycle time, and total quality. The difference between this twenty-first century Taylorism and the original is that now companies are asking employees, rather than 'experts', to redesign processes and workflows. Interestingly enough, though it is the ostensible goal of reengineering to focus each and every process on customer satisfaction, it is almost always the promise of reduced costs rather than heightened customer satisfaction, that convinces a top team to sign up for a reengineering project. Far from being a tribute to senior management's steely resolve or far-sightedness, a large restructuring and reengineering charge is the penalty that a company must pay for not having anticipated the future.[11]

It is entirely possible, Hamel and Pralahad say, for a company to downsize and to re-engineer without ever confronting the need to regenerate its core strategy, without ever being forced to rethink the boundaries of its industry, without ever having to think what customers might want in ten years' time, and without ever having to redefine its 'served market'. No company, they believe, can escape the need to reskill its people, reshape its product portfolio, redesign its processes, and redirect resources.

> However lean and fit an organization, it still needs a brain. But the brain we have in mind is not the brain of the CEO or strategic planner. Instead it is an amalgamation of the collective intelligence and imagination of managers and employees throughout the company who must possess an enlarged view of what it means to be 'strategic'. In business, as in art, what distinguishes leaders from laggards, and greatness from mediocrity, is the ability to uniquely imagine what could be.[12]

Strategic intent

Strategic intent aims at establishing the company as the intellectual leader in an industry, in terms of influence over the direction and shape of that industry's transformation. Such strategic intent helps managers answer three critical questions.

First, what new types of customer should we seek to supply in 5, 10, or 15 years?

Second, what new competencies should we seek to build or acquire to offer these benefits to customers? And third, how will we need to reconfigure the customer interface over the next several years?

That intent, moreover, and the accompanying strategic architecture, must be grounded in a deep understanding of potential discontinuities, competitor intentions and evolving customer needs. At the same time, it should represent an ambition that stretches far beyond the current resources and capabilities of the firm. When what is feasible drives out what is desirable, an ambitious strategic intent becomes impossible. Such intent must take precedence, furthermore, over the *realpolitik* of planning. Thus, Hamel and Pralahad argue, we need a view of strategy as stretch as well as fit. They believe that what is needed to close the gap between aspirations and resources is leveraging resources, rather than downsizing. This brings them onto 'core competence'.

From strategic intent to core competence

BUILDING WORLD LEADERSHIP

It is, for Hamel and Pralahad, the simple desire to build world leadership in the provision of a key customer benefit, and the imagination to envision the many ways in which that benefit can be delivered to customers, that drives the competence-building process. Clearly the competencies that are most valuable are those that represent a gateway to a wide variety of potential product markets. To take a financial analogy, investing in core competence leadership is like investing in options. Such a leader possesses an option on participation in the range of end-product markets that rely on that core competence. Sony's unrelenting pursuit of leadership in miniaturization, for example, has given it access to a broad array of personal audio products.

HIERARCHY OF COMPETENCE

A core competence, then, is a bundle of skills and technologies that enables a company to provide a particular benefit to customers. At Federal Express, for instance, the benefit is on-time delivery and the core competence, at a very high level, is logistics management. Because competence building represents more cumulative learning than leaps of inventiveness, it is difficult to 'time-compress'. Product cycles may be getting shorter, but the quest for core-competence leadership is still more likely to be measured in years than in months. A core competence, then, represents the sum of learning across individual skill sets and organizational units, that is a hierarchy of competencies. In the Fedex case, these descend from meta-competencies (logistics) to core competencies (package trading) to constituent skills (bar coding). A multitude of dangers await a company, Hamel and Pralahad maintain, that cannot conceive of itself and its competitors in core-comptence terms. First there is the risk that opportunties for growth will be needlessly truncated. Second, in few companies are there any explicit mechanisms for ensuring that the best talent gets aligned behind the most attractive opportunities. Third, as a company divisionalizes and fractures into ever smaller business units, competencies may become fragmented and weakened. Fourth, the lack of a core-competence perspective can also desensitize a company to its growing dependence on outside suppliers of core products. Fifth, a company focused only on end products may fail to invest adequately in new core competencies that can propel growth in the future. Sixth, a company that fails to understand the core-competence basis for competition in its industry may be surprised by new entrants who rely on competencies developed in other end markets. And seventh, companies insensitive to the issue of core competence may unwittingly relinquish valuable skills when they divest themselves of an underperforming business.

Consistency of competent effort

Given that it may take five, ten or more years to build world leadership in a core-competence area, for Hamel and Pralahad consistency of effort is key. Consistency depends first on a deep consensus about which competence to build and support and, second, on the stability of the management teams charged with competence development. The goal is to develop a group of people who see themselves as corporate resources, and whose first loyalty is to the integrity of the company's core competences rather than to any single business unit. The goal is not to 'hardwire' the core competences into the organization through structural changes, but to 'softwire' the perspective into the heads of every manager and employee, building a community of people within the organization who view themselves as carriers of corporate core competences. We now turn from the 'hard' to the 'soft' rational branches and, to begin with, from total quality to quality circles.

The 'soft' rational branches

From social science to quality circles

The father of total quality in America after the war was not Philip Crosby but W. Edwards Deming. Yet, as is now well known, for many years Deming's work was followed in Japan and ignored in his home country. For Deming was too much of a holist for the American scientific management establishment. From the 1980s onwards, however, armed now with his Japanese successes, he became a prophet in his own land. What, then, is the cause for which he has become such a veritable champion?

Deming was alarmed by the devastating effect on people of the annual appraisal of performance, the futility of management by numbers or by objectives.[13] For such a results orientation, Deming lamented, takes account of just numbers, not quality or methods. For Deming, a company's role was not to make money but to

provide jobs through innovation, research, constant improvement and maintenance. People are eager to do a good job, Deming maintained, and are distressed
when they cannot, so that barriers to doing a good job must be removed. It is
necessary, he said, for better quality and productivity, that people feel secure. Both
managers and workers will need to be educated in the new methods, including
statistical techniques and teamwork, so as to secure their long-term futures.
Whereas the focus on statistical methods led towards quality control, the focus
on teamwork led towards the concept of 'quality circles'.

Japan's Kaoru Ishikawa was a leading light, in the sort of quality-oriented
context established by Deming, in the introduction of so-called quality circles.
Their purpose, for Ishikawa, was to:

> Contribute to the improvement and development of the enterprise;
> respect humanity and build a worthwhile and happy workshop; display
> human capabilities fully, and eventually draw out infinite possibilities.[14]

Quality circles arose in Japan following the Second World War. To win for their
exports a better reputation in the world market, the Japanese focused on quality.
With the help of Deming in the early 1950s, the Japanese began by first implementing statistical quality control, then by expanding the responsibility for control
of quality throughout the company.

In 1961, Kaoru Ishikawa, then an engineering professor at Tokyo University,
with the backing of the Japanese Union of Scientists and Engineers, suggested that
small groups of workers be formed to address problems in their respective work
areas. Ishikawa drew on many of the American organizational and behavioural
specialists, including Maslow and Herzberg, whose writings were already well
known in Japan. He was also influenced by the Japanese tradition of interdependence that had derived from their limited space and from their rice-farming
technology. The collective goals that Ishikawa established for Japanese quality
circles were as follows (emphasis added):

1 to contribute to the improvement and *development* of the enterprise
2 to respect *humanity* and build a worthwhile, lively, happy and bright workshop
3 to display human *capabilities* fully and eventually draw out infinite possibilities

Whereas Ishikawa was writing in the 1960s and 1970s, and no end of theory, and
also practice, has since emerged in such related areas as participative management, self-managed teams, and overall empowerment, I have chosen to focus in
this text on two of the 'farther reaches' of the 'soft' rational branches. Whereas the
first is focused upon the emerging virtual organization, the second is oriented
towards the 'informated' one. Interestingly enough, both major exponents of the
'soft' rational approach are women. Solveig Wikstrom is a Fin, based at the
University of Stockholm, and working with her Swedish associate Richard
Normann; Shoshana Zuboff is based at the Harvard Business School. We start

with Zuboff's so-called 'informed organization', which in this informed sense takes over from where quality circles leave off.

From quality circles to informated organization

From craftwork to scientific management

Shoshana Zuboff subtly traces a path from the 'soft' primal world of the craftsperson, through the 'hard' rationality of scientific management up to the 'soft' rationality of her informated organization. Specifically, then, she says, the work of the skilled craftsperson may not have been 'intellectual', but it was knowledgeable. These nineteenth-century workers participated in a form of knowledge that had always defined the activity of making things. It was knowledge, she says, that accrues to the sentient body in the course of its activity; knowledge inscribed in the labouring body – in hands, fingertips, wrists, nose, eyes, ear, skin, muscles, shoulders, arms and legs – as surely as it was inscribed in the brain. It was knowledge filled with intimate detail of material and ambiance – the colour and consistency of metal as it was thrust into the blazing fire, the smooth finish of clay as it gave up its moisture. These details were known, though in the practical action of production work they were rarely made explicit. Few of those who had the knowledge were able to explain, rationalize or articulate it. Such 'tacit' knowledge – as Nonaka and Takeuchi intimate in chapter 18 – was acquired through observation, imitation and action more than it was taught, reflected upon or verbalized.

The agenda for scientific management, though, was to increase 'explicit' productivity by streamlining and rationalizing factory production from cost accounting and supervision to the dullest job on the shop floor. Efficiency was the mania, according to Zuboff, and to achieve efficiency it would be necessary to penetrate the labour process and force it to yield up its secrets. In order to rationalize effort, workers' skills had therefore to be made more explicit. In many cases skills did not yield themselves easily to explication; they were embedded in the ways of the body, in the knocks and know-how of the craft worker.

Instead, then, of depending upon judgement, scientific management depends upon knowledge in its task of administration. Judgement is the instinctive and subconscious association of impressions derived from previous experience. But even the best judgement falls short of knowledge. This knowledge, for the scientific manager, is carefully and systematically collected and the data thus obtained are classified and digested until the knowledge is instantly available whenever a problem is presented to management. Behind the form of the organization is a knowledge of the needs and the work of the plant. Behind the plan of wage payment is a knowledge of psychology and sociology. Behind the instruction sheet is a knowledge of the sciences of cutting metals and of handling work. And now we come to the nub of the matter as far as Zuboff is concerned:

By redefining the grounds of knowledge from which competent behaviour is derived, new information technology lifts skill from its historical
dependence upon a labouring sentient body. While it is true that
computer based automation continues to displace the human body
and its know-how (a process that has come to be known as deskilling)
the informating power of the technology simultaneously creates pressure for a profound reskilling.[15]

From scientific management to informated work

For workers it was as if their jobs had vanished in a two dimensional space of
abstractions, where digital signals replace a concrete reality. As the medium of
knowledge was transformed by computerization, the placid unity of experience
and knowledge was disturbed. Accomplishing work depended upon the ability to
manipulate symbolic, electronically presented data. Instead of using their bodies
as instruments to act on equipment and materials, the task relationship became
mediated by the information system. According to a pulping manager:

> With the evolution of computer technology you centralize controls and
> move away from the actual physical process. If you don't have an
> understanding of what is happening and how all the pieces interact it
> is more difficult. You need a new learning capability because when you
> operate with the computer you can't see what is happening. There is a
> difference in the mental and conceptual capabilities that you need – you
> have to do things in your mind. You have to be able to imagine things
> that you have never seen, to visualize them. For example, when you see
> a dash on the screen you need to be able to relate that to a 35 foot
> square by 25 foot high room full of pulp. It has a lot to do with
> creativity and the freedom to fantasize.[16]

Developing intellective skills

Information Technology (IT) combines abstraction, explicit inference and proce-
dural reasoning. Taken together these elements make possible a new set of competencies that Zuboff calls 'intellective skills'. At this level, the problem was not only to
clarify the significance of individual data elements, but also to construct from those
elements, and particularly from their combinations, an interpretation of abstract
properties of the production process. Instead of a problem of correspondence, the
data now presented an opportunity for insight into functional relationships, states,
conditions, trends, likely developments and underlying causes, none of which can be
reduced to a concrete, external referent. For an 'informated' banker, then:

> To navigate in the database you need a conceptual model of the
> business, the data, the logic. Users have to define their conceptual

211

model of the bank, to make the model in their heads explicit. For the first time they will need to know the meaning of their work. The new technology makes you look at the whole.[17]

In an informated environment, therefore, the electronic text displays the organization's work in a new way. Much of the information and know-how that was private becomes public. Personal sources of advantage depend less upon maintaining earlier forms of private knowledge than upon developing mastery in the interpreting and using of the public electronic text.

Communicative competence, then, for Zuboff, requires psychological individuation, which introduces a new sense of mutuality and equality into group life. To the extent that technology is used only to intensify the automaticity of work, it can reduce skill levels and dampen the urge towards more participatory forms of management. In contrast, an approach that emphasizes its informating capacity uses the new technology to increase the intellectual content of work at every organizational level, challenging the distinction between mental and manual work.

> Intelligent technology, then, textualizes the production process. When that text is made accessible to the operators, the essential logic of Taylorism is undermined. For the first time, technology returns to the workers what it took away – but with a crucial difference. The worker's knowledge had been implicit in action. The informating process makes that knowledge explicit: it holds up a mirror to the worker, reflecting what was known but now in a precise and detailed form. Intellective skill becomes the means to engage in the kind of learning process that can transform data into meaningful information and, finally, into insight.[18]

Automation for Zuboff preserves what is already known and assumes that it knows best. It treats as negligible the potential value to be added from learning that occurs in the living situation. The informating process takes learning as its pivotal experience. Its objective is to achieve the value that can be added from learning in the situation. Informating assumes that making the organization more transparent will evoke valuable communal insight. From this perspective, learning is never complete, as new data, new events, or new contexts create opportunities for additional improvement, insight and innovation.

From drivers of people to drivers of learning

In a traditional system, managers are drivers of people. You focus on driving people to work as hard as possible. With our new technology environment, Zuboff maintains, managers should be drivers of learning.

Learning requires a learning environment if it is to be nurtured as a core organizational process. Based on what Zuboff has seen of life at the data interface, a learning environment would encourage questions and dialogue. It would support shared knowledge and collegial relationships. It would encourage play and experimentation as it acknowledged the intimate linkages between the abstraction of the work and the requirements for social interchange, intellectual exploration and heightened responsibility.

The traditional system of imperative control, which was designed to maximize the relationship between command and obedience, depended on restricted hierarchical access to knowledge, and nurtured the belief that those who were excluded from the organization's explicit knowledge base were intrinsically less capable of learning what it had to offer. In contrast, an informated organization is structured to promote the possibility of useful learning among all members and thus presupposes relations of equality. However, this does not assume that all members are considered to be identical. Rather, the organization legitimates each member's right to learn as much as his or her temperament and talent will allow. The new division of learning, for Zuboff, produces experiences that encourage a synthesis of members' interests, and the flow of value-adding knowledge helps legitimate the organization as a learning community.

Such a new division of learning, moreover, requires another vocabulary, one of colleagues and co-learners, of exploration, experimentation and innnovation. Jobs are comprehensive, tasks are abstractions that depend on insight and synthesis, and power is a roving force that comes to rest as dictated by function and need. The contemporary language of work is inadequate to express these new realities.

> We remain, in the final years of the twentieth century, prisoners of a vocabulary in which managers require employees, superiors have subordinates, jobs are defined to be specific, detailed, narrow and task related, and organizations have levels that in turn make possible chains of command and spans of control. The guiding metaphors are military.[19]

The informated organization therefore is a learning institution, and one of its principle purposes is the expansion of knowledge, not knowledge for its own sake (as an academic pursuit) but knowledge that comes to reside at the core of what it means to be productive. Learning, Zuboff emphasizes, is not something that requires time out from being engaged in productive activity, learning is the heart of productive activity, it is the new form of labour. As the intellective skill base then becomes the organization's most precious resource, managerial roles must function to enhance its quality.

The concentric organization

Members can be thought of as being arrayed in concentric circles around a central core, which is the electronic database. Because intellective skill is relevant to the work of each ring of responsibility, the skills of those who manage daily operations

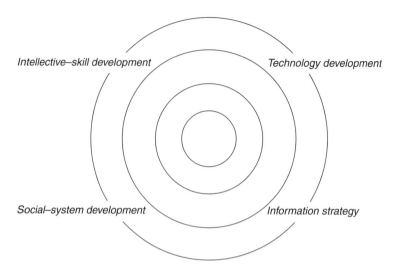

Figure 11.1 The concentric organization

form an appropriate basis for their progression into roles with more comprehensive responsibilities. The activities arrayed on the responsibility rings at a greater distance from the core include at least four realms of managerial activity – intellective-skill development, technology development, information strategy and social-system development (see Figure 11.1). This means that some organizational members will be involved in both higher order analysis and conceptualization, as well as in promoting learning and skill development among those with operational responsibility. Their aim is to expand the knowledge base and to improve the effectiveness with which data is assimilated, interpreted and responded to. They have a central role in creating an organizational environment that invites learning.

As such they help those in other managerial domains to develop their talents as educators and learners. Learning, moreover, increases the pace of change. For an organization to pursue an informating strategy it must maximize its own ability to learn and explore the implications of that learning for its long range plans with respect to markets, product development and new sources of comparative advantage. Some members will need to guide and coordinate learning efforts in order to lead an assessment of strategic alternatives and to focus organizational intelligence in areas of strategic value. The increased time horizons of these managers' responsibilities provides the reflective distance which they need in order to be able to gauge the quality of the learners' environment and guide change that would improve collective learning.

The skills that are acquired at the data interface nearest to the core of daily operating responsibilities provide a coherent basis for the kind of continual learning that would prepare people for increasingly comprehensive responsibilities. The relative homogeneity of the total organizational skill base suggests a vision of organizational membership that resembles the trajectory of a professional career, rather than the two-class system marked by an insurmountable gulf between workers and managers. The interpenetration between rings provides a key source of organizational integration.

In a conventional organization a manager's action-centred skills are shaped by the demands of achieving smooth operations and personal success under conditions of hierarchical authority. In an informating strategy the relationships to be managed are both more intricate and more dynamic than earlier patterns. The shape and quality of relationships will vary in relation to what people know, what they feel, and what the task at hand requires. Relationships will need to be fashioned and refashioned as part of the dynamism of the social process, like enquiry and dialogue that mediate learning.

Such relationships are more intricate, moreover, because their character derives from the specifics of the situation that are always both pragmatic – what it takes to get the work done best – and psychological – what people need to maintain motivation and commitment. The abstract precincts of the data interface heighten the need for communication. Interpretive processes depend on creating and sharing meaning through enquiry and dialogue. New sources of personal influence are associated with the ability to learn and to engender learning in others, in contrast to an earlier emphasis upon contractual relationships or the authority derived from function and position.

Social-system development

The demands of managing intricate relationships reintroduce the importance of the sentient body, for Zuboff, and so provide a counterpoint to the threat of hyperationalism and impersonalization that is imposed by computer mediation. The body now functions as the scene of human feeling rather than as the source of physical energy or as an instrument of political influence. Human feelings operate here in two ways. First, as members engage in their work together, their feelings are an important source of data from which intricate relations are structured.

Second, a manager's felt sense of the group and its learning needs is a vital source of personal knowledge that informs the development of new action-centred skills to foster the formation of relationships. In a traditional approach to work organization, employees could be treated as objectively measurable bodies, and, in return, they gave of their labour without giving of themselves. But when work involves a collective effort to create and communicate meaning, how people feel about themselves, each other and the organization's purposes is closely linked to their capacity to sustain the high levels of internal commitment and motivation that are demanded by the abstraction of work and the new division of learning.

The relationships that characterize a learning environment, Zuboff maintains, can thus be thought of as post-hierarchical. This does not simply imply that differentials of knowledge, responsibility and power can no longer exist; rather, they can no longer be assumed. Instead, they shift and flow and develop their character in relation to the situation, the task and the actors at hand. Managing intricacy calls for a new level of action-centred skill, placing a high premium on the intuitive and imaginative sources of understanding that temper and hone the talents related to working with others. We now turn from Shoshana Zuboff to Solveig Wikstrom, and from a focus on the informated organization, within itself, to the value network that characterizes the post-hierarchical organization, in the world without.

From quality circles to value networks

Driving forces stimulating creation of value

The general thrust of an informated business, for Wikstrom, stimulating value creation towards a greater density of resources and activities per unit of space and time, can be made available to the individual user, in various ways:

- new technology is used not only to automate but also to informate, thus to influence behaviour more dynamically than hitherto
- relations between the economic actors are less sequential, and more reciprocal and synchronous
- more value is created as networks are developed and mobilized
- the resources of the networks can be mobilized increasingly at an individual level, and can be adapted to the individual customers and their particular situations
- inter-actor channels work more efficiently and information flows in all directions
- customers are regarded as partipants in the co-production of value; thus the borderline between supplier and customer often becomes blurred

The value-creating process whereby a producer produces something and delivers it to a customer, who then uses it, therefore becomes less common. As the integration between company and customer processes accelerates, it becomes necessary for one to reinforce the other. More specifically, the company offers something that complements the resources and knowledge which the customer already possesses.

> The tendency now is for corporate resources and knowledge to collaborate in time and space with the customer's resources and knowledge; the output of this combination is a jointly produced value. The old picture consisted of a producer–consumer–user sequence; the new one which reflects reality better, consists of co-production.[20]

From value chain to value star

As a mental model, Porter's 'value chain' then proves to be a special rather than a general case. In a society in which the production of value was largely a question of transferring and refining physical resources, such a model provided a good mental approximation of what happened.

But when transactions became increasingly concerned with knowledge and information – which can exist at several places at once, and which do not cease to exist when they have been used – and when the creation of value builds on reciprocal and synchronous rather than sequential logic, then the model has to be so extended and adjusted that it loses its validity. Such complex offerings, combining products and services in a *value star*, call for co-production not only with the customer but also with other partners representing various productive resources and types of knowledge. This explains the remarkable proliferation of joint ventures, strategic alliances and networks in the business world. Today, according to Wikstrom, it is offerings rather than companies which compete with one another on the market.

Whereas companies in the industrial society focused on 'relieving' the customer of certain activities and functions which could be performed more efficiently in large-scale production based on the specialization of productive resources, the emphasis now has shifted, for Wikstrom, to enabling. If value creation is to be measured in terms of what company and customer can produce together, then the customer is an important production resource which the company must handle accordingly. The customer's learning, therefore, is at least as important as the company's.

Many industries therefore are coming to consist of loosely structured networks of companies specializing in particular activities or services and collaborating with each other on a long-term or *ad hoc* basis. The same companies can turn up in different roles in the relationships with one another – as suppliers, competitors or customers.

Change and integration

From a knowledge perspective the key words on the production side are change and integration. During the 1990s we can expect the increasingly intensive interaction between the actors in the business systems, and the growing emphasis on value creation between them, to affect production systems. When design and product development occur increasingly in dialogue with the customer, and temporal integration increases as the design and manufacturing of the product are the result of integration, more value will be created, more integration established and the rate of technological development speeded up.

Production's capacity for renewal, flexibility and optimization used to conflict with the very idea of job enrichment. Fragmentation, a long-lasting state of affairs with its roots in industrialism's infancy, was, for Wikstrom, the key word. The new

Decentralization

Integration   Multiplicity

Information technology

Figure 11.2 Information-technology production

key word, she and co-author Richard Normann say, is integration. The trend towards vertical disintegration, in the sense that large monolithic companies with everything under one roof are being broken up, coexists with the opposite process of integration. The apparent paradox for Wikstrom, that vertical disintegration can result in increased integration, stems from the fact that the new information technology makes greater cohesion possible even for loosely scattered units, in what she and Normann would call a form of technically conditioned integration.

When it comes to reducing lead times for new products, for example, attempts are made to see that interconnected processes occur in parallel and under integrated forms, rather than sequentially and in a disintegrated mode, as before. As the global division of labour increases, so also does firstly *spatial integration*, that is the bridging of geographical distances within and between organizations and between various actors, facilitated by modern electronics.

At more tactical and strategic levels, integration ambitions are connected with attempts to counteract the negative effects of specialization, such as poor linkages between design and production or between design and processing. This *functional integration*, secondly, also often leads to greater emphasis on the importance of management groups in organization. Thirdly, a cohering element in the organization as internal deregulation takes over, and the old hierarchies and instructions have to be replaced, consists of shared values and visions – a case, for Wikstrom, of *normative integration* (see Figure 11.2).

Early mechanization and automation developments, Wikstrom maintains, were mainly concerned to get rid of human resources, to make people dispensable. The new technological resources available today support creative human competencies, mediated through a knowledge system, rather than replacing them.

The company as a knowledge system

If the company is observed as a producer of knowledge, then the offering of the customer – the product and/or the service – will be a manifestation of the information, the skill and the theoretical knowledge which, according to Wikstrom, the company posseses in order to be able to supply the offering.

The company as such a knowledge system generates and transforms knowledge. The system contains different kinds of knowledge: information, skill, explanations and understandings. People, machines, documents (blueprints, computer programs,

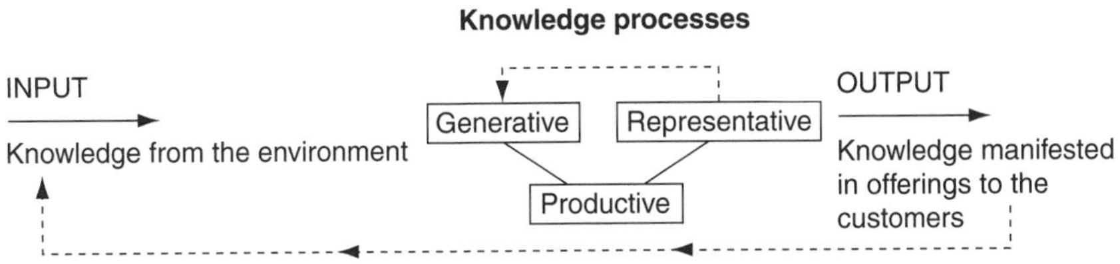

Knowledge processes

Figure 11.3 Knowledge management as a synchronous process

technical and administrative systems), and patents are all bearers of such knowledge.

New knowledge, then, is generated, firstly, by activities aimed at solving problems. Wikstrom calls these *generative* processes. This new knowledge is then secondly used in *productive* processes, which provide the basis for the offerings and commitments which the company undertakes *vis-à-vis* its customers. The productive processes also generate knowledge of a kind which is manifest and used. Just how this manifestation takes place will be determined by the nature of the company's operations. Thus a drill is manifest knowledge deriving from the knowledge processes (see Figure 11.3) of a manufacturing company. Other processes in the company transmit manifest knowledge to the customer. Wikstrom calls this third element a *representative* process. Through a combination of these three processes, knowledge is made available to the customers for their own value-creating processes. At different times, or in different places at the same time, one piece of knowledge can therefore be part of generative, productive or representative processes. This can be illustrated in the case of a drill.

The technical principle on which a drill is based may be tested in a new type of wood; this is a generative process. At the same time the drill is being manufactured as part of a batch; this is a productive process. Finally, discussions held with customers about the purchase of drills constitute a representative process.

If you adopt a traditional view of these three knowledge processes, that is knowledge transformation as a whole, you can describe them as a sequential process: the generative process first leads into the productive process, which in turn ends up as part of the representative process. But the sequential interpretation, for Wikstrom, is no longer sufficient for explaining the transformation of knowledge in companies today. For example, discussion with a customer can lead to new business ideas. The representative process can thus trigger important spin-offs into the generative process. And it is just this – that one activity can fulfil several functions at a time – that distinguishes the successful learning company. In this way it is possible to exploit knowledge, in the shape of ideas and experiences, regardless of whereabouts in the company they have originated, and thus to gain in both creativity and innovative potential. Consequently, both time and money can be saved, since transitions from one function to another can be scrapped, as they are integrated systems such as CADCAM, where the same database is used for design, manufacture, production and quality control.

219

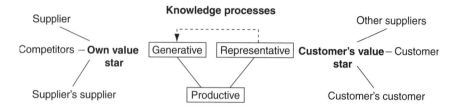

Figure 11.4 Knowledge system for creation of value

Value creation through processing knowledge

Value, for Wikstrom, can be created by various means, not only in offerings embracing both products and services, but also by developing new ways of collaborating with the customer, by training and education, by incorporating others into the collaboration and thus creating networks. Added value is also created by the very fact that exchange relationships become more lasting and far-reaching.

In other words, the customer relationship expands to what Wikstrom and Normann call the 'value star', in which different kinds of knowledge meet and are synthesized. The point of the metaphor is the multiplicity of knowledge accruing from different directions.

On the one hand, then, the capacity for constructive and creative collaboration across the dividing lines in the customer–supplier relationship is important to optimum value creation. On the other hand, it is necessary for people in the company to be able to collaborate by crossing old boundaries and bringing together existing knowledge from different levels and different parts of the organization. As the exchange of knowledge grows, and more and more parties are involved, the value star expands. Thus the openings in the company system turn increasingly towards the environment, and the boundary lines become blurred. In fact, for Wikstrom, what the model in Figure 11.4 demonstrates is the erosion of the traditional boundaries of the corporate system and the company's replacement by a series of value stars. The creation of value, finally, is crucial. Value can be created as a result of synergies or partnerships or through the creation of new knowledge. The company's search for efficient value-creating processes occurs primarily in two dimensions – cost and market efficiency. The one means that the company tries to increase its efficiency by exploiting the resources at its disposal, while the other means trying to develop just those offerings that inject a high value into the customer's own value-creating processes.

Conclusion

In conclusion, we can see the way in which the rational branches of management have drawn on their historic roots, that is on Taylor's 'hard' roots and Parker

Follett's 'soft' ones, respectively. Elliot Jaques, firstly, whose work constitutes the mainstem, has elevated Taylor's, Weber's and Fayol's scientific and hierachical approach into an organizational stratification that, also following Parker Follett, is 'requisite' for human nature. TQ and BPR, moreover, have been set up, notwithstanding Crosby's and Hammer and Champy's more contemporary orientations, very much in Frederick Taylor mode. Womack and Jones, as well as Hamel and Pralahad, on the other hand, have definitely taken on the 'hard' rational approach, because of their partial orientations towards the developmental. Both, moreover, are strongly lodged in the technological – more than the economic, social or cultural – domains of business.

Zuboff and Wikstrom, by way of contrast, are not only women as opposed to men, like Sandra Vandermerwe in comparison with Michael Porter, but they draw on information technology more than production technology. For both these 'soft' interpreters of the rational, moreover, the socio-technical aspects of management come to the fore, so that they transport Parker Follett, so to speak, from the mechanical into the electronic era. Also, in the case of Wikstrom and Normann, the systematic and collective approach of the Scandinavians, albeit with a softly networked touch, is clearly in evidence. Interestingly enough in Zuboff's case, perhaps because of the similar lack of a strong collective orientation in America, she has more recently shifted her attention towards a more individualistic orientation towards career development. We now turn from the rational branches to the rational fruits, represented by a German executive and an English agent of change.

12

EXECUTIVE AND CHANGE AGENT

The fruits of rational management

Introduction

From primal to rational

As a business evolves from a pioneering enterprise to a managed organization, so it requires a new or transformed cast of leading managerial characters. No longer do entrepreneurs and animateurs dominate the show. A youthful Bill Gates and Ricardo Semler need to 'grow up', as they both have done, or else step aside. The world has grown too complex for a youthful orientation to prevail on its own. Hence companies in Germany or Japan often supersede those in the UK or even the US as models of efficiency.

The primal age of enterprise/entrepreneur and community/animateur gets left behind or is pushed into the background. The rational age of the 'hard' hierarchy and 'soft' network takes over. In fact the era between the 1950s and the 1970s was dominated, in the industrialized nations at least, by the 'hard', hierarchically based rationality. The more recent era has been characterized by more adaptive networks, with more flexible structures and systems. Hence so-called managers of change have gained ground over their more establishment counterparts.

The executive and the change agent

The hard edge of rational management is provided by the executive, who asserts his or her strategic intent arising out of core organizational competence. The softer edge is provided by the change agent, who establishes an 'informated' organization that becomes part of a 'value star'. While the executive establishes order, the change agent instils freedom; between the two of them they achieve the right rational balance.

To recap, then, the entrepreneur and animateur have an important part to play in the managed organization, but not the primary one. They occupy the wings rather than the centre field, creating and nurturing new business ventures. The centre field is now occupied by executives, differentiated by function and integrated by means of a hierarchy of fixed command; and by change agents, differentiated by project and integrated via networks of temporary relationships. Let me begin, then, with the executive, and then move on to the agent of change.

The executive – the 'hard' rational fruits

Are you an executive?

As such an anaytically oriented manager:

- your direction is clear-cut
- you have a strategic intent
- your communications are clear
- you set clear objectives at all levels
- your mission is clearly and fully articulated
- your mission is internally consistent and collectively exhaustive
- you have explicitly recognized the business you are in
- you effectively link line and staff functions
- you stratify organizational levels clearly/appropriately
- you plan, organize, direct and control efficiently
- you link up with other business functions effectively
- you purposefully delegate authority and responsibility
- you operate horizontal and vertical communications effectively
- you ensure the organization functions smoothly as an integrated whole
- you serve your customers efficiently and with integrity
- you make a recognized contribution to the community

As an executive, then, you have a particular, and rational management orientation. As such you are more of a planner, a coordinator and a controller rather than a schemer, a networker or a self-starter. As a bureaucrat, in the 'requisite' sense that Jaques identifies, it is the qualities of impartiality, fairness, and justice which should mark you out rather than those of, say, regimentation and impersonality. As a prospective leader, like Dr Liebinger at Trumpf (see below), you are a conciliator or referee, a person of integrity who rises above the competitive fray.

Do companies recruit executives?

The systematic recruitment of 'analytical' managers has been going on for the past two decades, both from the business schools and from within the managed organizations themselves. If anything, too many prospective executives have been sought because of the recruiter's narrowly based – in our terms 'hard' and rational – frame of managerial reference. There is one other problem, though, to be addressed.

Prospective executives have been traditionally recruited from the ranks of men rather than women. Although this is rapidly changing in Europe and America, particularly in the retailing sector and in the human-resource function, there is still a long way to go before equality of opportunity becomes a reality. In particular, women in clerical and secretarial positions, who may well have latent executive potential, are not brought into the limelight.

The functional areas which place a premium on this kind of practical and organized mind are management accounting and control in the Anglo-Saxon world, production or systems engineering in Europe more generally, the analytical side of marketing, and human-resource management. Interestingly enough, in the United Kingdom, where I am based, there is a glaring absence of this managerial character, in the 'finely honed' sense, in management.

The executive, then, who is being sought in such a context, has a clear direction within his or her function or unit; can structure such a unit efficiently and effectively; has a well-defined concept of business in his or her mind; communicates clearly at all levels; understands succinctly his or her management discipline or function; and is both able and willing to serve the organization and the wider community.

How do you reward executives?

Sophisticated schemes have already been developed for rewarding executives. For it is the potential executives amongst you who particularly appreciate the increasing authority and responsibility, as well as the enhanced remuneration and status, that goes with conventional job promotion. Moreover, once it is recognized that it is only executive types who seek that particular form of remuneration, there will be less pressure, within the organization, for a single line of promotion. The organizational ladder – whether functionally, sectorally or territorially based – should serve only the hierarchically inclined amongst you. At the moment our one-dimensional 'hard' rational orientation, especially with the advent of de-layering in the 1990s, leads to unnecessary overcrowding.

How do you develop as an executive?

While small-scale enterprise flourishes in Anglo-Saxon cultures, including small-within-large, Germany is noted for its middle-sized, family-owned concerns. Such companies are characteristically run by the kind of executive to whom we have alluded here. Trumpf, employing some 3,000 people, is one such.

In fact Trumpf is to machine tools in Germany what Microsoft is to computer software in the US. Such notably German- and Japanese-made tools can be defined as power-driven machines that are used to cut, form or shape metal.

Such machine tools, just like the managers or engineers associated with them, can be distinguished along four dimensions: (1) specialization, that is flexible, general-purpose tools versus fixed, special-purpose ones; (2) standardization, whereby standard engineered tools can be differentiated from tailor-made custom-engineered ones; (3) integration, whereby stand-alone machine tools are distinguished from those system-integrated tools which form part of a coherent manufacturing system; and (4) control, in that conventional tools are manually or mechanically controlled, whereas machine tools with numerical control use hard-wired circuits. Moreover, under so-called 'direct numerical control' (DNC), several machine tools are controlled by a single computer. Such DNC is the key to flexible manufacturing cells, that is groups of machine tools set up to handle different subprocesses, and flexible manufacturing systems. Let us now hear directly about the way Trumpf has evolved.[1]

Rationality and precision

Today Trumpf GmbH, more than seventy years after it was founded by Christian Trumpf, develops and produces such machine tools for sheet-metal working, punching presses, electrical tools and laser equipment. In the field of laser technology it is an industry leader. The main production sites are in Germany, where the company employs 2,000 of its 3,000 employees. The Trumpf philosophy is communicated through a logo that comprises a simple blue square, associated with rationality, precision and accuracy.

This is embodied in the rationally based, technological orientation of the current MD, Dr Liebinger: 'I am heavily involved in determining the general direction of our research and development. There is no area that our R & D director does not talk to me about'. Technik, it would seem, is all! The cultural environment of Germany's southwest – with its pietistic focus on rationality, cleanliness and precision – has heavily influenced Trumpf, together with, for example, Daimler Benz and Porsche. In fact this southwestern region, around Stuttgart, is well known for its large number of flourishing, medium-sized firms. Respect for authority and technical competence, unremitting diligence as well as infinite politeness, are therefore central features of Trumpf, and indeed Mercedes Benz or Porsche, culture.

As one employee put it, 'leaving the job each day after only eight hours work would leave me with a bad conscience'. At the same time, interestingly enough, Trumpf is heavily influenced by Japan. Both Dr Liebinger himself, whose mother traded in Far Eastern works of art, and his son-in-law, the production director, have spent many years in that country.

Enlightened patriarch

In Liebinger's words 'I have always admired the Japanese for their devotion to the task, their eagerness and politeness'. This mix of German and Japanese elements might serve to explain the somewhat paradoxical relationship between leadership and delegation at Trumpf. Liebinger is very much a paternalist, or even an autocrat, albeit a benevolent one. 'I believe in the necessity of authority in life. My ideal is to be an enlightened patriarch, someone who is responsible for a task and who knows that he must care for others, and who is aware that he is dependent on others.' We see here a mixture of northern dependence and eastern interdependence. Close supervision and guidance in the company is instilled through both personal and also technocratic measures of coordination, within each of the functional areas of the business. At the same time, more recently, a 'management by projects' system has been introduced. This incorporates clear objective setting amongst project teams; close cooperation between project team members; clear definition of responsibilities; a competence-based approach to the allocation of such responsibilities; and coordinated interdependence between functional areas.

Duty and performance

Two criteria, finally, play an important role in Trumpf's selection and development of its personnel. Firstly, employees are required to have an excellent education in relevant areas of science and technology. Secondly, all employees are expected to have internalized the values which form the very basis of Trumpf's corporate culture. These are unpretentiousness, a sense of duty, a strong performance orientation, as well as self-confidence coupled with unselfishness. Until recently Trumpf had an implicit policy of lifetime employment. Having been forced to lay off people in the 1990s, the company reduced the 'shock effect' by effectively cutting wages so that staff cuts could be minimized. The earnings of high-level employees, in the process, were reduced more drastically than those of blue-collar workers. Moreover, the good relationship that management had with its works council helped to smooth the transition.

How then do you characteristically develop into a captain of industry such as Liebinger?

How do you develop towards executive leadership?

Youthful management trainee

The formal, credential-based training programmes which are run by business and management schools are geared towards the typically rational manager, eager to establish his or her authority. Each business discipline has a body of knowledge that underlies such hard won authority. However, where the greatest difficulty is still found is in schooling individuals for a more generalist role. For it is in fact the school of working life which offers some of the best forms of training for such general abilities. In your youth, then, you are likely to either undertake formal business or engineering, legal or economic studies, or else enter the practical business school as a trainee manager. Dr Liebinger took the first route, studying engineering, rather than the second. Your dream, in fact, is to become a responsible leader in society.

Adultlike functional manager

It may well be, in adulthood, that progressively more challenging job assignments, coupled with an action-learning approach, provide the best of both theory and practice. For within such action-learning groups, and live projects, scope is provided for design and implementation, as well as for objective knowledge and subjective insight. In your thirties, though, your major managerial activities are likely to be within a functional management role.

Midlife general manager

To develop in midlife from a section or functional manager, as Dr Liebinger did, into a business executive on the board, requires, as Liebinger found, wide-ranging exposure. Such exposure typically covers a wide range of business disciplines, situations, problems and opportunities. It also requires, amongst ordinary management mortals, the kind of wisdom, empathy and perspective that comes with age and experience.

Mature spirit of leadership

As you enter midlife and then maturity, in your fifties, you may be able to provide that extra amount of authority and conviction that comes with depth as well as breadth of perspective. Your determination to make a fundamental contribution to society will be embodied in the spirit of leadership that you, like Dr Liebinger in Swabia, have now built up. Together with your flexible counterparts, the agents of change, you will be in a position to adapt your organization to its fast-moving environment, as has recently been the case for Trumpf. Let us now turn to the role and functioning of that softer manifestation of rational management, the agent of change.

Change agent – the 'soft' fruits of management

Are you a change agent?

As a prospective agent of change, you:

- are a professional
- have in-depth knowledge and experience in your field
- have greater loyalty to your profession than to your firm
- learn from change
- observe, conceptualize, experiment, validate
- accommodate variety through flexible communications
- troubleshoot
- rapidly identify opportunities for change
- derive alternative courses of action in order to exploit them
- adapt to change by mapping out the internal and external environment
- create systems and procedures for dealing with change
- experiment with change
- continually form temporary project groupings
- solve ongoing problems in interdisciplinary teams

- plan for change
- monitor changes and adapt your plans accordingly
- construct long-term plans with contingencies built in
- embody the spirit of change
- become respected as a free thinker
- embody the organization's, or a social, cause

The scope for the change agent is rapidly growing in today's managed organizations, albeit more so within the Anglo-Saxon or Nordic worlds than in the Germanic or Japanese ones. Typically, you can be found in technical research and development, in computer programming and management services, in management training, in market research and public relations, in the emerging and flexible end of financial services, and on an MBA programme!

Who recruits change agents?

There is a potentially rich crop of change agents to be picked from amongst the rapidly growing body of knowledge workers. However, because you change agents are characteristically freedom-loving souls, like Steve Shirley (see below), you are often put off by the large and established organizations.

You either choose to remain independent freelancers or else join flexible design groups, advertising agencies, computer software houses and consultancy groups. Should you choose to join a large corporation, you are often kept well away from the corridors of power so as not to disrupt things, unless an enlightened boss or mentor recognizes your potential. This 'contrary' behaviour turns into self-fulfilling prophecy in that prospective change agents might not become sufficiently mature or politically streetwise to develop and implement desirable changes.

Typically, then, you will be involved in project, rather than in line, management. However, in recent years there has been a welcome rise to power of designers and electronics buffs, many of whom are beginning to act in such a change-making capacity. They are adding weight and strength to the opportunities for change being opened up every day by changes in lifestyles and by the emerging communications technologies.

How should companies reward change agents?

You agents of change, by definition, want to be free to make the sorts of change you consider appropriate. Such adaptations in products and processes, systems and procedures often cut across conventional functions. As a result you want to be able to move across functional boundaries freely and constantly. As a change agent you seek continual mental stimulus, preferring to work cross-functionally rather than within an established department.

If you do not feel you are learning and developing yourself, you will seek a change. Bureaucratic, unadaptive organizations can be particularly stifling for you in that respect. Your primary motivation is neither financial reward nor formal promotion but variety of experience and opportunity for self-expression, as has been the case for Steve Shirley, whose story is told in the next section (personal interview).

Becoming a change agent

Prelude to liberation

My life began in 1933 in Dortmund, West Germany. In 1939, when I was five years old, my family was scattered by the Nazis to the four winds. I was brought over to England by a Quaker family. I progressed from village to grammar school, via a Roman Catholic convent, and loathed all three. I would have liked to go to university, but the family could not afford it. At school I loved maths and literature, and I was fascinated by language and European culture.

Rebel with a cause

My passions at 18 were different from those of other children my age. I campaigned for homosexual law reform, lobbied for changes in the law on suicide, and campaigned for birth control. I was very extreme. These things were so important to me. While I was campaigning I went to London, at 18, to look for a job and took one with the Post Office research station. There was something very special in the atmosphere at Dollis Hill, where the research station was based. There was an aura of scientific boldness. I had three bosses in eight years; the last, T. H Flowers, had been at Bletchley Park, scene of the dramatic cracking of Germany's Enigma code during the first World War. Meanwhile I was busy developing myself.

Four years later, with the help of a college's day release facilities, I obtained my BSc in maths. At evening classes I came across computers for the first time. They really were primitive in the 1950s, when I was still working with mechanical calculators, albeit to investigate complex phenomena. Then I joined a new company called Computer Developments Ltd, jointly owned by GEC and ICL's predecessor, ICT. During my years there I helped design one of the early computers, the 1301, and I also became one of the first of a new breed of software engineers. The job was highly skilled, and well paid for those days.

But my career as an employee was coming to an end. For one thing, something in me was saying that my future did not lie in being an employee. My era of conformity, you might say, was coming to an end. For another thing, I wanted to have children, preferably five. Matters were brought to a head, when, at a staff meeting, I made a suggestion and was told 'that has nothing to do with you; you're technical'. I was furious. 'That's it, I thought to myself, I'm off'.

I decided to go freelance, thinking I was so good that people would come knocking at my door. Nobody came for three months, until a former colleague – he was then working for a large management consultancy – gave me a break. The firm had set up a computer consultancy division, and I was asked to design the management controls for a data-processing group. By the time I finished the job I was eight and a half months pregnant. When I was asked how many people worked for me, I said 'one and a bit'. I called 'our' business Freelance Programmers. When my son was born I lost interest in work for three months. That was the happiest time of our lives, for my son and me together. I was so pleased we had at least that little time. He is severely mentally handicapped, and has been hospitalized since he was 13 years old. It wasn't practicable to have any more of my five anticipated children.

Perhaps if I'd had them I would never have developed my other family, 'F International'. In 1964, then, I incorporated Freelance Programmers. That was a turning point. It was like laying an official foundation stone. The operation became more credible to my customers and to myself. Business was growing into more of a stream than a trickle. I had earned the status. It was also the time when I began to build up my panel of homeworkers. They were the real foundation stones, and they enabled the business to extend beyond myself. They have also become the business's reason, my reason, for being.

A *Guardian* article, in January 1964, gave our business publicity and context. Entitled 'Computer Women', it said: 'One of the fanatics is Mrs Steve Shirley, a maths graduate who, considering herself merely competent at research mathematics, found in computer programming an outlet for her artistic talents – working out patterns. She describes the essential quality required in programming as "seeing the wood for the trees". Now "retired", with a young baby, she has found that computer programming can be done at home, between feeding the baby and washing nappies'. If we look at the company policy today, we can see how it emerged out of the need and opportunity to utilize, wherever practicable, the services of people with dependents who are unable to work in a conventional work environment.

Managing change

As our dependents grew, so did our problems, particularly with regard to cash flow. In the late 1960s I realized I needed someone to share the burden of the company with, not just my husband or a friend, but someone with the commitment and commercial acumen to share the load. I found such a person within my panel, and we set up a dual management system. That's when the recession hit. Hardly a month would go by without news of the liquidation of a former client. And in the middle of all this my partner left and took a precious chunk of business from me. That experience scarred me for life, but it's where I got my toughness from. When I had originally started out in business most people I knew thought I was too soft. But, by now, I had found out what hard times were like and I realized how much I cared. These two factors together toughened me considerably. It was also in the early 1970s that the idea of going international first came to us. I had already altered the structure of Freelance Programmers, and renamed it F (for flexible) International. We had one or two European customers, but it was our chairman at the time who suggested we establish an overseas operation.

The idea was that the company spread its employment philosophy, as well as its computing services, elsewhere. By then we were offering a comprehensive range of data processing services. They included consulting, hardware and software evaluation, business and systems analysis, software development and computer installation support. The basic demand for our service was there in most countries but cultural and legislative differences could make it hard to winkle out a formula for implementing our unique employment policies. They were exportable, but not in their pure, original form.

Spreading wings

We developed operations in Holland, though, and in France, as well as in Denmark. Once I entered my early fifties, I chose no longer to be involved with day-to-day operations. I saw my main responsibility in spreading out our operations overseas, and in holding the ethos of the company together. Our turnover, in the 1980s, was 90 per cent UK-based. I wanted this to be reduced to 50 per cent over time, as we became truly international. Whereas I used to see my literary interests as a side track, now I could see how my involvement with different cultures became important for our work.

We also set up regional headquarters in the UK, and delegated project management responsibilities accordingly. Our turnover went up, from a few thousand in the 1960s, to over £10 million in 1987 (close to £100 million in 1997), and we had more than a thousand women involved with us, most of whom worked from home.

Controlling destiny

In the 1990s, I have been seduced into becoming more of a public figure. Between 1979 and 1982 I had been Vice-President of the British Computer Society. During the International Year for Disabled People I developed several IT-based projects. I am also preoccupied with the damaging effect that computers can have on the human spirit. In the end, of course, it's not money that motivates me. I've been determined to prove a point; I wanted to liberate a few hundred women from the constraints of motherhood, and I wanted to control my own destiny, while they should be able to control theirs. I have since passed over my shares to a trust, and a shareholding structure has been created for the company's employees. I developed, at the same time, a credo, a charter to cover the non-quantifiable aspects of our business. You need to be able to express those absolute qualities that are so important to business and to life. The twinning of technical excellence with the recognition of employees as whole people – writing programmes or attending their children's sports days – is essential to our philosophy and structure. I hate the way life and people get divided up. I started the business as an outsider, with a whole new approach to employment. Now, 35 years and over a thousand people later, we're putting across a new, revolutionary message to the world.

So how do you go about developing yourself as a change agent such as Steve Shirley?

How do you develop yourself as a change agent?

Youthful troubleshooter

Characteristically you start out in organizational life as a professionally qualified designer, computer programmer like Steve Shirley, training officer, or technologist. In your youth you may be called in as a troubleshooter, to investigate problems and opportunities of a technical, commercial or human nature. You will typically be involved in a variety of time-bound tasks and projects. Your dream is to be free to be yourself.

Adultlike management of change

As you develop through adulthood, in your thirties, you are likely to have attended specific and often short courses, travelled around the company, and visited different locations. You thus become a more knowledgeable agent of change, able to take on more significant assignments. You will be called in not only to solve particular problems but to apply more generalizable solutions. Ultimately you become involved in managing change with a particular function.

Midlife agent of change

In midlife, as you evolve your role across functions, or in your own organization as with Steve Shirley, you become a widely spread agent of change. Your need for variety and mental stimulus will be tempered by a willingness to focus on longer-term problems and opportunities. Your own need for self-expression will be matched by your desire to help others express themselves by spreading their wings within project-based activities.

Embodying the mature spirit of freedom

Finally, as you mature, your role will become more symbolic than practical, as is the case now with Steve Shirley in F International Services. You then come to embody the spirit of freedom rather than continuing to rush mentally and physically from one project or product to another. In other words, you will come to represent and even lead a particular cause, like 'shaping work around the individual' or 'giving people the freedom to pursue wild ideas', rather than solely managing a particular and adaptable function or project. As such you ultimately pursue your vocation.

Conclusion

Stability and change

As an agent of change on your own, however, even with the support of entrepreneurs and animateurs, you may be unable to steer your company in the right direction.

For all the intellectual and adaptive leadership that you are able to provide, you may lack the necessary stability, staying power, and sense of continuity to provide rounded leadership. That is where your counterpart comes in, the executive. On the other hand, if you round out into a fully fledged manager of change, then you may come to represent all the qualities of rational management in yourself.

Developing your rational individuality

Both the 'hard', hierarchically oriented executive and the 'soft', network-oriented agent of change need each other in order to mature. If you are to remain open over the course of your working life, moreover, then your rational qualities will be tempered, at first primally, and subsequently developmentally and metaphysically. In other words, and for example, while the management of human resources may be of paramount importance for you, in your youth you may be open to people as people; in midlife you may become involved in organization development; and in maturity you may become engaged in the transformation of your corporate culture. While all these activities, for you, will fall within the management of human resources, this function will take on broader and deeper connotations than would have been the case had you not matured.

Similarly, for you, while management services may be your source of primary identity, in your youth you may open yourself to risk-laden projects undertaken in new disciplines and in foreign lands; in midlife you may broaden your base from technology to people, and from project control to management control; finally, in maturity, you may progress from ongoing individual and group learning to the creation of a companywide learning community. In the process you advance from job to role, and from calling to vocation. While all this evolving activity would still be contained within management services, the nature and extent of this rationally based function would be rounded out.

In the process of maturing, then, whether as an executive or change agent, you maintain your fundamental rationality, but gradually round out, thereby imbibing qualities from the other three domains. This is not a smooth and continuous process. Collectively and individually such a development is interspersed with transitions, during which your evolving identity becomes confused. If you are able to withstand these periods of doubt and uncertainty, suitably reassured by your image of change and development, you should be able to realize your rational potential, and in the process interweave qualities both soft and hard. This was achieved by both Dr Liebinger and Steve Shirley, starting from their differing management perspectives. We now turn from a rational to a developmental orientation.

13

DEVELOPMENTAL ROOTS –
BIOLOGY AND ECOLOGY

Introduction

From rational to developmental management

Developmental management is founded upon the laws of growth and change that underpin the development of living organisms. It is rooted particularly in the life sciences, that is more within biology and ecology, rather than within classical physics or the social sciences. It is based, moreover, neither on purely instinctive behaviour nor on wholly rational conduct, but on a process of conscious evolution.

In fact this text so far, while enabling you to manage such growth – through competitive strategy or strategic intent – has not yet introduced you to the laws of growth and evolution, such as they may be. This is the aim of this chapter. Biologists, ecologists and some developmental psychologists, in recent years, have uncovered such laws of growth and evolution, with a view to their being applied to the management of organizations. Unfortunately, until very recently, they have been largely ignored by the OD (organization development) establishment, and have certainly been bypassed by those involved in product, market and systems development. It is my job in this chapter to uncover the 'hard' and 'soft' roots of such developmental management, then to follow up in the next chapter with the mainstem theory of 'organizational dynamics', before revealing, in chapter 15, the branch theories and applications, that have recently become available to us, as managers. We begin, inevitably enough, with Charles Darwin.

The 'hard' developmental roots – Darwin's
evolutionary biology

Natural selection – survival of the fittest

The roots of the 'hard' developmental, or evolutionary, orientation are contained within the Darwinian theory. Darwin accepted that the major phenomenon of life that needs to be accounted for is the adaptation of organisms to their habitats. Moreover, he believed that this could be explained in terms of random hereditary variations among the members of a species, and natural selection of the better variants over long periods of evolutionary time. This has become the basis for explaining innumerable aspects of life on earth. No aspect of human life is untouched by Darwin's theory of evolution – surivival of the fittest.

Darwinism, like all theories, has distinct metaphorical associations that are familiar from the use of descriptive terms such as survival of the fittest, competitive interactions between species, selfish genes and survival strategies. The criterion of value here is purely functional; species either work or they do not. They have no intrinsic value. Darwin sees the living process in terms that emphasize competition, inheritance, selfishness and survival as the driving forces of evolution. Such Darwinism, for the biologist Brian Goodwin[1] at Britain's Open University, has been phenomenally successful as a scientific theory. It is often ranked with Newton's theory of motion as one of those rare, enduring achievements of the scientific imagination.

Paley, Malthus and Darwin – religion, economics and biology

Scientific theories are based on decisions about basic problems that characterize some area of enquiry. Before Darwin, biology was largely about morphology, the structure of organisms. Darwin belonged to an age that had 'discovered' historical explanations.

As such it was becoming preoccupied with change and the reasons for it as Europe experienced increasing rates of social and political transformation. In biology, then, the continuous accumulation of fossils made their history more and more problematical: why did all these species become extinct? Why do the ones we see about us survive? Darwin cast about for a solution. One of the most prominent books in Darwin's day was by a theologian called William Paley (*Natural Theology*, 1802), who described in detail the remarkable and diverse ways in which organisms are adapted to their environments. This was interpreted as a major proof of God's existence, since only an intelligent creator could have generated such a good fit between an organism and its habitat. Inheritance was the other concept that Darwin made use of. It was the Lamarckian view that Darwin came to accept, whereby organisms have the capacity to adapt to their environments and pass their adaptations on to their children. But Darwin needed an idea to account for extinction. And he found it in the notion of competition for limited resources, which he got from Malthus' study of population growth. So here was the third ingredient that gave Darwin the recipe for a dynamic theory of evolution that accounted for adaptive change as well as for evolution. As the environment changes the pressures of survival force changes on populations. This is natural selection, the emergence of new, adapted types of organisms and the extinction of those that fail to change adequately.

Original sin and the selfish gene

So we enter a new world, one of perpetual change in which history, heredity and adaptation through competitive interaction are the ingredients of an evolutionary biology. This was Darwin's vision, a magnificent, inspiring unification of the biological realm. All organisms are joined together in the tree of life rooted in one common origin of life on earth, whose branches and twigs are the diverse forms that have evolved to adapt to different circumstances. Richard Dawkin,[2] the most renowned contemporary interpreter of Darwinism, has summarized Darwin's principles of evolution as follows:

1   Organisms are constructed by groups of genes whose goal is to leave more copies of themselves. The hereditary material is basically 'selfish'.
2   The inherently selfish qualities of the hereditary material are reflected in the competitive interactions between organisms that result in the survival of fitter variants, generated by the more successful genes.
3   Organisms are constantly trying to get better (fitter) in order to surpass their competitors. However, this landscape keeps changing as evolution proceeds, so the struggle is endless.[3]

Are these metaphors beginning to look familiar, Goodwin enquires. Here, he says, is a very similar set:

1   Humanity is born in sin; we have a base inheritance.
2   Humanity is therefore condemned to a life of conflict and
3   Perpetual toil.
4   But by faith and moral effort humanity can be saved from a fallen, selfish state.[4]

So we see, Goodwin maintains, that the Darwinism described by Dawkins has its metaphysical roots in one of the deepest cultural myths, the story of the fall and the redemption of humanity. Darwin saw competitive struggle as the path to civilization. In fact for Goodwin, all theories have metaphorical dimensions which he regards as not only inevitable but also as extremely important. For it is these metaphysical dimensions that give depth and meaning to scientific ideas, and indeed to managerial ones, as we shall see with our final domain.

'Soft' developmental roots – the leopard that changed its spots

From natural selection to morphogenesis

For Brian Goodwin, it appears, Darwin's theory works for the small-scale aspects of evolution: it can explain the variations and the adaptations within species that produce fine tuning of varieties to different habitats. The large-scale differences of form between different types of organism that are the foundation of biological classification systems are different. They seem to require a principle other than natural selection operating on small variations, some process that gives rise to distinctly different forms of organism. It is here that new theories which have recently emerged within mathematics and physics offer significant insights into the origins of biological order and form. What has developed from the widespread use of computers to explore the dynamic potential of interacting systems that can process information, such as biological molecules, cells or organisms, is a new theory of dynamic systems collectively referred to as the sciences of complexity.

Goodwin therefore argues that Darwin's view of species arises from a limited and inadequate view of the nature of organisms. The sciences of complexity lead to the construction of a dynamic theory of organisms as the primary source of the emergent properties of life that have been revealed in evolution. These properties are generated during the process known as morphogenesis, the development of the complex form of the adult organism from simple beginnings such as an egg or a bud. Darwin's emphasis on competition and survival, then, points to aspects of the remarkable drama that includes the history of our own species.

> But it is a very incomplete and limited story, both scientifically and metaphorically, based on an inadequate view of organisms, and it invites us to act in a limited way as an evolved species in relation to our environment, which includes other cultures and species. Darwin short-changes us as regards our biological natures. We are every bit as co-operative as we are competitive, as altruistic as we are selfish, as creative and playful as we are destructive and repetitive. And we are biologically grounded in relationships which operate at all different levels of our beings as the basis of our natures as agents of creative evolutionary emergence, a property we share with all other species.[5]

Focusing upon the generative field

Goodwin's focus is on 'the generative field', which has been left out by Darwin. It is the organized context within which inherited particulars act, and without which they have no effect. Putting this back into biology leads to a new definition of an organism as the fundamental unit of life. With this, for Goodwin, comes the need to look again at evolution. What emerges, for him, is no longer a spotted leopard struggling for survival, but a rather different kind of creature described by different metaphors. However, the leopard will be there if you want to see it. The Darwinian, evolutionary metaphor of organisms constantly struggling up the slopes of 'fitness landscapes', trying to do better than others in order to survive, does capture a particular quality of the living process, despite its excessively Calvinist work-ethic image. It represents organisms as agents that actively engage in the process of evolution. On the other hand, the physical notion of doing what comes naturally by seeking the path of least effort, like a marble falling into the centre of a bowl, suggests a different kind of agency, one that tends to harmonize its actions with the environment and go with the flow. In neo-Darwinism, organisms actually have no agency because they don't exist as real entities, reduced as they are to genes and their products, which assemble by local interaction into the structure of the organism. The genes are selected for their survival properties by natural selection, a cause external to the organism. So there is no agency left and organisms are purely mechanical consequences of internal and external forces, despite the metaphor of struggle and effort.

Autopoiesis – the capacity for self-generation

Quantum mechanics, however, reveals a world of action that is anything but mechanical. What about biology then? Organisms can regenerate and produce. These are expressions of the property of self-completion or individuation that is distinctive to the living state. Maturana and Varela[6] define this as 'autopoiesis', the capacity of active self-maintenance and self-generation that underlies regeneration, reproduction and healing. These, in fact, are all manifestations of the capacity of organisms to generate coherent wholes. We have now recovered organisms as irreducible entities that are engaged in the process of generating forms and transforming them by means of their particular qualities of action and agency, their causal powers. Species of organism are therefore natural kinds, not historical individuals as they are in Darwinism. The members of a species express a particular nature. Moreover, there is as much cooperation as there is competition. Mutualism and symbiosis are an equally universal feature of the biological realm. The immensely complex network of relationships between organisms involves all imaginable patterns of interaction, and there is absolutely no point in focusing on competitive interactions, singling them out as the driving force of evolution. The problem of origins, moreover, requires an understanding of how new levels of order emerge from complex patterns of interaction and what the properties of these emergent structures are, in terms of their robustness to perturbation and their capacity for self-maintenance.

A theory of emergent order

The reason why competition, selfish genes, struggle, adaptation, climbing fitness peaks, doing better and making progress are so important as metaphors in neo-Darwinism is that they make sense of evolution in terms that are familiar to us 'westerners' from our social experience of culture. Darwinian metaphors are grounded in the myth of human sin and redemption. This works in a limited way to describe selected aspects of small-scale changes that go on in organisms and populations. But these small changes do not add up to the emergence of a new species or new types of organism. For this we need a theory of emergent order, one that shows how patterns arise spontaneously from the complex, chaotic dynamic of the human state. When life is at 'the edge of chaos', all the parts of the system are in dynamic communication with all other parts. Thus the potential for information processing in the system is at a maximum. This state provides maximal opportunities for the system to evolve dynamic strategies of survival. Instead of focusing on quantities, things that can be measured, we look at the unique qualities of organisms that give us a sense of their unique value and what it means to seek quality in life. We thereby pick up again, Goodwin maintains, on many of the values that were left behind in the seventeenth century, when the modern age began. In fact this all provides the backdrop for the more specifically managerial emphasis that we are now going to provide, drawing on the contemporary work of two American management consultants, Jim Moore and Margaret Wheatley.

'Hard' roots – the age of business ecosystems

The death of competition

Thinking of whole systems

In 'The Death of Competition',[7] American business consultant James Moore signals the birth of a new business and economic era. Ironically, Moore, while substantively informed by Darwin's evolutionary biology, nevertheless heralds the demise of competitition, as we know it. The new paradigm, to begin with, he says, requires thinking in terms of whole systems, that is specifically seeing business as part of a wider economic ecosystem.

The basic idea for Moore is simple. Understand the economic systems evolving around you and find ways to contribute. Start with an understanding of the big picture rather than of products and services. So far so good, but nothing said up to now is revolutionary. There is, however, more to follow, and now Moore's more radical perspective starts to come into its own.

Evolution comes first

For evolution, he says, is a more important concept than simply competition or cooperation. The job of top management, in that respect – and this is the key – is to seek out potential centres of innovation where, by orchestrating the contributions of a network of players, they can bring powerful benefits to bear for customers and producers alike. As they hasten the coming together of disparate business elements into new economic wholes, new businesses, new rules of competition and cooperation and new industries can emerge. The presumption that there are distinct, immutable businesses within which players scramble for supremacy is, for Moore, a tired idea whose time is past. In place of 'industry' Moore suggests an alternative, more appropriate term: business ecosystem. The term, leading on from where Michael Porter's business cluster leaves off, implies intense co-evolution coalescing around innovative ideas. Moreover, such business ecosystems, like natural ones, for Moore as for myself, evolve in four stages, albeit somewhat different ones in each case.

The developmental stages

From pioneering to renewal

First, for Moore, a business is engaged in *pioneering*, when the basic paradigm of the ecosystem is being worked out. Second, *expansion* occurs, when the community broadens its scope and consumes resources of all types.

Third, *authority* arises, when the community architecture becomes stable and competition for leadership and profits within the ecosystem becomes brutal. Fourthly and finally, there is either *renewal*, when continuing innovation must take place for the community to thrive, or *death*. We shall review each in turn.

Exploratory pioneering

Entrepreneurs, for Moore, struggle to form embryonic ecosystems that, while hardly mature, are at least complete enough to fulfil the needs of initial customers. Offering a dramatic increase in value, compared with what is already available to customers, is the sine qua non of the early exploratory days of a business ecosystem, prior to expansion or consolidation. Out of the available range of environmental conditions and enabling genetic material, the pioneer must find a set of interdependent relationships through which this fundamental cycle of trapping and converting energy can be established.

In most cases a new ecosystem emerges on the edge of a more established one, or is grafted onto it, or else it comes about through the transformation of some aspect of the existing business. In all cases the community of customers and suppliers must work harmoniously because they are creating something new. Moreover, the ability of the network to learn together is crucial. The lead company, though, must provide the structure for the alliance, must provide end-to-end performance oversight, and must make sure that a key portion of the value cannot be replicated by others or targeted by competitors.

Expansionary consolidation

As a result of the pioneering stage 1, a new ecosystem has been colonized. Pioneer micro-organisms and fungi, in an ecological context, will have established themselves.

The territory will have become flecked with mats of vegetation and clumps of small bushes. Moreover, for an ecosystem to gain distinction, its population and species must expand to the extent that the ecosystem literally teams with life. Such teaming life characterizes, by analogy, what happens during stage 2 of the evolution of a business ecosystem.

240

One of the central observations of so-called bio-geography, for Moore, is that ecological communities mature in at least two ways. Firstly, they expand in biomass – for example, grasslands get denser, trees grow taller and populations of animals multiply. Generally speaking, stage 2 expansion therefore requires a compelling vision of value, combined with the ability to scale up the ecosystem to provide that value. Volume enables these companies to anchor huge ecosystems, scaling and replication require well-designed, standard processes. These in turn depend upon well-managed organizations. The second way ecosystems mature is through increased genetic diversity. They thereby add species, elaborating synergistic relationships and becoming ever more artful and lively in turning resources into community life.

In business ecosystems there is also such an advantage to diversity of people, organizations and ideas. In general, the diversity of members makes the ecosystem more robust and resilient, providing variety to its offerings, alternative sources of supply when bottlenecks arise, and a host of creative ideas to help spawn further evolution. It is about combining a wide range of value elements, and even aspects of competing ecosystems, into one that can capture market territory and defend it against rival ecosystems. Stage 2, then, is about the race to move from a set of core synergistic relationships to a rich, robust ecosystem. This is the period when the successful paradigm must be more broadly applied and made more reliable and replicable. Additional waves of customers and other stakeholders must be recruited.

The focus is upon identifying and rounding up the most desirable potential allies available: the best customers, the strongest suppliers, the most important channels, while keeping reasonable control over the direction of the whole enteprise. Logistics, production, purchasing and financing therefore can all present significant problems for the growing ecosystem. Once the expanding enterprise has the critical mass, more conservative potential allies will join forces, which will in turn have the effect of generating business volume and achieving welcome economies of scale. Subsequently, the developing organization, for Moore, needs to renew itself so as to command a new authority in the expanded business ecosystem.

Established authority

In business and biology the developing organism wants to become part of the establishment if it can. To stay successful in this way, a lead company must maintain and fortify its ability to shape the future direction and investments of the ecosystem's key customers and suppliers. It must therefore be able to fend off rivals within the ecosystem, and to exceed the attractions of other ecosystems. A central challenge facing business strategists in maturing ecosystems is how to maintain their authority and the uniqueness of their contribution to the community while also encouraging community-wide innovation and co-evolution. Business ecosystems are also vulnerable to outsiders such as Microsoft in America or Direct Line in Britain, who can create alternative ecosystems and take business from the entire industrial community. They may be able to reverse engineer a well-defined architecture and then go one better, building an alternative around more advanced underlying technologies or paradigms. Once its niches become solidified and its species entrenched, a biological ecosystem, for Moore, reaches structural maturity. The amalgamation of the ecosystem has largely taken place and the species have developed a sustainable framework within which to live and co-evolve. The prevailing species have made clear their dominance.

The lesser species have accepted the smaller scale that will be their lot. This often heralds a long period of relative ecological stability. At the same time, a new wave of participants begins to thread its way into the mature ecosystem by taking advantage of the fixed structure, and adds vastly to its complexity.

When the structure of the ecosystem stabilizes, many new entrants and customers envision their own possibilities and are able to muster power they are eager to test. Tempted by the promise of joining an ecosystem overflowing with expansion, and potential profits, they are entirely comfortable exploiting the strategic architecture that another set of firms has built, and they often find a surprising receptivity amongst its customers. As fresh participants join the ecosystem, struggles may erupt between the new leadership and the old. Companies retreat into their core competencies as new entrants outdo the leaders in certain functions and market segments. Outsourcing (contracting out) becomes a key consideration.

The winners, therefore, in stage 3 are the firms that go beyond rationalizing their own contributions and learn how to influence the structure and evolution of their business systems and opportunity environments. The key to becoming a winner and a leader, moreover, is bargaining power. Specifically, then, a company must become absolutely vital to the community, most especially to its customers. In that respect its ultimate bargaining power is a function of the degree to which it is embedded in the business ecosystem, how critical it is to it, and the company's relative position within an innovation trajectory, that is extending from invention to commercialization.

Renewal or death

Longevity comes from finding ways to inject new ideas into the existing ecosystem. As a business system matures it must surmount four fundamental tests. Firstly, it needs to establish a system and sequence of symbiotic relationships that result in the creation of something of real value relative to what else is available. Secondly, it must establish critical mass as the ecosystem expands across the available customers, markets, allies and suppliers. Thirdly, the business must lead innovation and co-evolution across the business ecosystem in which it is lodged. Fourthly, it needs to ensure that the business sustains continuous performance improvement.

Biological communities erupt in fits and starts rather than unfolding in an entirely orderly and incremental fashion. After protracted periods of stability during which species and their relative populations remain basically the same, sudden bursts of massive biological change can result in the radical transformation or even wholesale eclipse of an ecosystem. Physical developments, such as

242

earthquakes or floods, can often trigger this change. On the other hand, biological ecosystems can often heal themselves or be restored with the help of conservationists.

Finally, biological ecosystems are being transformed constantly, in positive ways that enhance capability and/or diversity. The means by which this happens include co-evolution among members, the introduction of new species, and geographically splitting and evolving in parallel but distinct directions. The same sort of changes – declines and restorations – beset business ecosystems. A business ecosystem threatened by obsolescence slips into stage 4. But its destiny is not set. It faces renewal or death, not death alone. And even if it slips into irremediable decline, it will usually provide species and feedstock for its successors. In fact, coping with the threat of obsolescence is the ultimate challenge for a dominant company.

In nature, moreover, continuous renewal is the order of the day and primary colonization the rarity. The ability to recognize assets in a dying ecosystem and reuse them, Moore concludes, will be an increasingly vital talent in the twenty-first century. We now turn from Jim Moore's 'hard' strategically oriented realities of biology and ecology, as well as the new chemistry and physics, to Margaret Wheatley's organizationally oriented 'soft' ones.

'Soft' roots – leadership and the new science

Chaos and Gaia

Self-organizing dynamics

Margaret Wheatley, an American management consultant renowned for her *Leadership and the New Science*,[8] rose to prominence in the early 1990s. She sets her stage, as it were, by taking us back to the Ancient Greeks. Several thousand years ago, she says, when primal forces haunted the human imagination, great myths arose to explain the creation of all beings. At the very beginning was Chaos, the endless, yawning chasm devoid of form or fullness, and Gaia, the mother of earth who brought form and stability. In Greek consciousness, Chaos and Gaia were partners, two primordial powers engaged in a duet of opposition and resonance, creating everything we know.

A few thousand years later, the modern-day chemist Ilya Prigogine's work on the evolution of dynamic systems has served to demonstrate that disequilibrium is the necessary condition for a system's growth. He has called these systems 'dissipative structures'[9] because they dissipate their energy in order to re-create themselves into new forms of order. Faced with amplifying levels of disturbance, these systems possess innate properties to reconfigure themselves so that they can deal with the new information. For this reason they are frequently called self-organizing or self-renewing systems.

One of their distinguishing features is resilience rather than stability. For example, Wheatley maintains, in the early stages of an ecosystem, those species predominate that produce large numbers of offspring, most of which die. These species are vulnerable to changes in the environment. At this early stage, the environment exerts extreme pressure, playing a dominant (Darwinian) role in the selection of species. But as the ecosystem matures, it develops an internal stability, a resilience to the environment which, in turn, creates conditions that support a more efficient use of energy and protection from environmental demands. What comes to dominate the system over time is not environmental dynamics, but the self-organizing dynamics (autopoiesis) of the system itself.

As the process of exchange between system and environment continues, the system, paradoxically, develops greater freedom from the demands of the environment. In fact, the presence of a strong competency-based identity makes the organization or organism less vulnerable to environmental fluctuations. Yet such enterprises need to be remarkably sensitive to their environments, staying wide open to new opportunities that call upon their skills. They also develop capacities to shape the environment.

Self-reference and self-organization

These entities, for Wheatley, highlight a principle that is fundamental to all self-organizing systems, that of 'self-reference'. In response to environmental disturbances that signal the need for change, the system changes in a way that remains consistent with itself in that environment. The system is therefore 'autpoietic', as Maturana and Varela have indicated, focusing its activities on what is required to maintain its own integrity and self-renewal. As it changes, it does so by referring to itself; whatever future form it takes will be consistent with its already established identity.

The system, in that context, 'keeps the memory of its evolutionary path'. Self-reference, then, is what facilitates orderly change in turbulent environments. In human organizations, a clear sense of identity – of the values, traditions, aspirations, competencies and culture – is the real source of independence from the environment. When the environment demands a new response, there is a reference point for change. This, for Wheatley, prevents the vacillations and the random search for new customers and new ventures that have destroyed so many businesses over the past several years. Another characteristic of self-organizing systems is their 'global' stability over time, in the presence of many local fluctuations and instabilities. Any mature ecosystem experiences many changes and fluctuations at the level of individuals and species, but the total system remains stable, capable of developing its own rhythm of growth. The more freedom in self-organization, the more order.

When the system is far from equilibrium, as Ralph Stacey will illustrate in the next chapter, creative individuals can have enormous impact. The presence of a lone fluctuation gets amplified by the system, through the process of autocatalysis. A small fluctuation may start an entirely new evolution that will drastically change

244

the whole behaviour of the system. By way of its dynamic interconnectedness, evolution determines its own meaning. Stasis, balance, equilibrium, these are temporary states. What endures is dynamic, adaptive process.

Energy and information

For Wheatley, then, it is energy that matters. It is thus possible to think of organizational roles as minimally bounded, as focused on interactions and energy exchanges. Any role could be understood both as a reaction channel in which forms – specific tasks or accountabilities – appeared, and as a generative force, capable of contributing its energy to others.

In such an organization, you would draw structures to emphasize the interactions you needed, thereby creating organizations of processes and relationships. You have been so engaged in rounding things off as a manager, Wheately maintains, smoothing things over, keeping the lid on things, that your organizations have been dying, literally, for information they could feed on.

For such information is different, disconfirming, and filled with enough instability to knock the system into a new life. This information is always spawned out of uncertain, even chaotic, circumstances. The intent is not to push and pull but to give form to what is unfolding. Newer theories of the brain describe information as widely distributed, not necessarily limited to specific neuron sites. We are coming to understand the importance of relationships and non-linear connections, therefore, as the source of new knowledge. Our task, then, is to create organizational forms that facilitate these new processes. For example, in Semler's Semco, as we have seen, roles and structures are created from need and interest. Relationships, exchanges and connections among employees – almost everyone bears the name 'associate' – are nurtured as the primary source of organizational creativity and success. More and more there is an openness to inter-organizational and intra-organizational exchanges.

Natural systems, then, engage with the universe differently than we 'rationally' do. We may struggle to methodically build layer upon layer, while they unfold. We labour hard to hold things together, while they participate openly and complex systems emerge. While 'building up' emphasizes structure and the emergence of hierarchical levels, 'unfolding' implies the interweaving of processes which lead simultaneously to organizational stratification at different hierarchical levels. In quantum physics, for example, electrons are drawn into intimate relations as their wave aspects interfere with one another, overlapping and merging.

Their own qualities of mass, charge, spin, position and momentum thus become indistinguishable from one another. Indeed it is no longer meaningful to talk of the constituent electrons' individual properties as these continually change to meet the requirements of the whole.

We are engaging, Wheatley ultimately maintains, with a fundamentally new relationship with order that is identified in processes that only temporarily manifest themselves in structures. Order itself is not rigid, but a dynamic energy swirling around us. Relational holism (Gaia) and self-organization (Chaos) work in tandem to give us the living universe. Two dynamic processes, fed by information, combine to create an ordered world. The result is evolution, the organization of information into new forms. Life goes on, more creative than before, and yet, paradoxically, in a 'simpler way'.

A simpler way

The nature of living systems

Margaret Wheatley and her associate Myron Kellner Rogers, have developed the earlier ideas contained in *Leadership and the New Science*, applying chaos and complexity theory more specifically to the management of organizations in *A Simpler Way*.[10] In so doing they start out with the following assumptions:

- The universe is a living, creative, experimenting experience of discovering what's possible at all levels of scale, from microbe to cosmos.
- Life's natural tendency is to organize; life organizes into greater levels of complexity to support more diversity and greater sustainability.
- Life organizes around a self; organizing is always an act of creating an identity.
- Life self-organizes; networks, patterns and structures emerge without external imposition or direction – organizations want to happen.
- People are intelligent, creative, adaptive, self-organizing and meaning seeking.
- Organizations are living systems; they too are intelligent, creative, adaptive, self-organizing, meaning-seeking.

Wheatley and Kellner Rogers, then, add a humanistic touch to the more pragmatically based approach adopted by Jim Moore. They describe such an approach as 'a simpler way'.

Welcoming back ourselves

The world of 'a simpler way', for Wheatley and Kellner Rogers, is a world we already know. We may not have seen it clearly, but we have been living it all our lives. The world we had been taught to see, they argue, was alien to our humanness. We were taught to see the world as a great machine. But then we could find nothing human in it. Alienation spawned the need to dominate. Fear led to control. As we change our image of the world, then, we leave behind the machine and welcome ourselves back. We recover a world that is supportive of human endeavour. This world of 'a simpler way' has a natural and spontaneous tendency towards organization, that is through self-organization. In this world we can create, experiment, organize, fail, accomplish, play, learn, create again. It is life's invitation to recreation and play, to natural organization and to self actualization that welcomes us back. We start with play.

Life as work and play

What has kept us from seeing life as creative, even playful, Wheatley and Kellner Rogers ask? At least since Darwin, western culture, they maintain, has harboured some great errors. It has believed that the world is hostile, that we are in a constant struggle for survival. The Darwinian environment loomed over every living thing, ready to challenge, ready to destroy. Get it right or die.

These errors of thought, they maintain – as does Brian Goodwin – have guided most of our decisions. They have kept us from seeing a world which is continuously exploring and creating. Life is about invention, not survival. We are here to create, not to defend. Out beyond the shadows of Darwinian thought, for Wheatley and Kellner Rogers, a wholly different world appears. Such a world delights in its explorations. Such a world makes things up as it goes along. Such a world welcomes us into its explorations as good partners.

The key elements of this 'logic of play' are evident in recent work by scientists such as Goodwin and Prigogine that explores how life came into being:

- Everything is in a constant process of discovery – every organism reinterprets the rules, creates exceptions for itself, creates new rules.
- Life uses messes to get to well-ordered solutions – using redundancy, fuzziness, dense webs of relationships, and unending trials and errors to find what works.
- Life is intent on finding what works, not what's right – the capacity to keep changing, to find what works now, is what keeps any organism alive.
- There are no 'windows of opportunity', narrow openings that soon disappear forever – possibilities beget more possibilities - they are infinite.
- Life is attracted to order – it experiments until it discovers how to form a system that can support diverse members – this system then provides stability for them.
- Life organizes around identity - every living thing acts to develop and preserve itself – new information and relationships are interpreted through a sense of self.
- Everything participates in the creation and evolution of its neighbours – all participate together in creating the conditions of their interdependence.

All this messy playfulness then creates relationships that make available more expression, more variety, more stability, more support.

In our exploration of what's possible we are led to search for new and different partners. Who we become together will always be different from who we are alone. We do not parachute into a sea of turbulence, to sink or swim. We and our environments become one system, each co-determining the other.

Patterns of organization

Organization as play

Playful and creative enterprises, for Wheatley and Kellner Rogers, are messy. Errors are expected, explored, welcomed. Simultaneity reduces the impact of any individual enterprise. More errors matter less if the actors are not linked together sequentially. The space for experimentation increases as we involve more minds in the experiment, as long as they can operate independently. Bacterial colonies, for example, successfully locate food by sending out 'random walkers'. Such systems slosh around in the mess, learning all the time, engaging everyone in finding what works. Living in this discovery-focused, messy, parallel-processing world, Wheatley and Kellner Rogers maintain, cannot help but engage us with the world's diversity.

Organizations as relationships

There is an innate striving in all forms of matter, they assert, to organize into relationships. There is a great seeking for connections, a desire to organize into more complex systems that include more relationships, more variety. This desire is evident everywhere in the cosmos, at all levels of scale. Everywhere, discrete elements come together, cohere and create new forms. The system maintains itself, Wheatley and Kellner Rogers maintain, only if change is occurring some-where in it all the time. New food sources, new neighbours, new talents appear. As conditions change, individuals experiment with new possibilities.

Without constant change the system sinks into the death grip of equilibrium. The broad paradox of stability and freedom, they argue – as will Ralph Stacey in the next chapter – is the stage on which co-evolution dances. Life leaps forward when it can share its learnings. The dense web of systems allows information to travel in all directions, speeding discovery and adaptation. Access to mutual learning creates resilience and adaptability. All complex organisms have therefore evolved through tumultuous cooperative venturing.

Organization as organizing

When we view organizations as machine-like objects, Wheatley maintains there-fore, unavoidably they become complexities of structure, policy and roles. We build rigid structures incapable of responding. We box ourselves in behind hard boundaries breached only by hostile forays. We create places of fear. We shrink from one another. We therefore mistrust the elemental organizing forces of life. The struggle and competitiveness that we thought characterized life become the pre-eminent features of our organizations. Our analytical culture, then, according to Wheatley and Kellner Rogers, drives us to so many cover-ups that it's hard to see the self-organizing capacity in any of us.

To the extent that we do self-organize, though, we see a need to join with others, we find the necessary information or resources, we respond creatively, and we create a solution that works. How then do we support our natural desire to organize and the world's natural desire to assist us? It begins with a change in our beliefs. We give up believing that we design the world into existence and instead take up roles in support of its flourishing. We work with what is available and encourage forms to come forth. We foster tinkering and discovery. We help create connections. We nourish ourselves with information. We remember that people self-organize and trust them to do so.

In self-organization, structures emerge. They are not imposed. They spring from the process of doing the work. These structures will be useful but temporary. We can expect them to emerge and recede as needed. It is not the design of a specific structure that requires attention but rather the conditions that will support emergence of necessary structures. Patterns and structures emerge as we connect to one another. People support one another with information and nurture one another with trust. In life, as a result, systems create the conditions for both stability and personal discovery.

For Wheatley and Kellner Rogers it is a lovely and intricate paradox. We connect with others and gain protection from external turbulence. We become part of something greater and thereby gain more freedom so that we can experiment with ourselves. If we do not exercise that freedom to change, the organization cannot maintain its stability. We therefore see differentiation in nature and conventionally interpret it as the key to competitive advantage. We look at the prevalence of narrow specializations and see it as the road to supremacy. According to Wheatley and Kellner Rogers we could not be more wrong. Life, for them, creates niches not to dominate but to support. Symbiosis is therefore the most favoured path for evolution. Self-definition, through the identification of a niche and the specification of the food required for survival, frees up all other food sources for others in the system.

Dances not wars

Living systems, then, as was illustrated conclusively by James Moore, cannot be explained by competition alone. Brutal species always destroy themselves, leaving the world to those who have worked out how to coexist with each other. We are not independent agents fighting for ourselves against all others. There is no hostile world out there plotting our demise. There is no 'out there' for anyone to occupy. We are utterly intertwined.

If we see life as a brutal contest among separate entities, we focus on individual contribution, on individual change. This world view not only makes us feel afraid and isolated but it also causes us to hope for heroes. Yet in a systems-seeking, co-evolving world there is no such thing as a hero. Everything is the result of interdependencies lodged within systems of organization where we support, challenge and create new combinations with others.

No one forges ahead independently, Wheatley and Kellner Rogers maintain, moulding the world to his or her presence while the rest of us trail admiringly behind. We tinker ourselves into existence by unobserved interactions with the players who present themselves to us. Environment, enemies, allies – all are affected by our efforts as we are by theirs. The systems we create are chosen together. They are the result, they maintain, of dances, not wars.

Self and identity

Self-discovery

Self-organization therefore is the capacity of life to invent itself. This process of invention, for Wheatley and Kellner Rogers, always takes shape around an identity. There is a self that seeks to organize, to make its presence known. All living systems have this ability to create themselves, not just initially, but as the continuous process of their lives.

Life, free to create itself as it will, moves into particular forms, into defined patterns of being. Pathways and habits develop. We then 'see' the world through this self we have created. We encourage others to change only if we honour who they are now. We ourselves engage in change only as we discover that we might be more of who we are by becoming something different.

We therefore misperceive the role of boundaries, according to Wheatley and Kellner Rogers, if we interpret them only as separations. We misperceive ourselves if we think we exist isolated from others. We misperceive the world if we see it as individuals struggling against one another. Life in fact co-evolves. There are therefore no separated individuals as such. The co-evolutionary processes of life cannot support isolation. What we create has value only if others find meaning in us. If our system rejects the self we have created we are truly valueless. As such, self is an opening to connections, not a barrier behind which we fight for survival. When we reach out for a different level of connection, our search for wholeness is rewarded with a world made wholly new.

Selves organizing

The organizing tendency of life, moreover, is always for Wheatley and Kellner Rogers a creative act. We reach out to others to create a new being. We reach out to grow the world into new possibilities. At the heart of every organization, then, is a self reaching out to new possibilities. We therefore organize always to affirm and enrich our personal identity. But then we take this vital passion for self-actualization and instutionalize it inauthentically, that is apart from ourselves, we create a depersonalized organization. The people who loved the originating purpose grow to disdain the institution that was created to fulfil it. Passion mutates into procedures, into rules and roles. The organization no longer lives. We see its bloated form and resent it for what it stops us from doing.

How then do we create organizations that stay alive? We need to trust that we are self-organizing, and we need to create the conditions in which self-organization can flourish. Identity, for Wheatley and Kellner Rogers, is the source of organization. Every organization is an identity in motion, moving through the world, trying to make a difference.

We need then to explore why we have come together. If we took time to ground our work in the deep connections that engage us, they maintain, we would be overwhelmed by the energy and contributions so willingly given. People and organizations with integrity then are wholly themselves. No aspect of self stands different or apart. When they go inside to find themsleves there is only one self there. With coherence comes the capacity to create organizations that are both free and effective. They are effective because they support people's ability to self-organize. They are free because they know who they are. Coherent organizations thus experience the world with fewer threats and more freedom.

Emergence

Emergence and relatedness

Life therefore wants to discover itself. Individuals explore possibilities and, according to Wheatley and Kellner Rogers, systems emerge. They self-transcend into new forms of being. Newness appears out of nowhere. Life becomes a one-way street to novelty. Such 'emergence', moreover, they say, is the surprising capacity we discover only when we join together. So-called 'emergence' provides simple evidence that we live in a relational world. Relationships change us, reveal us, evoke more from us. We seek out one another because we want to accomplish something. And then life surprises us with new capacities. Life is playful and life plays with us. A system is comprised of fluid relationships that all too often we observe as rigid structure, which inhibits emergence. What then do we normally do with surprise? What do we do with a world which cannot be known until it is in the process of discovering itself? It requires constant awareness, being present, being vigilant for the newly visible. An emergent world invites us to use the most human of all our capacities, a heightened self-consciousness. It asks us to be alert for what is unfolding.

An emergent world welcomes us in as conscious participants and surprises us with discovery. Our plans are nothing compared with what the world so willingly gives us.

Emerging organization

In classical evolutionary thought, as we saw in the previous chapter, change occurs within individuals. Each of us invents our own survival strategies as we struggle against the environment. When we apply this thinking to organizations, it leads us straight to individual personalities. If a distasteful situation develops, or we don't like where the system is headed, we just pluck out the bad genes. We look for the

251

mutants in our midst and expel them. Emergent evolution, Wheatley and Kellner Rogers emphasize, explains systems quite differently. Evolution occurs in many ways, but always from the desire to work out relationships for mutual coexistence. Locale by locale, individuals and groups figure out what works for them. Systems comprise fluid relationships that are webby, wandering, non-linear, entangled messes.

A self-organizing system therefore reveals itself as structures of relationships, patterns of behaviours, habits of belief, methods for accomplishing work. These patterns, structures and methods are visible. We become entranced by their forms. We probe and dissect them down to microscopic levels of detail. Yet change efforts directed at exchanging material forms have not given us the results we hope for. We need to look past these mesmerizing effects of organization and notice the processes that give them shape. Beneath all structures and behaviours lies the real creator, that is dynamic processes. Structures and behaviours emerge in effect from dynamic relationships. They emerge from decisions about how to belong together. Identity is at the core of every organization, fuelling its creation. In a world of emergence, new systems appear out of nowhere.

But the forms they assume originate from dynamic processes set in motion by information, relationships and identity. Organizations spiral into form, cohering into visibility. Like stars on winter nights, according to Wheatley and Kellner Rogers, they fill our field of vision and enthrall us. But organizations emerge from fiery cores, from richly swirling dynamics. This is where we need to gaze, into the origins that give rise to such diversity of form.

Conclusion

The spiral of life

Life, then, for Moore and for Wheatley, is motion, 'becoming becoming'. The motions of life swirl inward to the creating of self and outward to the creating of the world. We turn inward to bring forth a self. Then the self extends outward, seeking others, joining together. Systems arise. Life takes form from such ceaseless motions. Life moves toward life. Life as a result accepts only partners or indeed opponents, not bosses. We cannot stand outside a system as an objective, distant director. There is no objective ground to stand on anywhere in the entire universe. Our disconnection – our alleged objectivity – is an illusion; and even if we fail to realize this, the system will notice it immediately. Systems work with themselves; if we are not part of the system, we have no potency. Systems do not accept direction, only provocation.

There is no type of a priori intervention that can transform the system or turn it masterfully in a desired direction. The system is spinning itself into existence. It creates itself by exercising its freedom to choose what to notice. It is not volume or quantity that stirs any system. It is interest and meaning. If the system decides that something is meaningful, it absorbs this information into itself. It will display connections we never dreamed of.

Therefore, if we want to work with a system to influence its direction, the place for us to work is deep in the dynamics of the system where identity is taking form. Every being, every organization, is an identity in motion, creating itself in the world and creating its world simultaneously. The identity of a system can turn in on itself and become rigid and closed. Or the identity can move out into the world, exploring new ways of being. But always it is the process of self-creation that sets organizing in motion.

Strategic management and organizational dynamics

The one person, in the 1990s, who has combined the developmental insights of Moore, Wheatley, Goodwin and Prigogine into a coherent theory of strategy and organization is Ralph Stacey, whom we are about to meet in chapter 14. In chapter 15 we will look at the major contributions of Henry Mintzberg and David Hurst, both based in Canada, to the 'hard' side of developmental strategy, and those of Britain's Reg Revans and MIT's Peter Senge to the 'soft' side of organizational learning and development. In chapter 16, the final one on the developmental domain, the fruits of these developmental efforts are exemplified by Takeo Fujisawa, who helped create Honda, and by Joseph Jaworski, who recently wrote the best-selling book *Synchronicity: The Inner Path of Leadership*,[11] and who now works with Peter Senge. We turn first to Stacey.

14

STRATEGIC MANAGEMENT AND ORGANIZATIONAL DYNAMICS

The development mainstem

Introduction

From economics to psychology via complexity

Ralph Stacey is an economics graduate of the University of the Witwatersrand, in Johannesburg, and of the London School of Economics. Having subsequently spent many years as a corporate planner with the John Laing construction group, based in the UK, Stacey gradually came to the conclusion that the ordinary 'rationality' supposedly underlying both macro-economics and also business strategy was something of a a smokescreen. In the 1980s, as Stacey approached his own midlife, two transformations began to occur within him. In the first place he began to transfer his academic orientation from economics towards psychology, as he became ever more interested in processes of group dynamics. Secondly, his own 'mental model' of the world began to shift dramatically from a classically linear to a 'chaotically' non-linear view of reality.

Stacey became the first management thinker to systematically apply to the world of business the new insights into the physical and life sciences that were being acquired by 'chaos' and complexity theorists. In *Strategic Management and Organizational Dynamics*,[1] as we shall soon see, he differentiated the conventionally 'rational' and 'ideological' – our 'primal' – wisdoms from his own 'developmental' approach. Moreover, in his seminal work, *Managing Chaos*,[2] Stacey applies these latest insights from 'chaos' theory to the process of management. Finally, in his latest work, *Creativity and Complexity in Organizations*,[3] he most concertedly applies his insights, as a developmental management thinker, from the physical and psychological worlds to the strategic and organizational ones.

Such an integrated work is substantively different from the 'conventional strategic wisdom' of our primal (Peters and Porter) and rational (Hamel and Pralahad) managerial day.

Conventional 'mechanical' wisdoms: ideological and rational

The conventional wisdom on strategic management, for Stacey, is built on one or more of the following propositions:

- A *'one best way'* of managing – the visionary/ ideological model popularized by Tom Peters, amongst others. In this 'western' approach, research into successful organizations shows that key behavioural attributes are the causes of excellence.
- A *'best contingent way'*: the technical/rational 'northern' model, whereby companies formulate long-term plans using given criteria, then select, implement and monitor these.
- A *'configuration'* constellation model, involving an appropriate combination of structure, strategy, environmental and other factors that fit together.

This composite of conventional wisdoms, for Stacey, is based on the assumption that organizations are 'mechanical' systems that are driven by laws producing predictable long-term futures. Such predictable laws establish clear-cut links between cause and effect, between an action and an outcome. As a result, organizations are successful when they are close to a state of stable equilibrium. The dyanamics of successful organizations, as a direct consequence, are those of stability, regularity and predictability. Tensions or contradictions need to be resolved either personally and decisively (western), based on shared values, or impersonally and rationally (northern), based on pre-set criteria for evaluation. Such success is assumed to flow from analysing observable facts, based on a single shared ideology, so that little attention is paid to the way in which managers actually make sense of the world.

When uncertainty, ambiguity and paradox is recognized, it is assumed that success results from these being resolved in a way in which the tension they create is relieved. Instead of holism and evolution we have mechanism and resolution. These 'western' and 'northern' conventional wisdoms, then, can be compared and contrasted with an unconventional wisdom, which can be seen to have more of a connection with the 'east' and the 'south'.

The unconventional wisdom – dynamic and developmental

Strategic management

The strategies of any organization, from Stacey's own holistic perspective, are the perceived patterns, over a long period of time, in the sequences of actions undertaken by decision makers in the organization. These patterns in action flow from the circular feedback processes of discovery (cognitive), choice (affective) and action (behavioural) employed by these people in the organization (see Figures

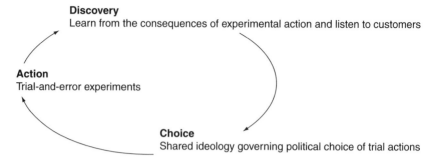

Figure 14.1 The 'western' excellence approach

14.1 and 14.2). How and what they discover (their paradigms and the perceptions they lead them to) directly affects what they choose to do. In effect, decision makers cannot choose what they have not perceived, and that choice in turn determines their actions. It is through their actions that they make further discoveries, leading to other actions and choices in a continuing loop.

Organizational dynamics

The following questions, for Stacey then, underlie these patterns of discovery, action and choice. What do people know about the operation of feedback systems, involving the circular processes of discovery, choice and action? What is the effect of uncertainty and ambiguity on that circular feedback process? What is the effect on management actions of shared or unshared ways of understanding the world? To what extent is organizational strategy the result of static organizational intention, as opposed to emergent evolving strategy?

What is the impact of group behaviour on the choices and actions of managers? What, moreover, is the role of the formal and informal organization in the successful management of the enterprise? What is the relationship between success and stability or instability? How do managers cope with paradox? What, ultimately,

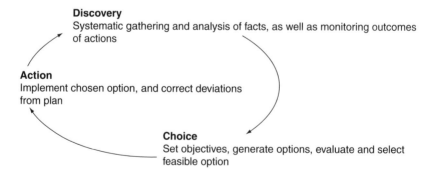

Figure 14.2 The 'northern' rational approach

can we say about the dynamics of organizations, that is the patterns of change in strategic management and organization development?

Statics and dynamics

Closed, contained and open-ended change

The way we frame our understanding of the world, as in the above terms, determines what we perceive or discover; what we perceive determines what we choose to do; what we choose determines what we actually do. The essence of mastering systems thinking, therefore, as a management discipline, lies in seeing whole patterns where others see only part events and forces to which to react. The more expert we become, therefore, the greater the risk that we will not question what we are doing. This gives rise to the need for complex learning, which involves not only adjusting our actions in the light of consequences, but also questioning and adjusting the unconscious mental models we are using to design these actions. Complex learning is therefore essentially holistic, destabilizing and revolutionary, but vitally necessary for creativity and innovation.

Managers in any organization, moreover, face a spectrum of change situations in every time frame, from the past to the present to the future. At each point the spectrum stretches from predictable *closed* change, through statistically predictable *contained* change, into unknowable *open-ended* change. In open-ended change situations the prime difficulty lies not in finding answers but in identifying what questions to ask. New mental models have to be developed and shared.

At the same time, people in a group facing change typically become anxious, and the dynamic of their interaction becomes complex, as will be indicated in the section on creativity and complexity below.

Closed change involves clear objectives, repetitive actions, measurable and known outcomes. Similar and yet different is contained change. It occurs when there are clear objectives and repetitive actions, but imperfectly measurable and largely unknown outcomes. Finally, and conversely, open-ended change means that there are ambiguous and conflicting objectives, unique actions, non-measurable and unknowable outcomes. In conditions near to closed change, therefore, control consists of routine-based monitoring and control. In conditions near to contained change, control can take the form of shared culture, political processes and trial-and-error actions. In conditions that are open-ended, control will be possible only in its intuitive, political and judgemental forms. Finally, whereas closed and contained change lend themselves to linear thinking, open-ended change is holistically based and intrinsically non-linear.

Linear and non-linear systems

The dominant way of thinking about the relationship between cause and effect in western (and northern) culture, for Stacey, is what might be called linear and unidirectional. The key point about all forms of such *equlilibrium* behaviour is that they are regular, orderly and predictable. Most primal and rational theories of management have been developed within a similarly mechanistic framework.

When we think of organisms and organizations as systems, as Peter Senge has done (see chapter 15), then we become aware of more complex forms of causality involving interconnection and interdependence, where everything affects everything else.

Such so-called mathematically 'non-linear' feedback systems can involve very complex and *dynamic* connections between cause and effect. Equilibrium, then, takes a stable form when the behaviour of a system regularly repeats its past. It takes an unstable form when behaviour diverges from the past, but in a perfectly regular way. The key point about all forms of equlibrium behaviour, Stacey emphasizes, is that they are regular, orderly and predictable. Most theories of management, the majority of which have originated from North America and a select minority from France, have been developed within such an equilibrium framework. Dynamics, conversely, is the the study of how a system evolves over time. It is concerned with the effects of tension in a system, with the manner in which contradictions or variations cause tension and so create energy which drives behaviour. Whereas such an approach is characteristic of psychodynamic psychology and also of the new physics and biology, it has until recently been singularly absent from management.

Conventional and unconventional strategic management

Central to the static conventional wisdom is the belief that successful organizations conform to one of a limited number of configurations covering mission, strategy, structure, style. This western orientation is best reflected in the now well-known 'seven Ss' illustrated in chapter 6. The static *posture* of an organization, in effect, is what you see when you stand at the organizational boundary and look inwards at its products and markets, technologies, organizational structure and controls, and its shared culture. The organization's *position*, moreover, is what you see when you stand at the organizational boundary and look outwards at market shares in particular segments, customer image, and core competence in relation to competitors. It is clearly reflected in the popular acronym SWOT – strengths and weaknesses, opportunities and threats – so characteristic of our conventional strategic wisdom.

A successful dynamic strategy, conversely, is determined by an organization's ability, and that of its people, to survive by innovating and transforming themselves. Everything managers do, therefore, depends at the most fundamental level on the mental models through which they understand their world, particularly the models they share. For Stacey, therefore, companies that succeed sustain contradictions which generate tension; tension creates energy; with such energy organizations transform themselves. Systems therefore can only be creative through experiencing instability; there is therefore a fundamental relationship between chaos and innovation. Such holistic and evolutionary thinking, moreover, is a distinct attitude of mind.

Ordinary and extraordinary management

The far-from-equlibrium organization

All organizations, from Stacey's holistic perspective, are webs of non-linear feedback loops connected to other people and other organizations (their environments) by similar webs. Such non-linear feedback systems are capable of operating in states of stable and unstable equilibrium, or in the borders between these states, that is far from equilibrium. All organizations, moreover, operate paradoxically, in that they are pulled both towards stability by the forces of integration, and also towards the other extreme of unstable equilibrium by innovation. If the organization gives in to the pull of stability or instability, it ossifies or disintegrates. Success lies in between, as a difficult-to-maintain 'dissipative structure', which we identified with the Nobel-prize-winning chemist Ilya Prigogine in the previous chapter. The dynamics of the successful organization are therefore those of irregular cycles and discontinuous trends, falling within qualitative patterns, or wholes. Through unravelling these holistic patterns, managers discover and create the long-term futures of their organizations.

Successful long-term planning, therefore, is a creative, innovative process that requires exposure to and management of contradiction. Instead of regularity and consistency it sees irregularity, contradiction and creative tension as the essence of the successful enterprise. Effective strategy formulation in fact requires management to maintain a position away from equilibrium, in a state of contradiction between stability and instability, between tight and flexible controls. Creativity is thus closely related to destruction, and instability is actually required to shatter existing paradigms, so making way for the new. Such a dialectic generates tension that will eventually force a 'chaotic' rearrangement of conflicting forces.

Self-organization

Such 'chaos' in its scientific sense is not utter confusion but a combination of qualitative patterns and specific randomness, as Wheatley has already identified. Such a combination of fuzzy categories, moreover, is accompanied by endless variability. Stable and explosively unstable equilibria are not the only attractors of systemic behaviour. Non-linear systems can operate at a level of bounded instability far from equilibrium, a state between differentiated and integrated extremes. This is a complex state of orderly behaviour which requires continual inputs of attention, time and resource to sustain the organization as a dissipative structure. Strongly shared cultures push an organization back to stability, while counter-cultures are required to sustain the dissipative structure far from equilibrium.

Those who succeed, therefore, in the borders between stability and instability will be strategic managers who see patterns where others search for specific links between causes and events. Since, for Stacey, little can be said about the future of complex systems, it makes sense to identify meaning retrospectively with a view to designing future action.

Ingrained habits need to be supplanted by a continual questioning of existing mental models, and the development of new ones to cope with the unfolding future. Moreover, it must be accepted that unconscious defence mechanisms against anxiety will be touched off when uncertainty and ambiguity levels rise, and when the nature of power is changed. These need to be accommodated as integral to change. Change cannot therefore be comprehensively anticipated; creative development depends, in effect, on some form of spontaneous self-organization, with management providing favourable conditions. This ultimately serves to differentiate what Stacey terms 'ordinary' from 'extraordinary' management, what Wheatley terms 'mechanism' from 'organism', and what Moore terms 'competitive strategy' from 'ecosystemic strategy'.

Passion, reason and emergence

Ordinary management, then, for Stacey, is practised when most of the managers in an organization share the same mental models or paradigm. Choices are made in some approximation to technically rational criteria as there is general agreement as to what the business is about. Control is practised in its planning/monitoring and ideological forms through the instruments of hierarchy and bureaucracy, deploying rational processes to secure convergence and fit. Such ordinary management can only be practised in closed- and contained-change situations. Effective top executives are 'ordinarily' in control of their organizations and their strategies because of their business missions, long-term plans, systems of rules and regulations. Such an organization should have a common and unified culture. The business should ordinarily identify what it is good at and deliver what its customers want. The trouble with such standard maps and traditional organizational principles, as Stacey emphasizes, is that they can be used only to identify routes that others have travelled before.

Extraordinary management involves questioning and shattering paradigms, and then creating new ones. It depends critically upon contradiction and tension, because it falls outside the known bounds of rational argument. It is a process of persuasion and conversion, requiring the contributions of champions. New paradigms have to emerge from the confusion created by anomalies in the existing paradigm, incorporating intuitive, political and group learning modes of decision making. (See Figure 14.3.)

Extraordinary management is the form managers must use if they are to change strategic direction and innovate. No one can know the future destination of an innovative organization. Rather, that organization's managers must create, invent and discover their destination as they go. To do that they must drop the old stable equilibrium mind-set and develop a new one that recognizes the positive role of

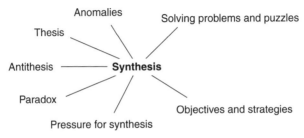

Figure 14.3 Ordinary and extraordinary management

instability and the fact that long-term futures are unknowable. A manager will use instability and crisis in a positive way to provoke the continual questioning and organizational learning through which unknowable futures are discovered and created. The resulting form of self-organizing and self-regulating control is a group phenomenon, occurring when political interactions and dialogues between members of a group produce coherent behaviour. Developing over time by passing through periods of instability, crisis or chaos and then spontaneously making choices at critical points, this evolutionary approach produces new wholes.

Politics and learning

Extraordinary managers, therefore, do not drive and control new strategic directions. Instead, they create favourable conditions for, and participate in, complex learning and effective politics. Instead of mission statements and plans, such managers focus on ever-changing agendas of strategic issues, challenges and aspirations. Multiple, contradictory cultures should therefore be developed to foster different perspectives and provoke the complex learning that is necessary to handle changing strategic agendas. Learning groups that work in spontaneously self-organizing networks that encourage open conflict, engage in dialogue, and publicly test assertions, become vital. Self-organizing political networks, according to Stacey, function to undermine the hierachically based status quo. Without the consequent tension between control and freedom there could be no change.

The most important learning that individuals and organizations undergo, moreover, flows from the trial-and-error action they take in real time, arising especially from the way they reflect on these actions as they take them. How well people learn under these circumstances depends on the way they interact with each other in groups. Continuing success flows from creative interaction with the market environment, not simply building on existing strengths but intentionally steering away from equilibrium. The result is organizational tension, paradox and never-ending contradiction, and this provokes conflict and learning, the source of creativity.

The only route to long-term success, for Stacey then, is through innovation and accelerated organizational learning, because no competitive advantage is inherently sustainable. This view of organizational development is a dialectical

261

one in which contradictory forces produce, through learning, a new synthesis of more complex strategies and structures.

Adapting to the environment is thereby replaced by creative interaction with other actors in the environment. Comprehensive control systems and culture-change programmes are replaced by organizations as complex, evolving systems where all managers can do is intervene at sensitive leverage points.

Corrective action will usually be experimental at first, so as to provide a vehicle for further learning. As unclear open-ended issues proceed through experimentation to emerge as potentially successful new strategies, the formal bodies play a more prominent role. Managers come to share memories of what has worked and not worked in the past. In this way they build up a business philosophy for the company. Activity is spontaneous and self-organizing in that no central authority can direct anyone to detect and select an open-ended issue for attention. The political activity of building support for attention to some detected issue is also self-organizing. It requires continuing inputs of energy and attention to sustain consensus within a far-from-equilibrium organization, conceived as a dissipative structure.

Dissipative structures

The border area between equilibrium and non-equilibrium, for Stacey, is a state of paradox in which stability and instability pull the system in different directions. Scientists, as Stacey has already indicated, have called this combination of specific unpredictability and qualitative pattern a chaos, fractal or change state. Only when a system operates in this chaotic, far-from-equilibrium state is it continually creative. Chaotic behaviour has an overall pattern within which specific random outcomes occur. Such 'chaos' is not utter confusion but bounded – rather than explosive – instability. A combination of order and disorder continually unfolds in irregular but similar forms. 'Chaotic' managers seize on small differences in customer requirements and perceptions, and build these into significant differentiators for their products, through amplifying feedback. Then they establish quality and cost targets against which they control production of the product to satisfy the demand they have created, through dampening feedback.

When non-linear feedback systems are pushed far from equilibrium, Stacey maintains, they follow a common sequence of steps in which they move from one state, through chaos, to unpredictable states of new order. These 'dissipative structures' are difficult to sustain because they require continual inputs of energy if they are to survive. Functional politics, then, involves continual dialogue around contentious issues. It is the means of attracting organizational attention to open-ended issues. Its function is to spread instability, within boundaries. Such instability is necessary to shatter existing patterns of behaviour and perceptions so that the new may emerge. At each point of transition, systems driven far from equilibrium move through patterns of instability in which symmetry is broken, confronting the system with choices at critical points. Through a process of spontaneous self-organization, involving a form of communication and cooperation among the components of the system, new order may be produced.

'Chaotic' strategic management

Strategy and learning

The strategic management process, then, as far as Stacey's extraordinary manager is concerned, goes something like this:

1 *Detect and select issues*   Open-ended change, the kind that strategic management is concerned with, is typically the result of many accumulated small events and actions.
2 *Gain attention and build support*   The birth of strategy involves some individual, at some level of the hierarchy, detecting some potential issue and beginning to push for organizational attention to be paid to it.
3 *Interpret and handle the emerging agenda*   The issue detected in 2 becomes part of the organization's strategic issue agenda – it becomes the focus of the organizational learning through which a business develops new strategic agendas.
4 *Clarify preferences*   At some critical point, pressure arising from power, personality or group interaction forces a choice, whose outcome is unpredictable depending on the power play and group dynamics.
5 *Take experimental action*   Action will usually be experimental at first, thus providing a vehicle for further learning – task forces may be set up to carry out experimental actions such as with new product development.
6 *Gain legitimacy and backing*   Before such informal action is built into a strategy, formal bodies and procedures are required to legitimize choices being made and to allocate resources.
7 *Incorporate outcomes into organizational memory*   In sharing memories of what has worked or failed to work in the past, managers build up a business philosophy; these recipes, taken together, become the company culture; they provide another boundary around the instability of the political and learning processes through which strategic issues are handled.

Anticipation and participation

Because trying to predict the future is a pointless exercise for an innovative company, according to Stacey, corporate strategy requires anticipation and participation. It must be based firmly on the qualitative nature of what is happening now and what has happened in the past, focusing particularly on the anomalies in the current situation. It means generating new perspectives on what has been going on. It means framing problems and opportunities. It means noticing potential and possibility. It means creating group dynamics that encourage participation in complex learning activities, making explicit and also exploring not only issues themselves but also the group's learning behaviours.

It involves trying to identify the mental models that have led to the way problems and opportunities are being framed, with a view to developing a different learning model and changing mind-sets. Complex group learning occurs far from equilibrium when individuals are in conflict and confusion, and it incorporates a newly shared meaning, and a willingness to engage in dialogue and listen.

Such far-from-equilibrium activities, in summary then, move the would-be extraordinary manager, in Stacey's terms:

- away from a concern with the individual expert or visionary towards a concern with the effects of the personalities, group dynamics and learning behaviours of managers in groups
- away from the stability of continuing consensus based on 'rational' reasoning and toward the creative instability of contention and dialogue
- away from condemning the messiness of real business decision making towards examining, understanding and dealing with organizational defence mechanisms and game playing
- away from the perception of group learning as a simple process relating to outcomes, and toward an understanding of group learning as a complex process affecting the way people develop
- away from the closure of problem solving toward the opening up of contentious and ambiguous issues
- away from trying to apply prescriptive models to many specific situations, and toward developing new mental models to design actions for each new strategic situation

Organizational dynamics

Patterns of learning and innovation

The developmental role of the extraordinary manager, therefore, as Stacey emphasizes, is not to invest in training programmes. Rather it is incumbent on him or her to create a context favourable to complex learning, from which challenges may emerge.

People interacting in an organization are more likely to produce a pattern in their actions through self-organization when the context in which they work enables them to discover and learn. Their focus will therefore be upon detecting anomalies in what is going on in the here and now, and upon using intuition and analogy to develop responses. At the same time, they will be examining and trying to improve the group dynamics upon which such processes in organizations depend. Finally, the concern for developing common cultures and cohesive teams will be replaced by actions designed to promote different cultures in order to generate new perspectives.

At the same time, for Stacey, an evolving, holistic perspective recognizes the great importance of hierarchy, unequal power and clear role definitions in the short-term control of a business. It also recognizes the importance of self-organizing political networks in managing the unknowable long-term future, and the necessary constraints on their operation provided by clear hierarchies. Both strong value sharing and also the failure to share culture at all have the effect of creating boundaries that are too tight or too loose, contexts inappropriate for complex learning. Loosely shared multiple cultures, on the other hand, both generate instability and provide a boundary around that instability. The more effective the interacting multiple cultures are at complex learning, the more they will be able to contain the instability that their learning inevitably generates. Self-organizing – as opposed to self-managing – teams thrive under such circumstances.

Self-organizing networks

Self-organization, then, is a fluid process in which informal, temporary teams form spontaneously around issues, whereas self-managed teams are permanent and formally established. Top managers cannot control self-organizing networks; they can only intervene to influence the boundary conditions around them.

Extraordinary participants decide who takes part in self-organizing networks and what the boundaries of their activities are, whereas ordinary managers decide who should constitute self-managing teams. Self-organizing networks therefore operate in conflict with and are constrained by the hierarchy, whereas self-managing teams replace the hierarchy. Unequal power, Stacey emphasizes, energizes self-organizing networks through conflict but also operates as a constraint, whereas dispersed powers in self-managing teams are supposed to lead to consensus. People in self-organizing networks empower themselves, whereas in self-managing teams the top management empowers people. The self-organizing process is both provoked and constrained by cultural difference, which is at least to some degree unknowable, whereas the self-managing process is based on a strongly and knowably shared culture.

Steps towards managing an unknowable future

In contrast, when the future is unknowable, Stacey concludes, managers cannot mechanistically install techniques, procedures, structures and technologies to control long-term outcomes. They can holistically manage boundary conditions, thereby pushing the organization far from equilibrium, where spontaneous self-organization may occur and new strategic directions may emerge. The key question managers face, in that case, is not how to maintain stable equilibrium but how to establish sufficient sustained instability to provoke complex learning. It is through political interaction and complex learning, then, that businesses create and manage their unknowable futures. More specifically this involves:

- *Developing a new understanding of control*   Ordinary managers, who view politics and group learning as forms of control devoid of organization-wide intent, operate on the boundaries of strategy, not on the process or the outcome. For extraordinary managers, political and learning processes are integral to planning and control.
- *Designing, applying and distributing power*   Where the organization faces an ambiguous, open-ended future, the application of force – Stacey maintains – is disastrous. Groups in a state of submission or rebellion are incapable of complex learning. The most powerful group members should sometimes withdraw and allow conflict, sometimes intervene with suggestions and influence, and sometimes impose authority, using power variably. If power is unequal but distributed and applied according to circumstances, we find a flexible, fluctuating boundary around the political process that enables complex learning.
- *Establishing self-organizing learning teams*   The heart of 'chaotic' management is a flexible, ever-changing agenda of open-ended issues that is identified, clarified and progressed by the self-organizing networks of the organization. Group members should be chosen on the basis of personality rather than on the basis of their position in the formal hierarchy, drawing membership from a number of different functions, units and levels. A team can only be self-organizing if it discovers its own goals and objectives. This means that top management must limit themselves to presenting the group with ambiguous challenges.
- *Develop multiple cultures*   Cross-cultural learning is finally promoted by rotating people between functions, companies and countries. New perspectives seldom appear when the same culture and unconscious mental models are shared. Their learning is complex because it is not simply the absorption of existing knowledge, techniques or recipes, but the continual questioning of deeply held and usually unconscious beliefs. The creative work needed to deal with open-ended issues ultimately takes time and resources, but without this investment new strategic directions will never emerge.

Creativity and complexity

In Ralph Stacey's most recent work, *Complexity and Creativity in Organizations*, his emphasis shifts towards the psychodynamics of creativity, set within an organizational context, focusing most particualrly on play and anxiety.

Play – space for creativity in the mind

Playing, he says, the basis of human creativity, takes place in a transitional space between an individual's rather disorderly inner fantasy life and the relatively orderly outer reality the individual encounters, the tasks he or she follows in the real world. Playing is the process of manipulating transitional objects, such as metaphors, objects that are one thing but stand for another. Creativity is also play because it is closely connected with the ability to use symbols and analogies, to construct and use metaphors – in other words, to allow one thing to stand for something else. Creativity, therefore, needs a feedback process between inner fantasy and outer reality.

Because play is not engagement with current reality but the use of real objects in fantasy, it cannot be driven by the dominant symbol system and so must reflect the contents of the 'recessive' symbol system. That system forms speculations, images, dreams, metaphors, analogies, fantasies and myths. In other words, such recessive schemata consist of the repertoire of thoughts and beliefs available to an individual but not currently being used in order to engage with reality. The recessive symbol system governs the inner life with which the individual engages others in play and in speculative, exploratory dialogue. This dialogue is the process of double-loop learning, which constitutes creativity. Innovation is new learning embodied in the performance of novel primary tasks or novel ways of performing old tasks. The two schemata are operating in tension with each other – play in the recessive system builds up potential destruction and renewal of at least parts of the dominant system.

However, potential creativity or innovation become actual only when they help an individual to survive better in his or her environment, that is to climb higher up a 'fitness peak', or better still to climb up a higher peak.

The fitness landscape for an individual is determined by the behaviours of those to whom this individual is linked in his or her own network – usually one or more of the immediate groups of which he or she is a part. Creativity, then, can never be an individual process but must always involve interaction with others in a group. An individual is creative only if she or he is a member of groups that are capable of assisting in the containment of anxiety. In the end individuals can only be said to be creative if they can engage with the creative activity of others, in both competition and cooperation of some kind.

Accommodating anxiety – space for creativity in the group

The key control parameter, Stacey says, in facilitating learning and development – thereby moving people between what he terms the stable and unstable zones of behaviour and into the space for novelty – is the level of the manager's anxiety and the degree of its containment. The individual can, regressively so to speak, be returned to the 'ordinary' stable zone by re-erecting the containing structures and thus reducing the level of anxiety. At some critical intermediate level, though, there is enough challenge and contention existing to provoke learners into some kind of exploration. However, this is only likely to arise if there is enough emotional containment of that anxiety to prevent managers from being submerged by defensive–aggressive behaviour.

At such critical points of 'anxiety containment', learners can avoid both the rampant fears of the unstable zone and the rigidly defensive behaviour of the stable one. It is the 'extraordinary' manager's role, then, to play a part in providing such containment. If, as a direct result, relationships within a small group, or within the organization as a whole, have the quality of trust and compassion, if for Stacey they are based on empathy and even love, then they operate as effective containers of anxiety. Given such high-quality interconnectedness, a group can contain anxiety and stay at the edge of chaos.

The second way of containing anxiety without abandoning the edge of chaos is provided by honest self-reflection, that is when members of a group jointly reflect upon the system they constitute. The third way to contain anxiety is through the quality of leadership and the way in which power is exercised – specifically, if a leader avoids authoritarian behaviour and exhibits a capacity for articulating issues and posing insightful questions. In this way, moreover, enabling conditions are established for role evolution, and the leader's role is to foster such a climate within his or her organization.

Conclusion

Extraordinary leadership

The leadership required in extraordinary management therefore includes the capacity to contain anxiety for others, on the one hand, and the ability to provoke and contribute to the 'double-loop learning' process (learning to learn) on the other. Anxiety-containing capacity is a function of the leader that has to do with the manner in which power is used and with compassion for the feelings and fears of others in the group. Leaders contain anxiety when they are able to empathize with others and articulate or intepret what they are experiencing.

Provoking such double-loop learning requires the capacity to play with metaphor and images and pose stretching challenges for others and the ability to listen and hold oneself open to changing one's mind. Complexity theories of management lead to a very rich, paradoxical theory of leadership in which leaders have to be both conventional directors of others and the far more subtle containers of their anxiety and provokers of their double-loop learning capacity.

Self-reflection – dialogue with others

Thus, extraordinary management is not a new process; it is what people in organizations are already doing in an automatic way without much awareness or reflection. What is new is a coherent overall framework for people to use in reflecting on what they are doing so that they can make their own more useful sense of it. The prescription, then, is to use the insights of complexity science as a framework for individual, group and organizational self-reflection, that is an examination of, and dialogue about, the processes of extraordinary management. This call for self-reflection – including how one is using power and what impact it is having on others – is perhaps the most important prescription of a complex adaptive system view of organizational life.

It involves true dialogue in which people engage with each other, not to be in control, but to provoke and be provoked, to learn and contribute to the learning of others, to change their own minds as well as the minds of others. This process is like play in that it invites activity in the transitional zone of the mind, whose reality and fantasy come together in the form of metaphors, analogies and images. Experience-based intuition, rather than sequential, logical analysis, leads to creative insight. Creativity and efficiency are therefore enemies. For the first requires slack resources and the second requires that there be no slack resources. Efficiency requires that there be no redundancy, no repetiton of the same tasks in different parts of the organization or at different times. Creativity, however, requires redundancy. Such a concept of 'redundancy' will be re-visited when we come to consider Nonaka's metaphysically based 'knowledge-creating company'. Before we do that, however, we need to reveal the branches, and fruits, of developmental management, starting with two noted Canadian strategists, Henry Mintzberg and David Hurst.

15

EMERGENT STRATEGY AND ORGANIZATIONAL LEARNING

The branches of developmental management

Introduction

Management and organizational development

The branches of developmental management are somewhat sparser than those in the rational domain. In fact, whereas on the one hand corporate strategy has been dominated by primal and rational orientations, so-called *organization development*,[1] which first emerged in the 1960s and 1970s, never really came of age. In its place, in the 1980s and 1990s, has been the stronger emphasis on *manager self-development*,[2] which has been isolated from the mainstream of management and organization. It is for that very reason that this book retains an intimate connection between a business's roots, mainstem and branches, and its managerial fruits.

Emergent strategy and organizational learning

Indeed, and as we shall soon see, a developmental approach to business, on the 'hard' side, stimulated in the 1990s by Ralph Stacey, had been spearheaded since the 1970s by Canada's Henry Mintzberg, duly *crafting strategy*.[3] However, its fuller articulation has been left to David Hurst, educated in South Africa and now resident in Canada, who has focused on commercial and industrial *crisis and renewal*.[4]

At the same time, during the 1990s, the focus on organizational learning has taken over from organization development. Whereas the originator in the field of managerial and organizational learning was Reg Revans, the British inventor of so-called 'action learning',[5] its most popular proponent today is Peter Senge.[6] This chapter places less emphasis on the work of Mintzberg and Revans and greater emphasis on the work of David Hurst and Peter Senge.

The 'hard' developmental branches – emergent strategy

Crafting strategy

Emergent strategies

Henry Mintzberg, based at McGill University in Montreal, has remained over the past twenty years something of an *enfant terrible* within the academic management establishment. Starting out in the 1970s,[7] he was critical of the rational approach to management, that is planning and organizing, directing and controlling, which had been originally derived from the Frenchman Fayol. For Mintzberg, management, for real, was a much more pragmatic combination of decision making, interpersonal and information-processsing activities. What he seemingly found, amongst senior managers, was that informal actions and interactions predominated over formal management activities.

Mintzberg, then, as indicated in chapter 7, was inclined to view the strategy-making process[8] in informal terms.

> Imagine someone planning strategy. What most likely springs to mind is an image of orderly thinking: a senior manager, or a group of them, sitting in an office formulating courses of action that everyone else will implement on schedule. The keynote is reason – rational control, the systematic analysis of competitors and markets, of company strengths and weaknesses, the combination of these analyses producing clear, explicit, full-blown strategies. Now imagine someone crafting strategy. An entirely different image most likely results, as different from planning as craft is from mechanization. Craft evokes traditional skill, dedication, perfection through the mastery of detail. What springs to mind is not so much thinking and reason as involvement, a feeling of intimacy and harmony with the material at hand, developed through long experience and commitment. Formulation and implementation merge into a fluid process of learning, through which creative strategies evolve. My thesis is simple. The crafting image better captures the process by which better strategies come to be. The planning image, long popular in the literature, distorts those processes and thereby misguides organizations that embrace it unreservedly.[9]

Mintzberg indicates that the first article he ever wrote on 'the science of strategy making', in 1967, alludes to the fact that the process was less of a 'grand plan' and more of a 'Darwinian evolutionary approach'. Indeed, for him, strategy making, which has been his central interest throughout his career, has always involved more than a set of rationally based prescriptions. Rather, as we can see from the quotation above, it has involved a process of 'crafting'. Such 'crafted' strategies, moreover, he and his colleagues at McGill typecast as 'emergent'. In other words, for Mintzberg as for Stacey, they appear without clear intentions. Actions simply converge into patterns. These may become deliberate, if they are recognized and legitimized by senior management, but this will be in hindsight rather than with foresight.

Strategic learning

For Mintzberg then, while deliberate strategy-making precludes learning, emergent strategy fosters it. People take actions one by one and respond to them, so that patterns eventually form. Strategies grow like weeds in a garden. They take root in all kinds of places, wherever people have the capacity to learn, because they are in touch with the situation, and the resources to support the capacity. These strategies become organizational when they become collective, that is when they proliferate to influence the organization at large. That having been said, though, Mintzberg asserts:

> In practice, of course, all strategy-making walks on two feet, one deliberate the other emergent. For just as purely deliberate strategy-making precludes learning, so purely emergent strategy-making precludes control. Pushed to the limit neither approach makes sense. Learning must be coupled with control.[10]

All in all, then, to manage strategy is to craft thought and action, control and learning, stability and change.

> The popular view sees the strategist as a planner or as a visionary, someone sitting on a pedestal dictating brilliant strategies for everyone else to implement. While recognizing the importance of thinking ahead and especially of the need for creative vision in a prosaic world, I wish to propose an additional view of the strategist – as a pattern recognizer, a learner if you will, who manages a process in which strategies (and visions) can emerge as well as be deliberately conceived. I also wish to redefine that strategist, to replace that individual with a collective entity, made up of many actors whose interplay expresses an organization's mind. This strategist finds strategies no less than creates them, often in patterns that form inadvertently in its own behaviour.[11]

Elements of strategic crafting

In the final analysis, for Mintzberg then, crafting strategy incorporates five distinct, though overlapping, elements. First it is necessary to *manage stability*. Indeed, most of the time senior managers should not be formulating strategies at all. They should be getting on with making their organizations as effective as possible in pursuing the strategies they already have. Like distinguished crafts people, he asserts, organizations become distinguished because they master the details. At the same time, the real challenge in crafting strategy is secondly to *detect* subtle *discontinuities* that may undermine an organization in the future. These can be dealt with only by minds that are attuned to existing patterns and yet able to perceive important breaks in them. There is no specific technique for this, Mintzberg stresses, only experience.

Thirdly, it is important for the strategic craftsperson to *know the business*. The kind of knowledge involved here is not intellectual knowledge, not analytical reports or abstracted facts and figures, but personal knowledge, intimate understanding, equivalent to the craftsperson's feel for clay. Fourthly, moreover, Mintzberg's emergent strategist needs *to manage patterns*, that is to detect emergent patterns and help them take shape. The job of such a manager, then, is not just to preconceive specific strategies but also to recognize their emergence elsewhere in the organization. To manage appropriately in this context, in fact, is to create a climate within which a wide variety of strategies can grow. In more complex organizations, this may mean building flexible structures, hiring creative people, defining broad umbrella strategies, and watching for patterns that emerge. Fifthly and finally, there is a need to *reconcile change and continuity*. There is a time to sow and a time to reap. Some new patterns must be held in check until the organization is ready for a strategic revolution, or at least a period of divergence. As patterns recognizer, the manager has to be able to sense when to exploit an established crop of strategies and when to encourage new strains to replace the old. Mintzberg concludes:

> While strategy is a word that is usually associated with the future, its link to the past is no less central. As the Danish existentialist philosopher Kierkegaard once observed, life is lived forward but understood backward. Managers may have to live strategy in the future, but they must understand it through the past. Like a potter at the wheel, organizations must make sense of the past if they hope to manage the future. Only by coming to understand the patterns that form in their own behaviour do they get to know their capabilities and potential. Thus crafting strategy, like managing a craft, requires a natural synthesis of the past, present and future.[12]

As we can see, Henry Mintzberg forges a unique blend between the primal and developmental domains of management, while almost bypassing the rational. Indeed, while I have included his work under the heading 'hard' developmental, because of the business and strategic connotations, there is much of the 'soft' primal within it. Moreover, unlike Stacey, who strongly embraces the rational, as well as the developmental, through his scientific inclinations, Mintzberg wants little to do with such rationally based sophistications. His fascination with 'tacit' knowledge overshadows any 'explicit' strategic notions, which, as we shall now see, are less alien to David Hurst.

Accommodating crisis and fostering renewal

Rhythms of renewal

David Hurst, though born in Britain, spent most of his youth and early adulthood in South Africa, before taking up an executive position in Canada. Moreover, he is one of those rare business executives who have taken the time and trouble to develop their own management concepts. In fact, his approach to 'crisis and renewal', while strongly lodged in the realms of the developmental, as we shall see, also has metaphysical connotations. For while Hurst draws explicitly on ecology and biology, he does pay his debts to the humanities.

Hurst, to begin with, takes on from where Mintzberg leaves off. To a considerable and unacknowledged extent, he reckons, modern business organizations advance strategically by accident, economically by windfall, and politically by disaster. A manager's influence, he says, is therefore often occasional, indirect and delayed rather than constant, direct and immediate. However, Hurst then takes a leap into metaphysical terrain that Mintzberg never dares to enter:

> In a modest way, I will try to restore management to life, to reintegrate it with the humanities, by reconnecting it with literature, philosophy, history and art. The humanities do not make progress the way that science does. They begin and end with human experience. Their great advantage over the sciences, however, is that they deal with ultimate human concerns.[13]

The concept of organizational renewal, Hurst goes on to say, assumes that in the beginning of an organization's life, at its founding, there was something of value, some shared experience that was authentic and meaningful. Over time, this original feeling of authenticity, of meaning, has either faded or been lost. Renewal involves going back to the founding values to reconnect the past to the present, to rediscover old in the new. Thus renewal is about continuty amid change, and about patterns that repeat themselves, the rhythms of life, about how we need to go backward in order to go forward – to travel back to the future. And the cycles of these movements are in the patterns of the stories we tell. They are the rhythms of renewal.

Hunting and gathering

In his journey through crisis towards renewal, Hurst starts out by orienting himself towards the ancient Bushmen of Southern Africa, who evidently touched a chord in him while he was living there. He, like me, recognized the developmental significance of the hunter and the gatherer in business's developmental journey.

I contend that the Bushmen's story is our story and that it is told over and over again at many levels in the lives of our organizations and our societies. We start off in the beginning in small-scale, informal organizations as naive hunters, not knowing much but capable of learning every day through trial and error. With success, and the learning of effective routines, we steadily become like herders. Soon we are protecting possessions and defending territories in large-scale hierarchical bureaucracies whose social dynamics are very similar to those in the Bushmen's herding mode of living.

Such large-scale organizations flourish in delayed-return economies in which significant investments, both of capital and time, may be required to generate a return. In the process of institutionalizing success, we build organizational structures that break down what were once novel, complex activities into simple, routine procedures. The easy formality that often characterizes small, entrepreneurial organizations is replaced by formality and rigid procedures. In this organizing process, the people who perform and manage the essential tasks are endowed with a variety of possessions, both physical and psychological, that enhance their status and hence their power in the formal organization. The products of success, the possessions, are protected and preserved in the boxes of the formal hierarchy, which is designed to formulate (or as will become clear, more accurately, to formalize) strategy, settle disputes, and perpetuate the static organization via a system of controls and sanctions against deviations from plan.[14]

Thus, for Hurst, our search for a learning organization involves the challenge of re-creating the dynamics of the original hunting band in contexts which are far removed from those in which it flourished naturally. For, as organizations and societies build structures, develop technologies and accumulate possessions in pursuit of progress, this sets them on an erratic course of change, with apparently smooth periods of evolution being interrupted by sudden disasters – disasters to which they become systematically vulnerable. It is during these periods of crisis that the social dynamics of the hunting band come into their own.

Hunters of the spirit

Interestingly enough, after assessing the role of the 'southern' Bushmen in our managerial and organizational psyches, Hurst then recalls the 'western' side of his English heritage, albeit set within the 'southern' Quaker realms of our pragmatic selves.

I have called the Quaker achievements 'accomplishments' because the original Friends did not set out to achieve anything for themselves; they set out to change the world. They lived their values, and as the saying goes, by doing good, they did very well . . . The Quakers were social activists from the very beginning. They were untiring in their activities to reform prisons, asylums and institutions of all kinds. Quakers such as Cadbury and Rowntree built libraries and schools, model living communities for workers, and established sick funds and pension schemes . . . Everywhere moreover, the Quakers were associated with invention and discovery. John Dalton, the discoverer of the atom, and Joseph Lister, the surgeon who researched and pioneered the use of antiseptics, were both Quakers. The Quaker emphasis on practice and experiment, coupled with the individual's search for the truth, fitted perfectly with the scientific temper of the times . . . From their humble beginnings as traders, finally the Quaker families became the leading entrepreneurs in cotton and wool, coal and brass, brewing (Burton, Truman), iron and steel, food (Cadbury, Fry, Rowntree), china and chemicals. From the primary industries the Friends moved into manufacturing and tertiary industries such as banking (Barclays, Lloyds) in which, in those unregulated times, their reputation for honesty and integrity gave them a natural competitive edge.[15]

Thus, and historically speaking, he rediscovers the Quakers, whom he considers to have had an inordinate effect on the industrial revolution, socially and economically, culturally and technologically. He then charts the 'model of change' that underlay their development, comprised of 'constrained', 'rational' and 'emergent' action.

Model of change

CONSTRAINED ACTION

Hurst begins (arbitrarily) with the constrained world of post-Elizabethan England in the 1620s and the stalemate between Parliament and the Crown. This situation is shattered by the Civil War and the subsequent execution of Charles I. The aftermath of this is a fragmented society, whose members are still constrained in their ability to act by the confusion of the destructive process.

RATIONAL ACTION

Soon, though, the individual begins to take on what one can call rational action. In the case of the Quakers, this action is taken by such people as George Fox, Robert Barclay and William Penn. Their actions are rational, not by virtue of their understanding of cause and effect, but by virtue of the values that these actions represent and express.

EMERGENT ACTION

These value-laden activities attract a large number of followers and result in the development of Quaker communities and networks. Behaviour in these is unconstrained and full of emergent novelty. Soon enterprises such as those at Coalbrookdale are started. At the heart of Hurst's developmental orientation, though, is a concept of growth and renewal.

Growth and renewal

PHASE 1 – EXPLOITATION

The first phase of the ecosystem, which, as for James Moore, is Hurst's knowledge ground, is characterized by a number of processes that lead to a rapid colonization of any space available. For example, when a gap appears in a forest due to, say, the fall of a large tree, a 'microclimate' is created, giving many organisms equal access to energy and resources. Many of these organisms will be what ecologists call 'r-strategists', that is hunters or pioneers, opportunists who can take quick advantage of the open space that has appeared.

PHASE 2 – FROM HUNTING TO CONSERVATION

As a forest ecospace becomes crowded, competitiveness grows and efficiency becomes increasingly important. Organisms that survive exhibit very different behaviours from those of the opportunistic pioneers. These so-called 'k-strategists' produce fewer progeny, invest their energy in protecting them for longer periods of time, and defend their territories. It is the operations of these 'herders' that leads to the emergence of large-scale, hierarchical organizations. Moreover, it is the very homogeneity of such systems, in terms of age, species and their specialized adapatation to protected niches, that renders them brittle and vulnerable to catastrophe.

PHASE 3 – FROM CONSERVATION TO CREATIVE DESTRUCTION

The third stage in the evolution of the ecosystem is the 'forest fire'. This phase is described as 'creative destruction' because the system is not destroyed completely: it is partially destroyed in order to be renewed. In contrast with its apparent steady state in phase 2, in phase 3 the ecosystem enters far-from-equilibrium conditions, acutely sensitive to small changes.

PHASE 4 – FROM CREATIVE DESTRUCTION TO RENEWAL

The fourth phase in the evolution of an ecosystem, for Hurst, involves the reconception of the system. After the structural integration of phase 3, it is often very difficult to distinguish the organization from its environment. Resources are no longer concentrated in specific structures, and are widely dispersed. In phase 4 of the ecocycle, via numerous regenerative processes, the resources become loosely connected in a large-scale network.

As we can see, then, Hurst, like Stacey and unlike Mintzberg, draws upon a developmental model from the life sciences – in his case from ecology – for his focus on strategy formulation. Moreover, because of his affinity with the 'southern' value base of indigenous as well as religious peoples, he adds a metaphysical touch to his developmental argument, in a way that sets him apart from, for example, 'westerner' James Moore. We now turn from the 'hard' developmental world of emergent strategy to the 'soft' developmental world of organizational learning.

The 'soft' developmental branches – organizational learning

Action learning

Bridging self and other: linking artisan and scribe

Reg Revans, arguably Great Britain's pre-eminent management thinker, paved his existential way towards managerial and organizational learning, which Senge, albeit on his own systemic terms, has since followed. Originally trained as a physicist, Revans found his way in the 1950s and 1960s, via coal mines and hospitals, into management. Twenty years later, I sought him out as a personal mentor. For Revans, who has all his life remained anti-establishment, especially in relation to the halls of academia, education has a role in helping the manager build bridges between his subjective self and the world.

> Human experience remains only partially accessible to external observation. Deep within the manager is the darkness of his subjective world. Education should play a part in helping us explore that darkness so that he may find his way through the solitudes of conscious experience.[16]

Revans has, no doubt, spent many years exploring his own inner world. Moreover, as he found, without the other, the self is incomplete. Revans alludes to learning situations in which there are neither 'Chiefs' nor 'Indians'. In this context, individuals, in seeking to enrich and enlarge their own subjective selves, help, reciprocally, to enrich and enlarge the subjective selves of others. Revans even refers – after the historian Arnold Toynbee – to a process of 'spiritual barter', whereby our latent capacity for warm and genuine exchanges manifests itself. He alludes constantly, moreover, to so-called 'comrades in adversity' learning from and through each others' moving experiences. In the following quote from Toynbee, Revans' ultimate, developmental mission may well be reflected:

> Real progress is found to consist in a process defined as 'etherealisation', an overcoming of material obstacles which releases the energies of society to make responses to challenges which henceforth are internal rather than external, spiritual rather than material.[17]

This vision of Revans' has evolved through a lifetime of so called 'action learning' – in himself and others – undoubtedly shaped by his experiences as Olympic athlete, Cambridge scientist, coal-face manager and worker. He has devoted some sixty years to developing his ideas and testing them in companies, the hospital service, in government and in education. Perhaps, more than anything, he has fought to bridge the class divide, particularly in Britain, between the 'artisan' and the 'scribe'.

> It is a virtue of action learning that, like truth itself, it is a seamless garment. With its help, all parties alike, 'scribe' and 'artisan', manager and workman, should tackle their common foe – the external problem. Their own opinions of each other – personal and interested – are strained by the antipathies of unforgettable tradition. They are teased and exacerbated, moreover, by every civilising process of the education establishment, and reinforced by every decision of our industrial tribunals. Advance therefore will not be easy.[18]

Linking thought and action

At a societal level, then, action learning digs at the root of Great Britain's problems. In his *The Rise and Fall of British Managers*, Alistair Mant puts the matter succinctly. He views Great Britain as being 'schizoid'. He describes a schizoid person or nation as one whose parts remain split, feeding off and sustaining each other. They are essentially unintegrated, incapable of resolution into a whole, fearing a fantasy of destruction. Such a nation, is, literally, without integrity. Mant argues that the obvious split in Britain is that between owners and workers.

> People in clerkish roles do not have an experience of, and cannot therefore properly comprehend, the three dimensional world of bulk, lumpiness, weight and unpredictability which lies outside their immediate perview. If there were two ingredients I most wanted to inject into clerkish veins, they would be inspiration and panic.[19]

Revans treats the whole question of integrity both in personal and in societal terms. Action learning is a means to link thought and action within the person, and scribe and artisan within the nation.

Learning – rate of change

In the process, Revans substitutes an ability to learn that exceeds the rate of change for Mant's 'inspiration and panic'. He maintains that anyone who cannot keep up with what is new, will lose control of their surroundings. Someone capable of taking innovation in their stride will profit by being able to turn it to advantage.

Therefore, in today's climate, he believes, the advantage must lie with anyone able to learn. For when he was working with the Coal Board, in the 1950s, Revans saw how management-worker relations impaired the nation's economic performance.

Revans' central argument, then, is that if the world does not change, the son may follow in his father's footsteps, simply by repeating what is already in the books. Programmed knowledge is sufficient. But, on the precipice, taking the climber into a new world at every rising of the sun, the primary need for learning is not programmed knowledge, but the ability to pose the proper questions about the microcosm of uncertainty, and then to answer these questions. Thereby, within so-called 'action learning sets' of comrades in adversity, meeting at regular intervals, and allowing each individual a time and space to reveal his or her primary concerns, such questioning insight, duly facilitated, is on call.

Management and learning

Revans calculated six essentials of managerial concern: the nature of *values*; the nature of *information*; the logic of *systems*; the theory of *decision*; the extension of *uncertainty*; as well as, most importantly, adaptation and *learning*.

A real decision, firstly, is always that of a particular person, with his own ends not to be neglected. He has his own fears to amplify his problems, his own hopes a mirage to amplify his resources, and his own prejudices, often called experience, to colour the data in which he works. A choice of goals, secondly, so much bound up with decision theory, is yet distinct from it. The ends for which one strives, deliberately or subconsciously, as an individual or with others, are but partly determined by the calculations of economic strategy. For behind them jostle the egocentric drives of the individual. Thirdly, there is the relevance of information, that product of which the raw material is data and the manufacturing process the personal sensitivities of the individual. Fourthly, the theory of systems describes the web in which the wordline of a particular manager is entangled.

The assessment of probability is, fifthly, that farrago of mathematical statistics and simple guesswork by which we attempt to assess our forgotten experience, our present wishfulness and our future hope. And, sixthly, the learning process integrates everything that one has so far become, and one's hope for future improvement.[20]

Management, for Revans then, is always an intermingling of self and other, subject and object, quality and quantity.

The project-based route to organizational learning

Action learning, as we have now seen, is a vehicle for management development and a route to organizational learning. One cannot proceed without the other. It is critical, therefore, that the organization as a whole should subscribe to the learning objectives, so as:

> to enable every enterprise to make better use of its existing resources, by trying to engender within it a social process of learning calculated to help it identify its internal strengths and weaknesses, to understand better its inertias and dynamics, and in other ways to make more effective use of its stored experience.[21]

Such a social process is engendered within the context of small groups, that is learning sets. Moreover, if a problem is seen as requiring a project report, this, in no way, interferes with the day-to-day operations of the company. However, if the organization is going to examine procedures, operations and methods, and subsequently, at the request of the action learner, change them, there is a substantial threat of disruption to present operations. These must be anticipated and negotiated. Organizational commitment to learning must be developed. In any dealings between facilitator of learning and learning organization, Revans has itemized 14 matters for consideration:[22]

1   choice of problems around which to form projects
2   role and responsibility of clients
3   qualities and selection of learning participants
4   monitoring of projects
5   development of set (small group) facilitators
6   representation of the firm in any consortium of learning organizations
7   role of training staffs
8   induction of participants into their projects
9   continued academic support for participants
10 continued role of line management in projects
11 supply of appropriate technical knowledge
12 extension of one project into another
13 issues of cost and benefit
14 concept of the organization as a learning system

We now turn from the originator of a concept of managerial and organizational learning, Revans in the United Kingdom during the 1970s and 1980s, to its major popularizer in the 1990s, Peter Senge based at MIT in the United States. For Senge there are five disciplines underlying organizational learning.

Towards the learning organization

Systems thinking

IN THE ABSENCE OF A SYSTEMIC WORLD VIEW

At the heart of Peter Senge's learning organization[23] is a shift of mind, from seeing ourselves as separate from the world to being connected to the world, from seeing problems as caused by someone or something 'out there' to seeing how our actions create the problems we experience. In the absence of such a systemic world view, managers are trained firstly to be loyal to jobs, to the extent, Senge maintains, that they confuse them with their own identities. When asked what they do for a living, most people describe the tasks they perform every day, not the purpose of their greater enterprise. When people in organizations focus only on their position, they have little idea of the results produced when all positions interact.

Secondly, moreover, when people focus only on their position, they do not see how their actions extend beyond its boundary. When those actions have consequences that come back to hurt people, they misperceive these problems as externally caused. Like a person being chased by his or her own shadow, they cannot seem to shake it off. All too often, Senge maintains therefore, 'proactiveness' is reactiveness in disguise. If managers simply become more aggressive fighting 'the enemy out there', they are reacting, regardless of what they call it. True proactiveness comes from seeing how managers contribute to the solution to their own problems. It is a product of a way of thinking, not of an emotional state. Thus conversations in such reactive organizations are dominated by events – last month's sales, the new budget cuts, the last quarter earnings, who got hired or fired. Focus on events leads to 'event' explanations. Such explanations may be true as far as they go, but they distract people from seeing the longer-term patterns of change that lie behind the events.

Learning to see slow, gradual processes, thirdly, requires slowing down your frenetic pace and paying attention to the subtle as well as to the dramatic. If you sit and look at a tidepool, Senge maintains, initially you will not see much of what's going on. However, if you watch long enough, after about ten minutes the tidepool will suddenly come to life. The world of beautiful creatures is always there, but moving a bit too slowly to be seen at first. The problem is that people's minds are so locked into one frequency, it is as if we can only see at 78 rpm; we cannot see anything at $33\frac{1}{3}$. We will not avoid the fate of the boiled frog until we learn to slow down and see the gradual processes that often pose the greatest threats. Fourthly, a core learning dilemma that confronts organizations, according to Senge, is that its people learn best from experience but never directly experience the consequences of many of their most important decisions. The most critical decisions made in organizations have system-wide consequences that stretch over years or decades.

They also stretch far beyond the bounds of one particular organization, economically and technologically, socially and culturally. In the same way, moreover, that organizations are lodged within a wider environmemt, individuals normally work within teams. All too often teams in business, Senge laments, tend to spend their time fighting for turf, maintaining the appearance of a cohesive team. If there is disagreement it is usually expressed in a manner that lays blame, polarizes opinion, and fails to reveal the underlying differences in assumptions and experience in a way that would enable the team as a whole to learn. People who are skilled in advocating their views are rewarded, as opposed to those who are good at enquiring into complex issues. Such complexity is inherent within the systemic world view.

SYSTEMS THINKING AS THE CORNERSTONE OF THE LEARNING ORGANIZATION

Systems thinking, as has by now become apparent, is first and foremost a discipline for seeing wholes. It is a framework for seeing ecosystemic interrelations rather than economic specifics, for seeing patterns of change rather than static 'snapshots'. Systems thinking is the antidote to the sense of helplessness that many feel as they enter the age of interdependence. It is a discipline for seeing the structures that underlie complex situations, and for discerning high from low leverage.

From the systems perspective, secondly then, according to Senge, the human actor is part of the feedback process, not standing apart from it. In mastering systems, thoughtful managers give up the assumption that there must be an individual responsible for masterminding the system as a whole. There is no more reliance on the one great leader to turn things around, whether in the company or in the country. The feedback perspective suggests that everyone shares responsibility for the problems, or opportunities, generated by a system. There are, moreover, two distinct types of feedback processes: reinforcing and balancing. Reinforcing or amplifying processes are the engines of growth or decline.

Balancing or stabilizing feedback operates whenever there is a goal-oriented behaviour. The state-controlled economy, for Senge, fails because it severs the multiple self-correcting processes that operate in a free market system. Furthermore, whenever there is resistance to change, we can count on there being one or more 'hidden' balancing processes. Aggressive action often produces instability and oscillation instead of moving you more quickly towards your goal.

Thirdly, therefore, rather than pushing harder to overcome resistance to change, Senge's artful leaders discern the source of resistance. They focus on the implicit norms and power relationships, rather than upon explicit results. Cultural renewal becomes more critical, as a point of leverage, than a more conventional form of reorganization. There are certain recurring patterns, or 'templates', moreover, that tend to control events. Such structures of which managers are unaware, Senge maintains fourthly then, hold them prisoner.

That is the essence of his systems perspective. In learning to see structures within which they operate, managers begin to free themselves from previously unseen forces, and they ultimately acquire the ability to work with them and change them. Certain patterns or structures – what Senge terms systems 'archetypes' – recur again and again. Within these 'generic structures' lies the key to your learning to see structures in your personal and organizational lives. If, moreover, reinforcing and balancing feedback and delays are like the nouns and the verbs of systems thinking, then the systems archetypes are analagous to basic sentences or simple stories that get retold again and again. Just as in literature there are common themes and recurring plot lines that get recast with different characters and settings, a relatively small number of these archetypes, for Senge, are common to a very large variety of management situations. We now turn to the second of Senge's five disciplines out of which organizational learning arises.

Personal mastery

The sense of connectedness and compassion characteristic of individuals with high levels of personal mastery naturally leads, according to Senge, to a broader vision. The discipline of seeing interrelationships gradually undermines older attitudes of blame and guilt. We begin to see that all of us are trapped in structures, structures embedded both in our ways of thinking and in the interpersonal and social milieus in which we live. For most of us, the structures within which we operate are invisible. We are neither victims nor culprits but human beings controlled by forces we have not yet learned how to perceive. We are used to thinking of passion as an emotional state, based on our concern for one another. But it is also grounded in a level of awareness.

In Senge's experience, as people see more of the systems within which they operate, and as they understand more clearly the pressures influencing one another, they naturally develop more compassion and empathy. People with a high level of personal mastery, therefore, share several basic characteristics. They have a special sense of purpose that lies behind their visions and goals. For such a person a vision is a calling rather than simply a good idea. You see current reality as an ally, not an enemy. You have learned how to perceive and work with forces of change rather than resist those forces. You are deeply inquisitive, committed to continually seeing reality more and more accurately. You feel connected to others, Senge claims, and to life itself. Yet you sacrifice none of your uniqueness. You feel as if you are part of a larger creative process, which you can influence but cannot unilaterally control. Finally, you make constructive use of mental models.

Mental models

Entrenched mental models will thwart changes that could come from systems thinking. Managers, Senge maintains, must learn to reflect on their current mental models. Until prevailing assumptions are brought into the open, there is no reason to expect mental models to change, and there is little purpose in systems thinking. If managers 'believe' their world views are facts rather than sets of assumptions, they will not be open to challenging those world views. If they lack the skills needed to enquire into their own, and other people's, ways of thinking, they will be unable to work truly collaboratively. Moreover, if there is no established philosophy and understanding of mental models in the organization, people will misperceive the purpose of systems thinking as drawing diagrams, or as building elaborate 'models' of the world, not improving their mental models.

Eventually what will accelerate the use of mental models as a practical management discipline will be a library of generic structures used throughout the organization. These 'structures', Senge concludes, will be based on the systems archetypes. There is more to learning and development, for him, than Jaques' cognitive processes or Revans' action learning. Organizational learning, for Senge, is dependent upon systems thinking, personal mastery, mental modelling, shared vision and team learning.

Shared vision

A shared vision, Senge tells us, is not an idea. It is rather a force in people's hearts, a force of impressive power. It may be inspired by an idea, but once it goes further, if it is compelling enough to acquire the support of more than one person, then it is no longer an abstraction. It is palpable. People begin to see it as if it exists. At its simplest level a shared vision is the answer to the question, what do we want to create?

Just as personal visions are pictures or images people carry in their heads and hearts, so too are shared visions pictures that people throughout an organization carry. They create a sense of commonality that permeates the organization, making diverse activities coherent. Shared vision then is vital for the learning organization because it provides the energy and focus for learning. While adaptive learning is possible without vision, generative learning occurs only when people are striving to accomplish something that matters deeply to them. Vision becomes a living force only when people truly believe they can shape the future. The simple fact is that most managers, according to Senge, do not experience that they are contributing to creating their current reality. So they don't see how they can contribute to changing that reality. Their problems are created by somebody 'out there' or by 'the system'.

But as people in an organization begin to learn how existing policies and actions are creating their current reality, a new, more fertile soil for vision develops. Specifically, then, a new source of confidence develops, rooted in deeper understanding of the forces shaping current reality, and of where there is leverage for influencing them. This new confidence, in its turn, spreads into the fifth and final element of organizational learning – arguably the most indicative of whether it is occurring or not – that is team learning, where Senge is particularly insightful.

Team learning

THE WISDOM OF TEAMS

Team learning, for Senge, is the process of aligning and developing the capacity of a team to create the results that its members truly desire. It builds on the discipline of developing shared vision. It also builds on personal mastery, for talented teams are made up of talented individuals. But shared vision and talent are not enough.

The great jazz ensemble has talent and a shared vision, but what really matters is that the musicians know how to play together. Individuals learn all the time and yet there is no organizational learning. But if teams learn, they become a microcosm for learning throughout the organization. Insights gained are put into action. Skills developed can propagate to other individuals and to other teams. The team's accomplishments can set the tone and establish the standard for learning together for the larger organization.

DIMENSIONS OF TEAM LEARNING

Shared minds Within organizations, Senge maintains, team learning has three critical dimensions. First, there is the need to think insightfully about complex issues. Here teams must learn how to tap the potential for many minds to be more intelligent than one. Second, there is need for innovative, coordinated action. All outstanding teams in organizations develop the same sort of relationship, that is an 'operational trust' where each team member remains conscious of other team members and can be counted on to act in ways that complement each other's actions. Third, there is the role of team members on other teams, that is inculcating the practices and skills of team learning more broadly. These include a juxtaposition of dialogue and discussion.

Dialogue and discussion Additionally then, for Senge, team learning involves mastering the practices of dialogue and discussion, the two distinct ways that teams converse. In dialogue there is the free and creative exploration of complex and subtle issues, a deep 'listening' to one another and suspending of one's own views.

By contrast, in discussion, different views are presented and defended and there is a search for the best view to support decisions that must be made at the time. The word 'discussion' has the same root as concussion and percussion. By contrast the word 'dialogue' comes from the Greek *dialogos* – *Dia* means through; *logos* means word, or, more broadly, meaning. *In dialogue a group accesses a larger pool of common meaning.* In dialogue people become observers of their own thinking. They also observe the difference between 'thinking', as an ongoing process, as distinct from 'thoughts', the results of the process.

If collective thinking is an ongoing stream, 'thoughts' are like leaves floating on the surface, according to Senge, that wash up on the banks. We gather up the leaves, which we experience as 'thoughts'. We misperceive the thoughts as our own, because we fail to see the stream of collective thinking from which they arise. In dialogue a 'kind of sensitivity' develops that goes beyond what we normally recognize as thinking. This sensitivity is 'a fine net', capable of gathering in the subtle meanings in the flow of thinking. This kind of sensitivity, for Senge, can be seen to lie at the root of real intelligence. For through dialogue people can help each other to become aware of the incoherence in each other's thoughts, and in this way the collective thought becomes more coherent. Senge identifies, more-over, three basic conditions necessary for dialogue. All participants must suspend their assumptions, as it were hanging them in front of them, constantly accessible to questioning and observation; participants must regard each other as colleagues, engaged in a mutual quest for insight and clarity; and there must be a facilitator who holds the context of dialogue. For example, the Quakers enjoined their members to say not simply what popped into their heads, but only those thoughts which were compelling, and caused the speaker to 'quake' from the need to speak them.

In team learning, finally, discussion is a necessary counterpart of dialogue. In a discussion, different views are presented and defended. In dialogue, different views are presented as a means toward discovering a new view. In a discussion, decisions are made. In a dialogue, complex issues are explored. When they are productive, discussions converge on a conclusion or course of action. On the other hand, dialogues are diverging; they do not seek agreement but a richer grasp of complex issues. A learning team masters movement back and forth between dialogue and discussion, duly bypassing defensive routines.

Conflict and defensive routines   Finally, teams need to avoid engaging, individually or collectively, in defensive routines. Defensive routines are entrenched habits we use, Senge maintains (as does Stacey), to protect ourselves from the embarrass-ment and threat that come from exposing our thinking. Defensive routines form a sort of protective shell around our deepest assumptions, defending us against pain, but also keeping people from learning about the causes of pain. One of the most useful skills of a learning team would be the ability to recognize when people are not reflecting on their own assumptions, when they are not enquiring into each other's thinking, when they are not exposing their thinking in a way that encourages others to enquire into it. In effect, defensive routines are like safes within which we 'lock up' energy that could be directed toward collective learning. As defensiveness becomes 'unlocked', that energy and insight are released, becoming available for building shared understanding, and advancing toward what the team members truly want to create. The approach taken by learning teams to defensive routines, therefore, is intrinsically systemic. Rather than seeing the defensiveness in terms of others' behaviour, the leverage lies in recognizing defensive routines as joint creations, and in finding your own role in creating and sustaining them.

If you only look for defensive routines 'out there', and fail to see them 'in here', Senge concludes, your efforts to deal with them will just increase defensiveness.

Team learning and the fifth discipline

Without a shared language, then, for dealing with complexity, team learning is limited. If one member of a team sees a problem more systemically than others, that person's insight will get reliably discounted, if for no other reason than the intrinsic biases toward linear views in our everyday language. On the other hand, Senge maintains that the benefits of teams developing fluency in the language of the systems archetypes are enormous, and the difficulties of mastering the language are actually reduced in the team. Language is collective. Learning a new language, by definition, means learning how to converse with others in the language.

While participative openness leads people to speak out, reflective openness leads to people looking inward. Reflective openness starts with the willingness to challenge our own thinking, to recognize that any certainty we ever have is, at best, a hypothesis about the world. No matter how compelling it may be, no matter how fond we are of 'our idea', it is always subject to test and improvement. It involves not just examining our own ideas, but mutually examining others' thinking. Such is the role, or at least one of them, of an authentic leader. In fact Peter Senge, in concluding his approach towards the learning organization, offers up an unconventional line on leadership, as we will see in the next section.

Conclusion

The leader's new work

Old views and new

Our traditional views of leaders, Senge maintains, as special people who set the direction, make the key decisions, and energize the troops, are deeply rooted in an individualistic and non-systemic world view. Especially in the west, leaders are heroes, who rise to the fore in times of crisis. At its heart the traditional view of leadership is based on assumptions of people's powerlessness, their lack of personal vision and inability to master the forces of change, deficits which can be remedied only by a few great leaders.

This new view of leadership in learning organizations centres on subtler and more important tasks. In a learning organization, leaders are designers, stewards and teachers. They are responsible for building organizations where people continually expand their capacities to understand complexity, clarify vision, and improve mental models, that is, they are responsible for learning.

Leader as designer

In essence, the leader's task, for Senge, is designing learning processes. These processes enable people throughout the organization to deal productively with the the critical issues they face, and develop their mastery in the learning disciplines. Crucial design work for leaders of learning organizations concerns integrating vision, values and purpose, systems thinking and mental models.

Leader as steward

Such a leader perceives a deep story and sense of purpose, a pattern of becoming that gives unique meaning to his or her personal aspirations and his or her hopes for the organization. This purpose story, for Senge, is both personal and universal. It is central to the leader's ability to lead. He or she becomes a steward of the vision. The vision is a vehicle for advancing the larger story.

Leader as teacher

The ultimate responsibility of a leader, Senge believes, is to define reality. Leaders can influence people to see reality at four distinct levels : events, patterns of behaviour, systemic structures and purpose story. Leaders in learning organizations pay attention to all four levels, but focus predominantly on the latter two. At the level of systemic structure, leaders are continually helping people to see the big picture. Moreover, when people throughout an organization come to share in a larger sense of purpose, they are united in a common destiny. Leaders in learning organizations, moreover, have the ability to conceptualize their strategic insights so that they become public knowledge, open to challenge and further improvement. They are masters of creative tension.

Mastering creative tension

In the final analysis, a leader's story, sense of purpose, values and vision establish the organization's direction and target. His or her relentless commitment to the truth and to enquiry into the forces underlying current reality continually highlights the gaps between reality and vision. Leaders generate and manage the creative tension, not just in themselves but in an entire organization. This is how they energize an organization. That is their basic job. That is why, for Senge, they exist.

Mastering creative tension throughout an organization, Senge claims, leads to a profoundly different view of reality from the norm. People literally start to see more and more aspects of reality as something they, collectively, can influence.

This is no hollow belief, which people express in an effort to convince themselves that they are powerful. It is a quiet realization, rooted in understanding that all aspects of current reality – the events, the patterns of change, and even the systemic structures – are subject to being influenced through creative tension.

In the words of the great Jewish philosopher Martin Buber:

> The free man is he who wills without arbitrary self-will. He believes in destiny, and believes that it stands in need of him. It does not keep him in leading strings, it awaits him, he must go to it, yet does not know where it is to be found. But he knows that he must go out with his whole being. The matter will not turn out according to his decision; but what is to come will only come when he decides on what he is able to will. He must sacrifice his unfree will, that is controlled by things and instincts, to his grand will, which is defined for destined being. Then he intervenes no more, but at the same time he does not let things merely happen. He listens to what is emerging from himself, to the course of being in the world; not in order to be supported by it, but to bring it to reality as it desires.[24]

At the same time, and unlike Elliot Jaques, for example, Senge has ultimately turned his learning orientation toward the individual – as a leader – through his mental models, within a team, managing systemically, sharing a vision. To that extent Senge has remained true to his Anglo-Saxon philosophical heritage. His orientation, therefore, is closer to that of his colleague Joseph Jaworski than to that of Takeo Fujisawa, both of whom we will meet in the next chapter.

16

ADOPTER AND ENABLER

The fruits of development management

Introduction

From rational to developmental management

The dominance of rational management

The change agent and executive, between the two of them, have established many a conventionally managed organization in Europe and America, that is in the 'north' and 'west'. While the one designs and implements adaptive systems and procedures, the other devises and maintains an overall business strategy and organization structure. However, it is only a certain proportion of you who are suited to developing along this path of rational management. Too often you are led to believe that, should you not be an entrepreneur, then functional or general management are the only paths open to you.

Our blindness to developmental management

So we resist real understanding of, as a critical example, the Japanese or Singaporeans in the east, because their particular brand of total quality and organizational harmony falls beyond our managerial ken. So while we find it relatively easy to identify with their primal aggression and sense of community, we find it very difficult to acknowledge their cooperative and developmental orientation. In addition, we are yet to see what particular brand of management emerges from China and from the different parts of Eastern Europe. For it is only now that these two 'eastern' regions of the world are beginning to evolve their own approaches, independent of the ideologies of Karl Marx or even Adam Smith – both of whom originated from Western Europe.

The developmental duo

The role of adopter

The 'hard' edge of developmental management has in fact emerged uniquely from the east, in the form of what I have termed an 'adopter'. Such an individual manager, as exemplified here by Honda's Takeo Fujisawa, is both similar to and different from an adaptive, or flexible manager. For the key to his personality lies in such Japanese concepts as *amae* – total dependence on a mother figure – and *mu* – total openness to the world around you. As an adopter, therefore, you have no inhibitions about adopting a belief, a technology, or a mentor, as long as you have total faith in them. Interestingly enough, the East Asians had such total faith in western technology, but not in Western Europe's or America's 'spirit' of management. For these they have trusted their own indigenous culture.

The Japanese, moreover, and more recently the Singaporeans, are by no means the only eastern culture to deny the self or the ego, thereby to submit themselves to the purposes of the organization. It is only that they have been particularly successful at it. Unfortunately, we in the north and west have been all too quick to dismiss such adoptive behaviour as paternalistic, or robot-like. We all too easily forget our own behaviour within the context of the church, where humility and devotion has its proper place.

The role of enabler

An interdependent, as opposed to dependent or indpendent, perspective, characterizes the enabler's new style of leadership, as identified in the previous chapter, by Peter Senge. In fact, stewardship, design and education are very much a part of such an enabling personality, as we shall see in the case of Joseph Jaworski's 'inner path of leadership'.

Moreover, as an enabler you do not limit yourself to the recognition of such interdependent potential in the external organization or market-place. You are also sensitive to your own potential, and to that of other people and environments.

The role of enabler, perhaps until the advent of the learning organization, has been very much underplayed in American and European organizations. Normally, in fact, it has been relegated to a fringe position, as perhaps a 'facilitator' lodged within the training and development function. The trouble is that this conventionally 'soft' character, at least in the west and north, has lacked a hard edge, as is provided by the 'adopter' in Japan. We start with that 'adopter' role that is so strange to those of us outside of the east and south.

The adopter

Are you an adopter?

As such an adopter:

- you are submissive
- you dedicate yourself to the purposes of your organization
- you submit to the will of your superior or mentor
- you place complete trust in people you know well

- as you develop trust, you merge into others' activities
- you are open
- your mind is empty and receptive, unbound by preconception
- your ears and eyes are constantly on the alert for opportunity
- you are humble
- you have no ego, no self to defend
- you give more than you receive
- you have peace of mind
- you are totally absorbed in and by your work
- you and what you do are as one
- you have faith in the company, and in its product or service
- your activities are attached to a higher spiritual purpose
- you see yourself as following a path of destiny

As an adopter, then, you are prepared to immerse yourself in the world around you, at least that part of it in which you have faith and trust. You draw such religious conviction from that trusted authority, literally or figuratively, that you are prepared to give your all. As you are aware, though, and this is the 'adoptive' downside, faith can be blind.

Do companies recruit adopters?

Adopters, as managers, are much better known in the east, and perhaps in the south, than they are in the west and north. However, any company with a strong culture, such as IBM used to have in America or Marks and Spencer still has in Great Britain, may be looking out for individuals who are prepared to submit themselves to such all-pervasive cultures.

Of course the fading practice of lifetime employment, whether in Japan as a whole or in a company such as Marks and Spencer in particular, lends itself to the adopter mentality. After all, you are being recruited for life – even though the chances of this happening are becoming ever less likely in today's business world. The manager being sought, then, in this adoptive context, has a weak individual ego – in that you are prepared to be absorbed by others; you are willing to place complete trust in the recruiting organization; you have evident humility – displayed through your obvious courtesy, respect and lack of self-centredness. You have faith in the purposes of the organization and want to attach yourself to its higher purpose.

You are open to influence – both in an organizational and market context, and are willing to immerse yourself in your work, through which you acquire ultimate peace of mind.

How are adopters rewarded?

The way in which you are rewarded, as an adopter, follows from your personality characteristics. The offer of lifetime employment, to begin with, enables you to place complete trust in your employer, which is a reward in itself. Moreover, should the organization espouse such higher purposes as service to God, or to the nation, which is certainly the case in Japan, then you will be provided with the meaning in life that you seek. Moreover, because your ego boundaries are very weak, you need the protection of an intimate group of trusted colleagues with whom to work. Similarly, you will seek to identify such intimate associates, as suppliers, as distributors, and as commercial partners, in order to reinforce your sense of both security and also opportunity. You will require a very close relationship with your superior, from whom you will both seek and gain trust. Finally, because there is no tight ego boundary surrounding yourself or your company, you will be rewarded by having the opportunity to work with government, and with other like-minded organizations, to attain the higher purposes to which you are attached.

Becoming an adopter

With the help of Sekeo Mito,[1] we now tell the story of 'adopter' Takeo Fujisawa, the complement to Soichiro Honda.

Youthful renunciation of the self – all men are equal

Takeo Fujisawa, his family business having been destroyed by the Great Kanto Earthquake, had to spend his middle school years in poverty. 'My father was a proud man, like the ancient warriers', Fujisawa later recalled. 'He used to say that I should never think badly of myself, no matter how poor I was.

'He also taught me that all men are equal, regardless of their social standing. And this served to encourage me a great deal, especially because I had no academic background.'

Fujisawa read many novels in middle school, often borrowing books from friends because the family was so poor. He was especially attached to the works of Soseki Natsume, who was greatly influenced by Buddhism and wrote about the conflict between the ego and the renunciation of the self. 'What I learnt from Soseki', says Fujisawa, 'was to put myself in other people's shoes when developing my thoughts.'

A would-be adult merchant

Fujisawa wanted to attend Tokyo Higher Normal School and become a teacher, but he failed the entrance examination because he had spent too much time reading novels instead of textbooks. More than anything he wanted to become a merchant. In that respect he had similar ambitions to Soichiro Honda, and ended up establishing his own manufacturing business, which he worked up during his twenties and thirties.

Alter egos meet

Fujisawa recalls that when he was first approached, in his early forties, by intermediaries with the possibility of joining Honda's small manufacturing operation, his wife warned him that two such unconventional Japanese characters would never be able to hit it off. It is hard to imagine two men more different. Fujisawa was large, heavy and introspective while Honda was waspish, small and gregarious. Fujisawa sometimed cloaked simple ideas in complicated language while Honda, contrary to Japanese custom, was blunt, sometimes to the point of rudeness. Honda and Fujisawa agreed with alacrity to team up together after a quick first meeting. Soichiro had always realized his deficiency in marketing and finance. More importantly, Honda always worked as a team member, recognizing that some of the most important members of any such cooperative group must have quite different talents and personalities than he. When Honda and Fujisawa – named director in charge of sales – opened an office in Tokyo in 1950, the move marked the transformation of the company into a modern enterprise. Tokyo was then emerging as the centre of Japanese finance and manufacturing.

Action and contemplation

After forming a team they often talked like two enthusiastic youths. Through these dialogues, Honda learned about Fujisawa's outlook on life and the knowledge he had gained from books, while Fujisawa learned about Honda's dominant personality and his enthusiasm for technology.

Honda spent most of his time at the factory and the research laboratory, teaching plant employees and engineers about technology, while Fujisawa devoted himself to sales and corporate management. Like many of his Japanese counterparts of the time, Fuijisawa patterned much of the company's activities on German industry. He was also a great admirer of German music, and missed only one Wagner Festival at Bayreuth in 25 years. He was also a great student of 'kabuki', traditional Japanese drama. Fujisawa was said to be a contemplative businessman. When a problem occurred, he would enter the tea ceremony room of his house and meditate to arrive at a solution. To him, the most important aspect of management was that the fundamental philosophy be understood and accepted by everyone.

In the early days of the company, Fujisawa not only found solutions, but also personally translated his thoughts into action, often in the role of dictator. Later his methods changed, and he would usually go no further than dropping hints about his theories. Fujisawa came to believe that true leadership meant not making all the corporate decisions, but rather doing nothing at all. Employees would take their own initiative based on theories they had learnt from him. Moreover Fujisawa had an almost animal-like intuition for delicate changes in the social condition.

One reason, moreover, for the ultimate success of Honda Motors, was that its founders were fully aware of their limitations. Over the course of their lives, and especially after their midlife transitions, both Honda and Fujisawa gradually abandoned their ego centred needs for control, ultimately welcoming unionisation rather than decrying its presence. Both acquired a degree of humility, and an appreciation of interdependence at a group as well as a personal level, that would have been anathema to their western or even northern counterparts.

Management by people's ideas

Except in the company's early days, Honda almost never attended the board of directors' meetings. After the establishment of the executive board system in 1964, Fujisawa stopped attending them as well. The entire corporate management was left in the hands of the four senior managing directors, including Kiyoshi Kawashima who subsequently became president. 'As vice president Fujisawa and I were the founders of the company', Honda says, we had much greater power than those who joined us later. Imagine what would have happened if we joined the board meetings with so much power. The other members would have simply listened to us and thought how to please us'.

Fujisawa's aim was to make experts out of as many company employees as possible. Honda Motors could not hope to become an international company unless it had as many experts as Honda in technology and Fujisawa in management. The organizational structure must not bind an individual expert by a single line to his immediate superior; lines must run both sideways and vertically. Fujisawa also created a system whereby each employee kept a notebook in which to record details of his work and his own creative activities. When he moved from one workshop to another he carried the notebook with him, so that whatever he achieved in the previous job was carried to the new workshop. Fujisawa viewed this system as the basis for fostering experts. 'When we were producing outstanding products ten years ago, we invested the best of our knowledge, ability and pioneering spirit; it follows that the joy and hardships we experienced at that time must be recorded.'

'Retirement' in maturity

In 1973 Honda and Fujisawa chose to withdraw from active day to day participation in the company. 'I can resign without anxiety', Honda said at the time, 'because I am convinced that the company can continue to move forward with vitality, cope with various situations with flexibility, without losing freshness.' Three years earlier both had begun to take more of a back seat, having appointed four senior managers in operational control.

'Each of us', Honda added, 'is only half a person, and only by combining the two can you get one real executive. That is why we agreed that it is natural for us to retire together. I want all of you (employees of the company) to realize that without harmony among people you cannot maintain, let alone develop, a business enterprise.' In continually talking about his company, its future, and the future of Japanese industry, Honda initially said it will be the spirit behind the business that will count. 'Honda's products are known all over the world not simply because they are good in quality but also because of the philosophy behind the products. Before technology there should be a way of thinking. Coexistence, mutual contribution through enterprise is the spirit needed.'

When Kiyoshi Kawashima became president of Honda Motor Company, the in house jargon he had developed during his years as head of Honda R & D began to spread to all the companies in the Honda group, and was elevated to the level of a company cult and a management system. Simultaneous competition among different approaches – also called individual play and team strategy – meant discovering the special abilities of each researcher and harnessing them for creative endeavour. It meant finding people's true calling through the shared experience of pursuing original research and all its joys and hardships. The relationship between the researchers and the managers was one of cooperation and conflict.

The mottos that Kawashima developed were:

- follow your *dreams*
- respect *theory*, new ideas and time
- *love your work* and make your workplace positive
- ensure a *harmonious flow* of work
- make research and *dedicated effort* a daily habit

Realizing a vision

Since they both retired in their sixties, in 1974, neither of the founders has said anything about the management of Honda Motors. Soichiro Honda has created the Honda Foundation devoted to technology and philosophy. The basic theme is Honda's thought that 'science and technology have contributed greatly to the happiness of mankind, but at the same time they have brought about many miseries'. Specifically, his movement is aimed at discovering problems of human beings and finding means of solving these. Fujisawa lives surrounded by the art that he loves so much. He seldom comes to the office, and spends time taking care of the garden.

How do you develop as an adopter?

Casting our eyes over Fujisawa's growth and development, as an adopter, what do we see?

Youthful apprenticeship

The first stage, as a prospective adoptive manager in your youth, is to submit yourself as an apprentice to a master-manager in the same way as Takeo Fujisawa submitted himself to the principles and practices of his father. In fact, the process is not unlike that followed by apprentices who submit themselves to master craftspeople. In the course of such submission, you are obliged to let go of your personal attitudes and beliefs, pride and prejudice, and absorb everything the master has to offer. That places a great developmental responsibility on the master's shoulders. You will be imbibing not only knowledge and skill, but also attitudes and beliefs from him or her.

Adultlike journeyman or women

In your adulthood, to continue the apprenticeship analogy, you become a journey-man or woman, making your way through the organization. In the process you acquire different disciplines and rub shoulders with different personalities, as

Fujisawa must have done in his journey through business. You engage, moreover, in a journey with a purpose, that is to build up business or managerial mastery, and to serve your chosen organization. Thus your journey takes place within a specific business and organizational context, and is not easily transferrable.

Midlife would-be master

In midlife, having acquired a wide range of knowledge and skills, you begin to develop mastery by applying them across a broad front. In other words, you graduate from specific applications to more general ones, and consciously interfuse with others.

This is what Fujisawa did, most particularly with Honda. As he did, you practise multi-leadership rather than becoming a single leader in your own right. In essence you are a coordinator of other people's energies rather than an energizer yourself.

Mature master

In maturity, if you have journeyed along your predestined path, you will finally acquire the power of mastery. In so doing you will enter into direct communion with powers higher than yourself, on whose behalf your mastery is being exercised. As Fujisawa began to enter that phase himself, he was able to make the direct link between material and aesthetic well being, with the latter firmly guiding the former. In his case, he also became fully aligned with Honda's higher purpose, that of creating the largest possible organization performing a service to humanity. As such he was at one with the totality. Now let me turn to the adopter's softer counterpart, the enabler.

The enabler

Are you an enabler?

As such an enabler:

- you are a harmonizer
- you have a talent for invoking consensus
- you focus on areas of mutual benefit
- you recognize potential for development
- you release potential by opening up hidden, connected pathways
- you help people and enterprises to fulfil their potential
- you are a link person
- you are moored by many interlocking lines of connection
- you build up alliances, as well as networks of mutual support
- you recognize the flow of energy

- you focus on energy's quality, velocity, vitality and direction
- you view changes in energy flows as evolutionary, not spasmodic
- you harness the power of interfusion, or flow
- you focus on mergers of individual or corporate entities
- you view all entities as both autonomous and interdependent
- you are in touch with evolution, and facilitate self-organization
- you can recognize an individual's, an organization's or a society's level of evolution
- you embody the spirit of development within your company

As an enabler, then, you are at home within an organization in midlife, whose prime focus is on development. You have an acute appreciation of subtlety and balance, amongst products and markets as well as people and organizations. Your approach is individually and collaboratively oriented rather than personality-based and competitive. This applies in person-to-person, business-to-business, supplier-to-customer or corporate-to-government dealings. You therefore enable people and organizations, or products and markets – as we shall see below with Jaworski – to realize their unique identity and potential. You achieve this by recognizing synchronicity, and harnessing opportunities for synergy, across space and time. You recognize that true individuality is acquired through genuine interdependence, and vice versa. At the same time you can be too much of an idealist, and not enough of a realist, seeing the wood in general but not the trees in particular!

Who recruits enablers?

The role of the enabler has only become widely recognized, in the west as opposed to the east, in the areas of management and organization development. As someone who can recognize and develop physical and human potential, you will often have a background in the life sciences, in social psychology or in industrial design. So you can indeed be recruited via conventional graduate channels. Personality-wise, you naturally seek out harmony in people or things; you recognize potential for development in one or the other; you are character-istically a link person within an organization; you have the distinctive capacity to recognize the qualitative flow of energy (though you often miss out on the quantitative); and you are uncannily in touch with the level of evolution of an individual or organization, product or market.

I have deliberately broadened the scope of the term 'enabler' to include industrial and product designers who are adept at recognizing and developing the potential of new products, materials and technologies – in fulfilling market needs. As design and technology becomes an integral part of business develop-ment, so the scope for recruiting the design-based enabler increases. Finally, fertile ground for potential enablers lies with the functional specialist or manager who has reached midlife, and who needs to broaden out rather than deepen his or her involvement with management. To the extent that such individuals could be redirected at mid-career, so the infamous plateauing of management could be stemmed.

How are enablers rewarded?

As an enabler you feel rewarded when you can see development – of people, of products, of businesses or of landscapes – arising before you. You hate to see physical or human potential go to waste.

You need to combine with other people, as Joseph Jaworski did in pursuing his 'inner path of leadership', often outside of your own organization, so as to enable change and evolution to take place. As a result, you find opportunities to step outside of the confines of your particular department or company most rewarding, particularly if you can create some joint venture that is of mutual benefit. Conventional salaries, derived from a single source, run counter to your interest in building up a combination of linked economic, personal and social benefits. You would rather, over time, build up a composite reward package, made up of a number of corporate constituents, than be limited to a single source. This has in fact been the case, in recent years, for Jaworski,[2] in his pursuit of synchronicity.

Becoming an enabler

Preparing to journey – a Disneyworld sort of life

Joseph Jaworski was an extremely successful partner in an international legal practice, based in Texas, USA. His father was not only a prosecutor at the Nuremberg trials, after the Second World War, but was also the chief Watergate prosecutor, who ultimately impeached President Nixon.

Life for the first part of my life was an absolute blur. I was popping from one activity to another without a moment's hesitation to reflect and consider my overall life direction. At the time, I considered this to be a great life, but in fact, I didn't really know life at all. Mine was a Disneyworld sort of life – inauthentic, narrow, utterly predictable, and largely devoid of any meaning. The end to this illusion would come to me, as it has done so for many, by means of a personal crisis after I had turned 40.

The journey begins – the world comes crashing down

In 1975, when I was 41, my world came crashing down around me. My wife announced to me, all of a sudden, that she wanted a divorce. She had found another man. During the subsequent days of separation, I went to work, but early in the morning and late at night, I remained alone. My older sister Joanie sensed the kind of pain I was in. One day after work I found a small package waiting at home for me. It was a book entitled *Notes to Myself*. I started writing in similar fashion on loose sheets of paper. In these moments of silent dialogue I gained important insights.

As my thoughts became clearer, I found myself spontaneously letting out my pain through deep, gut-wrenching crying. Maybe I was crying about the loss of my family, but I was also crying for the unreflective life I had led. And maybe I was releasing all the pent-up pain I had had over a number of years. For the first time, moreover, I was really allowing myself to feel.

The path to freedom

The essential elements of my life, overall, were so different from before. Instead of controlling life, I ultimately learnt what it meant to allow life to flow through me. Without the control, there are more intense highs and lows, and I felt much more at risk than ever before. But this sort of vulnerability goes with the path – that path that reveals itself as we walk.

A great deal of what I was experiencing was the need to break through from the conformity of my life over the previous fifteen years, as I fought the battle of living in the shadow of my illustrious father. But another notion of freedom was beginning to make its way into consciousness. Far below the surface lay the freedom to follow my life's purpose with all the commitment I could muster, while at the same time, allowing life's creative forces to move through me without control, without 'making it happen'.

The art of loving

The trip that I took to Europe around this time involved me in a lot of reading, writing and thinking in my journal. One of the books I read and re-read was Erich Fromm's *Art of Loving*. I was sitting in the bar in Cannes, on the last week of my trip, when an attractive young woman walked in. We smiled at each other. About ten minutes later she came up to me, and we ended up having dinner together. Her name was Bernadette. We talked and talked, well into the early hours of the next morning.

The alchemy of Fromm's teachings and my experience with Bernadette provided for me a key insight. When we are in the state of 'being' we open ourselves to life and all its possibilities, willing to take the next step as it is presented to us, then we meet the most remarkable people who are important contributors to our life . . . Alone in Europe, I had begun to reflect on the larger purpose of my life, and what I wanted out of it. I realized that I wanted to broaden my perspective and perhaps find a way to contribute to the larger social enterprise, not just in my narrow little niche in the practice of law.

Oneness – servant as leader

This created a new opening for me in my life, an emerging awareness about the impermanence of boundaries, and an opportunity to change my whole orientation about the possibilities of dialogue and interaction with others. Over time I came to see that the boundaries we create in life are imaginary; they don't exist, but we create them. Then we feel trapped by them. This type of awareness – sometimes called 'unity consciousness' – is natural to human beings, but because of early socialization, we progressively limit our world.

Over time I began to feel that the organizing principle of the universe is 'relatedness', and that this is more fundamental than 'thingness'. Robert Greenleaf, in his book on *The Servant as Leader*, describes the essence of leadership as the desire to serve one another and to serve something beyond ourselves, a higher purpose. Moreover, communication amongst the diverse leadership ele-ments – city hall, business, minorities – appeared to me to be the first condition for renewal in our communities and in our nation. By this point my sense of identity had expanded beyond me, and had embraced the whole world. I hap-pened to be in Cairo at the time, and I kept running to this place, which became a kind of sacred place for me, that is a small open area in the heart of Cairo. My time there was quiet and very reflective and peaceful. I felt at one with myself and the world.

Crossing the threshold

Every spare moment away from work, during evenings and weekends, I was engaged with my inner struggle, thinking about the prospect of setting up a new leadership forum, seeing pictures of it in my mind, of how it would be. Over time, the pictures of the new enterprise became all consuming. The vision began to pervade every part of my time. I became it and it became me, and it was to be that way for the next ten years.

At the moment I walked away from the firm, a strange thing happened. I clearly had no earthly idea of how I would proceed. I knew next to nothing about a leadership curriculum and development. I had no-one who could help me on the substantive side of things, no network of experts. The resources necessary for a national effort would be enormous, far exceeding my own capacity. I had none of this, only myself. Yet at this point, strangely enough, most of my concerns and doubts about the enormity of the project were erased. I had a great sense of internal direction and focus, and an incredible sense of freedom that I had never felt before in my entire life. I had committed to something far larger than myself.

The day I left our law firm I crossed the threshold. From that point on what happened to me had the most mysterious quality to it. Things began falling into place almost effortlessly – unforeseen incidents and meetings with the most remarkable people who were to provide crucial assistance to me.

The guide

In July of 1980, then, having resigned from the law firm, I began struggling with the philosophical underpinnings of the new enterprise I had decided to found. Picking up a copy of the English *Sunday Times* – my previous office had been based in London – I saw a headline in the education section: 'How Things Hang Together'. There was a picture underneath of Dr David Bohm, Professor of Theoretical Physics at London's Birkbeck College. Bohm maintained: 'Yourself is actually the whole of mankind. That's the idea of implicate order – that every-thing is enfolded in everything. The entire past is enfolded in each one of us in a very subtle way.' I made up my mind at this point that I would make contact with Bohm, immediately. It had been my feeling all along that a number of committed people could literally change the world. I realized now that this was not just an idle dream or unwarranted optimism, but a principle I could hang my hat on because it was consistent with the laws of natural order.

Synchronicity

I found myself, thereafter, devouring the literature on synchronicity, including the work of psychologist C.G. Jung and novelist Arthur Koestler. The doctrine that everything hangs together also runs as a leitmotiv through the teachings of

Taoism, Buddhism, and the philosophers of the early Renaissance. I felt at this time of my life I was working in the flow of things, in accordance with the natural unfolding of the whole system. I kept at the forefront of my mind Bohm's injunction: 'be alert, be self-aware, so that when opportunity presents itself, you can actually rise to it'.

I was also by now well aware of Joseph Campbell's work. In *The Hero with a Thousand Faces* he charts the hero's journey in terms of a circle, circumnavigating the 'threshold of adventure'. It starts with the 'call to adventure', followed by the recognition of a 'guide'. Having then embarked upon a 'crossing of the threshold', the hero undergoes a 'road of trials', again engaging with helpers with a view to undertaking the 'supreme ideal', or apotheosis of the journey. The 'return', penultimately, is followed by the passing on of the 'gift', or elixir, to those connected with the hero's journey.

The moment of swing

One day in London, after my meeting with David Bohm, I was walking down the street pondering the most pressing issue facing me. How could I find the necessary expertise to help me construct my leadership curriculum. The programme needed to be designed to take the fellows on a one year journey. I happened to pick up, from a newstand, a US News and World Report. There staring me in the face was an article on 'Leadership in America', written by Tom Cronin. It was clear that he was aligned with the principles of the Leadership Forum with which I had been struggling. So I flew to the States to find Cronin at Colorado Springs. Cronin immediately signed up to my Forum idea and urged upon me to meet John Gardner, founder of the White House Fellows programme. In fact Cronin picked up the phone and made an appointment for me. When Gardner realized how committed I was to the project he declared: 'What you are about is of great importance to me and to the world.' He made an appointment then for me to see Harlan Cleveland, who was Dean of the Humphrey Institute of Public Affairs. Cleveland subsequently signed on and became Chairman of our Programme Committee. All this proved to be a beautiful odyssey, and by the time it was over I had signed on seventeen leading thinkers, scholars and practitioners of leadership, people who could together construct the kind of curriculum I was dreaming about.

In the meantime, something else momentous had happened to me. I was on my way to catch a plane, accompanying my son to his prospectively new university, when I caught sight of a woman at the airport. I couldn't take my eyes off her. I told my son to carry on and catch the plane, and that I would follow soon after. I rushed up to the woman, and evidently her feelings towards me were as strong as mine toward her. She was in the course of transforming her own life by going to medical school. By May, 1981, Mavis and I were married.

Harlan and his committee, getting back to the business of leadership, formulated their views as a series of eight propositions. The trouble with American leaders is their lack of self knowledge. There is a lack of appreciation for leadership in and of itself. Such leaders focus on concepts that separate (communities, nations, disciplines) rather than ones that express our interconnectedness. American leaders lack worldmindedness. In their inattention to values they forget to ask, 'Why?' They are unable to establish an overall social architecture to encompass their efforts. There is insufficient appreciation of the implications of pluralism, nor finally of the broader context, or external environment, in which they operate.

The wilderness experience

The American Leadership Forum programme curriculum was tested and in place by 1983. Each class experienced a programme of approximately twenty days duration over the course of a year, starting with an orientation session to begin the process of connecting the fellows. A subsequent wilderness experience was designed as a six-day element. The full year's programme was ultimately designed to be an inner journey for the fellows, not unlike the journey of *The Hero with a Thousand Faces*. The quest was a transformative cycle consisting roughly of three phases: separation or departure; the trials, failures and victories, including a supreme ideal; and finally, the return and re-integration into society.

The return

By this time my life was a series of connections with people. Making these connections had become a natural way of working. I began learning how to move with the unfolding order, and to live out the principles, naturally. In December, 1988, I was asked whether I'd be willing to head up Shell's scenario planning group. There is a principle of economy of means that is in evidence more and more as we learn to operate with real mastery in life. For Bohm all matter and the universe are in motion. At a level we cannot see there is an unbroken wholeness, an 'implicate order' out of which seemingly discrete events arise. All human beings are part of that unbroken whole which is continually evolving. One of our responsibilities in life is to open and learn, thereby becoming more capable of sensing and actualizing emerging realities.

The Shell Group had always used scenarios to help their managers respond quickly to the changing business environment. But the concept of using scenarios to help shape the business environment was foreign to the mental models of many members of the team. They saw it as a naive approach which smacked of 'do-goodism'. My arguments centred upon the 'soft stuff', that we live in a relational, participative universe, that what is unfolding in the world is unique, and that this is an 'open' moment in history. Under these circumstances, small discontinuities can suddenly and significantly transform the whole system. We have enormous opportunities to create something new.

In South Africa we set up a team in 1991, spread across a spectrum of the country's diverse consituencies. In a series of meetings in Cape Town the team developed four scenarios, all focused on the nature of the impending political transitions. In 'Ostrich' the De Klerk government would stick its head in the sand.

'Lame Duck' suggested what might happen in a prolonged transition with a weakened transitional government. The third scenario, 'Icarus', suggested that a black government could come to power on a wave of public support and try to satisfy all the promises made in its campaign. It would embark on a huge, unsustainable spending programme, and crash the economy. 'Flamingos', finally, was the most positive of the four. The name was chosen because when flamingos fly, they rise slowly, but they fly together. In this scenario improvement is gradual and participatory. Events that subsequently unfolded in South Africa illustrated that the scenarios could be used to shape the environment, rather than merely respond to it.

Creating the future

The approach to scenarios is grounded in the deepest assumption that we human beings hold – that we cannot change things, so we must live our lives reacting to forces out of our control. A central purpose for me, at this stage of my life, is to propose an alternative: if individuals and organizations operate from the generative orientation, from possibility rather than resignation, we can create the future. All human beings in effect are part of that unbroken whole which is continually unfolding from the implicate and making itself manifest in our explicate world. One of the most important roles we can play individually and collectively is to create an opening, or to 'listen' to the implicate order unfolding, and then to create dreams, visions, and stories that we sense at our centre want to happen.

Out of this commitment a certain flow of meaning begins. People gather around you, and a larger conversation begins to form. When you are in this state of surrender, this state of wonder, you exert an enormous attractiveness – not because you are special, but because people are attracted to authentic presence and to the unfolding of a future that is full of possibilities. Doors open, a sense of flow develops, and you find you are acting in a coherent field of people who may not even be aware of each other. You are not acting individually any more, but out of the unfolding generative order. Out of all of my own experiences and meetings with remarkable people I have concluded that the fact that leadership can bring forth predictable miracles is more about being than doing. It is about our orientation of character, our state of inner activity. We stand in this open and interconnected state of being, we are like Samurai waiting expectantly with acute awareness for the cubic centimetre of chance to present itself. When it does, we must act with lightning speed and almost without conscious reasoning. It is at this point that our freedom and destiny emerge, and we create the future into which we are living.

Conclusion

Adopter and enabler

Whereas the adopter, firmly aligned to the organization's higher purpose, acts as a channel for the visionary thrust, the enabler ensures that such a thrust is received by the organization and its environment. In the pioneering context, the entrepreneur exploits potential and the animateur ensures that his or her aggressive exploits are warmly received both within and without. In the conventionally managed organization, the executive channels potential and the change agent ensures that such potential is adapted for the range of applications required within and without. In a developmental context, though, potential is not only exploited and channelled but also firmly aligned, thanks to the adopter, to an all-powerful vision. It is then the enabler's responsibility to ensure that human, product or market potential, thus aligned with the powers above, is suitably attuned to the people and things alongside and below.

Evolving as a developmental manager

The adopter and the enabler, a Fujisawa and a Jaworski, need one another in order to mature. For the one has fixity of purpose and the other has sensitivity of response. If both remain open, however, during the course of their working lives, their developmental orientation will be tempered. For example, in relation to the marketing function, the developmental manager in his or her youth will open himself or herself to aggressive salesmanship and to closeness to the customer, albeit in connection with a broader and deeper purpose. In adulthood, such a manager will espouse analytically based marketing, though again as a means to an evolutionary end. The longer-term end may be the development of the market as a whole, whereas the shorter-term means may be an effective marketing mix. We now turn, ultimately, from the developmental to the metaphysical.

17

METAPHYSICAL ROOTS –
PHILOSOPHY AND THE
HUMANITIES

The roots of metaphysical management

Introduction

From ancient wisdom to modern science

Two-way stretch

Having covered the primal, rational and developmental ground, we can now proceed to the realms of the metaphysical. In so doing we shall enter territory that has only explicitly been probed by management thinkers over the course of the last decade. Practising managers who plumb these depths range from engineer Alfred Nobel historically, to financier George Soros currently. This chapter is the most philosophical one in this text. If you are particularly averse to abstract thought, and therefore find the chapter a struggle, try and stay with it. For it is vital to the text as a whole. These metaphysical roots stretch all the way from ancient wisdom ('soft'), reaching down thousands of years, to modern physics ('hard') in the 1990s.

As we shall see in the next chapter, the major Japanese manufacturing corporations are a unique amalgam of traditional wisdom and contemporary knowledge. Somehow the traditional and the modern, when joined together, appear to produce a powerful combination. The same would seem to apply to the roots, or foundations, of management as a whole. The primal manager, firstly, draws on traditional anthropology and on contemporary economics. The rational manager, secondly, draws on traditional administrative and technical theory and on modern behavioural and communications sciences. The developmental manager, thirdly, draws on traditional ecologically based wisdom and on modern biological science. The metaphysical manager, finally, draws on traditional mystical beliefs about the functioning of the universe, and on the most contemporary philosophies of science.

A bridge between these ancient and modern approaches is formed by what Dennis Milner,[1] a modern philosopher of science, has termed 'consciousness'. First I shall explore the inner path of spiritual consciousness and the outer path of physical science, then I shall investigate the different levels of being that characterize the metaphysical approach, before returning to the nature and scope of the physical sciences.

The outer way and the inner way

There are essentially two ways in which a person such as you and I, and a manager in particular, can seek an understanding of his or her role and function. The first is the 'outer way', and the second is the 'inner way'. The outer way is based on the sense experience of the material world. This way has been espoused by both primal and rational managers. It is also the approach taken in classical and analytically based science by a Bill Gates or a Steve Shirley. By contrast, through the inner way, a person, or a manager such as Takeo Fujisawa or Joseph Jaworski, seeks to raise his or her level of consciousness. The aim is to gain direct perception of whatever forces and activities lie behind existence. This is more the approach of the developmental or, even more particularly, the metaphysical manager.

To understand phenomena, including those contained within and without organizations, we need both outer and inner viewpoints. Rational science provides a detailed knowledge of substances, that is of the bricks and mortar of the world, while metaphysics provides knowledge of the planning and organization behind the construction. To become a true organization builder you have to begin by learning how to deal immediately (primal) and prospectively (rational) with people and things. Once this has been mastered, you need to learn how to become an architect, and design (developmental) buildings or organizations. Finally, you have to learn how to perceive and actualize worthwhile products and purposes for which these are required (metaphysical).

Analysis and integration

When you apply the analytical, rationally based logic to the phenomena of your organizational experience, you find that the totality of your existence is far too great for you to grasp. You therefore divide and subdivide management into fragments small enough for you to comprehend. You then investigate these fragments in detail so that you can get a clear understanding of what they involve. Any knowledge you thereby gain is effective, detailed, working knowledge. But in the process of dividing and subdividing it into fragments you lose sight of the wholeness of management.

The metaphysical approach deals only cursorily with the detailed behaviour of people and things. Instead the metaphysical manager conceives and acts upon forces and activities that lie behind and beyond the material world. He or she is able to do this because of an 'expanded state of consciousness', or highly evolved state of managerial or moral being. Such perspectives on consciousness have been handed down to us, through antiquity, extending from classical Greece to Iroquois America.

Level of consciousness

Ancient wisdom

Aristotle's causes

According to the metaphysical view, every single thing in the universe has to be seen as existing at several levels of consciousness. The most common basis for such a division of levels is a fourfold one. Aristotle,[2] for example, the Ancient Greek philosopher, described four levels of causal influence:

1   A formal cause, e.g. the blueprint or concept of a table, affecting its shape and proportion. This formal cause corresponds with 'the objective general', with *body and substance.*
2   An efficient cause, e.g. the work of the carpenter in making the table. This efficient cause corresponds with the 'objective particular'. His or her work produced this particular table. He or she is concerned with *ends and means.*
3   A material cause, e.g. the wood or other raw substance of which a table is made. This material cause corresponds with the 'projective general'. Wood is general because it can make many things besides tables, being *full of potential.*
4   A final cause, e.g. the function of the table. This final cause corresponds with the 'projective particular', that is with the table's particular *function and purpose* of holding things.

Two thousand years later, an American physicist, albeit one informed by ancient wisdom, was drawing on Aristotle's original thinking.

The geometry of meaning

The American physicist Arthur Young,[3] from whom I discovered Aristotle's 'causes', also describes four levels of being, or of consciousness. Hydrogen for him is the first and most basic element, like the light that started it all. The second row of chemical elements – carbon, oxygen, hydrogen – are the ones that make up the carbohydrates, fats and proteins, that is the bulk of the body. These molecules are the building material and the fuel. They have no fixed character, no identity. The third row of elements contrast sharply with this. They are elements which make molecules which have a special purpose and retain their identity. The fourth row of elements also has special functions, but it would appear that the combining motif is emphasized.

For Young, as for David Bohm, as we saw in the previous chapter, atoms or molecules are not separate things but expressions of an evolving entity. At each state of its evolution the entity, be it a living cell or a human organization, acquires a new power. Since the powers are cumulative, an atom cannot achieve certain things, say, without previously having mastered molecular combinations. Furthermore, it cannot deal with genuine combination, as a molecule, unless it has previously learned personification, as an atom. We would argue that the same goes for a business enterprise, that is its powers are cumulative, stretching from primal to metaphysical.

In summary, for Young, as for the metaphysical manager, the geometry of meaning unfolds in the following way:

- the universe is a process, put in motion by purpose
- the development of process occurs in stages
- each stage develops a new power
- powers are cumulative; each one retains the powers developed in the previous stages
- powers are evolved sequentially in what ancient wisdom calls 'kingdoms'

Levels of being

This notion of different 'kingdoms', or levels of being, has been developed by the late E.F. Schumacher, the well-known German economic philosopher of the 1960s and 1970s, and author of *Small is Beautiful*. Schumacher describes four levels of being – matter, life, consciousness and self-awareness. They are 'in their fundamental nature' different, incomparable, incommensurable and discontinuous.[4]

Schumacher was a Christian economist and philosopher; his contemporary, Adin Steinsaltz,[5] has come to similar conclusions but, from a Jewish metaphysical standpoint.

The world of physical activity (matter), Steinsaltz says, is only one of a general system of four fundamentally different dimensions of being. He calls these dimensions, 'action' (primal), 'formation' (rational), 'creation' (developmental), and 'emanation' (metaphysical).

For Steinsaltz, the physical world in which we live, the objectively observed world around us, is only a part of a vast system of worlds. Three of these are of a different order from the immediately known world, which does not necessarily mean that they exist somewhere else, but rather that they exist in different dimensions of being. What is more, the various worlds interpenetrate and interact in such a way that they can be considered counterparts of one another, each reflecting itself on the one below or above it, with all the modifications, changes, and even distortions that are the result of such interaction. It is the sum of this infinitely complex exchange of influence back and forth, among the four different domains, that comprises the specific world of reality that we experience in every-day life, as well as within the whole of management.

Thus each domain or 'world' is distinguished from the others by the way that time and space is manifested in it. Moreover, for the reasons Steinsaltz gives, the interaction between the worlds often makes it difficult to distinguish, say, primal from metaphysical, or rational from developmental management. The spatial division between one world and another is as non-linear as the flow of time.

The flow of time

In our domain of experience, time is measured by the movement of physical objects in space. As we ascend the order of the worlds, this time system becomes increasingly abstract and less and less representative of anything we know as time in the physical world.

It becomes no more than the purest essence of change, or even the possibility of potential change. The concept of time, moreover, in the Jewish way of thinking, is not one of linear flow. Time is a process in which past, present and future are bound to each other, not only by cause and effect but also as a harmonization of two motions: progress forward and a counter-motion backward, encircling and returning. It is like the knowledge-creating spiral that Nonaka and Takeuchi allude to (see chapter 18), or like a helix, rising up from creation. There is always a certain return to the past, and the past is never a condition that has gone by and is no more, but rather one that continually returns, and begins again at some significant point, whose significance changes according to changing circumstances. There is therefore a constant reversion to basic patterns of the past, or prior knowledge grounds, although it is impossible to have a precise equivalent to the past at any moment of time.[6] (See Figure 17.1.)

The medicine wheel

Finally, having visited Ancient Greece and Jewish antiquity, we move across to indigenous America to review the Indian so-called 'medicine wheel'. Contemporary physicist David Peat, whom we shall meet again in his guise as a 'proper'

Figure 17.1 The spiral flow of time.

scientist, has alluded to this wheel in his most recent work, *Blackfoot Physics: A Journey into the Native American Universe.*

> The number Four is the four directions and the four winds. It is embodied within powerful concrete devices, images or algorithms. Through the Four Winds the cycles of the seasons are manifest on earth. And so the Four Winds are the animating powers or spirits or energies that bring about maturity, continuation, renewal, and refreshment. The Four Directions are pictured as spokes on the medicine wheel and refer not only to the transformation of the seasons but also to the movement from birth to death; to health and of healing; to the dynamics of the individual psyche; to the concept of justice; to the meaning of the sacred colours; to the history of a group; to the tasks that must be carried out by the different peoples of this earth.[7]

In many of the world's cultures, Peat maintains, four is the symbol both of balance and harmony, and of process and movement. Early medicine in the west (our 'north') spoke of the four temperaments and humours, and science pictured matter as an equilibrium of four elements. The great Swiss psychologist Jung believed that the human psyche was a dynamic process involving four forces, or psychological functions. Ideally, the human psyche should occupy a point of balance within the centre, but most of us – as managers specifically and as human beings generally – live out of balance. Arriving at a point of balance within the centre Jung called individuation. The four points, moreover, can be thought of as the different poles of two sets of dualities (north/south and east/west) while, at the centre, is the resolution of all conflict and duality. Thus the number four is created out of the opposition of dualities and resolved within unity.

> Within Indigenous science, therefore, the number four is not a thing, it is not a mental abstraction, but a living spirit; likewise the so-called sacred hoop is not a static diagram on a piece of paper, but an unfolding process. The hoop is a movement in which each of the sacred directions gives way to the other, for it is always in rotation. And so within the number four stands each of the sacred directions, each one also being a point of arrival and departure. Each number, therefore, also contains its neighbour – for it gives birth to and dies away from it. In the language of Carl Jung, and his friend the physicist Wolfgang Pauli, the centre is the speculum, the mystical mirror that stands between two worlds and reflects each into the other, yet belongs to neither.
>
> The essential processes of sacred mathematics then are dynamic, whereby the number five is born out of the number four.[8]

It is in that 'native' respect that the metaphysical domain represents, at one and the same time, a journey southwards and towards the centre. Such a journeying has radical implications for the organization, as well as for you as a manager, in the way we perceive, and work with, knowledge. These implications are specifically spelt out by Nonaka and Takeuchi, and in fact underly their so-called knowledge-creating company, which underlies the Japanese economic miracle.

> Western education predisposes us to think of knowledge in terms of factual information, information that can be structured and passed on through books, lectures and programmed courses. Knowledge is seen as something that can be acquired and accumulated, rather like stocks and bonds. By contrast, within the indigenous world, the act of coming to know something involves personal transformation.[9]

Having explored the metaphysical world of inner consciousness and levels of being, I now want to relate these concepts to the origins and development of physical science.

Modern science

Science and metaphysics

To what extent, then, is physical science, today, in a position to embrace these metaphysical viewpoints? Is there a place for Aristotle and for Young, for Schumacher and for Steinsaltz (at the centre), and for the indigenous (southern) peoples of our world, in the scientific world view? In other words, how might such ancient metaphysical knowledge grounds be revisited in the modern world, of science in general, and of management in particular?

There is no doubt that physical science is evolving in a direction which is able to accommodate such underlying metaphysical foundations. In fact, the contemporary physicists who will be represented in this chapter – the American David Bohm, the Swiss German Erich Jantsch and the Austrian Fritjof Capra – are not only noted scientists in their own right and trailblazers of the new physics, but also popular philosophers. Before we hear from these illustrious people, however, let us briefly trace the history of physical science, drawing on the insights of the Nobel prize winner whom we have already met, the Belgian Ilya Prigogine, and his French associate Isabelle Stengers.

From Greek atomists to quantum physicists

The Greek atomists' main aim, according to Prigogine and Stengers,[10] was to describe a godless, lawless world in which (primal) man is free, and can expect to receive neither punishment nor reward from any divine or natural order. By way of contrast, classical (rational) science was a science of engineers and astronomers, of action and prediction. Nature becomes law-abiding, docile and predictable instead of being chaotic and unruly. In the twentieth century we are again, via quantum physics (developmental), witnessing the clash between lawfulness and random events. In place of actuality and certainty the quantum physicists recognize only potential and probability. The recognition, and more particularly the actualization, of such a successive transition in scientific epochs, moreover, comes from a metaphysical consciousness.

A transition in epochs

Each epoch and each society is rooted in some fundamental beliefs and assumptions, which are acted upon as if they were true. They justify all other things that follow from them, while they themselves are accepted on faith.

A change in philosophy is a change in the accepted grounds of faith, whether of a religious or a secular character. And conversely, when a given people, society or civilization is shaken or shattered, this calls for fresh thinking, a new philosophical basis. This understanding, in the context of management, comes from Tom Peters, even though his thinking by itself would lead us down a primal cul de sac. We need then to create new myths to make transition in our society possible. Two myths in the making are: the myth of the unity of the family of man within the context of universal sympathy for all; and the myth which maintains that the cosmos is pervaded with spirituality, which leads to the reality that we are part of a sacred tapestry.[11]

I now turn to the new beliefs and assumptions that underpin the new physics, and that also underlie, in my view, so-called metaphysical management. The first person to publicly cross the bridge between modern physics and ancient wisdom has been the Austrian scientist Fritjof Capra, now working in California. He called his original book *The Tao of Physics*,[12] and he is more recently known for his work *The Web of Life*.[13] The 'tao', for the ancient Chinese, was the way of all things.

Self-renewal and self-transcendence

Fritjof Capra is a physicist who took the scientific world by storm, in the early 1980s, when he compared the concepts of contemporary western physics with the tenets of traditional eastern mysticism. Capra, accordingly, has a view of consciousness, also based on four levels, that evolves from the personal 'ego' to the collective and 'transpersonal'.

Firstly, at the *ego* level, specifically, one does not identify with the total organism, but only with a personal representation of it, known as the self-image. Hence, for us, the relevance of autonomy and entrepreneurship at this level. The second major level of consciousness he calls the *bisocial* because it represents an aspect of a person's social environment, including family relationships, cultural traditions and beliefs that profoundly affect the person's perceptions and behaviour. Hence, for us at this level, the importance of the behavioural sciences in management. The third *existential* level is the level of the total organism, characterized by the integrated individual who is exploring his or her full potential. At this third level of 'self-renewal', developmental management, for us, is of obvious relevance. The final *transpersonal* level is the level of the collective unconscious. The individual now feels connected to the cosmos as a whole, and so may be identified with the traditional concept of the human spirit (metaphysical). In the final analysis, for Capra, it is the processes of self-renewal and self-transcendence (levels three and four) which are of greatest interest.

'Re-ligio'

The late Erich Jantsch, a Swiss German physicist and contemporary of Capra's, initially established a reputation for himself, in industry, as a technological forecaster in the 1950s and 1960s. As he matured he broadened his perspective and in the 1970s wrote his seminal work *Design for Evolution*.[14] The book was addressed not only at corporate planners but also at executives and statesmen. He wrote as a physical scientist who had become increasingly interested in processes of social, as well as spiritual, evolution. We may experience evolution, according to Jantsch, in terms of roots branching in the direction of historical time, and accessible by means of 're-ligio', which literally means a linking back to the origin.

Re-ligio opens up the unformed with its wealth of open possibilities, and new evolutionary lines of development, thereby giving us a kind of dynamic security. In a civilization or an organization with a true history, therefore, the concept of irreversible time undergoes a significant modification. Not only does re-ligio, the linking backward to the origin, become the main spiritual concern, it also becomes, for Nonaka and Takeuchi, as we shall see in chapter 18, the core of creative action. This brings us onto the concept of the 'implicate order', promoted by David Bohm, another Nobel-prize-winning physicist, to whom Joseph Jaworski introduced us in the last chapter.

The implicate order

The matter–mind continuum

As Einstein brought us the space–time continuum, seeing space and time as one inextricably linked process, Bohm brings us the matter–mind continuum, seeing matter and consciousness as inextricably linked. Matter Bohm calls 'explicate order', and consciousness is closer to what he terms 'implicate order'. According to Bohm, ordinary consciousness (primal and rational) responds to the explicate because it had been trained, through acculturation, to screen out and suppress vast dimensions (developmental and metaphysical) of its implicate nature. One of the explicate forms of order that this explicate orientation adopts is a sense of personal or parochial identity.

Bohm believes, in fact, that there is a grave fallacy lurking in 'western' individual, or arguably 'southern' parochial consciousness. For him individual consciousness is an abstraction.[15] For when the binding power of the physical atom is released in an accelerator, the resulting energy – staggeringly huge – becomes freed. Analogously, huge amounts of binding energy are needed to sustain the ego and the illusion that it is an independent, ultimate entity.

Such polarized energy is thus unavailable for 'the high energy state' contained within the centre. Energy thus pre-empted, or indeed polarized, cannot flow into other grooves. The sage, or metaphysical manager, who has seen through this principle and understood it no longer exhausts himself or herself trying to hold his or her bonded energy together, but lets go of the ego and releases its energy, opening a channel to the limitless universal energy.[16] In classical physics the observer was separated from the observed. They were separate parts of the universe. With quantum physics some theorists proposed that the observed actually affects what is observed. Both these views subtly retain the idea that the observer is separate, though in the second case he or she and what he or she observes are 'interfacing'. For Bohm both observer and observed appear from the same under-lying, indivisible process and flow in and out of each other like a stream through vortices. They are both, in a sense, causing each other, and being caused, by the same movement. Bohm calls this the 'holomovement'.

Enfolded order and the holomovement

The implicate order then provides the ground for the explicate order that ranges from particles to planets, from silicon chips to cyberspace. A radio wave can carry 'enfolded' in its movement various orders that can be unfolded by the electronic circuitry of a TV into a two-dimensional image. With the hologram, the move-ment of interference patterns of coherent (laser) light enfolds a much subtler range of structures and orders. When these are recorded on a plate and retrieved by a laser beam, the reader sees three-dimensional scenes from many points of view. In a similar, but unthinkably vaster way, the whole movement or holomovement of the universe carries the implicate order and allows us to see and experience our four-dimensional space–time world.[17] In the implicate order, then, what is going to be visible is only a very small part of the enfolded order, and therefore Bohm introduces the distinction between what is manifest and what is non-manifest.

> It may fold up and become non-manifest or unfold into the manifest order and then refold again. The fundamental movement is folding and unfolding.[18]

In other words, there is much more to management than meets the primal or rational manager's eye. One reality, or domain, is enfolded within the other. Moreover, whereas the primal and rational domains are more 'explicate' or manifest, the developmental and metaphysical ones are more 'implicate' and non-manifest. Whereas, then, the adopter and the enabler as we have seen are primarily guided by the implicit, invisible order, the executive and change agent, entrepreneur and animateur, are guided by the explicit and visible.

Conclusion

Matter and consciousness, implicate and explicate order, self-determination and self-transcendence, are all familiar concepts to the manager grounded simultaneously in ancient wisdom and in the new physics. Your operating universe as such is, therefore, quite paradoxically, meta-physical; your invisible faculties, of imagination and intuition, are more focused than your visible orientations towards managing by objectives or by 'walkabout'. At the same time, you carry within you both yang and yin, both hard and soft edges to your management style.

Your hardness is reflected not so much in autonomy and enterprise but more in the creation of order through fluctuation. Through awareness of the implicate order, in which your enterprise is lodged, you are able to tap hidden sources of spirit and energy, thereby transforming them into successful business outcomes. Your softness, on the other hand, is reflected in a willingness to be absorbed by the cosmic dance of economic and technological, social and cultural activities.

In the chapters that follow, then, we shall first be exposed to the mainstem of metaphysical management, as conceived by Nonaka and Takeuchi, in their knowledge-creating company. Secondly, we shall review the so-called global businessphere, out of which the knowledge spiral arises, and through which it is activated. Thirdly, we shall review the 'stories we are', and the way that organizations, as well as individuals, harness spirit. Finally, in chapter 20, I shall reveal the fruits of metaphysical management in our role-model adventurer, the Englishman and explorer Richard Branson, and in our innovator, the Hungarian émigré and financier George Soros.

18

THE KNOWLEDGE-CREATING COMPANY

The mainstem of metaphysical management

Introduction

From primal to rational management

Primal managers, in their passion for excellence, build a business that competes successfully without, while establishing a cohesive community within. Rational management, in promoting a 'requisite' organization, effectively builds up the competence of the corporation, while adaptively managing change. Developmental managers, in the process of managing complexity, facilitate organizational learning while stimulating corporate renewal. Finally, metaphysical management, by virtue of organizational knowledge creation, continually turns a knowledge-based vision into physical action, and so enables individuals and organizations to live out their particular and unique stories.

Two Japanese industrial sociologists, Ikujiro Nonaka and Hirotaka Takeuchi,[1] have devoted the past twenty years to studying the ways in which Japanese companies such as Canon and Sony enhance the value of their products and services. They portray a company as enhancing its capacity to create new knowledge, disseminate it throughout the organization, and embody it in products, services and systems through the process of what they have subsequently termed 'organizational knowledge creation'. Moreover, they maintain that Japanese companies, faced with a crisis, have historically used this proactive approach as a means of breaking away from the past and moving into new and untried territories of opportunity. Such a knowledge-creating company, furthermore, as will be revealed in the next chapter, is the inner reflection of the outer businessphere.

Knowledge creation in the global businessphere

In the context of this text, therefore, what is most significant about the 'knowledge-creating company' is the fact that it draws on the full spectrum of managerial domains. In other words, it is a practical model of what we have termed 'four worlds management'.[2] Specifically then, and firstly at the global centre, Nonaka

318

and Takeuchi locate a company's *knowledge vision*. Secondly, connecting the core with the periphery is their so-called *knowledge crew* engaged in 'middle–up–down management'. Thirdly, the polar points, in our terms, north–south and east–west, are located within their so called *knowledge spiral*, which can be likened to the one identified by Adin Steinsaltz in the previous chapter. Fourthly and finally, the intermediate zones, serving to connect up adjacent managerial orientations, are contained within the so called *hypertext organization*. We start with the centre, or knowledge core, supported by what Nonaka and Takeuchi consider to be an 'eastern' view of knowledge, and what we perceive as a 'central' one.

Core and periphery

The global core

Knowledge creation as a dynamic human process

Japan's comparative economic advantage today, according to the two Japanese researchers, lies in the 'eastern' way it views knowledge. For, as they see it, in the west (including our 'north') the rationally based theory of business administration has long been dominated by a paradigm that conceptualizes the organization as an input–output system. Such a system 'processes' information or 'solves' problems in hierarchical 'north-western' fashion. A critical problem with this approach, as they see it, is its passive and static view of the organization.

Information processing is viewed as a problem-solving activity which centres on what is given to the business administration, without due consideration being accorded to what is created by it. Accordingly, we have designed this text so that you yourself are able to draw out of the knowledge grounds, or roots, and create a business organism uniquely your own.

A rationally based 'north-western' approach thereby emphasizes the absolute, static and non-human nature of knowledge, typically expressed in propositions and formal logic. Nonaka and Takeuchi, in contrast, as supposed 'easterners', consider knowledge to be a dynamic human process of justifying personal belief with a view to finding the truth or, I would add, goodness or beauty, with a view to promoting utility.

In fact I would argue that this approach to knowledge creation is less 'eastern' and more central or core (metaphysical) in nature and scope. For whilst a 'north-western' approach to information processing involves simply a flow of messages, from a core perspective, knowledge is created and organized by the flow of information anchored in the commitment and beliefs of its holder. The essence of innovation, therefore, from such a point of view, is the re-creation of the world according to a particular ideal or vision. To create new knowledge, then, means literally to re-create the company and yourself, and everything in each, as part of an ongoing process of individual and organizational renewal. It is not, therefore, just about putting together diverse bits of data and information, or even about generating 'wild ideas'. Your personal commitment, as well as that of others – inclusive of your emotional involvement with the organization and its mission – are indispensable to such knowledge creation. As a result such a process is not the responsibility of the few, for example a specialist in development or marketing, but that of everyone in the organization. How then is all of this achieved?

Creating a knowledge vision

A metaphysically oriented top management, to begin with, needs to create a knowledge vision and communicate it across the organization. Such a vision

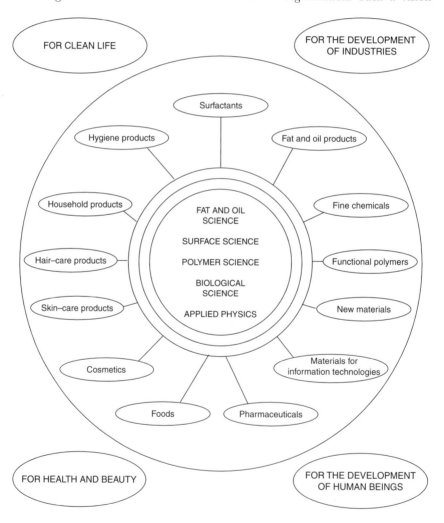

Figure 18.1 Kao's knowledge vision

should define the 'field' or 'domain' that gives corporate members a mental map of the world they live in. It thereby provides a general direction regarding what kind of knowledge you ought to seek and create. The essence of strategy for the knowledge-creating company, as a result, lies in developing the organizational capability to acquire, build up, and exploit the envisioned knowledge domain (see Figure 18.1).

Yet currently most companies, including even so-called learning organizations, only have products and services in mind when formulating strategy. This preoccupation can be somewhat limiting, since products and, to a lesser extent, services have clear boundaries. In contrast, boundaries for knowledge are much more obscure, which helps to expand the competitive scope as well as the technological horizon of the company. For example, in the spring of 1990, Japan's mighty Matsushita officially announced to the outside world its corporate vision of becoming a 'possibility searching company'. Under this vision, the global corporation set forth the following four areas of business, technology, people and globalization:

1 'Human innovation business' – a business that creates new lifestyles based on creativity, comfort and joy in addition to efficiency and convenience.
2 'Humanware technology' – a technology based on human studies such as artificial intelligence, fuzzy logic and neuro-computers as well as chips systems and networking technology, all necessary for the 'human innovation business'.
3 'Active heterogeneous group' – a corporate culture based on individuality and diversity.
4 'Multilocal and global networking management' – a corporate structure that enables both localization and global synergy.

At Kao, by way of a second example cited by Nonaka and Takeuchi, explicit knowledge is captured and recontextualized under the 'five scientific areas' which provide the company with a sense of direction regarding which new markets it should enter in the future. Kao – Japan's equivalent to Europe's Unilever and America's Proctor and Gamble – believes that there are five key scientific areas vital to their current technology. These comprise fat and oil science, surface science, polymer science, biological science and applied physics.

These five fields are closely related to Kao's historical development. Moreover, they allow Kao to move into markets that may at first seem distant from its core business. Interestingly enough from our global perspective, CEO Yoshio Maruta has been very conspicuous as a 'philosopher executive' and devout student of Buddhism. Maruta's philosophy can be seen to accord with three principles: (1) contribution to the consumer, (2) absolute equality of humans, and (3) the search for truth and the unity of wisdom. These philosophical principles, in turn, form Kao's tacit knowledge base. They provide the core knowledge context under which Kao's corporate culture is defined, and the knowledge content under-pinned, in Nonaka's terms, by epistemology and ontology.

Knowledge, epistemology and ontology

Knowledge creation, for Nonaka and Takeuchi, takes place through the combina-tions of tacit and explicit knowledge, originally brought to light by the Polish-born British philosopher Michael Polanyi. These, firstly then, serve to make up the 'epistemological' dimension to organizational knowledge creation, that is through the continual dialogue between the tacit and the explicit. Secondly, the extent of social interaction between individuals that share and develop knowledge is the 'ontological' dimension. A 'spiral' model of knowledge creation shows the interac-tion between the two of them. We start, then, with the epistemological dimension.

THE EPISTEMOLOGICAL DIMENSION: TACIT AND EXPLICIT

For Nonaka and Takeuchi, knowledge that can be expressed in words and numbers, as in balance sheets and computer programs, only represents the tip of the iceberg of the entire body of possible knowledge. Polanyi classified knowledge into two categories. On the one hand, 'explicit', explicate or codified knowledge refers to knowledge that is transmittable in formal language.

On the other hand, 'tacit' or implicate knowledge has a personal quality, which makes it hard to formalize and communicate. For tacit knowledge is deeply rooted in action, commitment and involvement in a specific context, that is character-istically for us 'south-western'. Both tacit and explicit knowledge, moreover, contain technical and cognitive dimensions. The tacit, abstract and, for us 'north-eastern', elements centre upon mental maps in which human beings form working models of the world by creating and manipulating analogies in their

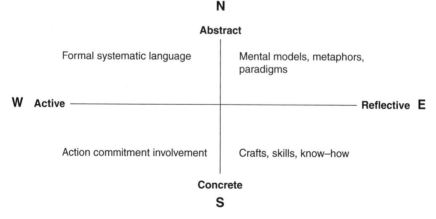

Figure 18.2 The connective knowledge-creating intelligences

minds. These working models include metaphors, paradigms, beliefs and view-points that provide 'perspectives' that help individuals to perceive and define their world. Explicit 'north-western' variations include codified systems of rules and regulations, policies and procedures, trading accounts and software programs. By contrast, the concrete, in our terms 'south-eastern', element of tacit knowledge covers specific know-how, crafts and skills that apply to particular contexts. (See Figure 18.2.)

Tacit knowledge, then, is a continuous activity of knowing and embodies an 'analogue' quality that aims to share tacit knowledge to build mutual understanding.

This understanding involves a 'parallel processing' of the complexities of current issues, as different dimensions of a problem are processed simultaneously. By contrast, explicit knowledge is discrete or 'digital'. It is captured in records of the past such as libraries, archives and databases, and is accessed on a sequential basis.

THE ONTOLOGICAL DIMENSION: LEVEL OF SOCIAL INTERACTION

Now we turn from epistemology to ontology. At a fundamental level, Nonaka and Takeuchi maintain, knowledge is created by individuals. Knowledge creation, therefore, should be understood in terms of a process that organizationally amplifies the knowledge created by its people, and crystallizes it as a part of the knowledge network of the organization. In this context it is possible to distinguish between several levels of social interaction at which the knowledge created by an individual is transformed and legitimized.

In the first instance, an informal community of social interaction provides an immediate forum for nurturing the emergent property of knowledge at each level. Since this informal community might span organizational boundaries, it is important that the organization is able to integrate aspects of emerging knowledge into strategic development. Thus the potential contribution of informal groups to organizational knowledge creation should be related to more formal notions of organization structure. This should arise both within the organization and without. For this to happen, in fact, certain enabling conditions are necessary, that is the 'developmental' part of the knowledge core.

Knowledge creation – enabling conditions

According to Nonaka and Takeuchi, there are five such enabling conditions for organizational knowledge creation, that is intention, autonomy, fluctuation, redundancy and variety.

ORGANIZATIONAL INTENTION

Intention is concerned with how individuals form their approach to the world. While, from a peripheral perspective, information processing models treat the mind as a fixed-capacity device for converting meaningless information into conscious perception, from a core perspective cognition is the activity of knowing and understanding as it occurs in the context of purposeful activity, that is Aristotle's level four! From the viewpoint of organizational knowledge creation, then, the essence of strategy lies in intentionally developing a corporate capability to acquire, create, accumulate and exploit knowledge. In our terms, therefore, such knowledge arises out of a raised consciousness.

The core element of such corporate strategy, then, is the conception of a vision that encompasses the kind of knowledge and culture that should be developed, and its implementation through the management system. Such implementation is dependent, in turn, upon the establishment of conditions favouring individual or group autonomy.

INDIVIDUAL OR GROUP AUTONOMY

The prime movers in the process of organizational knowledge creation are the individual members of the organization. Individuals who are in touch with their own centre, that is the core of their being, are continuously committed to re-creating the world in accordance with their own perspectives. As such they are fully autonomous, albeit as a conscious part of a larger whole. The principle of autonomy, in fact, can be applied at the level of individual, group or organization, separately or together. Such autonomy increases the possibility that individuals or self organizing groups will motivate themselves to form new knowledge. Autonomous individuals and groups in knowledge-creating organizations, furthermore, set their task boundaries by themselves, to pursue the ultimate goal expressed in the higher intention of the organization. Such intention is necessarily subject to fluctuation, and to creative chaos.

FLUCTUATION AND CREATIVE CHAOS

While intention is internal to the individual, and autonomy is intrinsic to one entity or another, knowledge creation involves continuous interaction with the environment. In this context, chaos or discontinuity can generate new patterns of interaction between within and without. As a direct result, individuals or groups have to re-create their own systems of knowledge if they are to take account of fluctuation. Specifically, when breakdowns occur, you may be led to question the value of longstanding habits and routine tools. The role of top management, in this respect, at least according to the chairman of Canon, Ryuzaburo Kaku, is to give employees a sense of crisis as well as a lofty ideal. This intentional fluctuation, which Nonaka and Takeuchi refer to as 'creative chaos', increases tension within the organization and focuses the attention of members on defining problems and resolving crisis situations. However, this knowledge creating process takes place only when members reflect on their actions.

Without reflection, in fact, the introduction of chaos tends to produce 'destructive' tension. As the American organizational psycholoist Edgar Schein has observed, 'when someone reflects while in action he becomes a researcher. He is not dependent on established categories of theory and technique, but constructs a new theory of the unique case'. The knowledge-creating organization, therefore, is required to institutionalize this reflection-in-action, in its processes as well as in its structures, to make it truly creative. Such reflectiveness, moreover, is reinforced by what Nonaka terms 'redundancy'.

REDUNDANCY OF INFORMATION

'Redundancy' is especially important at the concept-development stage, when it is critical to articulate images rooted in tacit knowledge. At this stage, 'redundant' information enables individuals to invade each other's functional boundaries and offer advice or provide new information from different perspectives. In short it brings about 'learning by intrusion' into each individual's sphere of perception. In organizational terms this means the conscious overlapping of company information, business activities and management responsibilities. Since members share overlapping information, they can sense what others are trying to articulate. There are two obvious ways, then, to institutionalize such redundancy. Internal rivalry, firstly, encourages teams to look at a problem from a variety of perspectives. A second way to build in redundancy is through strategic rotation, which helps members understand the organization from a multiplicity of perspectives. Alongside the notion of redundancy, as an enabling condition for knowledge creation, is that of 'requisite variety'.

REQUISITE VARIETY

According to the principle of requisite variety, an organization can maximize efficiency by creating within itself the same degree of diversity as the diversity it must process. To maximize such variety, everyone in the organization should be assured of the fastest access to the broadest variety of necessary information. Such variety is also enhanced by multi-functional, cross-cultural, or inter-organizational activities. These enabling conditions provide the support for the process of knowledge creating. The combination of the metaphysically based knowledge vision and the developmentally oriented enabling conditions make possible the establishment of the metaphysically based core of the knowledge creating company – not merely the rationally based core competence.

From core to periphery

The overall management of knowledge creation involves the establishment of dynamic linkages between the implicate knowledge core (metaphysical and developmental) and the periphery (rational and primal). This is accomplished, as we shall see, through a process of 'middle–up–down' management facilitated by a 'knowledge crew' that piggybacks on new product development, set in the context of a 'high-density field of interaction', ultimately building a knowledge network with the outside world. We shall now consider each of these facets in turn.

Developing a knowledge crew

Knowledge practitioners, engineers, and officers

Organizational knowledge creation, as we have seen, starts from your individual efforts, at core, to validate or justify your belief, or commitment, to the truth promoted by your job and by your company. Highly subjective insights and intuitions are therefore at the root of knowledge creation. To nurture these, a knowledge-creating company needs diversity in the pool of talent available.

Knowledge practitioners, that is frontline employees and line managers at the periphery, become responsible for accumulating and generating both tacit and explicit knowledge. They consist of 'knowledge operators', who interface with tacit knowledge for the most part (primal), and 'knowledge specialists', who deal primarily with explicit knowledge (rational).

For Nonaka and Takeuchi, so-called 'knowledge engineers', typically middle managers, need to take the lead in converting knowledge. In the process, and drawing upon the knowledge vision set in the context of the right enabling conditions, they will be actualizing a knowledge spiral through socialization, externalization, combination and internalization. In this respect these knowledge engineers become the project leaders of the organizational knowledge-creating process.

Finally, while knowledge engineers are responsible for converting tacit into explicit knowledge and vice versa – thereby facilitating the four modes of knowledge creation – knowledge officers are responsible for managing the total knowledge creation process at the corporate level. Specifically, moreover, they are required to create the knowledge vision (metaphysical), and the enabling conditions (developmental) for its realization. We can now describe the three roles more specifically.

Knowledge practitioners at the periphery

Knowledge practioners, the organization's knowledgeable frontline operating at the periphery, can be divided into tacit operators and explicit specialists. 'Hands-on' operators generally use their heads and hearts in close cooperation with their hands. In this way they constantly accumulate tacit knowledge in the form of experience-based, tacit skills. Knowledge specialists mobilize explicit knowledge in the form of technical, scientific and other quantitative data. Ideally, knowledge practitioners should have the following qualifications:

1 a high degree of practical or technical skill-based competence
2 a strong sense of commitment to a particular behavioural or cognitive perspective

3   a variety of both working and learning experiences in and outside the company
4   an ability and inclination to get practically involved, or socially network, with colleagues and customers
5   openness to active discussion and intellectual debate

We now turn from the practitioners to the knowledge engineers who mediate between core and periphery.

Knowledge engineers at the polar points

Knowledge engineers, then, synthesize the tacit knowledge of both frontline employees and senior executives, making it explicit, and incorporating it into new technologies, products or systems. As such they facilitate the creation of the knowledge spiral across epistemological and ontological dimensions. Knowledge engineers, therefore, need to:

1   be equipped with capabilities in project management and coordination, whether commercially or technologically, socially or culturally oriented
2   be skilled at coming up with hypotheses to create new business, technical, social or product concepts
3   have the ability to integrate various methodologies for knowledge creation
4   have the verbal or logical, intrapersonal or interpersonal communication skills to encourage dialogue and trust amongst team members
5   be proficient in employing stories or metaphors to help others imagine, and subsequently conceptualize, creatively

We now turn from the world of the knowledge engineer to that of the knowledge officer.

Knowledge officers at the centre

If the job of the knowledge practitioners on the periphery is to know 'what is', and that of the knowledge engineers is to know what 'might be', then the job of the knowledge officers at the core is to know 'what ought to be'. Such generally *innovative* or *enabling* knowledge officers, firstly therefore, are specifically expected to give a company's knowledge-creating activities a sense of direction, creatively using their powers of verbal persuasion to provide a clear commercial thrust. Secondly, they should be combining their imaginative powers with their logical minds to articulate grand concepts.

Thirdly, such concepts should be metaphorically enriched through a profound policy statement that lends itself towards deep contemplation. Finally, they should be setting far-reaching standards for justifying the social as well as commercial value of the knowledge that is being created. A senior manager should, ideally then, have the following attributes to qualify as a knowledge officer:

1   the ability to articulate a knowledge vision in order to give a company's knowledge-creating activities a sense of direction, coherence, profundity and value
2   the capability to communicate the vision dynamically or authoritatively, inspirationally or enthusiastically, to project team members
3   the capability to justify the quality of the created knowledge, based on commercial or technical, quality or social criteria
4   the ability to select the right project leaders, or knowledge engineers, for commercial or technological, design or development projects
5   a willingness to create chaos within the project team, for example, setting challenging commercial or technical, quality or social goals
6   skillfulness in interacting with team members personally or interpersonally, cognitively or intrapersonally, and soliciting commitment from them
7   the capability to direct and manage the whole of organizational knowledge creation, from a commercial or technical, product or process perspective

We now turn from the knowledge crew to the 'middle–up–down' style of organizational structure in which, according to Nonaka and Takeuchi, they operate. To start with, though, we shall compare and contrast this approach with the better-known 'top–down' and 'bottom–up' varieties.

Adopting middle–up–down management

Top–down management – the dominant centre

A 'middle–up–down' approach, serving to interlink core and periphery, stands, as we shall see, in distinct contrast to both the 'top–down' and the 'bottom–up' varieties. In the latter two cases, in fact, either core (top–down) or periphery (bottom–up) predominate. For the essence of a bureaucratic machine, firstly then, is top–down information-processing using a division of labour and a hierarchical structure of organization. Top management thereby create basic managerial concepts (the premises of decision making) and break them down hierarchically – in terms of objectives, and means – so that they can be interpreted by subordinates. These senior managers' concepts thereafter become operational conditions, according to Nonaka and Takeuchi, for middle managers who then decide how to realize such concepts. Subsequently, middle managers' concepts become operational conditions for lower managers, who implement their decisions.

To clearly break down the ends–means relations, it is necessary to get rid of any equivocality or ambiguity in the concepts held by top management. In sum, the concepts anchor on the premise that they have only one meaning. By implication, such concepts are also strictly functional, definitive and rational or pragmatic. An implicit assumption of this traditional model of organization, moreover, is that information and knowledge are processed most efficiently in a 'family-tree' structure. Moving from the bottom to the top of the organization, information is processed selectively so that people at the peak would get only simple, processed information. Moving in the reverse direction, on the other hand, information is processed and transformed from the general to the particular. It is this deductive transformation which enables human beings with limited information-processing capacity to deal with a mass of information. The centre thus predominates over the periphery.

Bottom–up management – the dominant periphery

A bottom–up organization, conversely, has a flat and horizontal shape. The periphery thereby calls the tune. Few orders and instructions are given by top managers, who serve as sponsors of entrepreneurially minded frontline employees, operating at the periphery. Knowledge is created by these employees, who operate as independent and separate actors, preferring to work on their own. Autonomy, not interaction, is the key operating principle. In the bottom–up model, those who create information are middle and lower managers, or 'intrapreneurs'. The two traditional models, then, that is top–down and bottom–up, may seem like alternatives to each other. Neither, in effect, is adequate as a process for managing knowledge creation, thereby linking core and periphery. The top–down model is suitable for dealing with explicit knowledge. However, in controlling knowledge creation from the top, it neglects the development of tacit knowledge that can take place on the frontline of an organization. Bottom–up management, on the other hand, is good at dealing with tacit knowledge. Yet its very emphasis on autonomy means that such knowledge is extremely difficult to disseminate and share within the organization. This brings us, finally, to the middle–up–down variety.

Middle–up–down management – balancing core and periphery

Unlike the above two models, the middle–up–down one takes all members as important actors who work together horizontally and vertically. Its major characteristic is the wide scope it offers for cooperation between core and periphery. No one department or group of experts has the exclusive responsibility for creating new knowledge. In other words, while top managers articulate the dreams of the firm, lower managers deal with the actual and perceived reality. The gap between these two is narrowed by and through middle management.

In this sense it is a leadership style that facilitates the parallel knowledge-creation process taking place simultaneously at top, middle and lower management levels respectively, as can be seen in Figure 18.3.

Frontline employees and lower managers, therefore, operating at the periphery, are immersed in the everyday details of particular technologies, products and markets. No one is more expert in the realities of a company's business than they

329

	Top–down	Middle–up–down	Bottom–up
Agent of knowledge creation	Top management	Self-organizing team	Intrapreneur
Management processes	Leaders as commanders	Leaders as catalysts	Leaders as sponsors
Accumulated knowledge	Explicit: documented/ computerized	Explicit and tacit shared diversely	Tacit embodied in individuals

Figure 18.3 A comparison of three management models

are. But while these managers and employees are deluged with highly specific information, they often find it extremely difficult to turn that information into useful knowledge. For one thing, signals from the market-place can be vague and ambiguous. For another, employees and lower managers can become so caught up in their narrow perspective that they lose sight of the broader perspective.

The main job of top and middle managers in the model of middle–up–down management, according to Nonaka and Takeuchi then, is to orient a chaotic situation towards purposeful knowledge creation. These managers do this by providing their subordinates with a conceptual framework which helps them make sense of their own experience. In both top–down and bottom–up management, a high emphasis is given to charismatic leadership. By contrast, middle–up–down management views managers as catalysts.

Top management gives voice to a company's future by articulating metaphors, symbols and concepts that orient the knowledge creating activities of employees. In other words they give form to organizational intention:

- What are we trying to learn?
- What do we need to know?
- Where should we be going?
- Who are we?

The final role of top management is to clear away the obstacles and prepare the ground for self-organizing teams headed by middle management. Such middle managers serve as team leaders who are at the intersection of vertical and horizontal flows of information. They work as a bridge between the visionary ideals of the top and the often chaotic reality of the frontline. They mediate between what is and what ought to be, even remaking reality according to the company vision.

In summary, middle managers synthesize the tacit knowledge of both frontline employees and top management, make it explicit, and incorporate it into new technologies and products. They are the true organizational engineers of the knowledge-creating organization. Senior managers, as so-called 'knowledge officers', thus become romantics who go in quest of the ideal. Middle managers as 'knowledge engineers', then, serve as a bridge between the visionary ideals of the top and the often chaotic reality of those on the frontline of the business. Such managers mediate between the 'what should be' mindset of the top, and the 'what is' orientation of the frontline 'knowledge practitioners', by creating mid-level business and product concepts. These, in their turn, become part of a knowledge network.

Constructing a knowledge network

Mobilizing tacit knowledge

Creating knowledge, finally, is not simply a matter of processing objective information about customers, suppliers, competitors, the local community or government. Crew members also have to mobilize the tacit knowledge held by these outside stakeholders through tacit interactions. Tapping the mental maps of customers is a typical example. Moreover, the knowledge-creating company is inevitably strongly networked into an outside world, which is only tenuously seperated from the inside one. As such the core and periphery are intimately interlinked, structurally through middle–up–down management and process-wise through the knowledge network.

A high-density field of interaction

To nurture the highly subjective and personal mind-sets of individuals within the company, a knowledge-creating organization should provide a place where a rich source of original experience can be gained. Within such a place, what Nonaka and Takeuchi call a high-density field, frequent and intensive interactions between crew members can take place between the organizational core and periphery. In other words, within such a field, typically, tacit knowledge is converted into explicit knowledge. More specifically our hunches, perceptions, mental models, beliefs and experiences are converted into something that can be communicated and transferred in formal and systematic language.

A high-density field is a place, then, where such knowledge conversion is triggered through some form of authentic dialogue. It is within such a context that crew members begin constructing a common language and synchronizing their mental and physical rhythms. It is also within such a force-field that product development takes place.

Piggybacking on product development

Organizational knowledge creation is like a derivative of new product development. How well a company manages the process of new-product development, therefore, becomes the critical determinant of how successfully organizational knowledge creation can be carried out. Firstly, companies must maintain a highly adaptive and flexible approach to such new-product development, which seldom proceeds in a linear manner. In fact, such development involves continuous, dynamic and iterative trial and error. Secondly, knowledge-creating companies must ensure that a self-organizing team is overseeing new-product development. Left to itself, the process begins to create its own dynamic order, beginning like a start-up company, while at some point the team develops its own concept. Moreover, such companies must provide autonomy to the team, and tolerate chaos and fluctuation. Thirdly and finally, knowledge-creating companies need to encourage the participation of non-experts who are willing to challenge the status quo. New-product development, in effect, is as critical to 'middle–up–down' management as efficiency and effectiveness is to the 'top–down' variety.

Knowledge, as we have seen, unlike more specific products and services, flows like water, resembling more of a free-flowing river course rather than a circumscribed channel. Moreover, the flow revolves around and is energized by, as it were, a central knowledge-creating vortex. Such a vortex, functioning as a kind of nucleus, is centrifugally centred upon a knowlege vision and centripetally enabling of such knowledge creation. Secondly, such a flow of knowledge energy has to be 'engineered' from core through to periphery, as well as vice versa. This is facilitated by a middle–up–down structure, combined with a networked process operating both within and without the fuzzily bounded enterprise. We now turn from the vortex-like core and the circumnavigating periphery to the two sets of knowledge-based polarities in between – the channels for the energy released from the centre.

The polarities – the pivotal knowledge-creating elements

The knowledge spiral

The assumption that knowledge is created through conversion between tacit and explicit knowledge allows Nonaka and Takeuchi to postulate four different modes of knowledge conversion, as can be seen in Figure 18.4. The first of these, that is the conversion of tacit input into tacit output, is what we likened to the *animateur*. The second, from explicit to explicit knowledge, is what we have indentified as the *executive* approach. The third knowledge mode, that converts tacit input into explicit output, is in our terms an *adopter*. Fourth and finally, the conversion of explicit into tacit knowledge corresponds with our *entrepreneur*.

	Tacit knowledge	Explicit knowledge
Tacit knowledge	**Socialization** (animateur)	**Externalization** (adopter)
Explicit knowledge	**Internalization** (entrepreneur)	**Combination** (executive)

Figure 18.4 The knowledge structure

The pivotal knowledge points

The stabilizing poles – north/south

NORTHERN – COMBINATION – EXECUTIVE

The first mode of knowledge conversion, typical of a French grande école, involves the combination of different bodies of *explicit* knowledge held by individuals. This takes place through such exchange mechanisms as formal meetings, office memos, formal papers and codes of conduct. The reconfiguring of existing information through the sorting, adding, recategorizing and recontextualizing of such explicit knowledge can lead to new combinations of knowledge. Modern computer-based data-processing systems provide a graphic example of such mathematically based knowledge 'combination'. It is this form of knowledge conversion which is the most visible within the north-west.

SOUTHERN – SOCIALIZATION – ANIMATEUR

Secondly, there is the knowledge conversion that enables knowledge workers on the Mediterranean coastline, or in an African village, to convert *tacit* knowledge in one person to tacit knowledge in another person through social interaction. Apprentices work with their mentors, for example, not through language but by observation, imitation and practice. The key to acquiring tacit knowledge, therefore, is through direct experience. The mere transfer of information will often make little sense if it is abstracted from embedded emotions and nuanced contexts, laden with interpersonally based intelligences. This process of creating tacit knowledge through shared experience, which Nonaka and Takeuchi call 'socialization', is therefore the second of the two stabilizing poles.

The dynamic poles – east/west

EASTERN – EXTERNALIZATION – ADOPTER

The third and fourth modes, finally, relate to patterns of conversion involving both tacit and explicit knowledge, capturing the idea that both are complementary and can expand over time through mutual interaction. It is these two mixed knowledge creating modes, in effect, which provide the dynamic conversion channels. In the typically Japense conversion of *tacit into explicit*, a metaphor or an image – portrayed orally or visually – plays an important role, alongside analogy and concept.

For such 'externalization', in Nonaka's and Takeuchi's terms, requires knowledge practitioners, engineers or officers to specifically transform metaphor into analogy and then analogy into product or organizational concept. In Japan, in effect, the interaction between tacit and explicit knowledge tends to take place at the group level, as a result of socialization. Middle managers lead knowledge-creating project teams, which play a key role in sharing tacit knowledge amongst team members. This tacit knowledge interacts with explicit knowledge, such as a grand concept advanced by top management and information sent from the business frontline. This intensive, human interaction produces mid-range concepts as well as concepts for target products, services, or business systems.

In terms of the knowledge-conversion modes, the western strength lies in internalization and combination. Japanese business people tend to rely heavily on tacit knowledge, and use intuition. They are relatively weak in analytical skills, for which they compensate through frequent interaction with people. Such south-eastern style knowledge creation is characterized by relatively ambiguous organizational intention, high redundancy of information and tasks, high autonomy at the group level, and requisite variety through cross-functional project teams.

WESTERN – INTERNALIZATION – ENTREPRENEUR

In the conversion of *explicit into tacit* knowledge, finally, that is 'internalization', action is important. In such a context the Battle of Waterloo was won 'on the playing fields of Eton' rather than in the English classroom! Individuals thereby internalize knowledge, tacitly, through direct, hands-on experience. Moreover, for explicit knowledge to become tacit, it helps if the knowledge is verbalized or diagrammed into manuals, documents, or stories. The quality of that knowledge is influenced by both the variety of the experiences and also the degree to which they are related. It is affected, moreover, by the degree to which the knowledge is embodied through deep personal commitment, thereby transcending the subject–object divide, providing access to 'pure experience'.

The interaction between tacit and explicit knowledge in the west tends to take place at the individual level, accompanied by internalization. Concepts tend to be externalized through the efforts of top leaders or product champions, and then are combined organizationally into archetypes of new products, services or management systems. Such north-western style knowledge creation, finally, is more receptive to certain enabling conditions, such as clear organizational intention, low redundancy of information and tasks, less fluctuation by top management, high autonomy at the individual level, and requisite variety through natural differences.

Unleashing the knowledge dynamics

Each of these four modes can convert knowledge independently. However, the central theme of the model proposed by Nonaka and Takeuchi is that organizational knowledge creation hinges on a dynamic interaction between the different modes of knowledge conversion, both in themselves, and also between them and the knowledge core.

That is to say, knowledge creation results from the interplay between an innovative knowledge vision and enabling conditions for knowledge creation, on the one hand, and the interweaving of both tacit and explicit knowledge on the other. Moreover, and in the latter context, the dynamic interchange between internalization and externalization is all important. There are various 'triggers' that induce shifts between different modes of knowledge conversion. First, the socialization mode usually starts with the building of a team or 'field' of interaction. This field facilitates the sharing of members' experiences and perspectives. Second, the externalization mode is triggered by successive rounds of meaningful 'dialogue'. In such authentic dialogue the use of metaphor or deep storytelling can be used to enable team members to articulate their own perspectives, and thereby reveal hidden tacit knowledge.

All too often, though, such a 'south-eastern' perspective on knowledge work is bypassed. For it is only with such a perspective that concepts formed by teams can be combined with existing data and external knowledge in a search for specifications that are more concrete and can be shared. This combination mode is facilitated by such triggers as coordination between members of the organization, and by documentation of existing knowledge. Through an iterative process of trial and error, concepts are then articulated and developed until they emerge in a concrete form. This experimentation can trigger internalization through a process of learning by doing. Participants in a field of action share explicit knowledge that is thereby gradually translated, through interaction and such a process of trial and error, into different aspects of tacit knowledge. The activation of the overall spiral, then, is dependent upon the innovative and enabling attributes to be found at the centre, as well as the *adventurous* and *change oriented* activities and information held at the periphery.

In summary, knowledge creation starts out from the centre, at the individual level, energized by a dynamic human process of justifying personal belief with a view to finding the truth. Thereafter, as a downward and inward centripetal movement, the individual and collective (group) level interconnect, together with the organizational level, sometimes even reaching out beyond the organization. The means whereby the centre is linked not only with the periphery but also with each of the pivotal points in between is established by what Nonaka terms the 'hypertext organization'.

The connective regions

The hypertext organization

In order for a company to qualify as a knowledge-creating company, as Nonaka and Takeuchi have said, it must have the organizational ability to create and develop, as well as to acquire, accumulate and exploit knowledge continuously and dynamically. It must therefore be able to recategorize and recontextualize such knowledge strategically for use by others in the organization or by future generations.

Unfortunately, Nonaka and Takeuchi argue, conventional organizations are not creative and flexible enough to perform all of these functions. In our terms, in effect, they are unable to incorporate the full spectrum of managerial orientations within their structures and processes. For while a hierarchy is the most efficient structure for the acquisition, accumulation and exploitation of knowledge, a task force is the most effective for the development of new knowledge originally created within the core. Or, to put it the other way around, recategorizing and recontextualizing the knowledge generated in these two structures or layers necessitates the establishment of a third layer that our two Japanese researchers call the 'knowledge base'.

The top layer, as we can see in Figure 18.5, is the 'project-team' layer, where multiple project teams engage in knowledge-converting activities such as new product development. The team members are brought together from many different units across the business system, and are assigned exclusively to a project team until the project is completed. At the bottom is the 'knowledge-base' layer, where organizational knowledge generated in the project layers and channelled in the business system is recategorized and recontextualized. This layer does not exist as an actual organizational entity, but is embedded in corporate vision, organizational culture, or technology. Corporate vision provides the direction in which the company should develop its technology or products, and clarifies the 'field' in which it wants to play. Organizational culture, then, orients the mind-set and action of every employee. While corporate vision and organizational culture provide the knowledge base to tap tacit knowledge, technology taps the explicit knowledge generated in the other two layers.

Once the task of a team is completed, they move 'down' to the knowledge-base layer at the bottom and make an 'inventory' of the knowledge acquired and created in the project. After categorizing, documenting and indexing the new knowledge they come back to the upper business-system layer and engage in routine operations until they are called again for another project. A key design requirement is to form such a circular movement of organizational members who are the fundamental source and subject of organizational knowledge creation. The ability to switch among the different contexts of knowledge swiftly and flexibly, so as to form a dynamic cycle of knowledge,

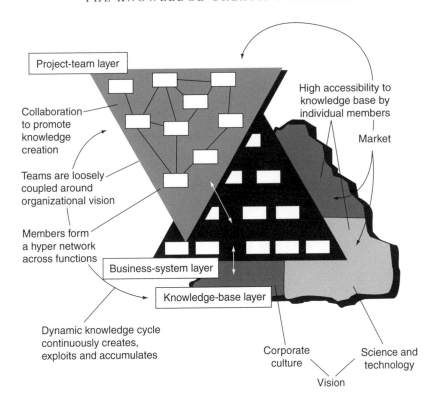

Figure 18.5 The hypertext organization

ultimately determines the organizational capability for knowledge creation. The knowledge base serves as a 'clearing house' for the new knowledge generated in the business-system and the project-team layers. Bureaucracy is more adept at accumulating operational knowledge (internalization) and systemic knowledge (combination), while the project team generates conceptual knowledge (externalization) and sympathized knowledge (socialization), both within and without.

Conclusion

In the final analysis, Nonaka's and Takeuchi's theory explains how knowledge held by individuals, organizations and societies can be simultaneously enlarged and enriched. In this sense, the theory of organizational knowledge creation is a basic theory for building not only a pragmatically and rationally but also a developmentally and indeed metaphysically based knowledge society beyond the limits of mere economic rationality. For organizations play a critically innovative, and enabling, role in mobilizing tacit knowledge held by individuals and providing the form for a 'spiral' of knowledge created through socialization, externalization, combination and internalization.

The implication of all of this for the 'branches' of metaphysical management is profound, and will be reviewed in chapter 19, as we enter more wholeheartedly into the global businessphere.

19

SPIRIT AND TRANSFORMATION

The metaphysical branches

Introduction

From managerial spectrum to global businesssphere

Over the course of this text, most specifically alluded to via our 'spectrum' of eight managerial orientations, we have spanned a 'global businesssphere' through which we have engaged in a managerial metamorphosis. Such a businesssphere, as we saw in the last chapter, contains a centre and a periphery, as well as four polar extremities. Within the context of the knowledge-creating company, the centre comprised the knowledge vision and the enabling conditions for its continuing renewal, whereas the periphery consisted of the energy and information that fuelled the knowledge network. Furthermore, the polar points consisted of the entrepreneurial west (internalization) and the adoptive east (externalization), the executive north (combination) and the animateurial south (socialization).

Such a spectrum of orientations, both hard and soft, can be reconceived as a 'force-field' of creative tensions. Altogether, and as we shall see in this chapter, they also make up a transcultural field, that is the global businesssphere.[1] While east and west, north and south, constitute the regional poles, the centrifugal and centripetal elements make up the global centre, and the energetic and informatic forces make up the local periphery.

In this chapter, we shall present both the 'hard' and 'soft' branches of metaphysical management. Whereas the former are lodged within culture and management, epistemologically, the other is contained within corporate culture, mythologically.

'Hard' metaphysical branches – managing across cultures

The global businesssphere

The central core

In pictorial terms, as can be seen in Figure 19.1, the centre is represented, firstly, by a vortex that comprises innovative and enabling attributes. Therein lie the *core*

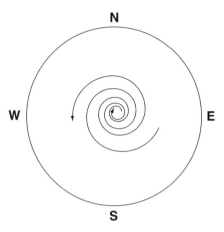

Figure 19.1 The psychosynthesis of organizations

intelligences.[2] On the one hand, the assertive and inspirational force spirals centrifugally, that is outward and downward, across an explosively global trajectory. On the other hand, the responsive and developmental force spirals centripetally, that is inward and upward. For example, in the case of Sony in its early days, its originator Maseru Ibuka was the explosive 'masculine' force as an innovator, and Akio Morita ('I want to realize Ibuka's dream') was the implosive 'feminine' influence as an enabler.

The local polarities

Such a global businessphere, secondly, like the atomic nucleus and its surrounding field, has two mediating polarities connecting the central core with the periphery. These comprise the *polar intelligences.* The east–west polarity is the dynamic or change-inducing one, with the adoptive nature of the collectively oriented east set against the enterprising one of the personality-focused west. The north–south polarity is the homeostatic or stabilizing one, with the institutionally based individual freedom of the north set against the communally based collective order of the south.

The peripheral hemispheres

Thirdly, the entire field is bounded by two semi-circular hemispheres. Therein lie the *peripheral intelligences.*

The whole of the southern hemisphere, forming a western-southern-eastern arc, is pulsating with physical activity. This is symbolized by the volcanic earth, constituted of sporting activity in the west, the rhythmical movement in the south, and martial arts in the east. Conversely, the whole of the northern hemisphere, forming a western-northern-eastern arc, flows through cyberspace, and is symbol-ized by the light of the sun. Technical ingenuity in the west, socio-technical systems in the north, and flexible manufacturing processes in the east represent the different forms of such informatically based activity.

The intermediate regions

Finally, there are four intermediate regions, as can be seen in Figure 19.2, that serve to connect up west and north, north and east, east and south, and south and west respectively. These then are the *connective intelligences*. Whereas, for example, the north-western quadrant links America with Western Europe, and the north-eastern one links Eastern Europe with the Far East, the south-eastern one con-nects Southeast Asia with the Middle East, while the south-western quadrant connects southern Europe with Africa and Latin America. We start, then, with the centre.

The global centre

The global centre, the business's nucleus, as it were, takes us back to the very roots of our global civilization, as well as down to the knowledge- and value-based vision of our global enterprise. Thereby, and on the one hand, the ability to create unity out of underlying variety, as the American 'melting pot' has endeavoured to do, has led to the development of the Microsofts of this world. Conversely, and on the other hand, the ability to develop variety out of an underlying unity, which has been the 'rainbow-like' task of Canada, the European Union and indeed South Africa, has led to the emergence of the Cashbuilds. While variety-in-unity leads to the leaps of innovation for which the US is famous, unity-in-variety leads to development and renewal, for which Japan is better known.

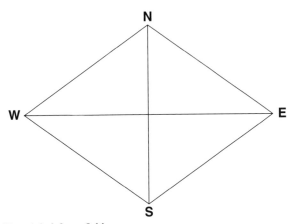

Figure 19.2 The global force-field

Unity-in-variety

These two centrifugal (melting pot) and centripetal (rainbow-like) forces, in fact, constitute the very roots of our global civilization. Firstly, the monotheistic Semites – including the Jewish, Islamic and Christian peoples – were forged out of a Middle Eastern crucible in which the belief in one God universally prevailed. Within this Middle East, moreover, in these ancient times, there was a coming together of peoples from the north and south, east and west. As a psychological parallel to this historical and geographical reality, Carl Jung has referred to the realization of self as representing the ultimate in what he terms 'individuation'. In effect, such a process serves to integrate our otherwise discordant personality. Such discord, in the global terms represented here, would mean that, either individually or organizationally, we exclusively orient ourselves administratively northwards or entrepreneurially westwards, adoptively eastwards or animatedly southwards, or hover about on the periphery.

As such, both individually and organizationally, we remain exclusive rather than inclusive, and in the process we never realize the whole of our selves. By analogy, a parochially based company develops and promotes a particular product line, or brand, without ever uncovering and releasing its globally based core competence, through its knowledge-based, value-creating centre.

This search for the centre of our personal or societal being, so long the quest of religion and more recently of psychology, has yet to find its wholehearted way into business and management. The pursuit of core competence, which is certainly a step along that centring road, gets all too quickly dislodged by the analytical or even enterprising mind. For such a mind seeks out multi-faceted competencies, rather than the core competence as a unity, prior to the emergent variety, or else the competence variety, but with a view to unity. In fact the secret of the enduring success of a company such as 3M lies in the fact that, in the 1950s, it identified 'coating and bonding technology' as its knowledge- and value-creating unity, out of which some 50,000 products emerged over time and space, in proliferating variety.

Similarly, the secret of President Mandela's success in providing a core competence for the new South Africa lies in his ability to stand at the centre. As such he has created a force for reconciliation between western enterprise, northern bureaucracy and southern community, even though eastern-style adaptivity may be somewhat missing from his core repertoire.

Variety-in-unity

While the Semitic peoples engaged in a monotheistic drive for unity-in-variety, the Indo-Europeans, secondly, strove for a variety-in-unity.

Ultimately stretching all the way eastwards from Ancient Greece to Persia, India and China, westwards towards Britain and France, and northwards towards Scandinavia, they formed the centripetal counterpart to the centrifugally oriented

Semites. As such they served to provide the evolutionary harmonic that complements, at core, the revolutionary dynamic.

Whereas, for example, Maseru Ibuka, co-founder of Sony, served to revolutionize the Japanese electronics industry after the war by creating product variety out of a unified quality orientation, Akio Morita's role[3] was to contextualize such a unified vision within the emerging variety of national markets around the globe. From a psychological perspective again, whereas the Swiss German Jung[4] ultimately strove for individual variety, stemming from a primal unity, or collective consciousness, the Italian Roberto Assagioli[5] strove for unity, or 'psychosynthesis' out of our variety of selves. Such a psychological synthesis was to be secured through a realization of the 'higher self', that would serve to unite the multiplicity that preceded it. Interestingly enough, neither the western notion of a holding company or conglomerate, nor the eastern notion of a Japanese *kereitsu* (group of companies) or Korean *chaebol* (group of family-owned companies), approach such a 'corporate psychosynthesis'. For before such a higher self can be realized, the multiplicity of selves – northern and southern, eastern and western – have to be identified. Moreover, the popular notion of our emergent 'global village', facilitated by the physical flow of goods and services around the world, and the electronic flow of information, is symptomatic of our explicit business focus upon periphery, rather than core. For neither our collective unconscious nor the multiplicity of our individual selves enters centre global stage.

The true recognition of diversity prior to unity, requires us, as authentically transnational managers, to enter into the core (see Figure 19.1) of the diverse cultures with which we come into contact, that is into their art and religion, their philosophy and psychology, rather than merely into the periphery. The visible habits and social encounters across the boardroom or restaurant table form that periphery, but do not constitute our core. Neither will electronic encounters, yielding surface data across the information superhighway, help in this respect.

The building up of a true cultural mosaic, in fact, requires diverse peoples to share each other's inner beings, as represented for example in their art and philosophy, rather than merely their outer doings, as reflected for instance within their eating habits and physical climate. Language, finally, represents a halfway house between the surface and the depths, depending upon the way in which it is appreciated and used. We now turn from the global core to the localizing polarities.

The local polarities

Polarity, centre and periphery

Within the global businessphere, emerging out of the centre, there are the *polar* intelligences, embodied in what we have termed the 'four worlds'.[6] These are symbolized by west and east, north and south, and characterized, in spectral terms, by entrepreneur and adopter, executive and animateur. In terms of

Howard Gardner's multiple intelligences,[7] the 'verbal' and 'logical' intelligences form the adjacent western/northern poles, typically adopted by the Americans, and the 'interpersonal' and 'intrapersonal' form the southern/eastern ones, characteristically adopted by the Japanese. Each of these four poles, as we shall see, moreover, is underpinned by an all-pervasive philosophy, and by typical forms of organization and management. For the first time in our global business history, in fact, these polar forces are combining cooperatively together in joint ventures, as well as fighting competitively apart within independent enterprises.

At the same time, knowledge work is being combined with physical labour, human with physical and financial capital, as well as information with energy. Through such combinations, the energetically based 'southern' (west-south-east), and information-centred 'northern' (west-north-east), hemispheres are being reintegrated. The extent to which the core of global learning and creativity is able to harness the worldwide periphery of such physical and informatic resources, moreover, will depend upon the strength and versatility of the polar forces. Each of these forces, as we shall be illustrating, is embodied, actually and potentially, in a particular kind of philosophy and economy, organization and management. In fact, the overall art, religion and philosophy of each lies close to the core. The specific managerial attributes, moreover, lie on the attitudinal or behavioural periphery.

Finally, the polar forms of economic and organization structure lie in between. We have related them, philosophically speaking, to pragmatism, rationalism, holism and humanism.

Global factors of production

Of the four polar factors of 'global production', then, *pragmatism* firstly, as we saw in chapter 3, is strongly rooted in *western* Anglo-Saxon culture, proliferating in the United States and in the UK, as well as in Canada, Australia and New Zealand. Such an empirical outlook has given rise to the market economy, to free enterprise, and to the business entrepreneur or enterprising manager. While its positive manifestation is in free-spirited individualism, its negative form of expression is in rampant materialism. Such a pragmatic approach can be closely aligned with the primal, economic and commercial domain. *Holism*, secondly, is most strongly rooted in far *eastern* cultures, such as China, India and Japan, but also has roots in the more easterly parts of Europe, such as in parts of Austro-Hungary and Germany. Such a holistic tradition has given rise to the social market economy in Germany, to the *Kereitsu* in Japan, and to the reflective style of adoptive management associated with a long-term business orientation. While its positive manifestation is in its total quality orientation, its negative expression is in totalitarianism. Holism, then, can be closely aligned with our developmental domain, and with the life sciences underpinning it.

Rationalism, thirdly, as we saw in chapter 4, is strongly rooted in *northern* Europe, most particularly in the Benelux countries, in France and northern Italy, in parts of Germany and Switzerland, as well as in Scandinavia. Such a rational outlook has given rise to the centrally directed or welfare-based economy, to bureaucratic organization, and to the analytically based professional administrator. While its positive manifestation is meritocratic, its negative expression is bureaucratic.

In its essence, then, it is strongly connected with our rationally based, technological and administrative domain. Finally, *humanism* is rooted at least in part in *southern* cultures, extending all the way from the south of Ireland to southern Europe – from whence came the Renaissance – to parts of Africa and Latin America. Such humanistic traditions have given rise to socio-economic networks, to familial 'clan'-based organizations, and to convivial styles of people management. While its positive manifestation is in its communal nature, it expresses itself negatively through nepotism and corruption.

These philosophically based factors of production, then, are parts of a global whole. In fact, while the artistic and scientific worlds have been noted for the intense interplay between the diverse philosophical systems that underlie each, until now, the same could not be said for our business and organizational ones. Whereas the advent of a 'global village' has been heralding ever greater peripheral connectivity, both physically and electronically, the central core, as well as the polar connections, have been left wanting.

Interestingly enough, moreover, the global force-field, as we can see in Figure 19.3, constitutes, more or less, the learning cycle popularized by American organizational psychologist David Kolb.[8] Following the basic methodology of scientific method, the global learner, depending upon his or her philosophical outlook, will start in one or other of the four positions, but will need to complete the cycle in order to wholly learn. In the process, we as learners actively experiment

CHANGE AGENT

Rationalism
Conceptualize
Deliberator – Executive

Imaginative – Innovator

Pragmatism   *Holism*
Experiment   **Observe**
Energized – Entrepreneur   Imitative – Adopter

Insightful – Enabler

Responsive – Animateur
Experience
Humanism

ADVENTURER

Figure 19.3 The polar forces in the global businessphere

(western), abstractly conceptualize (northern), reflectively observe (eastern) and concretely experience (southern). Because, then, in explicit management theory if not in implicit business practice, it is the pragmatically oriented, competitively focused, personality- and enterprise-based outlook which has predominated, our collective learning has been inhibited.

Interestingly enough, the managerial spectrum, as originally developed by my colleague, the British psychologist Kevin Kingsland,[9] not only reflects different personal orientations but also a full spectrum of learning and innovation. Learning in fact ensues through imitation (adopter), followed by rapid reaction (adventure), sympathetic response (animateur), and sensitive adaptation (change agent). Subsequently, energized commitment (entrepreneur), suitable deliberation (executive) is followed by profound insight (enabler), culminating in the act of creative imagination (innovator). This is what we term the learningful 'departure', in journey terms, to be followed by the innovative 'return', which we shall shortly be reviewing.

In the meantime it is the three perspectives which have been the much less clearly differentiated – rationalist, holist, humanist – that have suffered. The result has been, at a macro level, the over-generalized, and hence ultimately destructive, as opposed to creative, tension between capitalism and communism. Moreover, at a micro level, business enterprises have been under-performing radically, in relation to their global economic and technological, social and cultural potential. How then can that be obviated? Let us now turn to corporate culture.

The 'soft' branches – transforming corporate culture

The transformation journey

Hero with seven faces

The notion of the 'journey' serves to transport us from the 'hard' branches of metaphysical management, with their philosophical, secular and scientific connotations, to the 'soft' ones, with their mythological, religious and artistic overtones. In fact the problem with the processes of learning and innovation, as described up to now, is their somewhat clinical quality. Yet, in real life as we know, they are extraordinarily turbulent activities. As a result, the American student of mythology, the late Joseph Campbell,[10] identified seven phases in a hero's journey. The call to *adventure* (reaction), if taken up, is followed by the role of *protectors* (response), whereby others lend the hero a helping hand. A subsequent *road of trials* (adaptation) is followed by the *death of the self* (energized), whereby the old is surpassed by the new. Following this a *marriage of interest* (deliberation), combining the new self with a receptive organization, which paves the way for *plumbing the depths* (insight), where profoundly new insights are gained, so that ultimately *the power of creation* (imagination) is acquired.

346

From matter to spirit

However, the person who has done most to put such a 'soft' mythical imagination onto the management agenda is not Campbell, great thinker though he was. Rather it is the American business consultant, lay preacher, instigator of the 'organizational transformation' movement in the 1970s and 1980s, and, finally, close friend of mine, Harrison Owen.

> The point, is not that organizations become more spiritual, but rather that we might recognize that in their essence, they are spirit, and then get on with the important business of caring intelligently and intentionally for this most crucial and essential element.[11]

How then do we do this?

The use of the term 'transformation' by Harrison Owen, as opposed to development, is quite deliberate. For while – for him – development is evolutionary, transformation is revolutionary. Whereas the developmental manager (evolutionary) recognizes and enhances potential in people or things, the metaphysical manager (revolutionary) creates potential, where seemingly none existed before. In comparing and contrasting development and transformation, Harrison Owen uses the compelling analogy of the creation of a butterfly, as against a frog. Whereas a tadpole develops bit by bit into a frog, first losing its tail, then growing its legs, a caterpillar becomes a butterfly in a very different way. The essence of transformation, as the word suggests, is a movement across and through forms. Transformation takes place in the odyssey or passage of the human spirit as it moves from one formal manifestation to another. How this actually happens is indicated by the caterpillar transformation.

Butterflies start out as caterpillars, just as great organizations, symphonies, or technological breakthroughs start out as much simpler material forms.

These initial forms may range from a basic commodity, in the case of the organization, to a simple melody, in the case of the symphony, to a basic compound, in the case of a scientifically based innovation. Then, when the time is right, the caterpillar spins a cocoon about itself, and, after a period, emerges with beautiful colours and wings to fly. That might have been a 'development', but it is not. For once the caterpillar is inside it literally dissolves, as a small business enterprise or simple melody might dissolve rather than evolve.

The caterpillar has gone to its essence, which Owen terms 'spirit', and is then transformed into a butterfly, assuming that being a butterfly is a better way to be. The only way to get to that butterfly state is to allow the old form to dissolve, thus freeing the spirit of the thing to achieve a new form. This may seem, at first glance, to be like 'asset stripping'. The asset stripper, however, is dealing with material assets, at least that is the way he or she sees them, rather than with 'spiritual essence'. To achieve such transformation in a commercial context, then, the businessperson must be able to identify, release and reform 'spirit' rather than physical, economic or human matter. How, then, do you go about this?

Transforming the spirit – language, journey, storytelling

There are three specific parts, for Harrison Owen, as I see his work then, to transforming the spirit of a place. They cover, in a manner of speaking, 'meta' policy making, strategy formulation and operations management. The first *policy making* requirement is for the would-be transformative manager to learn a new *language*. The primal manager expresses himself or herself, for example, in terms of winning, of intrapreneuring, of sharing values, and of managing by wandering about. The rational manager uses the language of planning, organizing, directing and control. The developmental manager focuses on recognizing and realizing potential, identifying and fostering synergies.

As a metaphysical manager, finally, you express yourself, both verbally and non-verbally, through myth and ritual, through liturgy and covenant, through spirit and culture.

The second *strategic* requirement here – whether in an economic, technological, social or cultural context – is not to have a passion for excellence, to compete efficiently and effectively, or to subtley manage complexity, but to transform spirit into matter/energy or vice versa. In order to do either, such a manager needs to be capable of undergoing what Owen terms *the journey of the spirit*, or indeed the heroic journey. Finally, and in *operational* terms, the metaphysical manager must be able not to make things happen, to perform to standard, or to fulfil potential, but to uncover, translate, act out and reveal both original and derivative stories that convey the spirit/energy of the organization. Should you not be entirely successful in this operationally metaphysical respect, though, it is possible to intervene, indirectly, and facilitate effective transformation. This is achieved through a process of *collective storytelling*. For it is these stories – in their right form, in their right time, in their right place – that imaginatively and materially transform energy into spirit and back again. I shall now deal, via Harrison Owen, with these policy-making, strategic and operational elements.

Meta-policy – the language of spirit

MYTHOS

Mythos is the collective term for organizational myth and ritual. These two elements in combination make up the fundamental building blocks of the 'soft' side of the metaphysical manager. They represent to him or her what, for example, capital and labour represent to the primal manager. Myths are the stories of a group's culture which describe its beginning, continuance and ultimate goals.

These stories are so much part of the institutional fabric as to define it. To know the myth, according to Owen, is to know the institution in a way that balance sheets and organization charts can never tell. Ritual, moreover, is the dramatic re-enactment of the myth. In a ritual the group acts out its central stories in such a way that the members experience really being there and participating in the original event.

THE NATURE OF MYTHOS

A myth, then, may be defined as a likely (but not necessarily true) story, arising from the life experience of a group, through which it comes to experience its past, present and potential. The story does not reveal systematically the workings of the group or organization, but rather re-presents it in an immediate and gripping way. A myth is a good story that grips you, creates a world, and, to some significant degree, transforms it. Working with or in a given myth is like living in a good novel. The difference is that you cannot put the myth down. A myth not only reflects life. It becomes life. Whereas a rational manager, for example then, views his or her organization's systems and procedures as the natural channel for his or her activities, the 'soft' metaphysical manager sees myth and ritual performing that channelling function. Where the image of efficiency for the 'organization person' is reflected in return on investment, for the metaphysical manager the image of transformation is reflected in dreams turned into reality.

THE FUNCTION OF MYTHOS

The true function of mythos, according to Owen, is to say the unsayable, to express the ineffable, but, most importantly, to bring the participant employee, customer, or business associate into an immediate, self-validating relationship with the spirit of the organization. This means, of course, that the function of mythos in corporate policy making is not a static one.

It continues to grow, over time, as succeeding generations add their imagination – their spirit – to the original act and its re-creation. In the process of such re-creation, spanning both the imagination and also reality, those involved imbibe fascination, meaning, morality and even awe into their lives. Joseph Campbell has described the functions of myth in very distinct terms:

> The first function is to awaken us to the fascinating mystery of life. The second function is to interpret that mystery in order to give meaning to life. The third function is that of sustaining the moral order by shaping the individual to the requirements of his geographically or historically conditioned social group. The fourth function is the most vital one of fostering the unfolding of the individual, in accord with himself, his culture and the universe, as well as that awesome ultimate mystery, which is both beyond and within himself and all things.[12]

Myth and ritual moreover, just like the organization as a whole, goes through a life cycle. In the early days of a business's formation, stories are being acted out by the protagonist, and told, in real time. They are part of everyday reality rather than carriers of meaning. It is only later on, once the stories have become increasingly familiar (narrated) to an ever-growing number of people, that their presence begins to offer comfort and security as well as excitement and drama. Eventually it becomes important that the stories are told (read) in the right way, if they are to continue to be meaningful. In their more flexible form, for Owen, organizational stories provide an outlet for creativity and innovation. At the point where stories have become fixed in people's minds, they need to be broken in order to give them a fresh and updated touch. In fact, to the extent that mythos is alive and well in an organization, those who participate in it will experience the moment of breaking as one of release. Yet they will also experience such release as fearful.

Mythos completes its life cycle with renewal, whereby the individual or organization is infused with new meaning and purpose (re-authorization). This new spirit is generated during the time of 'breaking', and is created under conditions of what Owen terms 'open space'. As you and I participate in the story in such a climate of open space, and specifically its breaking, we discover that the spirit has been freed to explore new possibilities. The myth is ripe for renewal, rather than being stuck in rigidly formed tradition, which is quite deadly to the spirit.

ROLE OF MYTHOS

The role of myth and ritual, therefore, changes as it reaches different points in its life cycle. At first it tacitly embodies transformation. Secondly, moreover, it explicitly serves as a record of transformation. Such a transformation may involve the initial conversion of a speculative idea into a fully established business, the handover of a business from one generation to the next, or a diversification into a new product line. The intent of mythos at this second point is not just to talk about what transpired, but rather to create the conditions under which that prior journey of the spirit (adventurous, enterprising, innovative, or whatever) may be experienced.

The third role of myth and ritual is to become an agent of transformation. By virtue of the fact that mythos, within a dynamic regime, is being constantly broken, it exists within the corporate psyche as an uneasy bedfellow. Just as everybody has become accustomed to the tale, it shifts, and exposes some new area of meaning. This ongoing shifting continually creates new open spaces which invite the group spirit to consider new forms of expression. For example, a previously conceived act of bold diversification may be subsequently viewed as a deliberate attempt to catch the competition off guard.

This in turn leads to a new subtlety in corporate strategy and to a fresh sense of humour in its interpretation. A strategy of deliberate 'fun making' takes over from jungle-fighting tactics. Fourthly, and finally, mythos may itself be transformative. Clock time (Greek *chronos*) is replaced by *kairos*, that is meaning-filled time, which in turn defines time for the group or organization. In other words, eras, for example, pre- and post-merger, replace months or years as focal points in an organization's historical progression.

LITURGY

Liturgy, of which the raw material is myth and ritual and the manufactured process is form and structure, provides the peculiar sense of time, space and propriety indigenous to a particular people and culture. Liturgy, Owen tells us, is formed from two Greek words – *laos*, meaning people, and *ergos*, meaning work. In literal translation it means the people's work, or what people do. In fact it is the sum of what the people do and say as an expression of their deepest being. When myth and ritual are deeply and continuously integrated into the life of an organization, that is liturgy. Liturgy at its best, then, is the conscious production and orchestration of myth and ritual such that spirit is focused and directed in a particular, intended way.

SPIRIT AND BRAND IMAGE

Traditionally it has been the role of the priest to care for the story of the people, and to provide the means whereby that story can be continually remembered. In contemporary business organizations we now find the public-relations function sometimes taking on the role of guardian or protector of the spirit, the image or even the brand of the corporation, albeit oftentimes in a somewhat crass vein.

This modern preoccupation with 'brand image' is, at its best, an attempt to nurture, protect and convey the company's story to its consuming public. Perhaps the most pre-eminent example of this, in Great Britain, is the case of Richard Branson's Virgin Group. For every time that Branson embarks on another of his spectacular adventures he re-enacts the genesis story of a business that was founded upon exploration. This is both physically the case for Virgin Atlantic and artistically for Virgin Records.

COVENANT AND FORM

While the raw material of liturgy is myth and ritual, the processes for 'liturgy making', according to Owen, are form and structure. Form is the way we do things, as in the phrase 'good form'. Structure is the delineated field of operation within which things get done. To be effective in metaphysical terms, both form and structure should accord with, and be expressive of, the image and channel of the spirit of the organization.

At some point in the life of an organization this special sense of time and space, form and structure, will be given formal verbal expression. Initially this expression will be very sparse, limited to some general agreement about 'the way things ought to be done around here'. Over time it will become more detailed, eventually constituting some kind of 'rule book'. This is what Owen terms the organizational 'covenant'. For example, in the case of Sony in Japan, its founder's intital 'dream', in the 1940s, was later converted into such a covenant. We start, then, with Maseru Ibuka's dream:

> If it were possible to establish conditions where persons could become united with a firm spirit of teamwork, and exercise to their heart's desire their technological capacity, then such an organization could bring untold pleasure and untold benefits.[13]

This was converted in the 1960s into an organizational covenant, or 'mission statement':[14]

- We shall eliminate any untoward profit seeking, and shall constantly emphasize the real substance of our products, not seeking expansion in size just for the sake of it
- as such, we shall seek a compact size of operation through which the path of technology and business activities can advance in areas that large companies, because of their size, cannot, whereby
- we shall focus on highly sophisticated technical products that have great usefulness in society, regardless of the quantity involved
- thus utilizing to the utmost the unique features of our firm, we shall open up through mutual cooperation our production and sales channels, whereby
- we shall guide and foster subcontracting factories in directions which will help them become independently operable, and shall strive to expand the pattern of mutual help with them.

The extent to which the organizational covenant reflects the real behaviour of the people within an enterprise such as Sony varies enormously. It will all depend on the extent to which the spirit of the organization, reflected in and through myth and ritual, has inspired the people within it. How then might this, or might this not, come about?

Meta-strategy – the journey of spirit – the creation of potential

OUT OF THE DEPTHS

At the beginning of any organization's creation there is a moment when some individual, or some small group, has what amounts to an 'aha' experience. Something might be done, something of particular moment. We saw it, for example, with Steve Shirley of FI, when she came to realize she could give women, including herself, choice. This is the creative moment when something

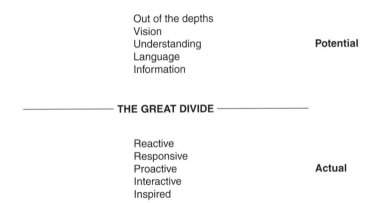

Out of the depths
Vision
Understanding   **Potential**
Language
Information

———————————— **THE GREAT DIVIDE** ————————————

Reactive
Responsive
Proactive   **Actual**
Interactive
Inspired

Figure 19.4 The journey of the spirit

emerges out of nothing. It appears, as it were, from out of the depths (see Figure 19.4).

One might think of Edwin Land, when the mere possibility of an instant camera popped into view, or a thousand other emergent moments when the pot began to boil. At that instant, the originator may not know precisely what to do, and where it all might lead. But the thing is definitely there, as Owen describes it, 'hot, powerful, and moving'.

As substance is created out of the void, so for Harrison Owen a vision may begin to form, that is literally a picture or image of where the future lies. In colour, shape and form the idea is embedded in some descriptive way. But the vision is not only clothed in garments of the world; the vision also reaches out to shape, form and change that world. The nascent organization expands its power base as sympathetic individuals are brought within the expanding energy field. What the vision may lack in concreteness it more than makes up for in raw power.

UNDERSTANDING

With 'understanding' the vision assumes clarity of form. Shape is measured, force is calibrated, products and goals are specified. Planning must be applied so that what emerges 'out of the depths' can move from vision to the real world.

LANGUAGE

Something arising out of the depths, represented in a vision, and located in a context that can be readily understood, must then be named. The possibility of expression comes through language. When something is named it is literally called into existence, as a conscious element in the life of the organization. In this way TTK came to be called Sony, Branson became Virgin, Soros became Quantum.

Until you know the name, the products and the functions of an organization, you cannot know it in a unique sense.

INFORMATION AND DATA

Harrison Owen does not separate out 'information and data' as impersonal abstractions devoid of spirit. In viewing them as a means whereby progress is measured and plans are measured and changed, he still sees a continuity of flow. In other words, such data are a record of the movement of spirit, along its journey from out of the depths onwards. The same spirit moves on through a sequence of manifestations. There is also a discontinuity of effect. Each appearance of spirit must end before the next emerges. That, for Owen, is the story of the butterfly, the story of transformation.

FROM POTENTIALITY TO ACTUALITY

Crossing the great divide separating 'might be' from 'is' brings the organizational spirit from the level of good idea to that of being there. In this process of 'actualization', the spirit brings about reaction, response, proactivity, interaction and, finally, inspiration.

REACTION

On the first days of business, Owen points out, things are more than a little confusing. Events and demands pile on top of one another. The style of management may be described as 'reactive'. You just keep things moving, with 'a bias for action'.

RESPONSIVE

Once things begin to move ahead without constant disruption, you will have learnt to distinguish what works from what does not. In other words, you will have learnt to respond appropriately. As Owen says, it becomes clearer who you are and what your business is, so that your organization may be responsive to your own needs, and to those of the outside world, thereby keeping 'close to the customer'.

PROACTIVE AND INTERACTIVE

Proactive organizations are at the opposite pole from reactive ones. They not only respond appropriately but they exhibit a strong sense of purpose. Proactive enterprises, moreover, approach particular problems, albeit purposefully, as they individually arise, whereas interactive ones have a more holistic and integrated approach. They merge with their environment, seeking progressively more interactive ways of expressing themselves. The distinction between 'in here' and 'out there' becomes increasingly more blurred, as boundaries and constraints are turned into linkages and opportunities.

INSPIRED ORGANIZATION

The journey of the spirit is completed when the matter it has infused becomes fully transformed. In other words, the organization as a whole now becomes totally inspired through its people.

Although the quality of inspiration is similar to that of the individual's original vision, it is now diffused throughout the organization. The whole enterprise has become 'spiritualized'. All forms of energy are vibrating with spirit!

SPIRIT – ENERGY – SPIRIT

The potential for the inspired organization is given by the out-of-depths experience with which the organization began. The experience was powerful in the sense that something dramatic and new appeared from nowhere. What it was and what it would become were all unknowns. Over the course of the succeeding stages of the odyssey, that primordial spirit, having emerged from out of the depths, became more focused and particular. The spirit appeared in successive modes of being, each one of which allowed for a fuller expression of its potential. Yet even at the interactive level, form and structure were important and constraining considerations. The inspired level, for Owen, brings the possibility of going beyond these constraints.

Meta-operations – the manifestation of spirit

FACILITATING THE JOURNEY

The journey of the spirit is an odyssey that a metaphysically aware manager may naturally undergo, over an extended period of time, but which can also be purposefully facilitated. At one stage, as such a manager, you will have emerged from out of the depths to gradually formulate your vision. You will thereby have established your meta-policy. Over time the vision will have been placed in context, and converted into a business language that those around you could understand. In your own mind you will also have planned a series of steps for its accomplishment. This process, whereby potential is created, will often recur during your managerial 'metaphysical' lifetime. This journey takes place, however, in the wider context of an organization.

The organization's culture is in its turn re-presented through myth and ritual (mythos). Japanese and Anglo-Saxon mythology, for example, whether pertaining to self-sufficiency (Sony) or exploration (Virgin), will have become part of the organization's fabric. The heroic exploits of their current and ancestral originators live on through stories acted out, ritualized and re-presented. Mythos for Owen, then, creates liturgy, that is the everyday activities of people in the organization, which is more or less infused with myth and ritual. Liturgy is codified, at a later stage of the organization's development, as the organizational covenant, which serves, in its turn, to produce a coherent spirit.

Harrison Owen, in enabling us to facilitate the journey of spirit, points to three distinct steps. In step 1 a general understanding of the organization is developed through a consideration of its *business history*. In step 2 the facilitator interviews the *leader*, getting to know his or her personal *vision and understanding*. In step 3, the most comprehensive and distinct one, the *organization's culture* is studied, in two stages as we shall see, and reflected back to its members.

STEP 1 – CONDUCTING A HISTORICAL SCAN

Through a historical scan, you uncover how the organization got started, where and under what conditions, who were and are now the major players. Moreover, you find out what is the structure of the organization, its major affiliations, and major products and services.

STEP 2 – UNCOVERING THE LEADER'S VISION

After completing this historical scan, and having identified several 'heavy words', or key repeated phrases, as a facilitator you interview the leader of the organization.

During this interview – step 2 – the essential question that you ask is where the organization thinks it is going, or where it would like to go. The discussion starts with facts and figures – production targets, plans for relocation and recitation of major problems and opportunities – but should proceed to the uncovering of the leader's personal and qualitative vision of the long-term future. The question 'What would it look and feel like if success were achieved?' addresses the quality of spirit desired.

STEP 3 – UNRAVELLING THE ORGANIZATION'S CULTURE

Step three begins at the conclusion of the interview with the leader, at which time he or she is asked to identify a dozen important people in the organization. 'Importance' may be defined in any way the leader chooses, though he or she would inevitably include several members of his or her senior staff. In interviewing these important people, you cannot begin by asking 'What are the key myths and rituals around here?'. Rather you centre upon three questions:

- Who are you and how did you get here?
- What is this place?
- What should it be?

The first question is designed to set the stage and allow the person to talk about him or herself. It serves to place him or her in the context of the organization, and its historical evolution. The second two questions go to the heart of the matter, but indirectly. Inevitably the person interviewed will initially respond with facts and figures, but will be likely to turn to stories and incidents that emerge out of, or exemplify, these. Their words might go something like this: 'You really don't understand this place . . . it's like . . . well last week . . .', and out comes the tale. In listening to the interview responses, it is important to remember what, in particular, you are investigating.

The factual information is of interest, but only in so far as it establishes the context. The real concern is for the 'little stories' that are told. Sometimes the telling of a tale will be an extended performance; other times it may involve just a few key words, for example 'John is a mysterious character'. Although only a select few stories will be told by the 12 or so people interviewed, in Owen's experience the seminal ones will recur. The actual number of major myths (stories 'pregnant' with meaning), in his opinion, is unlikely to exceed half a dozen, even within a major corporation. The first stage of step 3 comes to an end when the findings are presented to a pre-selected focus group of the organization's leader and his or her key associates. The function of this group is twofold – firstly, to validate the stories, and secondly, to assess the proposed interpretation and corrective actions.

In the second stage of step 3, stories are sought from all levels and sectors of the organization. Specifically this means interviewing a representative sample from the executive, middle management, and working levels of all major departments and divisions. This may involve a total of, say, one hundred people in an organization of ten thousand – the facilitator simply proceeds until stories begin to repeat themselves, continually, at any one level or in any one sector. In addition to uncovering these stories through interviews, it is important to observe closely the rituals that characterize different parts of the organization. These may range from board and departmental meetings, to sales drives, to 'rites of passage' for new recruits. You need to identify their precise range and character.

COLLECTIVE STORY-TELLING

The ultimate object is to create a new and composite story out of the existing elements contained within the stories and within the rituals uncovered. By using the existing mythos, the basic, conservative nature of culture is acknowledged.

However, the very power of the newly shaped story overrides the existing negativity. Specifically, for Owen, in constructing the new tale, a place must be found for the heroes and rebels of the past, as a basis and connecting point for the future.

The new mythos, moreover, cannot be created impersonally, but has to be installed through a process of collective story-telling. Weaving such a new tale is the essence of this 'soft' side of metaphysically based leadership, and lies at the heart of the process of organizational – as opposed to business or product

– transformation. In constructing it, it is necessary to consciously link back to the organizational potential, created through its depths, vision, and language, and also to the ways in which its potential may have become actualized in everyday business life. Whatever this new tale may be, it cannot simply jettison all that went before.

The leader may start with a 'story-line', but that is just the framework around which need to be orchestrated all of the other elements. In fact it should be possible to touch, smell and move with a story that is well told. Each part should be able to contribute in its own way, and none should be allowed to dominate. But most of all, the story should be constructed with sufficient open space to allow members of the organization to partake in its creation, through their own imagination. The story must become their story, 'our story'. Telling a four-dimensional story is a real art form. In Harrison Owen's view, it may be the ultimate form of twenty-first-century art.

A story once told, moreover, will be quickly eroded unless it is retold and embedded within the organization. It must become real, and an ongoing part of organizational life. In other words, it must become liturgy – or what the people do. No longer is it the leader's prime function to direct the organization.

Rather it is your responsibility, as a leader, to orchestrate the new story in all its forms. The structure of the institution, its physical fabric, the cycle of organizational activities – all need to reinforce it. Suitable 'rites of passage' for new recruits to the enterprise need to be developed. Celebrations, at regular intervals, must reflect the ethos, the mythos and the appropriate heroes.

Conclusion: the soft branches meet the hard

Mobilizing the spectrum

To retrace metaphysical steps, then, we may recall that the roots of metaphysical management were lodged, on one side, in ancient wisdom, and, on the other, in contemporary epistemology. Whereas the former leads directly on to Harrison Owen's 'mythological' approach to corporate culture, the other can be more easily aligned with my own 'philosophical' approach to culture and management. In the middle, moreover, lies Nonaka's 'knowledge-creating' company, which is rooted in spiritually inspired knowledge grounds, on the one hand, and is elevated through an epistemologically based knowledge spiral, on the other. However, for Nonaka and Takeuchi, the earth-bound grounds and the airy spiral are somewhat disconnected. In this concluding section, therefore, lying in between the 'hard' and 'soft' metaphysical branches, we are concerned to connect the two, through our managerial spectrum.

Innovating – imagining – creating

In mobilizing the spectrum of managerial orientations, then, we become more vividly aware of the links between the knowledge vision, the enabling conditions and the knowledge spiral circumscribing metaphysical management. The nucleus of knowledge creation – the knowledge vision – is constituted of the powerfully imaginative force that radiates *value*.

This is inspired by the pursuit of truth and goodness (Platonic) as well as of beauty, with a view to yielding manifold utility (Aristotelian). As we saw with the Quakers in chapter 15, such *moral* values that drive wealth creation originate in culture, meaning to 'work upon'. For example, the individual entrepreneurs in Britain, such as Cadbury and Leverhulme, who first organized production systematically, were steeped in nonconformist spiritual beliefs. A product or service was fashioned first and foremost in the image of the maker. If customers grew in number, the faith was economically and ethically redeemed.

Value *integrity*, secondly, for the individual or the organization, represents an accrued assurance of an investment in order and meaning, forming a conscious part of a world order. Only when you have faced the triumphs and disappointments that come with being a generator of products and ideas, and have been able to uncover the meaning contained therein, can you develop such integrity. Moreover, it involves an acceptance of your own and only life cycle, or journey, or indeed story, as something that had to be and that, by necessity, permitted of no substitutions. As such a visionary then, you know that all human integrity is at stake in the one style of integrity of which you partake.

Enabling – harmonizing – enhancing

That powerfully innovative force is only effectively mobilized if it becomes centripetally connected through a parallel enabling force, expanding and developing simultaneously inward and upward. Such a centripetal, transcultural orientation is more European than American or Japanese, emerging out of a cultural mosaic (diversity out of unity) as opposed to a melting pot (unity out of diversity). Business and technological vision, market and social context, product and organization design, financial and human capital, systems and processes, physical and social activities all need to resonate with each other.

Such a harmonic interconnection, or interfusion, forms a wholesome basis for so-called business process re-engineering. In other words, it is tension-resolving, pattern-making and harmonically unifying in its diversity, in the same way that the centripetal force creates diversity out of unity.

Such a tacit process of whole making, moreover, needs to be made explicit, what I term a 'virtual process', if full-scale 'externalization' is to ensue. The triumph of the great composers, for example a Beethoven or a Mozart, has been to extract musical ideas from out of the air, as it were, and to transform them into physical notations that can subsequently be interpreted by generations of performing musicians. The result may be a Beethoven symphony or a Mozart opera that is a creation of value. In other words, a tangible product and organization design needs to be established that will serve to externalize the intangible pattern of meanings and relationships contained within the business's unfolding story.

Executing – deliberating – formalizing

The development of a product or service, as a fusion of different material and social elements, needs to be contained within an organization. Such a simultaneously hierachical and networked form is an outcrop of both vertical and lateral thought patterns. Its eminently 'European' rationality turns intrinsic forms – scientific/technological, managerial/organizational or product/market concepts – into extrinsic forms, that is physical goods or services. Strong product concepts, such as a BMW or a Volvo, and organizational identities, such as Club Med or Michelin, result. The predominance of engineering, moreover, as a business-related discipline in such mathematically oriented societies is a notable feature of their institutional lives, with *informatique* in France and *Technik* in Germany being prominent cases in point.

Whereas continental Europe, including France and Germany, has predominantly embodied the hierarchical form of such bureaucracy, Scandinavia has embodied the more networked variety, with Sweden and perhaps the Netherlands occupying an intermediate position between the two. Across Europe, such companies as Michelin, Siemens, Volvo and Phillips epitomize such a logical and mathematical way of knowing and being. While they lack the centrifugal creativity of America and the centripetal harmony of Japan, they embody the best of Europe.

Enterprising – energizing – empowering

Whereas America specifically has played a unique role in the modern business world, as a creative force, the Anglo-Saxon world more generally has acted as harbinger of the free market, and as home of free enterprise. America's particular genius has been to turn the explicit knowledge – resulting in new business, managerial and product concepts – into tacit 'user-friendly' language, embodied in marketing and salesmanship. In that respect its management 'gurus' have acted as externalizers, and their disciples have combined the resultant knowledge into training 'packages'.

The result has been that such programmes as 'management-by-objectives', 'total quality management' and 'business process re-engineering' have taken the business world, around the globe, by storm. Within the context of their own business corporations, moreover, such American entities as Microsoft and Compaq in computing, and Macdonald's and Burger King in fast foods, have recently grown at lightning pace, rapidly internalizing, or applying, the business and product concepts, on a global basis. The United Kingdom, by way of comparison, with much of the entrepreneurial but little of the executive within its national psyche, has been stonger on internalizing – witness its advertising industry – and weaker on combining – witness the demise of its motor industry.

So the harvesting of green shoots, within Britain, has lacked the scale and scope of its cross-Atlantic neighbour, comparing, for example, Psion with Microsoft.

Changing – adapting – networking

The creation of networked systems, both technically and socially, that facilitate rapid adaptation has been a special prerogative of the Scandinavians. What has been termed 'relationships management', embodied in powerful communication systems, has been pioneered in these northern climes of Europe. Such value-adding networks, together with the services they provide, arise out of the highly developed 'visual–spatial' intelligence that is reflected in such companies as Autocon and Lego in Denmark, as well as Eriksson and IKEA in Sweden. Rapid adaptations take place across the synapses of these communication systems, linking up functions within, and suppliers and distributors without. Business and product concepts, duly promoted to the buying public, are continually adapted to its needs, and hence continually internalized. In fact it is this dual capacity both to combine and also to internalize knowledge that gave Sweden's IKEA an edge over Britain's Habitat, even though the latter, through Terence Conran, had led the way during the 1970s and 1980s, in the UK's design-led furnishing revolution.

Animating – responding – enthusing

The internalization of knowledge, through marketing and communications, has been a strong point of the Anglo-Saxons and the Scandinavians, respectively. Where the Japanese have scored is in linking internalization with socialization, thereby maintaining hands-on contact between employees, and with customers. The Japanese, in effect, have been much more animateurial than either the Anglo-Saxons or the north-western Europeans. Their collective orientation makes them more socially responsive than the other members of the triad.

Knowledge is more concertedly built up between highly motivated groups than within highly talented individuals. At the same time the 'southerners' within the businessphere, that is both Latin Europeans and also South Americans, as well as Africans and even perhaps some Middle Easterners, are much more of an unknown quantity. Such workers' cooperatives as Mondragon in the Spanish Basque country, and Cashbuild in South Africa, are intensely socialized. Their communal orientation is based upon a strongly developed interpersonal intelligence that leads to the socialization of knowledge. Unfortunately in apartheid South Africa, hitherto, this would-be socialization was curbed by a black–white divide, whereby the communal influence of the former was withheld from the individualistic orientation of the latter.

Adventuring – reacting – choreographing

It is only with the new South Africa that this imbalance is being significantly redressed. More particularly, of course, the images we have in our mind of dancing in the streets, at election time, are yet to be transformed into a proliferation of kinesthetic intelligence deployed in the southern workplace. Whereas the 'eastern' Japanese 'company song' has become a phenomenon of our busines time, the southern African or indeed Latin American equivalent is yet to make its influence felt. In Japan, as both interpersonal and kinesthetic intelligences combine forces to make up socialization, tacit knowledge, for Nonaka, is converted through co-experience into a common base:

> Such communication is like a wave that passes through people's bodies and culminates when everyone synchronizes himself with the wave. Such sharing of mental and physical rhythms among members of a field may drive socialization towards conceptualization.[15]

In effect, therefore, our image of the physical end of knowledge internalization is restricted to a western-type 'work hard, play hard' culture, and is thereby divorced from its more overtly and kinesthetically intelligent variety. In Albert Koopman's terms, 'the Divine Will of Africa', embodied in its communal rhythms, is yet to make its economic influence felt.

Adopting – imitating – contemplating

The ultimate in knowledge internalization, though, that is learning from and through doing, may not be the active 'western'-style 'trial and error', but more the reflective Japanese style of contemplation-in-action. For such 'reflective practice', in effect, serves to integrate internalization with externalization. Robert Pirsig, the American social philosopher who wrote the classic *Zen and the Art of Motorcycle Maintenance*,[16] describes quality in terms of realizing an 'at-oneness', or an overall peace of mind. Continuous improvement, or *kaizen*, is realized not so much through a desire to achieve, but more through a pursuit of perfection, facilitated by total immersion in the task at hand. Similarly, such a total immersion in the company encourages the employee to 'give his or her all' in a spirit of utter devotion that embodies an 'eastern' approach to socialization. Finally, his or her contemplative outlook enables him or her to subordinate his or her individual personality to the group ego.

We have now completed the metaphysically inspired journey from vision to perfectibility, thereby straddling the global businessphere, while harnessing the sprit of transformation. We now turn to the final two of our live managers, George Soros and Richard Branson, through whom we shall complete the spectrum of managerial orientations, this time incorporating the innovator and the adventurer.

INNOVATOR AND ADVENTURER

The fruits of metaphysical management

Introduction

From developmental to metaphysical management

A developmental manager, such as Fujisawa or Jaworski, may participate in a fundamental transformation of spirit, and of energy, but will lack the power to complete the revolution in which each has played an important part. For while adopter and enabler merge with, and harness, potential, innovator and adventurer – between them – actually create it. While, for example, Henry Ford in the America of yesterday created an entire automobile industry, Anita Roddick in Britain today is creating a new industry founded upon naturally based cosmetics. Both have combined innovation and adventure in their far-reaching activities. While Ford ventured out on the open seas, engaging in his somewhat bizarre peace missions, Roddick travels about the world, discovering and transforming traditional methods of skin and hair care. Both have missions that transcend the material world, and yet partake fundamentally of it.

While entrepreneur and animateur infuse an organization with enterprising activity and shared values; while executive and change agent provide stable organization and adaptive systems; while adopter and enabler align the organization to its ultimate vision and attune it to technological, social and economic evolution; the innovator provides the creative nucleus of the organism, and the adventurer infuses it with energy.

Innovator and adventurer

The most basic element of business life is not money, nor is it people, but it is energy. It is the adventurer who releases raw energy, in its purest form, and it is the genuine innovator who is able to create new energy forms. The most highly evolved corporations will take particular note of these two metaphysical managers. There is a strange bond between an adventurer such as Roddick, compelled to risk life and limb, and an innovator such as the original Ford, compelled to devote his whole life and livelihood to the realization of his dream. While the one enters into the physical unknown, the other enters a technical, social or artistic void. Both, like Englishman Richard Branson and Hungarian émigré George Soros chosen for our purposes here, are obsessive in their managerial pursuits.

The innovator

Are you a prospective innovator?

As such an innovator:

- you have the courage to dream
- you have the courage to tap powerful, subconscious images
- you remain close to the nature and to the spirit of your nation
- you can envisage the future
- you are connected with the distant past and the full present
- a little corner of the infinite has been revealed to you
- you impart fundamental values
- you express your vision in a language of uplift and idealism
- you raise your organization's emotional and spiritual level
- you are impassioned
- you experience pain and ecstasy through your work
- you love what you do, as an all-embracing obsession
- you are an originator
- you are in touch with the roots of your company's being
- you are newly connecting those roots with contemporary soils
- you transform people and things
- you are consciously transforming the world's physical resources

Broadly based innovators, as opposed to the purely technical variety, are few and far between in our society, and they are more visible in politics – Disraeli, Ghandi, Luther King – than in business. Yet this was not always the case. Brunel in the railways, Nobel in the chemical industry, and the first Henry Ford in the automobile industry – to mention just three – were powerful innovators of yesteryear. At the same time, as was certainly the case for Ford, you may be one of those geniuses who is on the edge of madness, or at least one so obsessed that you are blind to the destructive aspects of your vision.

Who recruits innovators?

Such innovators as described above are like gold-dust. Unfortunately the popular business press brackets innovators and entrepreneurs together as if they were the same breed. This is not strictly true. Innovators are to be found amongst the ranks of highly imaginative artists or scientists. If corporations can succeed in attracting such creative technologists and designers, they will do themselves a great service.

In order to attract you, as a budding innovator, a company will have to project its image in brilliantly imaginative terms. Companies, rather than being mere patrons of the arts, would need to create and project their own art forms, as the more innovative high-tech businesses are now doing. Innovation becomes central rather than peripheral to the company's existence – something towards which Apple, for example, in its heyday aspired.

As such a creative artist or scientist, then, you have the courage to dream; you are impassioned by your technological or social vision; you are in a position to transform the earth's resources; you impart fundamental values through your activities; you are an originator of a new technology or society, drawing from economic or technological, social or cultural roots.

How are innovators rewarded?

You innovators gain your ultimate satisfaction from seeing your dreams turned into reality. In other words, the far-reaching potential of your scientific, artistic, philosophical or social imaginations needs to be recognized, converted into a product or service, furnished with adequate resources, adapted to changing conditions and circumstances, and warmly accepted by people inside and outside the organization. To the extent, then, that your far-reaching idea was turned into reality you would feel duly rewarded. You might then see your creative idea spiral upwards and outwards like nuclear fission, just like what is happening to George Soros today. Landmarks along the road to transformation would be scientific, philosophical or design breakthroughs, together with the flashes of inspiration that served to achieve them. Ultimately you have no direct interest in progression along a career ladder. A progressive spiral, technologically or socially based, serves to elevate you from the bottom to a top which – in association with many others – is of your own making. In business terms you can but create your own products and markets.

Becoming an innovator

I have deliberately selected George Soros, the financier and philosopher, as a role model, in order to emphasize that our 'innovative' manager does not need to be a technologist. He tells his story in the following extracts from his book *Soros on Soros*.[1]

Tension as the driving force

Tension has been a driving force in my life. I have been acting out the drama of two different people within me. My father taught me how to deal with the world, my mother taught me how to be introspective. My father liked to stay on the surface; my mother was inclined to delve deeply.

In 1944, the year of the holocaust, I was 14 years old, and living as a young Jew in Hungary. I had a father whom I adored, who knew what to do, and how to help others. By the time I was 15 my father was encouraging me to strike out on my own, and I wanted to go to England. Two years later, after persisting and persisting with the English authorities, I got a passport. I had learnt how to survive from my father, a grand master, who had himself escaped from a Soviet prison. I left Hungary at the age of 17 and he had little more direct influence on the rest of my life.

Open society and its enemies

Upon leaving for England I first attended an Esperanto conference in Switzerland, because my father was an Esperantist. When I got to England I enrolled at the London School of Economics, where I met up with Carl Popper. Having lived through Nazi persecution and then the Soviet occupation of Hungary, I was not surprisingly deeply affected by Popper's book, *The Open Society and its Enemies*. It struck me with the force of revelation, showing me that fascism and communism have a lot in common, and they both stand in opposition to a different principle of social organization, the principle of the open society.

Having got a job with a broking house when I was 26, I was sent to New York, where I started trading in international arbitrage – that is buying securities in one country and selling them to another. I was a trader rather than an investor. I bought and sold quickly. However, in the course of making a study of German banks, showing that their stock portfolios were worth a great deal more than their total capitalization, I turned my interest to Allianz Insurance. Next I wrote a veritable book on the German insurance industry. Identifying a group of insurance companies that had cross-shareholdings in each other, I showed that you could buy some of the stocks at a tremendous discount.

But in the mid sixties, when I was entering my mid thirties, business was becoming scarcer and scarcer and I retired to philosophy, spending time rewriting my undergraduate thesis. I revisited my hypothesis, drawing on Popper, that our understanding of the world we live in is inherently imperfect. There is always a discrepancy between the participant's views and expectations and the actual state of affairs.

History is made by the participant's errors, biases and misconceptions. Testing your views is therefore essential in operating in the financial markets.

Establishing the quantum fund

My so-called Double Eagle Fund started with $4 million in 1969. It became the Soros Fund in 1973 with about $12 million. In 1978 I changed the name from Soros to Quantum Fund. I said it was to celebrate the quantum jump in the size of the fund, and of course I was intrigued by the uncertainty principle in quantum physics. But the real reason was to get my name off the line.

At the beginning of 1981, aged forty, I was running the fund all by myself, with a very small staff, and the strain became unbearable. In September of that year I retired from active management and farmed out the capital of Quantum Fund to the other managers. The issue was the degree of pain, tension, and insecurity I was willing to live with.

The period of turmoil

Then came a rather wild period. I separated from my longstanding partner Jim Rogers and from my first wife. This was all part of the psychological turmoil I went through. My style of management had been too tight and too cramped; so now I let it rip. I no longer insisted on knowing so much about every situation. I was able to establish connections that were not readily available to others, but I also thought that I was a depleting asset. The machine that I was, was running down. While the Fund grew from $100 million to $400 million, I felt that the controls were slipping from my hands. The pressure became almost too much to bear. It began to turn into an internal conflict whereby the Fund became an organism, a parasite, sucking my blood and draining my energy. I asked myself, who was more important, the Fund or me? Is the Fund a vehicle for my success, or am I the slave of my Fund? I wanted to get off the firing line.

When you are a serious risk taker you need to be disciplined. The discipline that I used was a profound sense of insecurity, which helped to alert me to problems before they got out of hand. In fact I think I went through a profound change in my personality during that period. I had some sessions with a psycho-analyst. At one point I had a stone in the salivary gland in my mouth, which was extremely painful. The doctor took it out in an operation, which was also very painful. The stone was a round, hard ball. I wanted to preserve it because of all the pain it had caused me. In a few days I looked at it and it had turned into dust. It was pure calcium which turns into dust when it dries.

The alchemy of finance

That is what happened to my hang-ups. Somehow, they dissolved when they were brought to light. I tell my second wife Susan the kind of person I used to be, and I don't think she can quite believe me. I certainly became a pleasanter person to live with.

In order to get myself intellectually engaged again in investing, I decided to try and write a book about my approach. I started what I called a real-time experiment, recording the decision-making process as it unfolded. It was less a scientific experiment than an alchemic one, because I was conducting the experiment to influence the results. My hopes were in fact fulfilled and we had a period of explosive growth. The book was eventually written, and published, in 1987, when I was in my mid fifties. It attracted Stan Druckenmiller, who was, at the time, a fund manager with Dreyfus. We got to know each other, and I asked him to join our firm. I remained the boss, but I was increasingly absent because of, as we shall see, my involvement in China and Eastern Europe.

Evolving my theory of reflexivity

When the chips are down, philosophy is the most important part of my life. I can summarize my main idea in two words: imperfect understanding. On the one hand, reality is reflected in people's thinking – this is the cognitive function. On the other hand, people make decisions that affect reality and these decisions are based on reality – I call this the participating function. The two functions work in opposite directions and in certain circumstances they can interfere with each other. The interaction between them takes the form of a two-way reflexive feedback mechanism. Instead of correspondence, there is almost always a discrepancy between perception and actuality. This divergence is the key to understanding historical processes in general and the dynamics of financial markets in particular. In my opinion, misconceptions and mistakes play the same role in human affairs as mutation does in biology. That is the core idea. It has, of course, a great number of ramifications. It may not be important to others, but it is terribly important to me. Everything else follows from it.

After the stirling crisis in 1992 I became known as 'the man who broke the Bank of England'. That is what gave me the reputation that I can move markets. Afterwards I had to be very careful about my statements. That complicated my life considerably. The market, in fact, always destroys the weak – that is inves-tors who don't have strong convictions. But having the courage of your convic-tions can get you wiped out if your convictions are false. So I prefer only to take a stand when I have strong convictions.

Towards an open society

In my late forties, when the Quantum Fund had reached a size of $100 million, and my personal wealth had grown to roughly $25 million, I determined after some reflection that I had enough money. After a great deal of thinking I came to the conclusion that what really mattered to me was the concept of an open society. In my philosophy, open society is based on the recognition that we all act on the basis of imperfect understanding. Nobody is in the possession of the ultimate truth. Therefore we need a critical mode of thinking; we need interests and institutions to live together in peace; we need a democratic form of government that ensures the orderly transfer of power; we need a market economy that provides feedback and allows mistakes to be corrected; we need to protect minorities and respect minority opinions.

As a Jew in Hungary I was hunted by the Nazis, then later I had a foretaste of communist rule in that country. Then I emigrated to England. It was as a student at the London School of Economics that I came to understand the difference between open and closed society. My first major commitment in 1980 was in South Africa. I gave 80 scholarships to black students. I did not do a lot more there, which I now regret, though belatedly I have set up an Open Society Foundation there. In that same year I started giving scholarships to Eastern European dissidents. I also began my support of human rights organizations, Poland's Solidarity, the Czechoslovak Charter 77 and the Sakharov movement in the Soviet Union. My aim was to support the people who had staked their lives on fighting for freedom, for open society. The Hungarian Foundation that I established became, from 1984 to 1989, the centre of intellectual life there. I also tried my hand in China.

In each country I identified a group of people who shared my belief in an open society and I entrusted them with the task of establishing priorities. I had an overall vision and, with the passage of time, I learned from the experience of individual foundations. I reinforced the initiatives that were successful and abandoned the ones that were not. But I did not impose anything from the outside. Open society is meant to be a self-organizing system and I wanted the foundations not only to help build an open society, but also to serve as a prototype of such. We started in a chaotic fashion and order emerged out of chaos, gradually. The scope for the foundations was practically unlimited. We tried to choose projects that made a real difference. What they were depended on the needs we identified, and the skills we could bring to bear. Our main priorities are education, civil society, law, the media, culture, libraries and the Internet.

In Czechoslovakia, after the Velvet Revolution of 1989, I recognized the need for an institution that would preserve and develop the spirit of revolution. As a revolution, 1989 was incomplete. It destroyed communism but it did not give rise to a new form of social organization. The Velvet Revolution was fought in the spirit of the open society, but the concept of open society was not elaborated, either in theory or in practice. There was a gaping intellectual need and I set up the Central European University in the hope that we might meet that need. It is not meant to propagate the notion of open society but to practise it. The aim is not only to educate a new elite but also to reach a new understanding. The university came into existence in a revolutionary fashion – without any planning, and without the proper legal structure. Classes started in September 1991. By now order has emerged from chaos and the university has been transformed into a solid institution.

Today the reversal from my starting point, when I disassociated myself from my philanthropy, is complete. I accept everything that I do, either as a benefactor or as an investor, as an integral part of my existence. And I am very happy about it because in a sense my whole life has been one long attempt to integrate the various facets of my existence. There is a remarkable parallel in the evolution of my attitude toward philanthropy and my attitude towards making money. At first I didn't want to identify myself with a business career. I felt there was more to me than making money. I kept my private life strictly separate from my business. Then I went through a rough patch in my early thirties, when I was practically wiped out, and it affected me deeply. I had some psychosomatic symptoms, like vertigo. It made me realize that making money is an essential part of existence. Now I am completing the process by doing away with the artificial separation between my activities as investor and philanthropist. The internal barriers have crumbled and I am all of one piece.

How do you develop as an innovator?

Youthful inventiveness

In your inventive youth you need to explore, to experiment, to risk your personal resources or identity in a new technological or social invention. Travel into the physically, economically, or philosophically unknown – all of which the young Soros did – is therefore a natural feature of healthy, youthful development.

Innovative adulthood

In adulthood, authority and responsibility now come naturally to the developing innovator. Thus the free-wheeling inventor needs to come to grips with the problems of managing innovation – from idea generation to commercialization – that is in Soros' case the Quantum Fund. Whereas your twenties and early thirties are therefore a time for raw enterprise, your thirties and early forties are prime time for managed innovation.

Midlife visionary

Midlife is the time to listen to your heart first, and to your head second. As a technological or indeed financial innovator you need to broaden your social

369

awareness, thereby becoming a true visionary. In fact it was only when Soros entered his fifties that his Foundations truly came into their own.

Mature spirit of creativity

Finally, if you have successfully undergone life's transitions, as a mature individual, like George Soros is now, you are ready to tap the very core of your being, your spirit of creativity. In so doing you also connect yourself with the roots of your company's, or indeed society's being. The relationship is a particularly powerful one, resulting in a fully developed vision. Let me now turn from George Soros to Richard Branson, and from the socio-economic to the physical-kinesthetic world.

The adventurer

Are you an adventurer?

As such an adventurer:

- you're always on the go
- you work long hours and travel to far-flung places
- you have lots of staying power
- you work hard and play hard
- you prefer physical to emotional and intellectual activity
- you take time off to unwind
- you are fit and healthy
- you exercise regularly, in your work or in your leisure
- you are full of energy
- you make a physical impact on others
- you galvanize people around you into activity
- you're an explorer
- you risk life and limb in some of your ventures
- you travel into the physically unknown
- you embody the spirit of adventure
- you are recognized as a wandering spirit
- you imbue your organization with the spirit of adventure

Adventurers have been part of our recorded heritage for centuries. Marco Polo, Vasco da Gama, Christopher Columbus, Francis Drake and Lawrence of Arabia are all prominent examples from the past, for both good and ill.

Today, in the business world, we have, for example, Armand Hammer, the itinerant oil magnate from the USA, and the famed Red Adair, who snuffed out the flames emanating from the Kuwaiti oil rigs after the Gulf War. The role model in point here, though, is Richard Branson of the Virgin Group, in the UK. With the advent of an increasingly leisure-oriented society, in which health and recreation has an increasing part to play, the role of a Branson-like adventurer becomes ever more evident.

Do companies recruit adventurers?

As companies spread their international wings, particularly towards the remoter parts of our globe, and even our planet, so the call for the adventurer is increasingly heard. As research take us up into outer space and down into the depths of the oceans, this demand for adventurers is likely to grow. The mercenary or merchant adventurer of old, then, is being replaced by a more sophisticated business adventurer of the 1980s and 1990s. At the same time, as the pressures of competitive business mount, the demand for adventure training, for adventure holidays, and the like, increases. Work hard, play hard, becomes both a desire and a psychological necessity. The particular parts of a business organization that are likely to be most interested in you, as an adventurer, are export sales, publicity and promotions, research and exploration, and the more physically hazardous operations.

How are adventurers rewarded?

Adventurers, such as Red Adair, Richard Branson, Armand Hammer and Anita Roddick, need to keep constantly – and physically – on the move. If they are not physically on the go, they feel no sense of achievement. So as an adventurer you have physical challenges to surmount, like Branson's attempt to cross the Atlantic in a hot air balloon, and Anita Roddick's desire to keep picking up skin and hair-care recipes from all over the world.

Equally, you may seek physical comfort in good food and wine, in exercise and massage, in sunny beaches on the Caribbean, or in pleasurable sporting holidays.

Becoming an adventurer?

Richard Branson is probably Great Britain's most prominent so called entrepreneur, though, for our purposes he is much more the adventurer or explorer. Here is his story, as told by Tim Jackson.[2]

Would-be money-making student

Richard's mother had grand ideas for her son, that he would one day be Prime Minister, albeit that he showed little more aptitude for conventionally based scholarship than his father had done. He neither wanted to do his 'A' levels nor to go to university. Instead he left school early to set up in business. In fact as a child he had already pursued several successful moneymaking ventures, from growing Xmas trees to breeding budgerigars. *Student*, the magazine he started when he left school, was an artistic and literary if not also a commercial success. Its list of contributors and interview subjects reads like a *Who's Who* of the 1960s counterculture. John Le Carré, Vanessa Redgrave, David Hockney, Henry Moore, James Baldwin, Jean-Paul Sartre.

It takes two to tango

Letters of support had been solicited from everyone from Peter Sellers to Lyndon Johnson. In fact the *Student* magazine was not an isolated venture. At the same time Branson and his girlfriend established a Student Advisory Centre, a voluntary organization set up to help teenagers solve their problems, and an employement agency which sought to match underemployed nurses with London families who wanted cleaners or babysitters. Branson in fact saw an opportunity to capitalize on the public sympathy for the low pay received by nurses. Personal experience, moreover, had led him to set up the Advisory Centre. For at 17 he had met a girl and made her pregnant, then spent 'three months of hell', not knowing what to do. So together he and his girlfriend set up an advice centre for young people. The Centre to this day, with Branson's financial support, continues to give advice on venereal diseases. In the final analysis though, perhaps because of the way Richard was spreading his wings, *Student* never really made money. New issues could never be produced at the rate of a proper magazine. So Branson diverted himself towards selling records by mail-order. What turned out to be the last edition of *Student* contained the first advert for 'Virgin' records.

Richard Branson, at 19, was the senior partner and his friend Nick Powell the junior one. He was also joined in the business by another of his friends, Steve Lewis, who had a passion for pop music, and managed to combine his undergraduate studies with working in the business. After three years moreover Branson came to realize that if he could make money by selling records, he should be able to make even more by manufacturing them. The idea of opening a recording studio was put in his mind by Newman, a guitarist and songwriter who had dabbled in amateur recording for a while. By 1971 Steve Lewis had discovered a kindred spirit. A young South African turned up at the Virgin offices, and announced himself to be Simon Draper, Richard's cousin, a literature graduate who had a passion for music. Draper relished the prospect of turning his life's great passion into a way of making a living.

Chance favours the playful

'Nik and Richard', Simon Draper would later recall, 'had no particular feel for the music business. They found themselves in it by accident. They were public school boys who had dropped out of education.' While the two budding entrepreneurs did what they were good at – Richard sweet-talking the press and striking daring deals – the more introverted Nik reading his management magazines and trying to think of ways in which he could cut costs – they needed some real musical expertise. So there was a vacuum for Draper to step into.

While meanwhile the new recording studio was preparing for its first formal booking in 1971, an obscure band that was recording there pulled out a demo tape and handed it over to Tom Newman, who was in charge of the studio. Simon Draper heard it a whole while later, after the young guitarist had been turned down by almost every record company in Britain, and pronounced it 'incredible'. He decided to tell Richard to sign up Mike Oldfield. *Tubular Bells* put Virgin on the map. It also unleashed a torrent of money into the company's bank account. Virgin Records was now in business as an independent label, and Simon now had enough money to sign the bands he wanted. As the venture grew, Powell and Branson assumed their complementary roles. Powell would produce financial figures for the bank, Branson would take the figures to the meeting and persuade the bank manager to lend a few thousand. It was Branson also whose gusto for life persuaded people that working for Virgin would be fun; it was Powell who stopped the biscuits in the coffee cupboard when times were hard. In common with almost everybody else working for Virgin, Draper, Lewis and Newman were not particularly bothered by money. Music was the passion of their lives.

Virgin gusto

A pattern seemed to emerge meanwhile whereby Draper could make the artistic decisions about which act to sign, Branson would knock out a broad agreement and then Ken Berry would be left to tie up the details in a formal contract. Later, as Branson withdrew from daily involvement in the label, it would be Berry who carried out the negotiations in all but the biggest deals. Richard, in the interim, devoted much of his time to establishing a network of record companies across Europe, paying attention to an aspect of the business, foreign distribution, that most of the other independents had neglected.

At the same time Virgin was willing to hire people who had an enthusiasm and love for music, but no formal experience in other record companies. Once inside, they would find themselves given important jobs to do. Everyone seemed to be friends. And although people took their jobs seriously, they did so as they would take seriously a game of tennis that they passionately wanted to win, rather than as a career. But it was the company's weekends abroad that did most to cement the team spirit. Starting on a Friday and ending on a Sunday the entire staff of the record company, publishing company and studio management team would decamp to a country house hotel. Business was banned. Instead the guests would spend the weekend playing tennis or golf, swimming and sunning themselves, eating and drinking with great gusto.

From records to aeroplanes

By the spring of 1981 it was ten years since Branson had closed down *Student* magazine to concentrate on selling records by mail order. A great deal had happened since then. Virgin had established a record label, a studio business, a chain of shops, a music publishing house. The record label was the engine of Virgin's growth. Powell parted from the Virgin company and became a Buddhist. Culture Club grew bigger and bigger. Boy George, who had signed on for Virgin, in the eighties, was the world's most successful musician. The sums that flowed into Virgin's bank made the Oldfield millions seem paltry.

The founder of Virgin Atlantic Airlines, meanwhile, the company that was to change Richard Branson's life, was a barrister named Randolph Fields. The young barrister realized that Laker's demise left a gap in the lucrative but highly regulated market for air travel between London and New York. He resolved, moreover, to turn in-flight entertainment into the most important selling point of his airline. Flying was to be not merely glamorous but also fun. Meanwhile Fields knew he had to find at least another million, so he approached Branson. Nobody in the Virgin Group knew the first thing about airlines.

Branson's most loyal lieutenants were flatly opposed to the idea. But as far as

Branson was concerned, if People's Express could be run by a Wall Street analyst and British Airways by a former executive of Avis rent-a-car, why coudn't a pop tycoon start an airline. In effect Boy George paid for Branson's airline!

Playing at retailing

By 1981, Virgin had 35 record shops up and down the country ranging from hole-in-the-wall to megastore, and with a bewildering variety of gimicky sidelines. Clothes had been sold in the record stores for a while, under the name Virgin Rags. By 1984 the retailing side was looking distinctly problematical. While turnover-wise it was the country's third biggest record chain, it was not, with the exception of the megastore in Marble Arch, making money. By 1988 it was decided to sell the chain of shops, lock, stock and barrrel, and W.H. Smith were approached. In the interim, though, Branson decided to keep the megastores, and see whether they could be turned around.

Simon Burke, a trained accountant, took over the balance of the retailing after the core had been sold off to Smith's. After a massive streamlining operation, Virgin Retail proceeded to make a steady recovery, and even opened up a new megastore in the centre of Paris. By 1992, moreover, Burke had opened up 30 video game stores around the country. Over the course of the next few years, and in collaboration with W.H. Smith itself, as well as with Chinese and Japanese partners, Virgin opened up megastores in Europe, America and the Far East. For a company, then, that had merely played at 'shopkeeping' during the first seventeen years of its existence, Virgin Retailing was now turning out to be an extraordinary success, with separate management running the American, European and Far Eastern operations.

From private to public

Ten years after the foundation of the record label, nearly fifteen years after the first discount LPs had been sold by mail order, Branson had decided to take Virgin public. Knowing that the group would need some tidying up before it could be sold to investors in the stock market, he had resolved to bring in a manager from outside who could groom the company, and reassure the City. In appointing Cruikshank, as in so many other cases, Branson relied on personal connections. Cruikshank had spent five years with McKinsey before he moved to the Pearson Group, where he was a managing director of the firm's information and entertainment group.

The group he was brought in to run in 1984 was generating £100 million in turnover, but making remarkably little profit. The record side was minting money but the rest was a rag-bag of different businesses, many of which lost money. What was more shocking to Cruikshank was that the group seemed to have no management structure. The firm was struggling to expand with working capital that was hugely inadequate, and an overdraft facility that was miniscule. Branson, he maintained, should not turn himself into an administrator, but devote his attention to acting as a catalyst, motivating others and enthusing them with his conviction. All that he needed was a couple of people to tidy up behind him, and to help him decide clearly what he was trying to achieve. Trevor Abbott was then brought in as Group Finance Director. Both he and Cruikshank were referred to as 'suits' by the more creative people. Undeterred by the initial hostility, they set about reorganizing Virgin into three divisions, Music, Retail and Vision.

The rest were to be got rid of. With that done, the next step had to be to ensure that each Division had a financial controller with enough experience and authority to handle a growing business. There was also a job to be done in disentangling some of Branson's private interests from the mainstream of the business. In appointing KPMG as the firm's advisers, Richard Branson had to say good-bye to the lawyers and accountants who had advised him for years. But Cruikshank was not satisfied with these management changes. Before joining the company, he had wanted assurances from Branson that their agreed mutual goal was to make Virgin public – to have its shares listed on the London stock exchange. The greater prestige of being a public company would enable Virgin to do bigger business deals. There was, of course, a downside. Once the company's shares were quoted on the stock market, Branson would have to exchange the relative freedom of a private limited company, in which his controlling share meant he could do almost anything he wanted, for the more constrained world of a public limited company. Virgin would have to publish a great deal more information than it had done before, and follow more detailed rules. To date Branson had run the Virgin group with a view to maximizing its value over the long term. If he were to become answerable to shareholders, he would have to run Virgin so as to achieve the greatest value to shareholders over a period of months rather than years.

Life and death and life

Branson was bored by finance, by accountancy, and by formal techniques of management. When he had been in partnership with Nik Powell he had pointed gentle fun at the jargon that Powell had picked up from his reading of American business magazines. Meanwhile Cruikshank saw himself trying to bring to Virgin standards of corporate governance.

Branson found it hard not to view this as an obstruction. Too often Cruikshank seemed to wish to scale back his ideas, to bureaucratize his relations with the staff. Whereas Cruikshank seemed to get in the way of Branson's ambitions, Abbott was someone who helped them become a reality. In 1988, Branson reported to the press that Virgin's strategy of investment for long-term growth, with its effect on short-term profitability, had had an adverse affect on the share price. As a result, the benefits of a listing which he anticipated had not been realized. In view of this he was exploring the possibility of a management buyout. A consortium of international banks led by Citibank provided the loan finance required. By 1989, when the buyout was complete, Virgin was twice the size of the company that had gone public in 1985. But the re-privatized Virgin was particularly highly leveraged. It was against this background that the group began to look for ways of raising capital to pay off debt. It was after all other possibilities had been exhausted that Branson had to face the inevitable: the sale of Virgin Music, the crown jewel of the empire. The decision was a gut-renching one, although the ultimate sale to Thorn-EMI ultimately yielded £560 million. At the ceremony marking the sale Branson and his fellow senior management were in tears.

Up, up and away

From Steve Lewis downwards the staff at Virgin Music were unanimously agreed that Branson had made them feel that they were working together in a cooperative enterprise from whose progress they would all benefit in the long term. In doing this, he had imbued them with a positive spirit, transmitting as if by telepathy his blind faith that every problem could be surmounted. Behind the jeans and T-shirts, Virgin Music had a clear corporate culture: it could be summed up in the view that it was idle to ask if something could be done. Virgin people would assume that it could and confine themselves to asking how. Branson had not only commanded loyalty but it had given many of the Virgin Music staff – particularly women – opportunity for promotion. The mid nineties heralded Virgin's diversification into soft drinks, via its own brand of Cola, and into financial services. Rowan Gormley, another South African who had approached Branson with a view to moving into financial services, explained the move by saying that Virgin had become a value-based brand, rather than one dependent on products. Gormley, who had been trained as an accountant, had been working for Electra Trust.

Branson had previously engaged Gormley to help him through the innumerable business propositions that landed on his desk. Meanwhile Gormley had become aware of the major revolution taking place in financial services. Essentially two trends were at work. First, consumers were becoming used to the idea of buying products over the telephone. Notable amongst the companies doing such were Direct Line, selling car insurance, and First Direct, a subsidiary of Midland Bank. Secondly, purveyors of financial products, from mortgages to unit trusts, were under pressure to disclose more clearly the commissions they paid to salesmen and other intermediaries. Gormley's conclusion was simple. The first company that devises a way of delivering products that consumers want by eliminating salesmen, he told Branson, will make a bundle. There was just one problem. How would such a company persuade customers to believe its promises, after all the half-truths the financial industry had peddled for years? Gormley told Branson then: 'What's required to make this work is not a computer system, nor is it capital. It's a name people will trust. There are only two names in Britain strong enough for this purpose. The one is Marks and Spencer, the other is Virgin.'

Branson took some convincing. He couldn't associate together in his mind financial services with the fun image of his company. Once he had eventually become convinced, they had to search for a partner. Branson wanted to team up with a mutual rather than a public company that had the technical knowledge and the capital to launch the new range of financial products. He wanted a company that was big enough to get the project through the regulatory hoops, and that was not too heavily focused on the short term. Soon Virgin settled on Norwich Union as its chosen bride. Recently humbled by a steep regulatory fine for the mismanagement of its pensions operation, Norwich Union was looking for ways of improving its way of dealing with customers. It also had some spare staff and an enthusiastic divisional MD, Phil Scott. The former venture capitalist, Rowen Gormley, therefore left Holland Park, and decamped to a new office in the suburbs of Norwich, close enough but not too close to Norwich Union itself, where he began to set up a clone of the Direct Line operation. The atmosphere, Jackson maintains, bore little resemblance to the stolid air of the average financial institution. The staff were younger, there were more women, and instead of a sea of polyester suits and drip-dry shirts, the new office was full of gelled hair and smart-casual clothes.

From king to kereitsu

By February of 1995, the new Virgin financial services company had sixty employees working at computer terminals. The firm's first product was to be a Personal Equity Plan (PEP), which allowed an individual to invest up to £6,000 a year in approved shares and bonds, and to receive both dividends and profits from rising prices free of tax. Until seven months before the planned launch of the business, according to Jackson, Branson had no idea of what a PEP was, so he was as keen as anyone else in the organization to ensure that the literature was jargon free.

The Virgin PEP's selling point, though, would be clear. Its charges would be low – an annual commission of one per cent on the portfolio value for both the PEP and its underlying unit trust investment – and it would keep dealing costs to a minimum. Instead of wasting money by buying and selling stocks in a vain attempt to buck the market, the fund would simply put its investors's savings in the blue-chip shares that comprised the stock market index, and leave them there. Gormley explained the move into financial services by saying that Virgin had become a value-based brand, rather than one dependent on products, while others looked to the Japanese *kereitsu*, a loose industrial group linked by cross-shareholdings that spanned a wide range of industrial sectors, for the Virgin Group's model.

Second to Mother Teresa and the Pope

When opinion pollsters asked young Britons in 1994 who they would most trust to update the Ten Commandments in the modern world, Branson came in a good third after Mother Teresa and the Pope. To the general public then, Richard Branson is the embodiment of all the great modern values, tolerance, informality and human warmth. It is a sobering thought, the biographer Jackson claims, that the very reason he stands out is that business is not usually associated with such values.

How do you develop as an adventurer?

Youthful action person

In your youth you may come across as an action man or woman. Like Armand Hammer, for example, you may have sold to more countries than anyone else in your company, by footslogging around the world. Like Richard Branson, you may have undergone physical risk or hardship.

Adultlike action manager

In young adulthood you become more visible in the company as a whole, as an action-centred manager. Like Richard Branson, you are physically 'on show' so as to publicize your product and your business, or, like Red Adair, you may have engaged in innumerable chancy escapades.

Midlife adventurer

In midlife you become less intensively involved in your own physical accomplishments, as Richard Branson is doing, and more so in activating others, in sales or in exploration, through coaching or through 'mentorship'.

Mature spirit of exploration

Finally, in your fifties, sixties and onwards, as has been the case with Hammer and may be the case for Branson, as you actualize your true self, you come to embody the spirit of adventure, by broadening the base of your physical accomplishments. Instead of leading from the front you inspire from up above, by, for example, transforming a physical environment rather than keeping yourself physically on the go. As you develop towards maturity, then, you come close to the role of innovator, your counterpart. Between the two – energy and imagination – a vision is materialized.

Conclusion

Vision and energy

The metaphysical paths of adventurer and innovator are somewhat more identifiable than those of enabler and adaptor, but as yet only barely accommodated within conventional organizations. Technological innovators and rugged adventurers are generally relegated to the mature business periphery, even though it is acknowledged that their role has been indispensable. Without Alfred Nobel there would have been no ICI; without George Eastman there would have been no Kodak; without Maseru Ibuka there would have been no Sony. Yet our commercial memories are short. All too quickly we lose sight of our real source of creativity, both in its conception and in its continued activation. Therein lies the creative nucleus, the 'soul' of the business.

For the metaphysical manager, in fact, be he or she an innovator or an adventurer, it is the dream rather than the reality which is the launching point for his or her managerial activity. Although this does become more evident as the person matures, it is always there in the background.

Saving people from contracting Aids, for Branson, or protecting people from raging fires, for Red Adair, may be material necessities, but they are a means to an imagined end. As the metaphysical manager grows and develops, so his or her dreams become tempered by the necessity to survive, the need to be productive, and the requirements of people around him or her. So primal, rational, and developmental management has its evolving place in the metaphysical manager's self-realization. But that place remains subordinate to his or her ultimate dreams.

In the final analysis, though the adventurer begins with action, and the innovator with imagination, both realize that the ultimate possibility and constraint is neither money nor organization, but the laws of nature, reflected in human energy.

Becoming your managerial self

In conclusion, there are eight managerial subdomains, or paths, each of which has been made visible to you, as 'fruits', over the course of this book. Each path makes

Table 20.1 Becoming your managerial self

Exploration (youth)	Consolidation (adulthood)	Renewal (midlife)	Individuation (maturity)
Action man/woman	Action manager	Adventurer	Spirit of adventure
Craftsperson	People manager	Animateur	Community spirit
Troubleshooter	Change manager	Change agent	Spirit of freedom
Entrepreneur	Enterprising manager	Entrepreneur	Spirit of enterprise
Trainee manager	Functional manager	Executive	Spirit of leadership
Artist/scientist	Developmental manager	Enabler	Spirit of development
Inventor	Innovative manager	Innovator	Spirit of creativity
Apprentice	Adoptive manager	Adopter	Spirit of mastery

its way through four stages of development, interspersed with transitional phases. In realizing your managerial individuality, you will probably be best suited to forge, or to follow, one or other of these. In the process, and should you continually grow and develop, you will explore in your youth, consolidate in adulthood, renew yourself in midlife, and become your ultimate, and managerial, self in maturity (see Table 20.1).

We now turn, finally, to a developmental programme, to help both managers and also the organizations in which they are based to become themselves, economically and technologically, socially and culturally.

Part III

HOW? MANAGERIAL METAMORPHOSIS – TRANSFORMING YOUR CAPABILITIES

21

DEVELOPING MASTERY

Poetry in motion

Introduction

Programme structure – Management MBA

Over the course of the last ten years, at City University Business School in London, we have developed a 'masters' programme that is oriented towards managerial and organizational learning, as well as knowledge creation. While being structurally underpinned by **m**anagement domains set in the context of **b**usiness realms, process-wise it is also a project-based programme, run in partnership with major public and private corporations. Whereas the management domains encompass the primal, rational, developmental and metaphysical, the business realms span the economic and technological, the social and cultural. Moreover, each domain and realm is divided up into 'hard' and 'soft' orientations.

Autopoietic process – POEM

While the Management MBA (MMBA) structure is underpinned by the management domains, and the business realms, the process is 'autopoietic'. 'Autopoiesis', as we saw in chapter 13, is a term used today by biologists and ecologists to describe the process of 'self making' that goes on in nature, as organisms evolve. That process is contextualized within the journey to **m**astery facilitated by our project-based, **a**ction-centred programme. We have adopted the umbrella term 'autopoietic', therefore, to encompass **p**reparatory training, **o**rdinary learning, **e**xtraordinary development and a **m**asterly process of transformation.

Whereas the managerial training courses – oriented towards individual knowledge, skill and self-development – are essentially '**p**reparatory' in nature, '**o**rdinary' action learning requires the manager to combine reflection with action, set within the context of a learning 'set'. Leadership, by way of contrast, additionally incorporates '**e**xtraordinary' development, of the manager and the organization, and the '**m**asterly' encompasses organizational knowledge creation.

Altogether, as an acronym, they form a POEM. Hence the 'poetics' of learning. The same original Greek word underlies both 'poetry', in the arts, and 'poiesis', in the sciences.

Preparatory training

Courses of instruction

Management domains

Preparatory courses of instruction, firstly then, provide the business and managerial structure underlying the curriculum. At the core of the MMBA programme is a course of instruction on management, spanning the four domains (see Figure 21.1). As a participant, having assessed your own managerial style in spectral terms, you are introduced to the entrepreneur and the animateur (primal), the executive and the change agent (rational), the enabler and the adopter (developmental), and the adventurer and the innovator (metaphysical). Thereafter, and over the course of the two-year programme, you are encouraged to develop yourself more fully, along your natural path within the spectrum, while at the same time developing, though to a lesser extent, along other chosen paths.

Realms of business

While the management domains apply to you yourself, as an individual manager, the realms of business (see Figure 21.1) apply to your enterprise, as a particular

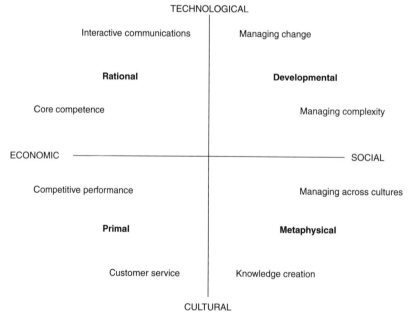

Figure 21.1 Realms and domains

organization. I have summarized below each of these business realms, which are represented on our MMBA within three-day modules of instruction.

ECONOMIC REALM

Competitive performance

- to help you understand the importance and relevance of competitive strategy, and strategic alliances, in today's world of globally based business
- to review managerial reporting systems, and discuss the nature and significance of performance evaluation, set in the context of other such systems across the globe

Customer service

- to enable you to develop an overall appreciation of the nature of economic and social activity, and how both have shifted away from mass production and distribution to the provision of customized solutions
- to appreciate the role of customer service, and a market (and communally sensitive) orientation, in your shifting from transactional to local/global relational strategies

TECHNOLOGICAL REALM

Core competence

- to acquaint you with the rapid changes in technology, and manufacturing methods going on around the world, and with ways of developing your strategic intent accordingly
- to offer you a comprehensive framework for linking research and development with product and process development in the context of global business strategy

Interactive communications

- to understand the role you may play, through information technology and information networks, in expanding business communications within and across organizations
- to accommodate the link between core competence and information technology, and to learn how you can develop a virtual organization to take due account of this

Managing of complexity

- to explore your sets of beliefs and theories about strategic management, organizational change and corporate renewal
- to widen your perspectives of, and provide opportunities for, your becoming more familiar with the management of uncertainty, anxiety, and complexity

Managing change

- to understand the socio-economic forces that are causing the restructuring of work and employment, and identify the implications for human-resource management
- to identify the advantages and disadvantages of organizations that are designed to be more flexible and faster responding

CULTURAL REALM

Knowledge Creation

- to recognize and enhance the knowledge-creating capacities of organizations, thereby enabling you to become more adept at managing knowledge creation
- to enhance your role as so-called 'knowledge engineer', thereby linking the emerging vision of your organization with ongoing business realities

Managing across cultures

- to enhance understanding of, and ability to manage, cultural diversity, both internally within your work group and externally amongst suppliers and customers
- to help you to build up a 'worlds class' organization, thereby incorporating the comparative cultural advantages of different nations in the global enterprise as a whole

In effect these modules of instruction, as revealed below, are run parallel to the relevant projects rather than prior to them, so as to enhance the relevance of each.

'Ordinary' learning

Individual learning in a group context

Action learning takes off, then, from where instructionally based preparation leaves off. In effect, three so-called projects constitute the heart of the MMBA

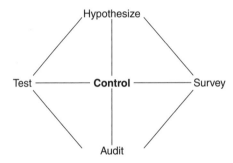

Figure 21.2 The 'ordinary' action-learning cycle

programme, the development of each one being facilitated within a group. Such a group faces both inwards towards the individual, via the learning 'set', and outwards toward the organization, via a self-organizing network. Learning within such a group, moreover, unlike individually based training, is both an interactive and also a cyclical process. For the first project, though, the group still serves the interests of the individual.

Such an individual cycle of learning, for which both student and facilitator are ultimately responsible, involves an interplay between action and reflection. You as managers can only learn from experience if you reflect on it. Without experience, you have no foundation on which to base learning. This specific model of the learning process is in fact a particular application of rationally based scientific method, otherwise known as 'single-loop' learning (see Figure 21.2). Faced with a problem (survey), you use your general understanding (hypothesis) of the situation in order to decide on a strategy and means of implementing it. You go into action phase (test) when trying to put ideas into practice. This is followed by a process of evaluation (audit), whereby the results expected are compared with what has occurred. The differentiation and integration of the learning cycle as a whole is identified as a 'control' process.

The 'learning set'

The 'learning set' provides a focal point for reflection, while the 'project' is the focal point for action. Such a small learning group is a source of challenge and support, a focal point for reflection upon action. It is through the set that the scientifically based learning cycle is socially channelled. Managers on our MMBA therefore learn with and from each other, duly facilitated, by supportive attacks upon real and menacing problems.

A set consists of some four to six individuals, and is convened by a facilitator. In the course of a meeting, which might last up to a day and which is arranged either monthly or bi-monthly over a two-year period, there will be:

- an exchange of *information*, that is of ideas, advice, contacts, hunches, concepts
- *interaction* between set members, offering each other support and encouragement as well as challenge and critical appraisal
- *behavioural* change resulting more often from the reinterpretation of past experiences than from the acquisition of fresh knowledge

Within the set, therefore, learning is facilitated through the interplay of thought (information), feeling (interaction) and action (behaviour). As a production manager, for example, who 'thought' that marketing was about 'bribery and lunches', you would never be able to take in fresh information about it until you came to 'feel' differently about the subject. Only when you had reinterpreted your past experiences would you be able to think and subsequently 'act' differently.

From a practical perspective, then, typically action-learning-based 'set meetings' are expected to provide the following:

1 an opportunity for members to *seek each other's help* in carrying out the project
2 an external *source of pressure* upon members to keep their individual projects moving
3 a source of *progress planning and review*
4 scope for the occasional provision of formal *inputs*
5 through reflection, the gaining of *insights*
6 mutual encouragement and *support*

As a participant on the MMBA, then – each of you being allocated 30–60 minutes to speak in the course of each meeting – you need to purposefully decide upon the orientation of your session prior to the meeting. For such an individually focused session is not merely intended to lead to discussion. Rather, it is a period to reflect on past actions and to make resolutions towards future ones, both intrapersonally and interpersonally, subjectively and objectively.

The 'ordinary' role of the set facilitator

The group facilitator, within the context of the first MMBA project, has a specifically 'ordinary' role to play. This can be divided among four major functions:

1 *scheduling* a minimum of four set meetings during the course of an eight-month period, for each of three projects, including a final meeting during which a project review takes place (see below)
2 *stimulating* the project-based progress of each person within the group, while at the same time enabling members within the set to support and challenge each other
3 *ensuring* that each individual develops knowledge-, skill and character-based

competencies, spread – in the knowledge case – across the four economic and technical, social and cultural domains

4   *monitoring* the progress of each person, through the different phases (AIR, SHARE and REView as indicated below) of the project, and building up peer-group pressure to safeguard completion

5   *reviewing* the 'ordinary' project according to the criteria set forth below, subject to ensuring that the project is up to scratch before it is finally submitted

'Ordinary' criteria for evaluation

The first project is set within an 'ordinary', primal/rational context, usually contextualized within the economic or social domain. As such the following criteria apply, drawing upon the action-learning process developed by Reg Revans:[1]

AIR

1   Identify what needs to be **a**chieved, the constraints that you need to **i**nvest in overcoming, and the **r**esources you will need access to.

SHARE

2   **S**urvey the practical business context – functional, cross-functional or general – in which your problem/opportunity is lodged, and the managerial skill and self on which the project will draw.

3   **H**ypothesize, that is establish the general and particular theoretical base for, primarily, your knowledge development, and, secondarily, your skill and self-development.

4   **A**ct, that is apply the newly acquired competencies to the problem/opportunity at hand, documenting the way in which you have experimented in each case.

5   **R**eview the results of your actions, drawing out the specific lessons learnt for each of the three sets of competencies.

6   **E**valuate the whole action-learning process, drawing out general conclusions and recommendations with respect to business performance, organizational know-how and corporate identity.

REView

7   Relate your project **r**esults – knowledge, skill and self-development – to **v**isible behavioural improvements in managerial performance of your self and your unit/organization/environment.

We now move from the 'ordinary' action-learning-based project, focused on the individual-in-the-group, towards 'extraordinary' development, oriented towards the group-in-the-organization.

'Extraordinary' development

The dynamic process

The second MMBA project is positioned halfway between ordinary *action learning* and the ultimately *masterly transformation* embodied in the managerial 'mastery'.

It thereby requires of you the kind of emotional commitment and conceptual prowess that *dynamic learning* warrants. Specifically, you need to develop significant self- and political awareness, a sensitivity to individual and organizational processes in flux, and an ability to cope psychologically, politically and commercially with such a dynamic environment. Such a dynamic process is laid out below, incorporating the kind of 'double-loop learning' whereby you are able to reflect upon your own 'mental models', and modify them according to personal and organizational need. The learning set and facilitator play a critical role in that respect. Such complex learning, moreover, takes place spontaneously in self-organizing networks that encourage open conflict, that engage in dialogue, and that publicly lead you to test assertions. At the same time, self-organizing political networks function to undermine the hierachically based status quo. Without the consequent tension between control and freedom, acccording to Stacey,[2] there can be no change. Therefore, the most important learning we do flows from the trial-and-error action we take in real time and especially from how we reflect on these actions as we take them.

Where Stacey parts company from Revans is in emphasizing that how well you learn, under these circumstances, depends on the way you interact both within and also across self-organizing groups. Continuing success flows from tension with people, socio-politically, and with the market environment, commercially and technologically. Moreover, this involves not simply building on existing strengths but intentionally steering away for equilibrium. The result is organizational tension, paradox and never-ending contradiction, and this provokes the conflict and learning which for Stacey is the dynamic source of learning development (see Figure 21.3). It is with all these 'extraordinary' tensions – both within the person and without – that the second MMBA project is concerned.

A chaos theory of organization

In the second project, therefore, the focus shifts from the individual-in-the group to the whole network of which you as a manager form a mere part. While as an individual you continue, therefore, to undertake your project in association with your learning set, it is an emerging network of people within the organization that now occupies pride of place. Set within the context of a dynamic organization, for

Manage diversity and complexity

Interpret emerging agenda

Clarify preferences   Incorporate into organizational memory   Recognize and dissolve dilemmas

Gain attention and build a support

Secure legitimacy

Figure 21.3 Dynamic development

Ralph Stacey, moreover, are webs of non-linear feedback loops connected to other people and organizations (their environments) by similar webs. Long-term development is a spontaneously self-organizing process, incorporating political interactions and learning in groups, from both of which new strategic directions emerge. In this way, and as an extraordinary manager, you discover and create the long term future of your organization, as an integral part of a process incorporating a network of associates.

The 'extraordinary' role of the facilitator

It is the facilitator's 'extraordinary' role, then, alongside the members of the learning set, to recognize and enhance such a process of emergent networking. For Stacey, as we have seen in chapter 14, the key control parameter in facilitating this – thereby moving you between what he terms the stable and unstable zones of behaviour and into the space for novelty – is the level of the participant's anxiety and the degree of its containment. You can be returned to the 'ordinary' stable zone by re-erecting the containing structures and thus reducing the level of anxiety. At some critical intermediate level, however, there is enough challenge and contention existing to provoke you into some kind of exploration, but also enough emotional containment of that anxiety to prevent you from being submerged by defensive–aggressive behaviour. At critical points of anxiety containment you can work and perform double-loop learning, avoiding both the rampant fears of the unstable zone and the rigidly defensive behaviour of the stable zone. It is the 'extraordinary' facilitator's role, then, together with that of the learning set, to provide such containment.

If relationships are based on empathy and love, then they operate as effective containers. Given high-quality interconnectedness, a group can contain anxiety and stay at the edge of chaos. The second way of containing anxiety without abandoning the edge of chaos is provided by honest self-reflection, that is when members of a group jointly reflect upon the system they constitute. The third way to contain anxiety is through the quality of extraordinary facilitation and the way in which power is exercised. Specifically, the facilitator needs to avoid authoritarian behaviour, and exhibit a capacity for articulating issues and posing insightful questions. In this way, moreover, enabling conditions are established for your role evolution.

The set facilitator in the second project, therefore, is involved in such activities as giving feedback on self-perceptions; serving as a role model for 'extraordinary' development; supplying mental, emotional and behavioural support and challenge; as well providing conceptual frameworks for modelling management. More specifically, tolerance for ambiguity, openness and frankness, patience, a desire to see others learn, and the ability to empathize are desirable facilitator attributes.

This calls upon the facilitative skills involved in:

1   *timing interventions*: too early and the intervention is not understood, too late and the opportunity has passed
2   *asking good questions*, that is ones which make set members think, and at the same time make them feel challenged and supported – not criticised
3   using the *language of managers*, thereby avoiding speaking down and intellectualizing
4   selecting and applying the *appropriate model* to reflect *processes* taking place at a particular time
5   hearing two or three *processes simultaneously*
6   *making statements truthfully*, while structuring them to be of maximum use
7   containing anxiety, by combining openness and *challenge* with empathy and *support*

'Extraordinary' criteria for evaluation

The non-linear 'extraordinary' criteria for evaluation, finally, are very different from the linear 'ordinary' ones, starting with your ability to recognize emergent patterns.

AIR – recognizing emergent patterns

1   Detecting and selecting an emergent project issue: What significant issues or opportunities are simultaneously emerging from the depths of the business or organization, and from your own work and life?

S H A R E – becoming a reflective practitioner

2   **S**urvey – gaining attention and building support: What important business or organizational project arises, addressed at resolving what dilemmas, who will be joining forces with you, and who will become a sponsor?
3   **H**ypothesis – interpreting/handling the emerging agenda: What conceptual

approaches to managing complexity are you acquiring – for self and organization – and how are both reflected in personal/business emergent strategies?

4   **A**ct – clarifying preferences: How have you been involving the emerging project stakeholders, with what resulting kind of involvement in political and learning processes?

5   **R**eflect – undergoing action and learning: What experimental actions have been engaged in, yielding what kind of business or organizational benefits, followed by what kind of reflection on the results?

6   **E**valuate – gaining legitimacy and backing: How have you, and your network of project associates, engaged with the formal authorities to legitimize initially experimental activities?

Review – internalizing experience

7   Incorporate outcomes into organizational memory: To what extent have the actions taken combined with the insights acquired led to the evolution of your role / the development of your business or organization?

We now turn from dynamic to so-called masterly or 'heroic' learning, or indeed transformation, and how it can be facilitated. In the process, we move from the action learner contained within the action-learning group, and from the dynamic developer within the self-organizing network, to the heroic transformer set within the context of the knowledge-creating company.

Masterly transformation

Triple-loop learning

As a master manager you are on the one hand able to encompass the whole of our so-called 'businessphere' and on the other hand able to completely 're-authorize' yourself. As such you must be able to withstand, indeed draw creatively upon, a field of 'businesspheric' tensions. As such a transformational leader you do so by maintaining the ultra-stability and super-vitality of your individual and organizational core. The result is so-called 'triple-loop learning'. In the process you become able to accommodate and harness those tensions within the self, within the organization, and within society at large. You do so, in fact, by aligning yourself with a higher cause. To develop such a transformative orientation is the ultimate object of our programme, focused not upon business administration but upon knowledge creation.

The knowledge-creating company

A knowledge-creating company, as we saw in chapter 18, is one which continually re-creates knowledge, and thereby products and services, through spirals of

Table 21.1 Stages of re-storying

Ordinary thesis
You can get your story out.
You identify your surface story-line.
Facilitator's function: confirmation.

Extraordinary antithesis
You step back from the story.
You identify conflicting underlying story-line.
Facilitator's function: contradiction.

Masterly synthesis
You develop a larger story.
You identify and integrate a new story-line.
Facilitator's function: continuity.

---

progressively enriched differentiation and integration. The core of this knowledge-creating activity lies within the 'poetic' human process of justifying personal belief with a view to finding the truth (or beauty or goodness).

On the MMBA such a pursuit of truth, goodness or beauty, with a view to realizing utility, is fostered through the mastery project, whereby individual managers build up their own perspectives on the world. Yet these perspectives remain personal, as the Japanese sociologists Nonaka and Takeuchi emphasize, unless they are articulated and amplified through social interaction, that is by a 'field' or self-organizing team in which individual members collaborate to create a new concept. On our programme, such a field is created, at least initially, through both in-company and also cross-company learning sets, which serve to foster continuous dialogue, and appropriate 'interaction rhythms'.

In order for a learning set to start the process of concept creation, it first needs to build up mutual trust, through *socialization* (humanistic) amongst its members. A key way to build mutual trust is to share original experience. Such a sharing is fostered through self-development in the context of others, as is illustrated in the 'storying' process (see Table 21.1).

For direct understanding of other individuals relies on shared experience that enables members to 'indwell' others and to grasp their world from 'inside'. This brings about an *externalization* (holistic) of the internal worlds (see Figure 21.4). Such sharing of mental and physical rhythms among learning-set members, facilitated through such 'storying', may drive socialization towards *combination* (rationalistic). This knowledge created in an interactive field needs to be crystallized into some concrete 'form' such as a product or a system, which serves the purposes of business development of the extraordinary MMBA project. As would-be master managers, at this point, you test through *internalization* (pragmatic) the reality and applicability of concepts created along the way. Such prolonged experimentation needs to be followed by justification. This is a process of final convergence and screening, whereby a learner judges whether the knowledge

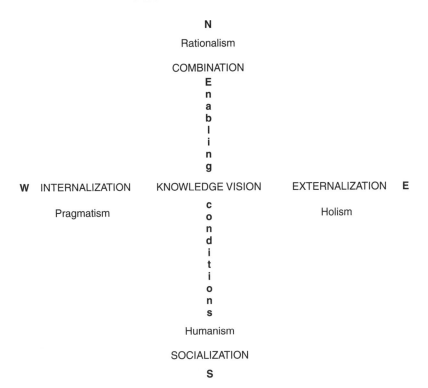

Figure 21.4 The knowledge-creating process

created is truly worthwhile for the organization and the society. Justification determines the 'quality' of the knowledge. Standards arising may include cost and profit, a product's contribution to a firm's development, as well as such criteria as adventure, romance and aesthetics. Through a third project, then, such a concept, created, chrystallized and justified in the organization, is integrated into a whole network of organizational knowledge. At the same time your self-concept is deepened and broadened through it becoming constituted of 'the stories we are'.

The stories we are

The poetics of learning

For William Randall,[3] a Canadian Professor of Literature, learning is making – making sense, making a life, making ourselves. In that respect it is synonymous with 'autopoiesis'. Learning for him, then, in the context of 'the stories we are', is synonymous with self-creation. The 'poetics of learning' is thus concerned with how we story and re-story both ourselves and our world.

Such stories, moreover, are incomplete: our lives and careers are still unfolding, mysteries yet unresolved, open books for whose endings we can but wait. It can also imply that each of us, in our own way and our own time, is 'legendary'. Judaeo-Christian tradition is founded on the conviction that reality itself – at least human reality – is inherently storied, that all events of our lives constitute one grand, unfolding plot. History is somehow purposeful, in that sense 'plotted', so that each event in our work and lives is novel, and thereby charged actually or potentially with significance.

Every one of you, during the course of your mastery project, then, must build – starting with the most natural territory of our own life – a work, an opus, into which something enters from the elements of the earth. When we speak of self-creation and the art of living and learning, we raise questions about how we resolve the tension between the determined and the undetermined dimensions of our existence. We are raising questions about how we weave the fabric of our work and lives from the warp of the new and the woof of the old. Such a fabric emerges from both the unprecedented and the pre-programmed, from what is coming into the present from the future and what is receding away from it into the past. In that context, moreover, you develop through your self in the same way that the knowledge-creating company's development is grounded in its vision. How each of you carries it out – that is, in what proportions you blend these elements – is one of the things that make you unique. Some of us approach our work each day as if it were a brand new page or chapter, an ever-unfolding adventure, while for others it amounts to the same old story, even the same chapter and verse, repeated over and over.

The story-lines

TENSION AND RESOLUTION

As with 'once upon a time' so with 'happily ever after' stories there are countless variations. What all of them have in common, however, is that they represent attempts to tie together the potentials and possibilities implied by their respective beginnings. It is the function of endings in general to bring to at least some resolution the problems your story has raised. Part of the allure of your story, therefore, and that which the experience of the ending keeps alive, relates to the 'catharsis' that the story provides. The middle is where you encounter the *agon*, the conflict required to fuel the story. A good story has to have conflict, within or between characters. The middle is the arena of continuous tension – between limits and possibilities, dangers and dreams, obstacles and goals, the real and the ideal. In particular it is in the tension – the push and the pull – between the exigencies of the plot and the existence of the characters that we find the central engine of your story, what keeps it pumping from chapter to chapter. Indeed no struggle, no story; no trouble, no tale; no ill, no thrill.

UNFOLDING PLOT

A story, your life story, your career story, unfolds. The greater the *energeia* inherent in its beginning, moreover, the more pregnant with possibilities the initial 'germ' of the story. Narration locates itself in the past in order to allow itself forward movement, as if your story's own future were a vacuum into which it is steadily sucked. This explains a paradoxical and yet common feature of following any story: your sense that how it unfolds is both unexpected and yet, in retrospect, inevitable.

As in literature so in work and life you – as a would-be master manager – begin at the middle, thrust into the midst of a particular organizational story, industry story, world story. As such you are suspended in time between a beginning you cannot recall and an end you cannot envision, constantly having to revise the plot as new events are added to your project. In projecting your self, as in reading a story, you tend to cling to the conviction that you are 'getting somewhere', that you are 'onto something', that the bits of your existence that seem so scattered today will eventually find their place. Such life and career narratives reflect the prevailing theories about 'possible lives' and 'possible vocations' that are part of our culture.

ROUNDED CHARACTERS

As flat characters you are simple, two-dimensional, endowed with very few traits, highly predictable in your behaviour. You are thus called 'stock' characters, or indeed ordinary managers. Your characteristics are steady throughout, your natures fixed, just like Belbin's team roles, Myers Briggs types, or indeed one point on the spectrum in isolation from the others. You are thereby 'ordinary'. However challenging the situations in which the story places you, you undergo little in the way of development. As rounded characters, on the other hand, you are complex, multi-dimensional, capable of unpredictable behaviour. You develop as the plot unfolds.

POINT OF VIEW

Storying, for Randall, involves four stages, which can be likened to our journey towards mastery. As a *protagonist* (preparatory) you are basically inside your story, acting and reacting in the present, unable to see the whole story or even any story. Operating by 'primal' reflex, you do things on the wing. For all intents and purposes, your life is the plot. You are as close to raw existence as one can get.

As *narrator* (ordinary), however, you are more outside your story in psychological time and space. You have greater 'rational' control over it as a story. As a *reader* (extraordinary), you are outside your life story even more, not controlling it so much as 'developmentally' monitoring it, recognizing it, discovering and enhancing its meaning. Finally, as *author-izer* (mastery), you create the story, 'metaphysically', that is your novel-ty.

The author-ity of the transformational leader

Poetry in motion

As you become a 'masterly' metaphysical manager or transformational leader, you use stories, or indeed parables, all the time. You use these to instruct and to provide insight; you work within, are constrained by, and contribute to, the unfolding stories of particular individuals, organizations and societies. The masterly facilitator is involved in enabling you to create and re-create the stories of your own work and lives. At the same time you are involved, indirectly if not directly, in enabling individual companies to become knowledge-creating enterprises. This means that besides being intellectual, emotional and practical, your vocation is poetic, as well as knowledge creating, in nature.

As we have seen, then, the search for a self-story and a company story are intertwined. To entertain a story on how your organization or industry hangs together – past, present and future – is by implication to entertain a theory on how your life and work hang together within it. The larger stories swirling about in the world around you shape your self-stories in turn. You soak in through your pores their plot-lines, their point of view, their conflicts, their morality, their modes of characterization, their themes, their atmosphere.

The more extensive and intensive your need to 'pull it all in', that is your self and your world, the more philosophical, the more artistic, the more 'metaphysical' you may be deemed, even when we accept that no sacred 'master-plots' can tell the whole story.

Facilitating re-storying

Re-storying involves a change not merely in the individual events of your work and life themselves, but in your master story. When such change happens, it is a genuine re-formation or even transformation. The first stage of this process involves you in *narrating* the story of your work and life with a new intensity and honesty. At this point the guiding question is simply 'What is your story?' The 'masterly' facilitator's role is primarily that of a listener, affirming your novelty. The second stage in re-storying is that of *reading* your story, that is re-viewing, re-cognizing and re-conceiving it. Here the key question is what kind of story is it – its themes, conflicts, characters, authority, plot-line, genre. It can also mean enquiring into the themes and characters of the larger stories that envelop your life, whereby the personal leads into the economic and technological, social and cultural. The role of the facilitator here is to help you, in conjunction with others, expand and deepen your story, thus releasing the energy bound within it. Through both the narrating and the reading, another key question comes – how can you *re-author* your story.

Resistance to re-storying

When you re-story, in fact, you and your facilitator step out of line. You undermine the authority of the script in which you have previously played your part. You move out of the ordinary into the extraordinary, with a possible view to mastery. You tip over whatever applecart you, and indeed your organizations, have been riding in hitherto.

Your co-actors, colleagues and co-authors might not like this. As a creation within a creation, your managerial mutiny, your tearing to pieces of the plot of your common larger story, may not be appreciated. Second, there will be resistance from your self and others. You know that you cannot change your story profoundly overnight. Besides, we grow accustomed to the stories we are. We feel cosy inside them. With them we have propped up an image of ourselves that is familiar. Thus we get in the way of our own re-storying.

The novelty of your life

Should you ultimately have the courage to be yourself, the story-world you create around you will differ from everyone else's in terms of its atmosphere, its openness and its integrity. As a living story, an embodied novel – with its unique vocabulary (fancy rather than plain), plotting (thick rather than thin), characterization (round rather than flat), and point of view (past, present or future) – each exudes a distinct atmosphere. We all carry within us a collection of questions we ask, conflicts we wrestle with, themes to which we continually return. But some of you are more aware of your collection than others. Such openness, or awareness, is a function of your compassion, that is – for Randall – the span of your emotional geography, and of your childlikeness, that is your ability to live with loose ends. The more complete the story, the more integrated your self. In other words, people with integrity can sustain diversion but maintain direction. You strike a balance between action and reflection, complexity and focus. The ability to bring integration out of wildly disparate tendencies is the mark of a master manager, duly enabled by a masterly facilitator.

To see the thread running through your work and life, finally, and to honour it, requires a particular discipline. Such a discipline is alert to the role of each event in the working out of the plot of the story as a whole, whatever that plot may be. In that context you are alert to how each event adds a significant dimension to the unfolding of that plot and contributes to its denouement, its destiny. It is as if each of your life's events could be read as a unique revelation of the movement of a larger, more authoritative reality within which it finds its ultimate source, whatever that reality be called: the Tao, the Higher Self, or even managerial Mastery.

The role of the masterly facilitator

From re-storying to self-creation

In effect the more unstoried existence you are enabled to transform into experience, and the more untold experience you are able to express, then the more powerfully and profoundly can self-creation proceed. Moreover, the more artistically coherent and ethically satisfying the story you can live and tell the more emotionally fulfilled you might feel. In other words, the wider your awareness of the stories you are, the more power you have in relation to others.

The masterly transformational process

In the final analysis, during the third mastery project, a complete spectrum of learning – evolving progressively from imitation to creation – replicates what goes on organizationally within the knowledge-creating company. For the individual learner, it takes the shape of a heroic journey, a fully fledged re-storying both encompassing and also surpasssing the 'ordinary' and 'extraordinary' parts of it, starting with total immersion, set within the context of socialization. It is the task of the facilitator, together with other members of a learning set, to enable such a journey to mastery. The journey, moreover, is not strictly sequential but iterative, though there is an overall developmental pattern to it.

SOCIALIZATION

1 *Undergoing immersion – adopting the faith* To start with, as a would-be master you have the courage to lay yourself completely open to the world, to *imitate* a wholly valued other, to still the mind through meditation, or to let go fully – opening out to the full power of metaphor.

2 *Pursuing activity – responding to the call to adventure* The pursuit of self-mastery continues with a sensual *reaction*, that sets your adrenaline flowing. You have a physical urge to do something about a situation, for fear of being left way behind. You cannot resist taking the plunge into the unknown, to respond to the call to adventure, by yourself or with others.

3 *Undergoing apprenticeship – attracting protectors* Once you are physically underway, but not sure which way to turn, you are willing if properly 'socialized' to become dependent on sympathetic others, *responding* enthusiastically to their every offer of help. Having been tough enough to strike out on your own, you become tender enough to invite in others, including the members of your own work group to please help. You now move on from socialization towards internalization.

INTERNALIZATION

4   *Improving performance – road of trials* As you *adapt* to the world, you now seek
    out alternative books and courses, people and experiences, and try out a
    variety of ideas and networks. In so doing, you seek to improve your own
    performance as managers, as well as that of other people.

5   *Creating a job of your own – from old self to new* Once you have acquired
    conventional wisdom, that is 'ordinary' know-how, you are ready to make
    it individually your own, that is to internalize it. You begin to personally
    energize your thoughts, feelings and actions with a view to making your mark.
    The new work that you do becomes so internalized that you begin to make
    it your own. You are now ready to combine experience more fully with the
    reality of the world around you.

COMBINATION

6   *Evolving a role – forging a new union* You are now ready to *deliberately* combine
    together the old work with your new role. A prospective marriage of
    interests arises between your aggressive new ego, or the new work you carve
    out for yourself, and a receptive environment, heralding the new work that
    needs to be done. Out of this newly forged union, an evolved role, alongside
    a new product or process, emerges.

7   *Invoking a calling – penetrating the depths* To the extent that you are able,
    through appropriate facilitation, to integrate your emergent role with your
    life's journey, so it may be identified with your *calling*, emerging out of the
    centre of your being. Moreover, to the extent that you are able to link
    together your own emergent purpose with that of your organization, if not
    also with that of your society, you will be all the more likely to realize this
    purpose. This is where, as a 'masterly' manager, you come fully into your
    own. You thereby fuse together yourself and others, your organization and
    environment. It is at this point that the full-scale externalization of what you
    and your knowledge-creating organization have so far become can take
    place.

EXTERNALIZATION

8   *Realizing a vocation – unravelling the core* As a 'master' manager you ultimately
    reach a point where you are able to grasp things as integrated wholes and
    turn them into newly differentiated parts. For the knowledge-creating com-
    pany this represents an ability to enter, business-wise, into the organization's
    knowledge grounds, lodged within the fundamental arts and sciences, and
    turn them over to yield commercial benefit. You thereby recognize your
    vocation in the process of building upon your organization's knowledge
    vision, and your own soul!

Criteria for evaluating 'mastery'

The 'ordinary' project, rooted in cognitive and behavioural psychology, was focused on action learning, whereby you became a classical scientist; the second 'extraordinary' one, rooted in the life sciences, was oriented towards dynamic development, whereby you became a quantum scientist. Now in the third 'mastery' project, you become an artist or author.

As such you are responsible for the 'novelty' of your life as well as that of your organization. In the process you develop from an action-centred or dynamic learner into a poetic or heroic one, following in the footsteps of the heroes and heroines in the myths of old:

AIR

1   Undergoing immersion – adopting the faith
    - To what extent have you adopted the 'learning faith', thereby becoming committed to lifelong learning, set within the context of an emerging vocation?
    - To what degree has your organization adopted a cause to which you have enabled it to become attached?
2   Pursuing activity – responding to the call to adventure
    - What has been the nature and scope of your heroic journey, over the course of your life and work in general, and over the past two years in particular?
    - To what extent have you enabled your organization to be engaged in such, with respect to both its structure building and structure changing phases of development?

SHARE

3   Undergoing apprenticeship – attracting protectors
    - What has been the part played, particularly during the course of the MMBA, by 'protectors', that is by colleagues, fellow learners, coaches, mentors, by friends and family?
    - How extensive is the process of socialization, whereby a learning community has been established around the MMBA, with a view to business and organization development?
4   Improving performance – road of trials
    - To what extent have the seminal ideas and experiences that have been acquired over the past two years been explicitly incorporated into your mind-set?
    - To what degree has the learning undergone during the MMBA been incorporated into the 'knowledge network' of the organization?

5   Creating a job of your own – from old self to new
- To what extent, and in what way, have aspects of your self been discarded as destructive, in favour of others newly adopted, as creative?
- How effectively have you internalized your learning, during the MMBA, with a view to exploiting such new knowledge commercially and/or organizationally?

6   Evolving a role – forging a new union
- How explicitly has a new union been forged between your newly established role and your recently reconceived organization?
- How methodically have you combined your learning with that of others, thereafter converting knowledge into new products/services or processes/systems?

7   Invoking a calling – penetrating the depths
- To what degree has a personal and business vision been emerging, in the light of current developments in the market-place, with technology, and in society?
- What is the nature and extent of the enabling conditions for organizational learning and knowledge creation that you have helped to establish?

REVIEW

8   Realizing a vocation – unravelling the core
- To what extent have you become a creative force in people's work and lives, having journeyed through the realms of the ordinary and extraordinary towards mastery?
- What is the nature and extent of the knowledge vision that you have helped to both realize and also actualize within your organization?

Conclusion

As an 'autopoietic' learner, set in the context of the management domains and the business realms, you need to be able to progressively reorient yourself and others, from the preparatory towards the ordinary, onto the extraordinary and ultimately the masterly, as indicated above.

You have now journeyed all the way, in the course of this text, from the metamorphosis of management, and of business, to the description of a masters programme, designed specifically to accomplish this journey. In the process you have traversed many of the major cultures of the world, and several of the most distinctive managers within them. I can only hope that the journey, for you, has proved to be an enlightening rather than a debilitating one, and that you have found your own path to developing as a manager, through cultural diversity.

NOTES

INTRODUCTION

1 R. Pascale and A. Athos, *The Art of Japanese Management*, Penguin, 1982.
2 C. Hampden Turner and F. Trompenaars, *Mastering the Infinite Game*, Capstone, 1997.
3 M. Piore and T. Sabel, *The Second Industrial Divide*, Basic Books, 1984.
4 A. Koopman, *Transcultural Management*, Blackwell, 1991.
5 T. Peters and R. Waterman, *In Search of Excellence*, Harper and Row, 1982.
6 E. Jaques and W. Clement, *Executive Leadership*, Blackwell, 1991.
7 S. Wikstrom, *Knowledge and Value*, Routledge, 1984.
8 P. Womack and D. Jones, *Lean Production*, HBS Press, 1996.
9 R. Stacey, *Strategic Management and Organizational Dynamics*, Pitman, 1993.
10 P. Senge, *The Fifth Discipline*, Doubleday, 1992.
11 H. Mintzberg, *Mintzberg on Management*, Random House, 1995.
12 I. Nonaka and H. Takeuchi, *The Knowledge Creating Company*, Oxford Univesity Press, 1995.
13 H. Owen, *Spirit, Transformation and Development*, Abbott, 1988.
14 R. Lessem and S. Palsule, *Managing in Four Worlds*, Blackwell, 1997.

1 DEVELOPING IN STAGES

1 J. Moore, *Leadership and Strategy in the Age of Business Ecosystems*, Wiley, 1996.
2 R. Heilbronner, *The Worldly Philosophers*, Penguin, 1968, p. 23.
3 D. Ricardo, *Principles of Economics*, 1817.
4 C. Tugendhat, *The Modern Multinational*, Eyre & Spottiswoode, 1971, p. 26.
5 T. Aitken, *The Multinational Man*, Allen & Unwin, 1973.
6 P. Drucker, *Management in Turbulent Times*, Heinemann, 1979, p. 93.
7 Drucker, *Management in Turbulent Times*, p. 96.
8 Drucker, *Management in Turbulent Times*, p. 98.
9 Drucker, *Management in Turbulent Times*, p. 101.
10 J. Walmsley, *Handbook of International Joint Ventures*, Graham & Trotman, 1982, p. 31.
11 Walmsley, *Handbook of International Joint Ventures*, p. 14.
12 K. Ohmae, *Triad Power*, Free Press, 1985.
13 Ohmae, *Triad Power*, p. 145.
14 Y. Stourdze, 'A Divided Continent in Search of Its Lost Vitality', *Financial Times*, 26 June 1985.
15 O. Kalthoff *et al.*, *Light and Shadow: European-ness and Innovation*, Capstone, 1997, p. 146.
16 M. Porter, *The Competitive Advantage of Nations*, Macmillan, 1990, p. 35.
17 J. Jaworski, *Synchronicity – The Inner Path of Leadership*, Berrett Koehler, 1996.

18 A. Roddick, *Body and Soul*, Bloomsbury, 1994.
19 R. Pascale and A. Athos, *The Art of Japanese Management*, Penguin, 1982.
20 A. Toynbee, *A Study of History*, Thames & Hudson, 1972.
21 R. Lessem, *The Roots of Excellence*, Fontana, 1986, p. 16.
22 R. Lessem, *Total Quality Learning*, Blackwell, 1991.
23 R. Horwitz, *Entrepreneurial Management*, Westhall Books, 1978, p. 37.
24 A. Chandler, *Strategy and Structure*, Doubleday, 1954.
25 W. Teague, quoted in S. Bailey, *The Shape of Design*, Design Council, 1982.
26 A. Maslow, *Motivation and Personality*, Harper & Row, 1964.
27 V. Mahesh, *Thresholds of Motivation – The Corporation as a Nursery for Human Growth*, McGraw Hill/Tata, 1994.
28 M. Porter, *The Competitive Advantage of Nations*.
29 P. Drucker, *The Post-Capitalist Society*, Butterworth-Heinemann, 1993.
30 I. Nonaka and H. Takeuchi, *The Knowledge Creating Company*, Oxford University Press, 1995.
31 T. Sakaiya, *The Knowledge-Value Revolution*, Bellew Publishing, 1992, p. 57.
32 T. Stewart, *Intellectual Capital*, Nicholas Brealey, 1997.

2 TRANSCENDING THE EAST–WEST DIVIDE

1 C. Hampden Turner, *Radical Man*, Duckworth, 1973.
2 C. Hampden Turner, and F. Trompenaars, *The Seven Cultures of Capitalism*, Doubleday, 1993.
3 C. Hampden Turner and F. Trompenaars, *Mastering the Infinite Game*, Capstone, 1997.
4 J.P. Carse, *Finite and Infinite Games*, Ballantyne, 1986.
5 M. Porter, *The Competitive Advantage of Nations*, Macmillan, 1990.
6 W. Ouchi, *The M-Form Society*, Addison & Wesley, 1986.
7 E. Schein, *Strategic Pragmatism*, MIT Press, 1996.
8 Kisho Kurokawa, *The Philosophy of Symbiosis*, International Thompson, 1996.

3 CROSSING THE NORTH–SOUTH DIVIDE

1 M. Piore and C. Sabel, *The Second Industrial Divide*, Basic Books, 1984, p. 4.
2 Piore and Sabel, *The Second Industrial Divide*, p. 5.
3 Piore and Sabel, *The Second Industrial Divide*, p. 135.
4 Piore and Sabel, *The Second Industrial Divide*, p. 216.
5 A. Koopman, *Transcultural Management*, Blackwell, 1991.
6 E. Bondi, 'South African Management Principles within a Building Supplies Organization, MBA thesis, Wits Business School, 1995, p. 17.
7 Bondi, 'South African Management Principles', p. 24.
8 ITISA, 'Value Sharing', internal publication, 1992.
9 ITISA, 'Value Sharing'.
10 H. Fayol, *Industrial and General Administration*, IMI, Geneva, 1930.
11 B. Lievegoed, *Managing The Developing Organization*, Blackwell, 1990.

4 THE SOFT AND HARD EDGES OF MANAGEMENT

1 R. Pascale and A. Athos, *The Art of Japanese Management*, Penguin, 1981.
2 T. Peters and B. Waterman, *In Search of Excellence*, Harper & Row, 1982.
3 A. Watts, *The Taboo against Knowing Who You Are*, Abacus, 1977, p. 130.
4 N. Foy, *The Yin and Yang of Organizations*, McIntyre, 1980.
5 S. Colegrave, *The Spirit of the Valley*, Virago, 1979, pp. 69–70.

6 Colegrave, *The Spirit of the Valley*, p. 56.
7 Colegrave, *The Spirit of the Valley*, p. 86.
8 G. Sheahy, *The New Passages*, Random House, 1996.
9 Colegrave, *The Spirit of the Valley*, p. 111.
10 F. Capra, *The Tao of Physics*, Shambala Press, updated edition, 1991.
11 F. Capra, *Mankind at the Turning Point*, Wildwood House, 1981.
12 T. Buzzan, *Use Your Head*, BBC Publications, 1974.
13 R. Ornstein, *The Psychology of Consciousness*, Pelican, 1975.
14 M. Ferguson, *The Aquarian Conspiracy*, Granada, 1980.
15 Ferguson, *The Aquarian Conspiracy*, pp. 82–3, 329.
16 Capra, *Mankind at the Turning Point*, p. 29.
17 R. Van Duyn, *Message of a Wise Kabouter*, Duckworth, 1972, p. 56.
18 Van Duyn, *Message of a Wise Kabouter*, p. 58.
19 J. Moore, *Leadership and Strategy in the Age of Business Ecosystems*, Wiley, 1996, p. 219.
20 R. Eisler, *The Chalice and the Blade*, Unwin, 1990.
21 R. Tarnas, *The Passion of the Western Mind*, Doubleday, 1992, p. 343.

5 PRIMAL ROOTS – CULTURE AND ECONOMICS

1 K. Polanyi, *The Livelihood of Man*, Academic Press, 1977.
2 M. Bookchin, *The Ecology of Freedom*, Cheshire Books, 1982, p. 62.
3 M. Gelfand, *Growing Up Shona*, Mambo Press, Zimbabwe, 1979, p. 80.
4 R. Heilbronner, *The Worldly Philosophers*, Allen Lane, 1969, p. 64.
5 A. Smith, *An Inquiry into the Wealth of Nations*, Penguin, 1970, Vols. I–III.
6 Smith, *Inquiry into the Wealth of Nations*, p. 124.
7 J. Schumpeter, *The Theory of Economic Development*, 2nd edn, Oxford University Press, 1954, p. 86.

6 PASSION FOR EXCELLENCE

1 T. Peters and B. Waterman, *In Search of Excellence*, Harper & Row, 1982.
2 T. Peters and N. Austin, *A Passion for Excellence*, Collins, 1985.
3 R. Pascale and A. Athos, *The Art of Japanese Management*, Penguin, 1982.
4 Peters and Waterman, *In Search of Excellence*, p. 11.
5 Peters and Waterrnan, *In Search of Excellence*, pp. 44–51.
6 Peters and Waterman, *In Search of Excellence*, p. 234.
7 Peters and Waterman, *In Search of Excellence*, p. 164.
8 Peters and Waterman, *In Search of Excellence*, p. 272.
9 Peters and Austin, *A Passion for Excellence*, p. 4.
10 T. Peters, *Thriving on Chaos*, Macmillan, 1987, p. xii.
11 T. Peters, *Liberation Management*, Free Press, 1992.
12 T. Peters, *Liberation Management*, p. xxxiii.
13 T. Peters, *The Pursuit of WOW*, Vintage Books, 1994.
14 T. Peters, The Tom Peters' Seminar, Vintage Books, 1995.
15 S. Krainer, *Tom Peters – From Corporate Man to Corporate Skunk*, Capstone, 1997.

7 STRATEGY, PERFORMANCE AND VALUE

1 J. Kay, *Foundations of Corporate Success: How Business Strategies Add Value*, Oxford University Press, 1993, p. 24.
2 ITISA, Management Strategy Workshop, unpublished document, 1985, p. 43.
3 M. Porter, *Competitive Strategy*, Macmillan, 1983.

4 M. Porter, *Competitive Advantage*, Macmillan, 1993.

5 M. Porter, *The Competitive Advantage of Nations*, Macmillan, 1990, p. 84.

6 R. Kaplan and H. Thomas Johnson, *Relevance Lost: The Rise and Fall of Management Accounting*, Harvard Business School Press, 1987.

7 H. Thomas Johnson, *Relevance Gained*, Free Press, 1993, p. 13.

8 R. Kaplan and D. Norton, *The Balanced Scorecard*, Harvard Business School Press, 1996.

9 R. Kaplan and D. Norton, *The Balanced Scorecard*, 1996, p. 96.

10 S. Vandermerwe, *From Tin Soldiers to Russian Dolls: Creating Added Value through Services*, Butterworth-Heinemann, 1993, p. 14.

11 V.S. Mahesh, *Thresholds of Motivation: The Corporation as a Nursey for Human Growth*, Tata-McGraw, 1993.

8 ENTREPRENEUR AND ANIMATEUR

1 D. Levinson, *Seasons of Man's Life*, Knopf, 1979.

2 R. Lessem, 'The Spectral Management Inventory (SMTI)', Copyright, 1993.

3 B. Gates, *The Road Ahead*, second edition, Penguin, 1996.

4 O. Kalthoff *et al.*, *The Light and the Shadow: European-ness and Innovation*, Capstone, 1997.

5 R. Semler, *Maverick*, Arrow Books, 1994.

6 G. Alexander, 'Internet Gamble Soars Sky High', *Sunday Times*, 4 May 1997, Business, p. 7.

9 RATIONAL ROOTS – ADMINISTRATIVE AND BEHAVIOURAL SCIENCE

1 P. Graham (ed.), *Mary Parker Follett – Prophet of Management*, Harvard Business School Press, 1995.

2 D. Wren, *The Evolution of Management Thought*, Wiley, 1979, pp. 21–5.

3 T. R. Mitchell and W. G. Scott, *Organization Theory*, Irwin Dorsey, 1972, pp. 18–19.

4 A. Chandler, *The Visible Hand*, Belknap Press, 1977, p. 1.

5 D. McCallum, 'Superintendent's Report', 25 March 1856, in *Annual Report for the New York Erie Railroad Co.*, 1855.

6 Wren, *Evolution of Management Thought*, p. 96.

7 H. A. Hopf, *Historical Perspectives in Management*, Hopf Institute of Management, 1949, p. 11.

8 Wren, *Evolution of Management Thought*, p. 157.

9 S. Kakar, *Frederick Taylor: A Study in Personality and Innovation*, MIT Press, 1970, p. 19.

10 F. Taylor, 'On the Art of Cutting Metals', speech to ASME, 1908.

11 F. Taylor, *Principles of Scientific Management*, Harper Bros., 1911, p. 39.

12 Taylor, *Principles of Scientific Management*, p. 73.

13 N. Wiener, *Cybernetics: or Control and Communications in the Animal and the Machine*, MIT Press, 1948.

14 D. Wren, *Evolution of Management Thought*, p. 412.

15 E. Mayo, *The Human Problems of an Industrial Civilisation*, Routledge & Kegan Paul, 1949, p. 18.

16 L. Henderson, *Fatigue of Workers*, Reinhold Publishing, 1941, pp. 12–13.

17 E. Mayo, *Human Problems*, p. 32.

18 M. Parker Follett, *The New State*, Longman & Green, 1929.

19 P. Graham, *Integrative Management*, Blackwell, 1991.

20 Graham, Mary Parker Follett, 1995.

21 Parker Follett, *The New State*, p. 112.

22 Parker Follett, *The New State*, p. 3.

23 Parker Follett, *The New State*, p. 3.
24 Parker Follett, *The New State*, p. 127.
25 Parker Follett, *The Creative Experience*, Peter Smith, 1926, p. 41.
26 L. Urwick (ed.), *Dynamic Administration*, Pitman, 1941.
27 Parker Follett, *The New State*, p. 74.
28 Wren, *Evolution of Management Thought*, p. 330.

10 REQUISITE ORGANIZATION

1 E. Jaques, *Requisite Organization*, Blackwell, 1991.
2 E. Jaques, *A General Theory of Bureaucracy*, Heinemann, 1976.
3 E. Jaques, *Executive Leadership*, Blackwell, 1991.
4 Jaques, *Bureaucracy*, p. 100.
5 Jaques, *Bureaucracy*, p. 295.
6 Jaques, *Bureaucracy*, p. 318.
7 Jaques, *Executive Leadership*, p. 83.
8 Jaques, *Executive Leadership*, p. 176.

11 CORE COMPETENCE AND CHANGE MANAGEMENT

1 P. Crosby, *Quality is for Free*, Mentor Press, 1979.
2 M. Imai, *Kaizen: The Key to Japan's Competitive Success*, McGraw Hill, 1976, p. xxix.
3 M. Hammer and J. Champy, *Reengineering the Corporation*, Nicholas Brealey, 1993, p. 27.
4 J. Womack, D. Jones and D. Roos, *The Machine that Changed the World*, Macmillan, 1990.
5 J. Womack and D. Jones, *Lean Thinking: Banish Waste and Create Wealth in Your Organization*, Simon and Shuster, 1996.
6 Womack and Jones, *Lean Thinking*, p. 19.
7 Womack and Jones, *Lean Thinking*, p. 29.
8 Womack and Jones, *Lean Thinking*, p. 59.
9 Womack and Jones, *Lean Thinking*, p. 278.
10 G. Hamel and C.K. Pralahad, *Competing for the Future*, Harvard Business School Press, 1994.
11 Hamel and Pralahad, *Competing for the future*, p. 17.
12 Hamel and Pralahad, *Competing for the future*, p. 25.
13 W. Edwards Deming, *Out of the Crisis*, MIT Press, 1986.
14 K. Ishikawa, *Guide to Quality Control*, Asian Productivity Press, 1976.
15 S. Zuboff, *In the Age of the Smart Machine*, Heinemann, 1988, p. 57.
16 Zuboff, *Age of the Smart Machine*, p. 71.
17 Zuboff, *Age of the Smart Machine*, p. 169.
18 Zuboff, *Age of the Smart Machine*, p. 304.
19 Zuboff, *Age of the Smart Machine*, p. 395.
20 S. Wikstrom and R. Normann, *Knowledge and Value*, Routledge, 1994, p. 30.

12 EXECUTIVE AND CHANGE AGENT

1 Kalthoff *et al.*, *The Light and the Shadow, European-ness and Innovation*, Capstone, 1997.

13 DEVELOPMENT ROOTS – BIOLOGY AND ECOLOGY

1 B. Goodwin, *How the Leopard Changed its Spots: The Evolution of Complexity*, Phoenix Books, 1996, p. xiv.
2 R. Dawkin, *The Blind Watchmaker*, Norton, 1987.

3 R. Dawkin, *The Selfish Gene*, Oxford University Press, 1976, p. 77.
4 Dawkin, *The Selfish Gene*, p. 84.
5 Goodwin, *How the Leopard Changed its Spots*, p. xiv
6 H. Maturana and F. Varela, *Autopoeisis and Cognition: The Realization of the Living*, D. Reidel, 1980.
7 J. Moore, *Leadership and Strategy in the Age of Business Ecosystems*, Wiley, 1997.
8 M. Wheatley, *Leadership and the New Science: Learning about Organization from an Orderly Universe*, Berrett Koehler, 1992.
9 I. Prigogine and I. Stengers, *Order out of Chaos*, Bantam Books, 1984.
10 M. Wheatley and M. Kellner Jones, *A Simpler Way*, Berrett Koehler, 1997.

14 STRATEGIC MANAGEMENT AND ORGANIZATIONAL DYNAMICS

1 R. Stacey, *Strategic Management and Organizational Dynamics*, Pitman, 1993.
2 R. Stacey, *Managing Chaos*, Kogan Page, 1994.
3 R. Stacey, *Complexity and Creativity in Organizations*, Berrett Koehler, 1996.

15 EMERGENT STRATEGY AND ORGANIZATIONAL LEARNING

1 B. Lievegoed, *Managing the Developing Organization*, Blackwell, 1990.
2 J. Parikh, *Managing the Self*, Blackwell, 1991.
3 H. Mintzberg, *Mintzberg on Management*, The Free Press, 1989.
4 D. Hurst, *Crisis and Renewal*, Harvard Business School, 1996.
5 R. Revans, *Action Learning*, Blonde Briggs, 1980, p. 37.
6 P. Senge, *The Fifth Discipline*, Doubleday, 1992.
7 H. Mintzberg, *The Nature of Managerial Work*, Harper and Row, 1973.
8 J. Quinn, H. Mintzberg and R. James, *The Strategy Process*, Prentice Hall, 1988.
9 Quinn, Mintzberg and James, *Strategy Process, p. 26.*
10 Quinn, Mintzberg and James, *Strategy Process*, p. 32.
11 Quinn, Mintzberg and James, *Strategy Process*, p. 38.
12 Quinn, Mintzberg and James, *Strategy Process*, p. 42.
13 Hurst, *Crisis and Renewal*, p. 3.
14 Hurst, *Crisis and Renewal*, p. 27.
15 Hurst, *Crisis and Renewal*, p. 34.
16 R. Revans, *Management Education and Development* 10, 1975.
17 A. Toynbee, *A Study of History*, Thames & Hudson, 1985.
18 Revans, *Action Learning*, p. 240.
19 A. Mant, *The Rise and Fall of British Managers*, Pan, 1979, p. 57.
20 R. Revans, *Science and the Manager*, Macdonald, 1965, p. 48.
21 R. Revans, *Developing Effective Managers*, Longmans, 1971, p. 33.
22 R. Revans, *The ABC of Action Learning*, Chartwell Brett, 1985, p. 37.
23 P. Senge, *The Fifth Discipline*.
24 M. Buber, *I and Thou*, Charles Scribner and Sons, 1970.

16 ADOPTER AND ENABLER

1 S. Mito, *The Honda Book of Management*, Kogan Page, 1990.
2 J. Jaworski, *Synchronicity: The Inner Path of Leadership*, Berrett Koehler, 1996.

17 METAPHYSICAL ROOTS – PHILOSOPHY AND THE HUMANITIES

1 D. Milner (ed.), *Explorations in Consciousness*, Neville Spearman, 1978.
2 Aristotle, cited in A. Young, *The Geometry of Meaning*, Delacorte Press, 1976.
3 A. Young, *The Geometry of Meaning* p. 63.
4 E.F. Schumacher, *A Guide for the Perplexed*, Jonathan Cape, 1977, p. 32.
5 A. Steinsaltz, *The Thirteen Petalled Flower*, Basic Books, 1980, p. 3.
6 A. Steinsaltz, *Thirteen Petalled Flower*, p. 124.
7 D. Peat, *Blackfoot Physics: A Journey into the American Native Universe*, Fourth Estate, 1994, p. 165.
8 D. Peat, *Blackfoot Physics* p. 166.
9 D. Peat, *Blackfoot Physics*, p. 6.
10 I. Prigogine and I. Stengers, *Order out of Chaos*, Fontana, 1984, p. 37.
11 H. Skolimowski, Eco-Philosophy, Marion Boyars, 1981, p. 37.
12 F. Capra, *The Tao of Physics*, Shambala, 1975.
13 F. Capra, *The Web of Life*, Harper Collins, 1996.
14 E. Jantsch, *Design for Evolution*, Brazillier, 1974.
15 J. Briggs and D. Peat, *Looking Glass Universe: The Emerging Science of Wholeness*, Fontana, 1985.
16 D. Bohm, 'The implicate and the explicate order', cited in R. Weber, *The Search for Unity*, Routledge & Kegan Paul, 1987, p. 27.
17 Weber, *Search for Unity*.
18 Briggs and Peat, *Looking Glass Universe*, p. 122.

18 THE KNOWLEDGE-CREATING COMPANY

1 I. Nonaka and H. Takeuchi, *The Knolwedge Creating Company*, Oxford University Press, 1995.
2 R. Lessem and S. Palsule, *Managing in Four Worlds*, Blackwell, 1997.

19 SPIRIT AND TRANSFORMATION

1 A. Morita, *Made in Japan*, Collins, 1987.
2 A. Stevens, *On Jung*, Penguin, 1990.
3 Morita, *Made in Japan*.
4 Stevens, *On Jung*.
5 J. Hardy, *A Psychology with a Soul: Psychosynthesis in an Evolutionary Context*, Routledge & Kegan Paul, 1987.
6 R. Lessem and S. Palsule, *Managing in Four Worlds*, Blackwell, 1997.
7 Lazear, D. *Seven Ways of Knowing*, Skylight Publishing, 1991.
8 D. Kolb, *Experiential Learning*, Prentice Hall, 1989.
9 K. Kingsland, *The Personality Spectrum*, unpublished manuscript, 1985.
10 J. Campbell, *The Hero with a Thousand Faces*, Princeton University Press, 1969.
11 H. Owen, *Spirit and Transformation and Development in Organisations*, Abbott Publishing, 1987.
12 Campbell, *Hero with a Thousand Faces*, p. 39.
13 Morita, *Made in Japan*, p. 52.
14 Morita, *Made in Japan*, p. 60.
15 I. Nonaka and H. Takeuchi, *The Knowledge Creating Company*, p. 172.
16 R. Pirsig, *Zen and the Art of Motorcycle Maintenance*, Black Swan, 1976.

20 INNOVATOR AND ADVENTURER

1 G. Soros, *Soros on Soros*, Wiley, 1995.
2 T. Jackson, *Virgin King*, Viking, 1995.

21 DEVELOPING MASTERY

1 R. Revans, 'Action Learning', in *Business as a Learning Community*, R. Lessem, McGraw Hill, 1993.
2 R. Stacey, *Strategic Management and Organizational Dynamics*, Pitman 1995.
3 W. Randall, *The Stories We Are*, Toronto University Press, 1995.

INDEX